Beginning ASP.NET E-Commerce

Cristian Darie
Karli Watson

Wrox Press Ltd. ®

Beginning ASP.NET E-Commerce

Printing History
First published: November 2002

Published by Wrox Press Ltd.,
Arden House, 1102 Warwick Road, Acocks Green,
Birmingham, B27 6BH, UK
Printed in the United States
ISBN 1-86100-750-7

Trademark Acknowledgments

Credits

Authors
Cristian Darie
Karli Watson

Commissioning Editor
David Barnes

Technical Editors
Catherine Alexander
Helen Callaghan
Mike Footer
Robert FE Shaw

Managing Editor
Jo Mason

Project Manager
Darren Murphy

Author Agent
Nicola Phillips

Technical Reviewers
Andreas Christiansen
Chris Crane
Ben Galbraith
Brad Maiani
Johan Normen
Larry Schoeneman

Production Project Coordinator
Sarah Hall

Illustrations
Sarah Hall

Cover
Natalie O'Donnell

Proof Reader
Chris Smith

Index
Adrian Axinte
Martin Brooks
Andrew Criddle

Special Thanks

We would like to thank www.the-joke-shop.com and its suppliers for kindly allowing us to use their product images in our book

About the Authors

Cristian Darie

Cristian is an independent IT consultant specializing in Microsoft technologies. He has worked with computers since he was a child, he won his first prize at the age of 12 in the first programming contest he ever entered. Now, with more than five years of professional programming experience, he tries to get involved in projects that are somehow connected to the .NET Framework, a product he likes very much. He is actively involved with Wrox Press as a technical reviewer, having checked more than 15 Wrox titles in the last year, and he also contributed the OOP parts for *Visual C# – A Guide for VB6 developers*. He is the author of MCAD preparation material and various SkillDrill tests, such as C# Programming, Microsoft COM+ and DB2 Development – these can be taken at www.skilldrill.com.

Cristian is at Politehnica University of Bucharest, one of the most famous technical universities in Romania and Europe, studying Automatic Control and Industrial Informatics. He can be contacted at CristianDarie@xnet.ro or through www.CristianDarie.ro.

> *Many thanks David – your vision made this book what it is right now, and I am honored that you chose me to write it (which was, of course, a very wise decision). Helen, Cath, Mike – I'm glad I had the chance to work with professionals like you; thanks pals for improving my writing – who said bestsellers are easy to write? Last, but most important, I'd like to thank Alina, my girlfriend, for constantly providing me with food and cans of Red Bull – I couldn't have done this without them. I love you!*

Karli Watson

Karli Watson is a freelance author and IT specialist with a penchant for multicolored clothing. He started out with the intention of becoming a world famous nanotechnologist, so perhaps one day you might recognize his name as he receives a Nobel Prize. For now, though, Karli's computing interests include all things mobile and Everything.NET. Karli is also a snowboarding enthusiast and wishes he had a cat.

Table of Contents

Table of Contents

Table of Contents

Table of Contents

Introduction

Welcome to *Beginning ASP.NET E-Commerce*. The explosive growth of retail over the Internet is encouraging more small to medium size businesses to consider the benefits of setting up E-Commerce web sites. While there are great and obvious advantages to trading online, there are also many hidden pitfalls that may be encountered when developing a retail web site. This book provides the grass roots reader with a practical, step by-step guide to setting up an E-Commerce site. Guiding you through every step of the design and build process, this book will have you building high quality, extendable e-commerce web sites quickly and easily.

Over the course of the book, readers will develop all the skills necessary to get their business up on the Web and available to a worldwide audience, without having to use high-end web solutions based on Microsoft Site Server. We present this information in a book-long case study, the complexity of which develops as the reader's knowledge increases through the book.

The case study is presented in three phases. The first phase focuses on getting the site up and running as quickly as possible, and at a low cost. That way, we reduce the financial implications of customers not using the site, and also, should customers use the site, we can start to generate revenue quickly. At the end of this phase, readers will have a working site that they can play with or go live with if they want to.

The revenue generated above can be used to pay for further development, and in phase two, we concentrate on increasing revenue. This is achieved by improving the shopping experience, and actively encouraging customers to buy more using cross selling and up selling techniques, as well as providing enhanced customer service. Again at the end of this phase, we have a fully working site that readers can go live with if they wish.

By the third phase, we've got a site up and running, and it's doing very well. We now want to look at increasing our profit margins by reducing our costs through the automating/streamlining of order processing and administration, and by handling credit card transactions ourselves.

This book is a *Beginning...* series book and we aim to take you from knowing nothing about e-commerce to a point where you'll be able to set up a web site that will make money for your business. That's a tall order and we don't pretend that there aren't points in the book where you'll have to take some professional advice (after all, we're going to show you how to take credit card orders, so there's some pretty serious stuff in here!). We do signpost those points clearly though, and a careful reading of this book will help you understand the questions you need to ask... and the answers you get.

What Does This Book Cover?

In this book you will learn to:

❑   Build a product catalog that can be browsed and searched, with administration facilities for adding, modifying, and removing products

❑   Integrate your site with PayPal, a popular, easy-to-use online payment system with no start up costs

❑   Create your own shopping basket and check out in ASP.NET

❑   Increase sales by up selling and cross selling your products

❑   Market products direct to customers through automatic e-mails

❑   Process orders using Microsoft Transaction Server

The book's P2P forum is a platform for exchanging code and ideas, helping to extend the web site with new modules and modifications.

The following is brief roadmap of where this book is going to take us:

Phase One:

Chapter 1: Starting an E-Commerce site

In this chapter we see some of the principles of e-commerce in the real, hostile world. We see the importance of focusing on short-term revenue and keeping risks down. We look at the three basic reasons why an e-commerce site can make money. We then apply those principles to a three-phase plan that provides a deliverable, usable site at each stage and continues to expand throughout the book.

Chapter 2: Laying Out the Foundations

The previous chapter gave a overview of e-commerce in the real world. Now we we've decided to develop a web site, we start to look in more detail at laying down the foundations for the future WroxJokeShop web site. We will talk about what technologies and tools we'll use, and even more importantly, how we'll use them.

Chapter 3: The Product Catalog: Part I

In the previous chapter, after learning about the three-tier architecture, we implemented a bit of our web site's main page. In this chapter we'll continue our work by starting to create the product catalog for our site. Because the product catalog is composed of many components, we'll create it over two chapters. In this chapter, we'll create the first database table, implement access methods in the middle tier and learn how to create stored procedures – and by the end of it we'll finally have something dynamically generated on our web page.

Chapter 4: The Product Catalog: Adding Content

In the previous chapter we provided our web site with a selectable list of departments. However, there is much more to a product catalog than that list of departments. In this chapter we continue by adding the rest of the product catalog features.

Chapter 5: Searching the Catalog

In the previous chapters we implemented a functional product catalog for our site. However, it lacks an important feature: it cannot be searched. Our goal in this chapter is to allow the visitor to search the site for products by entering one or more keywords.

It will be interesting to see how easy it is to add new functionality to a working site, and this happens in part because of the three-tier architecture we implemented. We will implement the search functionality by adding the necessary components to each of the three tiers.

Chapter 6: Receiving Payments using PayPal

Any e-commerce web site needs a way of receiving payments from customers. While the preferred solution for established companies is to open a merchant account, many small businesses choose to start with a simpler solution to implement, where they don't have to process credit card or payment information themselves.

There are a number of companies and web sites that can help individuals or small businesses that don't have the resources to process credit card and wire transactions, and can be used to intermediate the payment between companies and their customers. In this chapter we will demonstrate some of the functionality provided by one such company, PayPal, as we use it on our web site in the first two stages of development.

Chapter 7: Catalog Administration

In previous chapters we worked with catalog information that already existed in the database. In this chapter we implement a Catalog Administration page. This is the last thing we to do before we can get our site up and running.

Phase Two:

Chapter 8: The Shopping Basket

Welcome to the second phase of development! This is when we start improving and adding new features to the already existing, fully functional e-commerce site. In this chapter, we will implement the custom shopping basket, which will store its data into the local WroxJokeShop database. This will provide us with more flexibility, compared to the PayPal shopping basket over which we have no control and which cannot be saved into our database for further processing and analysis.

Chapter 9: Dealing with Customer Orders

The good news is that our brand new shopping cart looks good and is fully functional. The bad news is that it doesn't allow the visitor to actually place an order, making it totally useless in the context of a production system.

As you have probably already guessed, we'll deal with that problem in this chapter, in two separate stages. In the first part of the chapter we will implement the client-side part of the order placing mechanism. In the second part of the chapter we'll implement a simple orders administration page where the site administrator can view and handle pending orders.

Phase Three:

Chapter 10: Customer Details

So far in this book we've built a basic (but functional) site, and have hooked it in to PayPal for taking payments and confirming orders. In this section of the book we'll take things a little further. By cutting out PayPal from our ordering process we can obtain much better control over things – as well as reducing overheads.

In this chapter we'll be laying out the groundwork for this, by implementing a customer account system.

Chapter 11: Order Pipeline

Our e-commerce application is shaping up nicely. Now we have added customer account functionality, and we are keeping track of customer addresses and credit card information, which is stored in a secure way. However, we are not currently using this information – currently we are delegating responsibility for this to PayPal.

In this chapter we will build our own order processing pipeline that deals with credit card authorization, stock checking, shipping, e-mail notification, and so on. In actual fact we'll leave the credit card processing specifics until the next chapter, but we will show where this process fits in here.

Chapter 12: Implementing the Pipeline

This is where we implement the class library we built in the last chapter into our WroxJokeShop application.

In this chapter we will build our own order processing pipeline that deals with credit card authorization, stock checking, shipping, e-mail notification and so on. In actual fact we'll leave the credit card processing specifics until the next chapter, but we will show where this process fits in here.

Chapter 13: Credit Card Transactions

There is one last thing we need to do before we can launch our e-commerce site: we need to enable credit card processing. In this chapter we'll look at how we can build this into the pipeline we created in the last chapter.

Chapter 14: The End

Here we wrap up our example application, and give resources in order for interested readers to search out more advanced topics.

Who Is This Book For?

Beginning ASP.NET E-Commerce is aimed at developers looking for a tutorial approach to building a full e-commerce web site from design to deployment. However, it's assumed that you:

❑ Have some knowledge of using ASP.NET with VB.NET

❑ Have experience using Visual Basic .NET Standard or Visual Studio .NET Professional or above

❑ Want to build e-commerce web sites

The book may also prove valuable for ASP3 developers who learn best by example, and want to experience ASP.NET development techniques first hand.

What You Need to Use This Book

The examples are designed to be run with Visual Studio .NET Professional and SQL Server 2000 or MSDE, running on Windows 2000 or Windows XP Professional Edition.

The complete source code for all the samples is available for download from our web site, http://www.wrox.com/.

Style Conventions

We use a number of different styles of text and layout in this book to help differentiate between the different kinds of information. Here are examples of the styles we use and an explanation of what they mean.

Code has several font styles. If it is a word that we are talking about in the text – for example, when discussing a For...Next loop – it is in this font. If it is a block of code that can be typed as a program and run, then it is in a gray box:

```
Private Sub Button1_Click(ByVal sender As System.Object, _
    ByVal e As System.EventArgs) Handles Button1.Click
End Sub
```

Sometimes, you will see code in a mixture of styles, like this:

```
Private Sub Button1_Click(ByVal sender As System.Object, _
    ByVal e As System.EventArgs) Handles Button1.Click

    MsgBox(TextBox1.Text)

End Sub
```

In cases like this, the code with a white background is code that we are already familiar with. The line highlighted in gray is a new addition to the code since we last looked at it. Code with a white background is also used for chunks of code that demonstrate a principle, but which cannot be typed in and run on their own.

Advice, hints, and background information comes in this type of font.

> **Important pieces of information come in boxes like this.**

Important Words are in a bold type font.

Words that appear on the screen, or in menus like the File or Window, are in a similar font to the one you would see on a Windows desktop.

Keys that you press on the keyboard like *Ctrl* and *Enter* are in italics.

Commands that you need to type in on the command line are shown with a > for the prompt, and the input in **bold**, like this:

```
>something to type on the command line
```

Customer Support and Feedback

We always value hearing from our readers, and we want to know what you think about this book; what you liked, what you didn't like, and what you think we can do better next time. You can send us your comments, either by returning the reply card in the back of the book, or by e-mail to feedback@wrox.com. Please be sure to mention the book ISBN and the title in your message.

Source Code and Updates

As you work through the examples in this book, you may decide that you prefer to type in all the code by hand. Many readers prefer this because it is a good way to get familiar with the coding techniques that are being used. However, whether you want to type the code in or not, we have made all the source code for this book available at the Wrox.com web site.

When you log on to the Wrox.com site at http://www.wrox.com/, simply locate the title through our Search facility or by using one of the title lists. Then click on the Download Code link on the book's detail page and you can obtain all the source code.

The files that are available for download from our site have been archived using WinZip. When you have saved the attachments to a folder on your hard drive, you need to extract the files using a de-compression program such as WinZip or PKUnzip. When you extract the files, the code is usually extracted into chapter folders. When you start the extraction process, ensure your software (WinZip, PKUnzip, and so on) has Use folder names under Extract to: (or the equivalent) checked.

Even if you like to type in the code, you can use our source files to check the results you should be getting – they should be your first stop if you think you might have typed in an error. If you don't like typing, then downloading the source code from our web site is a must! Either way, it will help you with updates and debugging.

Errata

We have made every effort to make sure that there are no errors in the text or in the code. However, no one is perfect and mistakes do occur. If you find an error in this book, like a spelling mistake or a faulty piece of code, we would be very grateful for feedback. By sending in errata, you may save another reader hours of frustration, and of course, you will be helping us provide even higher quality information. Simply e-mail the information to support@wrox.com, your information will be checked and if correct, posted to the errata page for that title, or used in subsequent editions of the book.

To find errata on the web site, log on to http://www.wrox.com/, and simply locate the title through our Search facility or title list. Then, on the book details page, click on the Book Errata link. On this page you will be able to view all the errata that have been submitted and checked through by editorial. You will also be able to click the Submit Errata link to notify us of any errata that you may have found.

Technical Support

If you wish to directly query a problem in the book then e-mail support@wrox.com. A typical e-mail should include the following things.

- ❑ The **book name**, **last four digits of the ISBN** (7507 for this book), and **page number** of the problem in the Subject field.

- ❑ Your **name, contact information**, and the **problem** in the body of the message.

We *won't* send you junk mail. We need the details to save your time and ours. When you send an e-mail message, it will go through the following chain of support:

1. **Customer Support** – Your message is delivered to one of our customer support staff, who are the first people to read it. They have files on most frequently asked questions and will answer anything general about the book or the web site immediately.

2. **Editorial** – Deeper queries are forwarded to the technical editor responsible for that book. They have experience with the programming language or particular product, and are able to answer detailed technical questions on the subject. Once an issue has been resolved, the editor can post the errata to the web site.

3. **The Authors** – Finally, in the unlikely event that the editor cannot answer your problem they will forward the request to the author. We do try to protect the author from any distractions to their writing, however, we are quite happy to forward specific requests to them. All Wrox authors help with the support on their books. They will mail the customer and the editor with their response, and again all readers should benefit.

Note that the Wrox support process can only offer support to issues that are directly pertinent to the content of our published title. Support for questions that fall outside the scope of normal book support is provided via the community lists of our http://p2p.wrox.com/ forum.

p2p.wrox.com

For author and peer discussion, join the **P2P mailing lists**. Our unique system provides **programmer to programmer™** contact on mailing lists, forums, and newsgroups, all *in addition* to our one-to-one e-mail support system. Be confident that your query is being examined by the many Wrox authors, and other industry experts, who are present on our mailing lists. At p2p.wrox.com you will find a number of different lists that will help you, not only while you read this book, but also as you develop your own applications.

To subscribe to a mailing list just follow this these steps:

1. Go to http://p2p.wrox.com/ and choose the appropriate category from the left menu bar

2. Click on the mailing list you wish to join

3. Follow the instructions to subscribe and fill in your e-mail address and password

4. Reply to the confirmation e-mail you receive

5. Use the subscription manager to join more lists and set your mail preferences

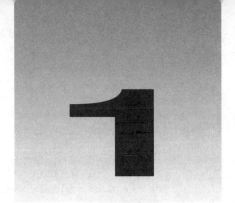

Starting an E-Commerce Site

In this book we're going to build an e-commerce site in ASP.NET. We'll be using Visual Basic .NET, and working in the Visual Basic .NET Standard or Visual Studio .NET IDE.

The book will mainly focus on programming, and associated disciplines such as creating, accessing, and manipulating databases. Before we jump into that, however, we need to have some understanding of the business decisions that lead to the creation of an e-commerce site in the first place.

The word 'e-commerce' has had a remarkable fall from grace in the past few years. Just the idea of having an e-commerce web site was enough to get many businessmen salivating with anticipation. Now it's more likely to leave them drooling with terror. If you want to build an e-commerce site today, you have some tough questions to answer. We're going to have a go at answering them in this chapter:

- ❏ So many big e-commerce sites have failed. What can e-commerce possibly offer me in today's tougher environment?

- ❏ Most e-commerce companies seemed to need massive investment. How can I produce a site on my limited budget?

- ❏ Even successful e-commerce sites expect to take years before they turn a profit. My business can't wait that long. How can I make money now?

The good news is these questions do have answers. In this chapter, we're going to find them out.

Why Go E-Commerce?

It's no longer good enough to just say "e-commerce is the future – get online or get out of business." You now need compelling, realistic, and specific reasons to take your business online.

There are hundreds of possible reasons, but they'll tend to fall into the following groups:

- ❏ Make customers spend more
- ❏ Get more customers
- ❏ Reduce the costs of fulfilling orders

Let's look at each of these.

Get More Customers

This is the most immediately attractive reason. With an e-commerce site, even small businesses can reach customers all over the world. It can also be the most dangerous, because many people set up e-commerce sites assuming that this will just happen. It won't. In the offline world, you need to know a shop exists before you go into it. This is still true in the world of e-commerce – you need people to know you exist before you can hope to get a single order.

This is largely a question of advertising, rather than the site itself. We won't really cover this aspect of e-commerce in this book. However, an e-commerce site is always available, and it is just possible people will stumble across it. It's certainly easier for customers to tell their friends about a particular URL than to give them a catalogue, mailing address, or directions to their favorite offline store.

Make Customers Spend More

Assuming your company already has customers, you probably wish that they bought more. What stops them? Well, it could be that they don't want any more. There's not really a lot that e-commerce can do about that, but the chances are there's other reasons too:

- ❑ Getting to the shop/placing an order by mail is a hassle
- ❑ Some of the things you sell can be bought from more convenient places
- ❑ You're mostly open while your customers are at work anyway
- ❑ Buying some products just doesn't occur to them

An e-commerce site can fix that. People with Internet access will find placing an order online far easier than any other method – meaning that when the temptation to buy strikes, it'll be far easier for them to give in. Of course, the convenience of being online will also mean that people are more likely to choose you over other local suppliers.

Because your site is online 24 hours a day, rather than the usual 9 to 5, your customers can shop with you outside of their working hours. But having an online store brings a double blessing to you if your customers work in offices – they can indulge in retail therapy right from their desks.

Skilful e-commerce design can encourage your customers to buy stuff that they wouldn't usually think of. You can easily update your site to suggest items of particular seasonal interest, or to announce interesting new products.

Lots of the big e-commerce sites encourage you to buy useful accessories along with the main product, or to buy a more expensive alternative to the one you're considering. Others give special offers to regular shoppers, or suggest impulse purchases at the checkout. We'll be seeing how to do some of these things in the later chapters, and by the end of the book you'll have a good idea of how to add more features for yourself.

Finally, it's much easier to learn about your customers via e-commerce than it is in face-to-face shops, or even mail order. Even if you just gather e-mail addresses, you can use these to send out updates and news. More sophisticated sites can automatically analyse customer's buying habits to make suggestions on other products they might like to buy.

Convincing Them to Come Back

Another related benefit of e-commerce is that there's no real cost in having people browse without buying. In fact, there's great value in getting people to visit the site as often as possible. For this reason, you should consider building features into the site that are designed purely to make people visit regularly. These can include community features such as forums, or free content related to the products you're selling. We won't be explicitly covering these in this book – but by the end of the book you will have learned enough to easily add them for yourself.

Reduce the Costs of Fulfilling Orders

A well-built e-commerce site will be much cheaper to run than a comparable offline business. Under conventional business models, a member of staff needs to somehow feed an order into the company's order processing system. With e-commerce, the customer can do this for you – the gateway between the site and the order processing can be seamless.

Of course, once your e-commerce site is up and running the cost of actually taking orders gets close to zero you don't need to pay for checkout staff, assistants, security guards, or rent in a busy shopping mall.

If you have a sound business idea, and you execute the site well, you can receive these benefits without a massive investment. What's important is to always focus on the almighty dollar: will your site, or any particular feature of it, really help you to get more customers, get customers to spend more, or reduce the costs and therefore increase your margins?

Now it's time to introduce the site we'll be using as our example in this book, and see just how all of these principles relate to our own shop.

Let's Make Money

We're going to build an online Joke Shop. If you are unfortunate enough to live in a country without joke shops, move house or read on. They tend to sell fancy dress costumes and accessories, along with equipment for magic tricks and practical jokes. Pepper sweets, soap that makes your face dirty, and weighted dice are freely available.

On all the e-commerce sites I've worked on, there's been a great deal of tension between wanting to produce a really amazing site that everybody will love, and the need to create a site with a limited budget that will make money. Usually, I'm on the trigger happy, really amazing site side – but I'm always grateful that my ambitions are reigned in by the real business demands. If you're designing and building the site for yourself, and you are the client, then you have a challenge – keeping your view realistic while maintaining your enthusiasm for the project.

This book will show you a fairly logical way to build an e-commerce site that will deliver what it needs to be profitable. However, when designing your own you need to think carefully about exactly who your customers are, what they need, how they want to place orders, and what they are most likely to buy. Most importantly of all, you need to think about how they will come to your site in the first place. If you're serious about building a profitable e-commerce site, you should really spend at least a day thinking about the customer and their needs. This should happen before you start to visualize or design the site, and certainly before you start programming. A helpful framework is to go through the following points:

- ❏ Getting customers – how will you get visitors to the site in the first place?

- ❏ Offering products – what you will offer, and how you expect customers to buy. Will they buy in bulk? Will they make lots of repeat orders? Will they know what they want before they visit, or will they want to be inspired? These factors will influence how you arrange your catalog and searching, as well as what order process you use. A shopping basket is great if people want to browse. If people know exactly what they want, then they may prefer something more like an order form.

- ❏ Order processing – how to turn a customer order into a parcel ready for mailing. Your main consideration here is finding an efficient way to process credit cards, and deliver orders to whoever manages your stocks or warehouse. How will you give your customers confidence in your ability to protect their data, and deliver their purchases on time?

- ❏ Customer service – will customers require additional help with products that they buy from you? Do you need to offer warranties, service contracts, or other support services?

- ❏ Bringing them back – how will you entice customers back to the site? Are they likely to only visit the site to make a purchase, or will there be e-window shoppers? Are your products consumables – can you predict when they'll need something new?

Once you've answered these questions you can start to design your site, knowing that you're designing for your customers – not just doing what seems like a good idea at the time. It will also help you ensure that your design covers all the important areas, without massive omissions that will be a nightmare to fix.

The example presented in this book has deliberately kept quite a generic approach in order to show you the most common e-commerce techniques. But to really lift yourself above the competition, you don't need fancy features or Flash movies – you just need to understand, attract, and serve your customer better than anybody else. Think about this before you launch into designing and building the site itself.

Risks and Threats

All this might make it sound as if your e-commerce business can't possibly fail. Well, it's time to take a cold shower and realize that even the best-laid plans often go wrong. Some risks are particularly relevant to e-commerce companies, such as:

- ❏ Hacking

- ❏ Credit-card scams

- ❏ Hardware failure

- ❑ Unreliable shipping services

- ❑ Software errors

- ❑ Changing laws

We can't get rid of these risks, but we can try to understand them and defend ourselves from them. The software developed in this book goes some way to meeting these issues, but many of the risks have little to do with the site itself.

Perhaps the most crucial way to defend yourself from these risks is to keep backups. You already know backups are important. But if you're anything like me, when it gets to the end of the day saving five minutes and going home earlier seems even more important. When you have a live web site, this simply isn't an option.

We haven't talked much about the legal side of e-commerce in this book, because we are programmers not lawyers. However if you are setting up an e-commerce site that goes much beyond an online garage sale, you will need to look into these issues before putting your business online.

While we're on the subject of risks and threats, one issue that can really damage your e-commerce site is unreliable order fulfilment. This is a programming book, and focuses on offering products to customers, and communicating their orders to the site's owner. An essential part of the processes is getting the products delivered, and to do this you need a good logistics network set up before launching your shop. If your store doesn't deliver the goods, customers won't come back or refer their friends.

> Webmonkey provides an excellent general e-commerce tutorial, which covers taxation, shipping, and many of the issues you'll face designing a site, at:
>
> http://hotwired.lycos.com/webmonkey/e-business/building/tutorials/tutorial3.html
>
> It's well worth checking it out before you start designing your own site.

Designing for Business

Building an e-commerce site requires a significant investment. If you design the site in phases, you can reduce the initial investment – and therefore cut your losses if the idea is a complete disaster. You can use the results from an early phase to assess whether it's worthwhile adding extra features, and even use revenue from the site to fund future development. If nothing else, planning to build the site in phases means that you can get your site online and receiving orders much earlier than if you build every possible feature into the first release.

Even once you've completed your initial planned phases, things may not end there. Whenever planning a large software project, it's important to design in a way that makes unplanned future growth easy. ASP.NET makes this fairly easy if you use it properly. In our software we've used User Controls, a new feature of ASP.NET, as well as using an *n*-tier architecture to make future modification and expansion easy. These techniques can be applied to any sizable web project, and aren't limited to e-commerce.

If you're not sure what User Controls or n-tier architecture is, you'll find out in the next chapter when we start building them. For now you just need to know that they both offer ways to make your web applications more scalable and easier to maintain.

If you're building a site for a client, they will like to think their options are open. Planning the site, or any other software, in phases will help the customer feel comfortable doing business with you. They will be far more able to see that you are getting the job done, and can decide to end the project at the end of any phase if they feel – for whatever reason – that they don't want to continue to invest in development.

Phase I – Getting a Site Up

In the early chapters we're going to concentrate on establishing the basic framework for our site, and putting our product catalog online. We'll start by putting together our basic site architecture, deciding how the different parts of our application will work together. We'll then build our product catalog into this architecture. You'll see how to:

❑ Design a database for storing a product catalog, containing categories, sub-categories, and products

❑ Write the SQL and VB.NET code for accessing that data

❑ Provide a free-text search engine for that database

❑ Give the site's administrators a private section of the site where they can modify the catalog online

Once we've built this catalog, you'll see how to offer the products for sale by integrating it with PayPal's shopping cart and order processing system, which will handle credit card transactions for you and e-mail you with details of orders. These orders will be processed manually – but in the early stages of an e-commerce site, the time you lose processing orders will be smaller than the time it would have taken to develop an automated system.

Phase II – Our Own Shopping Cart

Using PayPal's shopping cart is OK, and really easy. But it does mean that we lose a lot of advantages. For example we cannot control the look and feel of PayPal's shopping cart, whereas if we use our own we can make it an integral part of the site.

This is a significant advantage, but it's superficial compared to some of the others. For example with our own shopping cart we can store complete orders in our database as part of the order process, and use that data to learn about our customers. With additional work we can also use the shopping basket and checkout as a platform for selling more products. How often have you been tempted by impulse purchases near the checkout of your local store? Well, this also works with e-commerce. Having our own shopping cart and checkout gives us the option of later offering low-cost special offers from there. We can even analyze the contents of the cart, and make suggestions based on this. These optional features are outside the scope of this book, but will be easy to plug into the infrastructure we develop here – remember, our site is designed for growth!

So, in the middle chapters of the book we are going to:

❑   Build our own ASP.NET shopping cart

❑   Add a database table for storing complete orders

❑   Pass our complete order through to PayPal for credit card processing

Once again, at the end of Phase II our site will be fully operational. If you want, you can leave it as it is – or add features within the existing PayPal-based payment system. But when the site gets serious, you'll want to start processing orders and credit cards yourself. This is the part where things get complicated, and you need to be very serious and careful about your site's security.

Phase III – Processing Orders

The core of e-commerce – and the bit that really separates it from other web development projects – is handling orders and credit cards. PayPal is our friend because it's helped us put this off, but there are many good reasons why – eventually – you will want to part company:

❑   Cost – PayPal is not expensive, but the extra services it offers need to be paid for somehow. Moving to a simpler credit card processing service will mean lower transaction costs, although developing our own system will obviously incur upfront costs.

❑   Freedom – PayPal has a fairly strict set of terms and conditions, and is really designed for residents of the United States. By taking on more of the credit-card processing responsibility yourself, you can control the way your site works far more. As an obvious example, it means you can accept payment using regional methods such as the Switch debit cards common in the UK.

❑   Integration – if you deal with transactions and orders using your own system, you can integrate your store and your warehouse to whatever extent you require. You could even automatically contact a third-party supplier and have them ship the goods straight to the customer.

❑   Information – when you handle the whole order yourself, you can record and collate all the information involved in the transaction – and then use it for marketing and research purposes.

By integrating our order processing with the warehouse, fulfilment center, or suppliers, we can reduce costs significantly. This might mean that it reduces the need for staff in the fulfilment center – or at least mean that business can grow without requiring additional stuff.

Acquiring information about customers can feed back into the whole process, giving us valuable information about how to sell more. At its simplest this could simply mean e-mailing customers with notice of special offers, or just keeping in touch with a newsletter. It can also mean analyzing buying patterns and using that data to formulate targeted marketing campaigns.

During phase three you will see how to:

❑   Build a customer accounts module, so that customers can login and retrieve their details every time they make an order

❑   Establish secure connections using SSL (Secure Socket Layer), so that data sent by users is encrypted on its travels across the Internet

❑   Authenticate and charge credit cards using third-party companies such as DataCash, and their XML web services

❑   Store credit card numbers securely in a database

This third phase will be the most involved of all of them, and requires some hard and careful work. By the end of it, though, you will have an e-commerce site with a searchable product catalog, shopping cart, secure check out, and complete order processing system.

The Wrox Joke Shop

As I said earlier, we're going to build an online joke shop. We'll call it the Wrox Joke Shop. If this was a real business situation, and a customer asked me to build a site for their shop, I'd find out about the size of business that they had, and how they expected to attract customers.

For the purposes of this book, we'll assume that the company already exists as a mail order company, and has a fairly good network of customers. It is not completely new to the business then, and really wants the site to make it easier and more enjoyable for its existing customers to buy – in the hope that they'll end up buying more.

Knowing this, I'd suggest the phased development because:

- ❑ The company is unlikely to get massive orders initially – we should keep the cost of orders down as much as possible

- ❑ The company is used to manually processing mail orders, so manually processing orders e-mailed by PayPal will not introduce many new problems.

- ❑ The company doesn't want to invest all its money in a massive e-commerce site, only to find that people actually prefer mail order after all! Or it might find that, after Phase I, the site does exactly what it wants and there's no point in expanding it even further. Either way, I hope that offering a lower initial cost gives my bid the edge! (It might also mean I can get away with a higher total price.)

However, if it's already a mail order business it'll almost certainly already have a merchant account, and can therefore process credit cards itself. It'll therefore be in its interests to get on to Phase III as soon as possible, so that it can benefit from the preferential card-processing rates.

Summary

In this chapter we've seen some of the principles of e-commerce in the real, hostile world. We've seen the importance of focussing on short-term revenue and keeping risks down. We've looked at the three basic reasons why an e-commerce site can make money:

- ❑ Acquiring more customers

- ❑ Making customers spend more

- ❑ Reducing the costs of fulfilling orders

We've applied those principles to a three-phase plan that provides a deliverable, usable site at each stage and continues to expand throughout the book.

I've presented my plan to the owners of the joke shop. In the next chapter we'll put on our programming hat, and start to design and build our web site (assuming we get the contract, of course).

Laying Out the Foundations

Great! Now that we have convinced our client that we can create a cool web site to complement their store's activity, it's time to stop celebrating and start thinking about how to put into practice all our promises. As usual, when we lay down on paper the technical requirements we must meet, everything starts to seem a bit more complicated than initially anticipated.

In order to ensure this project's success, we need to come up with a smart way to implement what we have signed the contract for. We want to make our life easy and develop the project smoothly and easily, but the ultimate goal is to make sure our client is satisfied with our work. Consequently, we aim to provide our site's increasing number visitors with a pleasant web experience by creating a nice, functional, and responsive web site, by implementing each one of the three development phases described in the first chapter.

The requirements are pretty high, but this is normal for an e-commerce site nowadays. To maximize the chances of success we'll try to analyze and anticipate as many of the technical requirements as possible, and we'll implement our solution in such a way as to support changes and additions with minimal effort.

In this chapter we will lay down the foundations for the future WroxJokeShop web site. We will talk about what technologies and tools we'll use, and even more importantly, how we'll use them. Let's see a quick summary of our goals for this chapter before moving on.

- ❑ Analyze the project from a technical point of view
- ❑ Analyze and decide an architecture for our distributed application
- ❑ Decide which technologies and programming languages we'll use
- ❑ Decide what tools we'll need for our project
- ❑ Talk about the naming and coding conventions we'll use
- ❑ Create the basic structure of the web site and set up the database

Designing for Growth

The word *design* in the context of a web application can mean many things. Its most popular usage probably refers to the visual and user interface design of a web site.

This usage has a crucial importance because, let's face it, the visitor is more impressed with how a site looks and how easy it is to use than about which technologies and techniques are used behind the scenes, or what operating system the web server is running. If the site is hard to use or easy to forget, it just doesn't matter what rocket science was used to create it.

Unfortunately, this truth makes many inexperienced programmers underestimate the importance of the way the invisible part of the site is implemented – the code, the database, and so on. The visual part of a site is what gets the visitor interested to begin with, and then its functionality is what makes them come back. A web site can be implemented very quickly based on certain initial requirements, but if not properly architected, it can become very hard, if not impossible, to change.

For each project, depending on its size, there is a minimal amount of preparation that needs to be done before starting to code, and still, no matter how much preparation and design work is done, the unexpected does happen and hidden catches, new requirements, and changing rules always seem to work against our deadlines. Even without these, we can be asked to change or add new functionality many times after the project is finished and deployed. This will also be the case for our site, which will be implemented in three separate stages, as we learned in Chapter 1.

We will learn how to create our web site in such a way that it (or us) will not fall apart when functionality needs to be extended, or updates have to be made. Instead of focusing on how to design the user interface, or on marketing techniques, we'll pay close attention to designing the code that makes them work.

The term, *designing the code*, can have different meanings, for example, we'll need to have a short talk about naming conventions. Still, the most important aspect that we need to take a look at is the *architecture* we'll use when writing the code. The architecture refers to the way we split the code for a simple piece of functionality (for example, the product search) into smaller components. We'll see that although it may be easier to implement that functionality as quickly and as simply as possible, in a single separate component, we gain great long-term advantages by creating more components that work together in order to achieve the desired result.

Before talking about the architecture itself, first let's see what we want from this architecture.

So What Do We Want?

Each of the phases of development we talked about in the first chapter brings new requirements that need to be met. It is obvious that every time when we proceed to a new stage, we want to be able to **reuse** most of the already existing solution. It would be very inefficient to redesign the whole site just because we need to add a new feature to it, and I'm not only talking about redesigning the visual part of the site, but about the code behind it as well! We can make it easier to reuse the solution by planning ahead, so any new functionality that needs to be added can slot in with ease, rather than each causing a new headache.

When building our web site we'll implement a **flexible architecture** composed of pluggable components, so that when we need to add new features like the shopping cart, the departments list or the products search feature, we code them as separate components and just plug them into the existing application. Achieving a good level of flexibility is one of our goals regarding our application's architecture, and in this chapter we'll talk about the way we can put this into practice. We'll see that the flexibility level is proportional to the amount of time required to design and implement it, and we'll try to find a compromise that will provide us with the best gains without complicating the code too much.

The last major requirement that is common to all online applications is that we need a **scalable architecture**. Scalability refers to the way the application reacts when the number of clients increases. We can expect that in the first period of activity our web store won't have much traffic, and in these conditions any web site would handle very well the small number of requests. But since we're very optimistic about the number of customers and because we aim high, we need to be sure that our site will be able to deliver its functionality to a high number of clients without throwing out errors or performing sluggishly.

Throughout the development of the site we'll implement good programming practices in order to get good performance for our site.

The Magic of Three-Layered Architecture

Generally, the architecture refers to splitting each piece of the application's functionality into separate components based on what they do, and grouping each kind of components into a single logical tier.

The three-tier architecture has become very popular nowadays because it answers most of the problems we have discussed so far, by splitting an application's functionality into three logical tiers:

- ❑ The **presentation tier**
- ❑ The **business tier**
- ❑ The **data tier**

Almost every module that we'll create for our site will have components in all these three tiers.

The **presentation tier** is the tier that contains the user interface elements of the site, and includes all the logic that manages the interaction between the visitor and our business. This is the tier that makes the whole site feel alive, and the way we design it has a crucial importance for our site's success. Since our application is a web site, its presentation tier is composed of web pages and their components.

The **business tier** (also called the *middle tier*) is what receives requests from the presentation tier and returns a result back to it depending on the business logic it contains. All events that happen in the presentation tier usually result in the business tier being called. For example, if the visitor is doing a product search, the presentation tier calls the business tier and says, "Please send me back the products that match this search criterion". Almost always, the business tier will need to call the data tier for information to be able to respond to the presentation tier's request.

The **data tier** (sometimes referred to as the *database tier*) is responsible for storing our application's data, and sending it to the business tier when requested. For our e-commerce site we'll need to store data about products, their categories, and their departments, about users, about shopping carts, and so on. Almost every client request will finally result in the data tier being interrogated for information, so it is very important to have a fast database system. We'll learn in the following chapter how we can design our databases for optimum performance.

Note that these tiers are purely logical – there is no constraint on the physical location of each tier. We are free to place all of the application, and implicitly all of its tiers, on a single server machine, or we can place each tier on a separate machine. It all depends on the particular performance requirements of the application and this kind of flexibility allows us to achieve many benefits, as we'll soon see.

An important constraint in the three-layered architecture model is that information must flow in sequential order between tiers. The presentation tier is only allowed to access the business tier, and never directly the data tier. The business tier is the 'brain' in the middle that communicates with the other tiers and processes and coordinates all the information flow. If the presentation tier directly accessed the data tier, the rules of three-tier architecture programming would be broken. If we decide to implement a three-tier architecture, as we do, we must be consistent and obey to its rules, otherwise we will not reap the benefits.

The following diagram is a simple representation of the way data is passed in an application that implements the three-tier architecture.

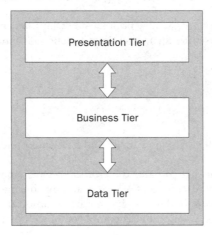

A Simple Scenario

It is easier to understand how data is passed and transformed between tiers if we take a closer look at a simple example. To make the example even more relevant to our project, we analyze a situation that will actually happen in WroxJokeShop. This scenario is a typical one for three tier applications.

Like most e-commerce sites, WroxJokeShop will have a shopping cart, which we will discuss later in the book; but for know it's enough to know that the visitor will add products to the shopping cart by clicking their "Add to Cart" button. The following diagram shows how the information flows through the application when that button is clicked.

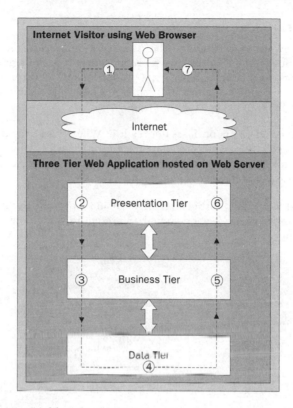

When the user clicks on the "Add to Cart" button for a specific product (Step 1), the presentation tier (which contains the button) forwards the request to the business tier – "Hey, I want this product added to my shopping cart!" (Step 2). The business tier receives the request and understands that the user wants a specific product added to their shopping cart. It handles this by telling the data tier to update the visitor's shopping cart by adding the selected product (Step 3). The data tier needs to be called because it is the one that stores and manages the entire web site's data, including users' shopping cart information.

The data tier updates the database (Step 4) and eventually returns a success code to the business tier. The business tier (Step 5) handles the return code and any errors that might have occurred in the data tier while updating the database, and then returns the output to the presentation tier.

Finally, the presentation tier generates an updated view of the shopping cart (Step 6). The results of the execution are wrapped up generating a HTML web page that is returned to the visitor (Step 7), where the updated shopping cart can be seen in their favorite web browser.

Note that in this simple example the business tier doesn't do a lot of processing and its business logic isn't very complex. However, the business tier is the one to change if new business rules appear for our application. If, for example, the business logic specified that a product could only be added to the shopping cart if its quantity in stock was greater than zero, an additional data tier call would have been made to find out the quantity. The data tier would only be requested to update the shopping cart if there are products in stock. In any case, the presentation tier is informed about the status and the visitor gets human readable feedback for its action.

What's in a Number?

It's interesting to note how each tier interprets the same piece of information differently. For the data tier, the numbers and information it stores have no significance. It is an engine that saves, manages, and retrieves numbers, strings, or other data types – not product quantities or product names. In the context of our previous example, a product quantity of 0 represents a simple, plain number without any meaning to the data tier (it is simply 0, a 32-bit integer).

The data gains significance when the business tier reads it. When it asks the data tier for a product quantity and gets a "0" result, this is interpreted by the business tier as "Hey, no products in stock!" This data is finally wrapped in a nice, visual form by the presentation tier, for example, a label saying, "Sorry, at the moment the product cannot be ordered."

Even if it is unlikely that we want to forbid a customer to add a product to their shopping cart if the product is not in stock, the example is good enough to present in yet another way how each of the three tiers has a different purpose.

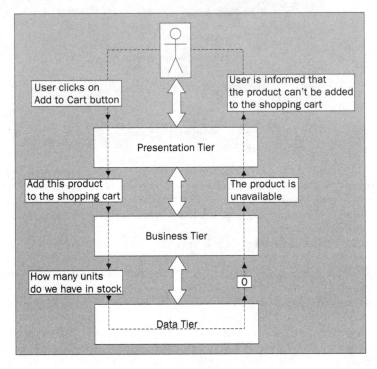

The Right Logic for the Right Tier

Since each layer can contain its own logic, sometimes it can be tricky to decide where exactly to draw the line between the tiers. In our above scenario, instead of reading the product's quantity in the business tier and deciding if the product is available based on that number, we could have a stored procedure in the database named `IsProductAvailable` that simply returns a value of `True` or `False` depending on the availability of the product. This way, the simple logic (an `if` statement) deciding if a product is available would be transferred from the business tier to the data tier.

As an alternative, instead of first checking if the product is available and then adding it to the shopping cart, we could directly call a database stored procedure named `AddProductToCart`, which first tests if the product is available before adding it, or returning an error code if it is not available. This way the whole operation is made with a single call to the data tier, which may result in better performance, but in a less clear architecture.

Note that in both of the hypothetical changes presented above some logic is transferred from the business tier to the data tier. There are many other scenarios where the same logic can be placed in one tier or another, or maybe in both. In most cases there is no single best way to implement the three-tier architecture, and there will be many times when we'll need to make a compromise or a choice based on personal preference or external constraints.

Furthermore, there are occasions where even though you know the *right* way (in respect to the architecture) to implement something, you may choose to break the rules in order to get a performance gain. As a general rule, if performance can be improved this way, it is OK to break the strict limits between tiers *just a little bit* (for example, add some of the business rules to the data tier or vice-versa), **if** these rules are not likely to change in time. Otherwise, keeping all the business rules in the middle tier is preferable because it generates a 'cleaner' application that is easier to maintain.

Final advice for this section: don't be tempted to access the data tier directly from the presentation tier. This is a common mistake that is the shortest path to a complicated, hard-to-maintain, and inflexible system. In many data access tutorials or introductory materials you'll be shown how to perform simple database operations using a simple user interface application. In these kinds of programs all the logic that is stored in separate tiers in a three-tiered application, is probably all written in a single file, with fewer lines of code in total. While it might be very good material, keep in mind that most of these texts are meant to teach you how to do different individual tasks (for example, access a database), and not how to correctly create a flexible and scalable three-tiered application.

A Three-Tier Architecture for WroxJokeShop

Implementing a three-tiered architecture for our WroxJokeShop web site will help us achieve the goals we were talking about at the beginning of the chapter.

When the site is built using an established architecture it is simple to add new components and features to it after deciding how to split their functionality along the tiers. The coding discipline imposed by a system that may seem rigid at first sight allows for excellent levels of flexibility and extensibility in the long run.

Splitting major parts of the application into separate, smaller components also encourages reusability. More than once when we add new features of the site we'll see that we can reuse some of the already existing bits. Anyway, adding a new feature without needing to change much of what already exists is in itself a good example of reusability. Also, smaller pieces of code placed in their correct place are easier to document and analyze at later times.

Another advantage of the three-tiered architecture is that, if properly implemented, the overall system is resistant to changes. When bits in one of the tiers change, the other tiers usually remain unaffected, sometimes even in extreme cases. For example, if for some reason the backend database system is changed, the business tier should work exactly the same with the new database, provided it supports the same stored procedures and exposes the same public interface as the old database. If you don't know what a stored procedure is, don't worry – we'll take a look at them in the following chapter.

Keep in mind that these advantages happen only if the architecture is correctly implemented. Changing the backend database *does* affect an application if its business tier contains logic that should have been in the data tier, for example, if it includes raw SELECT statements instead of calling database stored procedures. We'll talk more about that a bit later.

Why Not Use More Tiers?

The three-tier architecture we've been talking about so far is, a particular (and the most popular) version of the *n*-Tier Architecture, which is a very commonly used buzzword these days. *n*-Tier architecture simply refers to splitting our solution into a number (*n*) of logical tiers. In very complex projects, sometimes it makes sense to split the business layer into more than one layer, thus resulting in architecture with more than three layers. However, for our web site, it makes most sense to stick with the three-layered design, which offers most of the benefits while not requiring too many hours of design.

Maybe with a more involved and complex architecture we would achieve even higher levels of flexibility and scalability for our application, but we would need much more time for design before starting to implement anything. As with any programming project, we try to find a fair balance between the time required to design the architecture and the time spent to implement it. The three-tier architecture is best suited to projects with average complexity, just like the WroxJokeShop.

You may also be asking the opposite question, "Why not use fewer tiers?" A two-tier architecture, also called *client-server* architecture can be appropriate for simpler, less-complex projects. In short, it requires less time for planning and allows quicker development in the beginning, but it generates an application that's harder to maintain and extend on the long run. Because it is not appropriate for our application we won't discuss it any further in this book.

Now that we know what the general architecture is going to be, let's see what technologies and tools we are going to use to implement it. After a brief discussion about the technologies we'll create the basic part of our site's presentation tier by creating the first page of the site, and we'll also set up the data tier by creating the backend database. We will start implementing functionality in each of the three tiers in the following chapter when we will create our web site's product catalog.

Technologies and Tools

No matter which architecture is chosen, a major question that arises in every development project is the one regarding the technologies, programming languages, and tools that are going to be used, bearing in mind that external requirements can seriously limit your options.

Since this book is about ASP.NET and VB.NET, the fact that we'll use these technologies will not be a big surprise to you. We'll also talk about Visual Studio .NET and SQL Server 2000. Although the book assumes a little previous experience with each of these, we'll take a quick look at them and see how they fit into our project and into the three-tier architecture.

ASP.NET

ASP.NET is Microsoft's newest technology for building dynamic, interactive web content. Perhaps the simplest example of dynamic web content is the search results page of a search engine. If you go to www.google.com and search for "Beginning E-Commerce by Wrox", you'll see a web page as a response that obviously doesn't exist on the web server as a static HTML document. It would be impossible to store a separate web document for each possible search string, not to mention updating this tremendous number of result pages. ASP.NET pages contain a template that applies to all response pages, but their content is dynamically generated by the underlying code.

ASP.NET is not the only server side technology around for creating dynamic web pages. Among its most popular competitors are JSP, PHP, ColdFusion, and even the outdated ASP and CGI. Between these technologies are many differences, but also some fundamental similarities. For example, pages written with any of these technologies are composed of basic HTML, which draws the static part of the page (the template), and code that generates the dynamic part. Even Google's dynamically generated search pages have a static structure that applies to all of them. Of course, this could be also generated dynamically, but it's always better to write plain HTML for the parts that don't change because it results in better performance.

The Code Behind the Page

The following diagram shows what happens to an ASP.NET web page from the moment it is requested by the client browser and the moment the browser actually receives it.

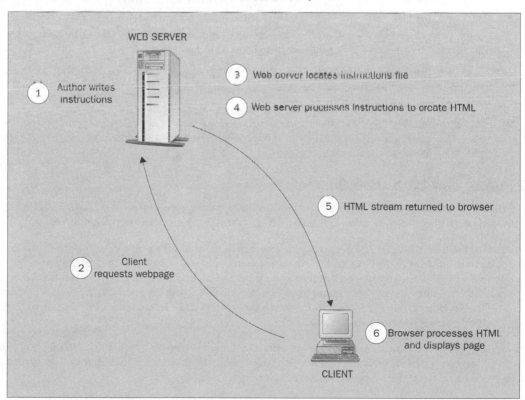

As you can see the page is first processed at the server before being returned to the client, this being the reason for which ASP.NET and the other mentioned technologies are called server-side technologies. When an ASP.NET page is requested, its underlying code is first executed on the server. This code can be written in any .NET-compatible language, and it is used to populate or generate the dynamic part of the page. After the final page is composed, the HTML is returned to the visitor's browser.

Note that HTML web pages can also contain client-side script code, which is always sent unmodified to the visitor's web browser that directly interprets it. The most popular client-side scripting technologies are JavaScript and VBScript. JavaScript is usually the better choice because it has wider acceptance, whereas only Microsoft's Internet Explorer recognizes VBScript. Other important client-side technologies are Macromedia Flash and Java Applets but these are somewhat different because the web browser does not directly parse them – the first one requires a specialized plug-in, the second a Java virtual machine.

Regarding the server-side code, ASP.NET has the nice advantage of allowing this code to be written separately from the static part of the file. All the code that belongs to a certain page can be saved as a **code-behind file** this being an advance over regular ASP pages where the HTML layout and the server-side code were mixed in a single file.

Before going to other details, let's summarize the most important general features of ASP.NET:

❑ The server-side code can be written in any .NET-enabled language. The .NET Framework is supplied with three languages (C#, Visual Basic .NET, and JScript.NET), but the whole infrastructure is designed to be language independent.

❑ The server-side code of ASP.NET pages is fully compiled and executed as opposed to being interpreted line by line, this resulting in excellent performance.

❑ The concept of code-behind files helps a lot in separating the visual part of the page from the (server-side) logic behind it. This is a nice advantage over ASP where both the HTML and the server-side code resided in the same file.

❑ Visual Studio .NET, an excellent and complete visual editor, represents a good weapon in the ASP.NET programmer's arsenal even though it's not required to have it in order to create ASP.NET Web Applications.

Web Forms and Web User Controls

An ASP.NET web page along with its code-behind file is called a **web form**. We learned that it is composed of server-side code and HTML (which in its turn may contain client-side script).

Web forms are files with the ASPX extension. Their code-behind files don't have to follow any particular naming convention except for the final extension specific to the language they are programmed in. The recommended naming system is the one implicitly used by Visual Studio, which automatically creates `.aspx.vb` code behind files for VB.NET projects, or `.aspx.cs` if working with C#. So, in our project, the `default` web form will be created in a file named `default.aspx`, and its code=behind file will be `default.aspx.vb`.

A web form may also contain **server-side controls**. Server-side controls act just like web forms, except they can't be requested directly by a client web browser. Instead, they are included in web forms, the parent web form acting like a client for the control.

There are a number of server-side controls provided by the .NET Framework. These include simpler controls like `Label`, `TextBox` or `Button` and more complex controls like `DataGrid` or `Calendar`. Finally when sent to the client browser, these are also transformed to simple HTML controls and maybe more complex HTML code, depending on the complexity of the control. The main advantage of having server-side controls is the ability to programmatically access them and set their properties, just as in Windows Forms applications or old VB6 programs. With ASP.NET it's nothing unusual to set a label's property like this, in the code-behind file:

```
descriptionLabel.Text = "This is an interesting description"
```

The best news about server-side web **user controls** is that we can create our own. When creating WroxJokeShop we'll write many smaller components (web user controls) that will be placed on the main web page to fill its contents. Web user controls have a `.ascx` extension, and their code behind files have an additional extension depending on their programming language.

Having a site structure based on user controls provides an excellent level of flexibility; if we want to change the layout of the site, sometimes it's enough to change the location of certain user controls, or change the look of a particular user control without interfering with the rest of the site.

ASP.NET and the Three-Tier Architecture

The collection of web forms and web user controls form the presentation tier of the application. They are the part that creates the HTML code loaded by the visitor's browser.

The logic of the user interface is stored in the code-behind files, for both web forms and web user controls. Note that although with ASP.NET you don't need to use code-behind files (you are free to mix code and HTML just as we did with ASP), we'll exclusively use code-behind files for the presentation-tier logic.

In the context of a three-tier application, the logic in the presentation tier refers to the various event handlers we may have, like `Page_Load` and `someButton_Click`. As we learned earlier, these should call business-tier methods to get their job done, and never call the data tier directly.

VB.NET

Visual Basic .NET is one of the languages that can be used to code the web forms' logic. Unlike its previous version (VB6), Visual Basic .NET is a fully object-oriented language that takes advantage of all the features provided by the .NET Framework.

Because of its similarity to VBScript, which was used as the server-side language for ASP files, Visual Basic .NET is currently the most popular programming language for developers.

This doesn't mean that using VB.NET is an absolute requirement. On the contrary, given the power and flexibility provided by the .NET Framework, we could use any .NET-enabled language. We have already learned that .NET comes by default with another two languages that can be used for the same purpose: C# and JScript.NET. Moreover, we can use different .NET languages for different modules of the project, because they will be perfectly interoperable. For more information about how the .NET Framework works I recommend you to read a general-purpose .NET book.

Apart from using VB.NET for the code-behind files, we'll use the same language to code the middle tier classes. We'll create the first of them in the following chapter when building the product catalog, and we'll learn more details there.

Visual Studio .NET

Visual Studio is by far the best tool you can find to develop your .NET applications. It is a complete programming environment capable of working with many types of projects and files, including both VB.NET and C# Windows and Web Forms projects, setup and deployment projects, and many others. Visual Studio can also be used as an interface to the database to create tables and stored procedures, implement table relations, and so on.

Although we'll exclusively use Visual Studio for writing our project, it is important to know that we don't have to. ASP.NET and the C# and VB.NET compilers are available as free downloads at www.microsoft.com, and a simple editor like Notepad is enough to create any kind of web page.

We'll explore various features of Visual Studio as we create WroxJokeShop.

SQL Server

SQL Server is Microsoft's player in the relational database management systems (RDBMS) field. It is a complex software program with the sole purpose of storing, managing, and retrieving large amounts of data as quickly as possible. We will use SQL Server to store all the information regarding our web site, which will be dynamically placed on the web page by the application logic. Simply said, all data regarding the products, departments, users, shopping carts, and so on will be stored and managed by SQL Server.

SQL Server in its commercial versions is also shipped with various management utilities. Perhaps the most popular of them is the Enterprise Manager, a program that allows us to perform almost any operation on a database, including set-up security and backup strategies. The other utility very much loved by programmers is the Query Analyzer, a simple yet powerful application that allows the execution and analysis of the execution of SQL statements. If you aren't familiar with SQL, we'll learn more about it in the next chapter.

Visual Studio .NET ships with a lightweight, free version of SQL Server named MSDE – Microsoft Database Engine – and we will use this as the database backend system. If you have SQL Server Standard or Enterprise edition, you can use that instead.

MSDE has some performance limitations, but it is free and totally compatible with the commercial and expensive version of SQL Server. This means that we can use MSDE on our development machines and then simply transfer the database to the full SQL Server versions at the client site. This is an advantage over the old way of using Access on development machines and then upsizing to SQL Server when moving the application to the client site.

MSDE doesn't ship with the management programs mentioned earlier, so we will use Visual Studio to interact with the database engine. We'll make the first steps in interacting with SQL Server a bit later in this chapter when we create the WroxJokeShop database.

SQL Server and the Three-Tier Architecture

It should be clear by now that SQL Server is somehow related to the data tier. However, if you haven't worked with databases until now, it may be less than obvious that SQL Server is more than a simple store of data. Apart from the actual data stored inside, SQL Server is also capable of storing logic in the form of stored procedures. These stored procedures are part of the data, and are called from the business tier. The stored procedures in turn access the data store, get the results, and return them back to the business tier.

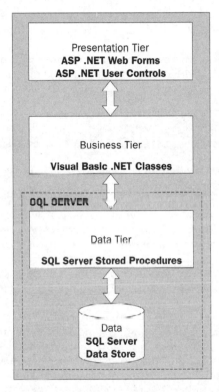

The stored procedures in the database are written in a language named T-SQL (Transact-SQL), which is the SQL dialect recognized by SQL Server. SQL, or Structured Query Language, is a language used to interact with the database. SQL is used to transmit to the database instructions like "Send me the last 10 orders" or "delete product #123".

Coding Standards

Although coding and naming standards may not seem that important at first, they definitely shouldn't be overlooked. Not following a set of rules for your code will almost always result in code that's hard to read, understand, and maintain. On the other hand, when you follow a consistent way of coding you can say your code is already half documented, which is an important contribution towards the project's maintainability, especially when more persons are working at the same project at the same time.

> Some companies have their own policies regarding coding and naming standards, while in other cases you'll have the flexibility to use your own preferences. In either case the golden rule to follow is *be consistent in the way you code*.

Naming conventions refer to many elements within a project, simply because almost all a project's elements have names: the project itself, web forms, web user controls, instances of web user controls and other interface elements, classes, variables, methods, method parameters, database tables, database columns, stored procedures, and so on. Imagine that without some discipline when naming those, after a week of coding you'll come to realize you don't just understand a line of what you wrote two days ago.

In this book we will try to stick to Microsoft's recommendations regarding naming conventions. Now the philosophy is that a variable name should express what the object does, and not its data type. We'll talk more about naming conventions while we'll build the site. Right now, it's time to play.

Creating the Visual Studio .NET Project

So far we have dealt with theory regarding the application we're going to create. It was fun, but it's even more interesting to put into practice what we have learned until now.

> *Before reading on, note that we assume you have Visual Studio .NET, ASP.NET, IIS 5.0, and MSDE or SQL Server installed on your computer. If you are not sure, please consult the appendix that explains how to do all the installation work.*

The first step towards the successful WroxJokeShop site is to open Visual Studio .NET and create an ASP.NET Web Application. From Visual Studio we will be able to manage all of the application's code for all three tiers.

Visual Studio .NET does a great job at automating some tasks. For example, when creating a new ASP.NET Web Application, you just need to specify the web location where you want it to be created, for example http://localhost/BegECom, and Visual Studio will automatically create the folder structure in the wwwroot folder (by default located at \Inetpub\wwwroot). However, we prefer (not that it's required) to physically have our project located in a different folder. For this, we'll need to take a few steps that are explained in the following *Try It Out*:

Try it Out – Creating a New ASP.NET Web Application in a Custom Location

1. Create a new folder named BegECom, which will be used for all the work we'll do in this book. We are creating it in the root folder of C:\ so it will be easier to work with it, but we will use relative paths in the code so you may choose another location or drive if you prefer.

2. In the BegECom folder please create another folder named WroxJokeShop. This folder will contain the WroxJokeShop project. If you created BegECom in C:\, right now the complete path to WroxJokeShop should be C:\BegECom\WroxJokeShop.

3. In Windows, open Control Panel, go to Administrative Tools and double-click on the Internet Services Manager tool. Here make sure the Default Web Site located in *local computername*\Web Sites is visible. Your Internet Information Services (IIS) tool should look like the following screenshot:

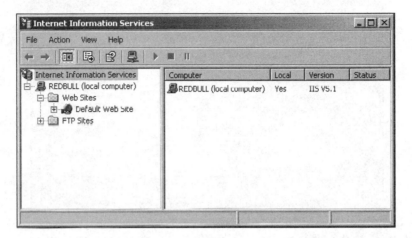

4. Right-click on Default Web Site, and select New | Virtual Directory. Click on Next, and in the Wizard that pops up, type WroxJokeShop for Alias:

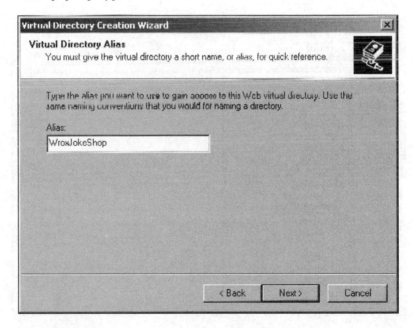

5. Click Next. In the window that appears you need to type or browse to the WroxJokeShop folder that we have just created:

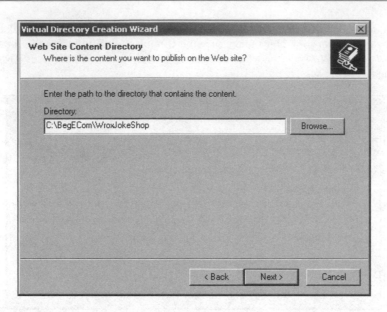

6. Click Next. In the next window leave the default options of Read and Run scripts checked. Click Next again, and then Finish to close the wizard. At this point the WroxJokeShop virtual directory should be selected in the IIS management console:

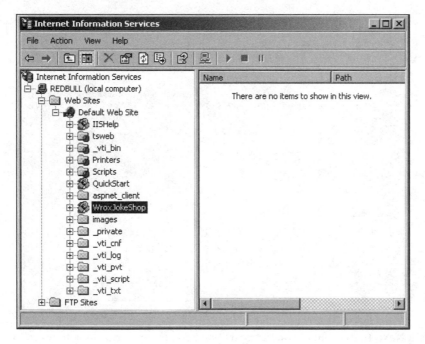

After creating this virtual directory, trying to load the address http://localhost/WroxJokeShop in Internet Explorer would attempt to load the site located in the BegECom\WroxJokeShop folder. Since the location is empty, right now we get an error. So, let's create a new Web Application in the mentioned folder.

7. Start Visual Studio .NET, select File from the main menu and then New | Project. A dialog box will open. Select Visual Basic Projects as the project type, and then ASP.NET Web Application from the Templates panel. Enter http://localhost/WroxJokeShop for the project location. The New Project window should look like the following screenshot:

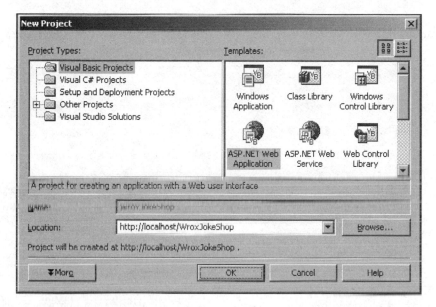

Click OK. Visual Studio now creates the new project in the WroxJokeShop folder that we created at the beginning of this exercise.

8. In the new project a new web form is created by default, WebForm1.aspx:

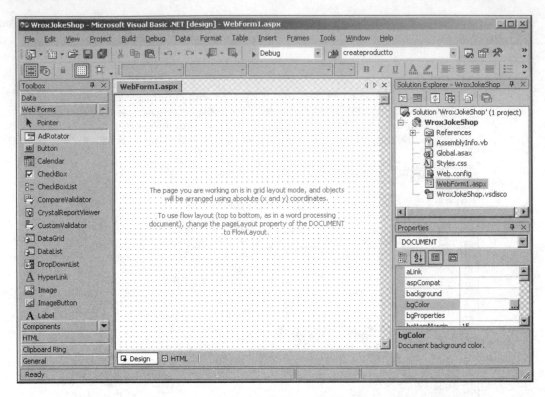

Congratulations! You have just made the first step for creating your cool e-commerce store!

How It Works

We have created a physical directory on the hard disk, and then a virtual folder associated with it. This means that the web address http://localhost/WroxJokeShop points to the application located in the BegECom\WroxJokeShop folder we created.

Keep in mind that we don't have to manually create the virtual directory. When creating a new ASP.NET Web Application, Visual Studio asks for a web location for the application. If we type http://localhost/WroxJokeShop there and the WroxJokeShop virtual folder doesn't exist, it is created and is associated with a physical WroxJokeShop folder that is created in InetPub\wwwroot.

We have done these steps manually because we wanted to have the application in a custom folder instead of the default one. If you're curious to see which files were automatically created by Visual Studio, open the BegECom\WroxJokeShop folder in Explorer:

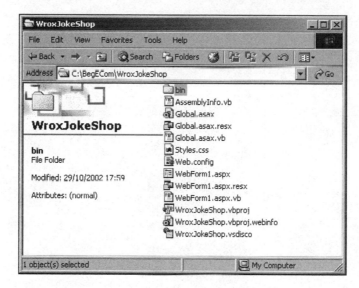

We will take a look at some of these files later. Right now it is interesting to see the web form that was created by default by Visual Studio, `WebForm1.aspx` and the code behind it, `WebForm1.aspx.vb`. This web form (empty by default) can be loaded in Internet Explorer by opening http://localhost/WroxJokeShop/WebForm1.aspx.

Implementing the Site Skeleton

The visual and functional design of the site is usually agreed upon after a discussion with the client, and in collaboration with a professional web designer. As noted earlier, since this is a programming book we won't focus too much on design issues. Furthermore, we want to have a pretty simple design that will allow us to learn how to create an e-commerce site quickly, without spending time with unnecessary details.

We finally agree that all pages in WroxJokeShop, including the first page, should have the following structure:

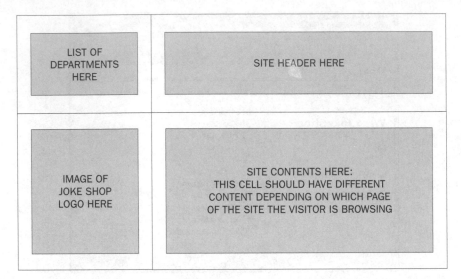

Although we will discuss the detailed structure of the product catalog in the next chapter, right now we know that we'll have a main list of departments that needs to be displayed on every page of the site. We also want the joke shop logo and the site header to be visible in any page the visitor browses.

In order to implement this structure as simply as possible, we will use user controls to create the separate parts of the page:

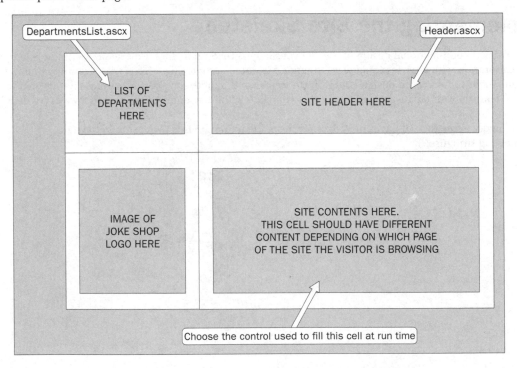

As the picture suggests we will create two web user controls, DepartmentsList and Header, which will help us to populate the first page. For the joke shop logo we will simply add an image in that table cell.

Having user controls to implement different pieces of functionality brings benefits that we talked about earlier in the chapter. Having different, unrelated pieces of functionality logically separated from one another gives us the flexibility to modify them independently, and even reuse them in other pages without having to write HTML code and the supporting code behind again. It's also extremely easy to change the place of a feature implemented as a user control in the parent web page; all we need to move is a user control, which is anything but a complicated and lengthy process.

The list of departments, the joke shop logo, and the site header are elements that will be present in every page of the site. The only part that changes while browsing through the site will be the contents cell, which will update itself depending on the site location requested by the visitor. For implementing that cell we have two main options. We can either add a user control that changes itself depending on the location, or use different user controls to populate that cell depending on the location being browsed. There is no rule of thumb about what method to use, as it mainly depends on the specific of the project. For WroxJokeShop we will create a number of user controls that will fill that location.

In the remainder of this chapter we will create the main web page and the header web user control. We'll deal with the other user controls in the following chapters. Finally, at the end of the chapter we will create the WroxJokeShop database, which will be the last step in laying the foundations of our project.

Building the First Page

At the moment we have a single web form in the site, WebForm1.aspx, which was automatically added by Visual Studio when we created the project. In order to work with more familiar names, in the next *Try It Out* exercise we'll delete this form from the project and add a new form called default.aspx instead. It is also possible to rename WebForm1.aspx to default.aspx but this wouldn't change the contents of the code-behind file, so we prefer to start with a new, 'clean' form.

We will write default.aspx with placeholders for the three major parts of the site – the header, the table of departments and the page contents cell, and in the lower-left side we'll add the joke shop logo.

Try It Out – Creating the Main Web Page

1. First, please download the files for this chapter from www.wrox.com. We'll need to use the Images folder, which contains background pictures for the main web page. Please copy the Images folder from the downloaded files to the WroxJokeShop folder that we created in the previous section.

2. Open the WroxJokeShop project in Visual Studio, if it is not already open. Let's first delete the automatically generated Web Form file, WebForm1.aspx. To do this, first make sure Solution Explorer is visible by pressing *Ctrl+Alt+L*. Then right-click on WebForm1.aspx in Solution Explorer and select Delete. Press OK when asked for confirmation.

3. To add a new web form, Right-click on the project's name WroxJokeShop in Solution Explorer, then choose Add | Add Web Form. Enter default.aspx for the name of the new web form. If you simply type default, Visual Studio will add the .aspx extension for you. Select Open.

4. Right-click on `default.aspx`, and click on the **Set As Start Page** option. This way, when we press *F5* to execute the project, `default.aspx` will be loaded in Internet Explorer. If you test this, make sure you close the Internet Explorer instance opened by Visual Studio before proceeding to the next step.

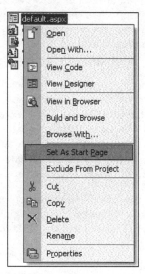

5. Now open `default.aspx` web form by double-clicking on it in Solution Explorer. You should be presented with a form like this:

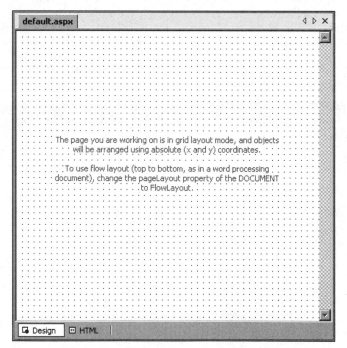

The screenshot shows the **designer window** of Visual Studio .NET. This allows you to edit a web form using either the **Design View** or the **HTML View** modes. In the screenshot we can see the web form in Design View mode, this being indicated by the Design button being highlighted at the bottom of the window.

When using Design View, we can visually edit the form in a WYSIWYG (What You See Is What You Get) editor, by dragging and dropping components from the toolbox into the form or by directly writing text on it. The other way of editing a web form is using HTML View mode, where we can directly edit the HTML of the web form.

No matter which edit mode we use, Visual Studio always keeps both views synchronized. If we edit the form in Design View and then switch to HTML View we'll see the changes there, and when directly changing the HTML, we'll see the results when switching back to Design.

While creating WroxJokeShop we will use both Design View and HTML View, depending on which one takes less time for the task at hand. Also, sometimes we will prefer to use HTML because we have better control of the code.

When using the Design View there are two layout modes that can be used to edit the form. As you can see in the screenshot, the default working mode is *grid layout mode*. This means that when we drag and drop components form the toolbox, these will be placed at the exact position where we dropped them because their location is stored using absolute coordinates. This mode is similar to the way controls are placed in Visual Basic 6 or in Windows Forms projects in Visual Studio .NET. However many developers prefer to work in the *flow layout mode*, where the HTML generated is similar to that which we know from 'regular' web pages.

6. While developing WroxJokeShop we'll work using flow layout mode. If the Properties window is not visible, press *F4* to see it. Make sure the design window is selected by left-clicking on it, and then modify its pageLayout property to FlowLayout in the Properties window:

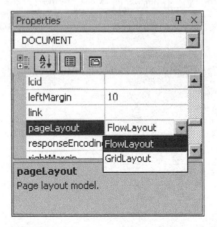

7. Then, enter the HTML View by selecting the HTML button at the bottom of the designer window:

8. Here we can see the code Visual Studio generated for us. While in HTML View mode, let's update the web form like this:

```
<%@ Page Language="vb" AutoEventWireup="false" Codebehind="default.aspx.vb"
Inherits="WroxJokeShop._default"%>
<!DOCTYPE HTML PUBLIC "-//W3C//DTD HTML 4.0 Transitional//EN">
<html>
  <head>
    <title>WroxJokeShop</title>
      <meta name="GENERATOR" content="Microsoft Visual Studio.NET 7.0">
      <meta name="CODE_LANGUAGE" content="Visual Basic 7.0">
      <meta name="vs_defaultClientScript" content="JavaScript">
      <meta content="http://schemas.microsoft.com/intellisense/ie5"
                                             name="vs_targetSchema">
  </head>
  <body>
    <form id="Form1" runat="server">
      <table height="100%" cellSpacing="0" cellPadding="0" width="770"
                                             border="0">
        <tr>
          <td width="200" height="100%">
            <table background="Images/backgr.gif" height="100%" width="100%"
                cellspacing="0" cellpadding="0">
              <tr>
                <td vAlign="top" height="100%">Place List of Departments Here
                </td>
              </tr>
              <tr>
                <td>
                  <IMG src="Images/Wrox.jpg" height="369" width="197"
                                               border="0">
                </td>
              </tr>
            </table>
```

```
        </td>
        <td vAlign="top" width="550"><br>
          <table>
            <tr>
              <td>Place Header Here</td>
            </tr>
            <tr>
              <td id="pageContentsCell" runat="server">
                Place Contents Here
              </td>
            </tr>
          </table>
        </td>
      </tr>
    </table>
  </form>
 </body>
</html>
```

9. After making these changes, let's switch back to Design View mode. If no errors were made, the page you see should resemble the following screenshot:

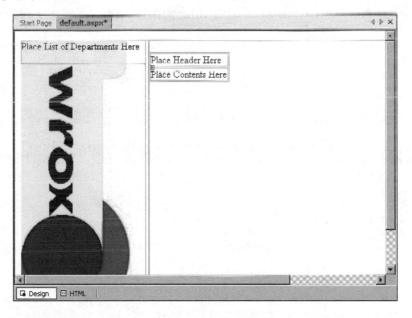

10. Note in the picture that the Place Contents Here table cell is marked with a little green arrow sign. This specifies that it is marked as being executed server-side (on the server). If you take a look at the HTML you'll see the runat="server" clause:

```
        <td id="pageContentsCell" runat="server">
          Place Contents Here
        </td>
```

All server-side controls and components (including Labels, TextBoxes, and so on) on the page will be marked with the same green symbol. We need the table cell to be executed server-side because we'll want to programmatically fill it with contents from the VB.NET code, and this is only possible if it is executed server-side. Remember that for the other cells we know for sure which user controls will be used, and we will populate them at design time, but the page contents cell will need to be populated from code.

When adding a server-side control to the form Visual Studio automatically generates an object in the code-behind file, which will allow us to access the control programmatically. To access the code-behind file default.aspx.vb, right-click on default.aspx in Solution Explorer and select View Code. Alternatively, you can click on the View Code icon at the top of the Solution Explorer window when default.aspx is selected.

Here you can see the declaration of the pageContentsCell object, at the beginning of the file:

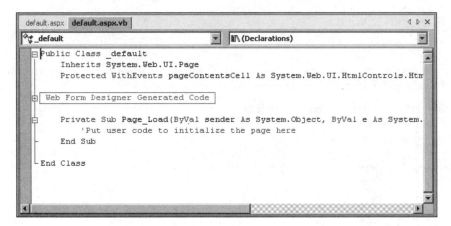

In certain situations when adding the control while in HTML mode, Visual Studio doesn't generate that line automatically for you. If this is the case, make sure that line is there by manually adding it:

```
Public Class _default
    Inherits System.Web.UI.Page
    Protected WithEvents pageContentsCell As _
                        System.Web.UI.HtmlControls.HtmlTableCell
```

How It Works – The Main Web Page

We've done a lot of things in this exercise. It took quite a long time because we learned about some of the features Visual Studio .NET provides us with along the way.

The main web page contains three major sections, plus the logo. There are three table cells that we will fill with user controls. We will write two of these – the one for the list of departments and the one for the page contents – in the following chapter. We will create the header control a bit later in this chapter. When these three controls are in place, the first page of the shop will look like this when loaded in Internet Explorer:

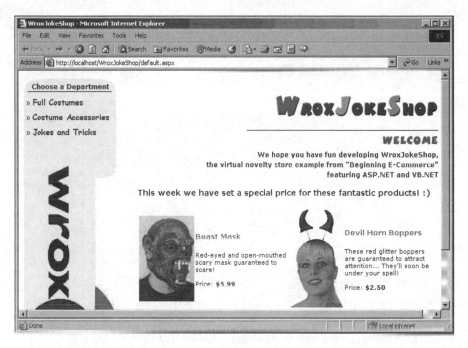

Notice the departments list placed on the left side, the header at the top, and the contents cell filled with information regarding the first page. As previously mentioned, this contents cell is the only one that changes while browsing the site – the other two controls will look exactly the same no matter what page we are visiting. This explains why the contents cell is the only one marked to run at the server. Now let's see how to create a web user control by implementing Header.ascx.

Adding the Header to the Main Page

Finally, after having talked so much about how useful user controls are, we get to create one. The Header control will populate the upper-right part of the main page and will look like this:

In order to keep our site's folder organized, we'll create a separate folder where we will place all the user controls. Having them in a centralized location is helpful, especially when the projects grows and contains lots of files.

Try It Out – Creating the Header User Control

1. First, let's create a separate folder that will hold our user controls. Make sure the Solution Explorer is visible in Visual Studio. If it is not, press *Ctrl+Al+-L*. Here, right-click on WroxJokeShop and select Add | New Folder.

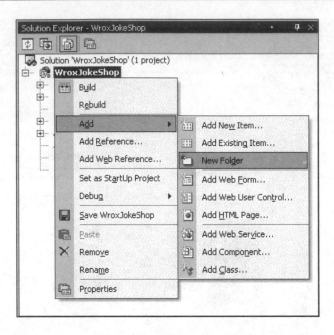

2. Enter UserControls as the name of the new folder.

3. Now let's create the Header user control in the UserControls folder. Right-click on UserControls in Solution Explorer, and then choose **Add | Add Web User Control**.

4. You'll be asked for the name of the new user control. Type Header.ascx and press *Enter*.

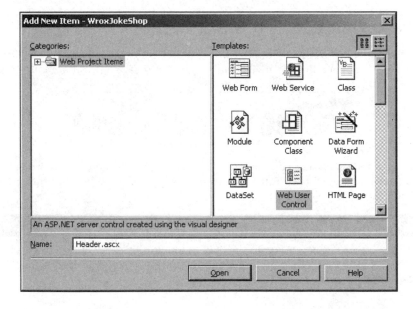

5. Now open the Header web user control by double-clicking on it in Solution Explorer. Enter the HTML view mode by clicking on the **HTML** button at the bottom of the design window. Modify the HTML code like this:

```
<%@ Control Language="vb" AutoEventWireup="false"
Codebehind="Header.ascx.vb" Inherits="WroxJokeShop.Header"
TargetSchema="http://schemas.microsoft.com/intellisense/ie5" %>
```

```
<table border="0" width="550" cellspacing="0" cellpadding="0">
  <TR align="right">
    <td>
      <a href="default.aspx">
        <img src="Images/WroxJokeShop.gif" border="0">
      </a>
    </td>
  </TR>
  <TR align="right">
    <td>
      <img src="Images/1n.gif" border="0" width="350" height="1">
    </td>
  </TR>
</table>
```

Note that if you switch the control to Design view right now, you won't be able to see the images. This happens because the `Images` folder in which they are located is not in the `UserControls` folder, where the user control is. However, when executed, the user control is included in its containing web form and the relative path used for the pictures will point to the correct location.

6. Press *Ctrl-Shift-B* to build the solution. Now open `default.aspx` in Design view, drag `Header.aspx` from the Solution Explorer and drop it in the **Place Header Here** table cell. Then delete the **Place Header Here** text from the cell. The design view of `default.aspx` should look like this:

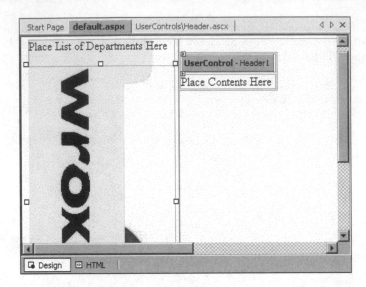

7. Press *F5* to execute the project. The web page will look like this:

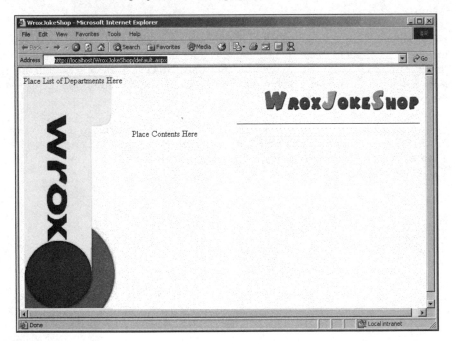

How It Works – The Header User Control

We created this control by editing its HTML source, but we could use the Design View to drag and drop items to the form as well. When executed alone, this piece of HTML generates the following output:

The Header control isn't particularly exciting, but it is interesting to see how we can create a user control and then add it to a web form. This User Control can be reused on other web forms pages; hence, it is an easy way to create toolbars, menus, headers (obviously), and other reusable elements.

Creating the SQL Server Database

The final step we make in this chapter will be to create the SQL Server database, though we won't get to effectively use it until the next chapter. If you have SQL Server you might prefer to use the Enterprise Manager to create the data structures. However, Visual Studio .NET does provide a great interface to the database engine and we'll use that to work with the database.

All the information that needs to be stored for our site, such as data about products, customers, and so on, will be stored in a database named, unsurprisingly, WroxJokeShop. We create the database in this *Try It Out exercise*.

Try It Out – Creating a New Database using Visual Studio .NET

1. In our Visual Studio project, make sure the Server Explorer window is open. If it is not, you can either open View | Server Explorer, or press the shortcut keys *Ctrl+Alt+S*.

2. In the Server Explorer, open Servers/*localservername*/SQL Servers. Right-click on the name of your SQL Server instance, and select New Database.

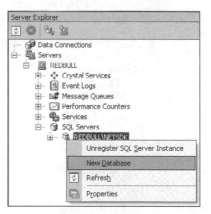

3. In the dialog that appears, you need to choose a name for the new database, and the way to log in to SQL Server. The database name will be WroxJokeShop, and for authentication you can either select Use Windows NT Integrated Security, or select SQL Server Authentication using the sa login account, which has a blank password by default. Be aware that the Windows Authentication might be disabled from SQL Server and you may need to use a SQL Server username/password combination.

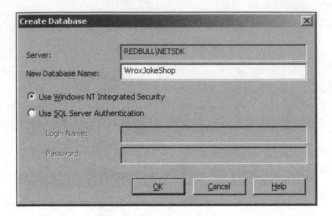

How It Works

That's it! We have just created a new SQL Server database. The Server Explorer window in Visual Studio is very powerful and allows us to control many details of our SQL Server instance. After creating the WroxJokeShop database, you can expand its nodes and see what it contains. Since we just created an empty database, its nodes are quite empty, but we'll take care of this detail in the following chapters.

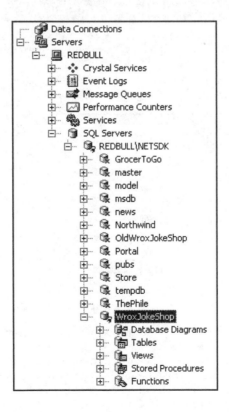

Code Download

The code you have just written is available in the download for this book from www.wrox.com. It should be easy for you to read through this book and build your solution as you go; however, if you want to check something from our working version, you can do. Instructions on loading the chapters are available in the README.TXT document in the download.

Summary

We covered a lot of ground in this chapter, didn't we? We talked about the three-tier architecture and how it helps us create great flexible and scalable applications. We also saw how each of the technologies we use in this book fits into the three-tier architecture.

So far we have a very flexible and scalable application since it only has a main web page and a header user control – but we'll feel the real advantages of using a disciplined way of coding in the next chapters. In this chapter we have only coded the basic, static part of the Presentation Tier, and we created the WroxJokeShop database, which is the support for the data tier. In the next chapter we'll implement the product catalog and we will learn a lot about how to dynamically generate visual content using data stored in the database, with the help of the middle tier, and with smart and fast controls and components in the presentation tier.

Creating the Product Catalog

In the previous chapter, after learning about the three-tier architecture, we implemented a bit of our web site's main page. This allowed us to discover some of the features of Visual Studio .NET we also created a web user control and added it to the front page.

In this chapter we'll continue our work by starting to create the product catalog for our site. Because the product catalog is composed of many components, we'll create it over two chapters. In this chapter we'll create the first database table, implement access methods in the middle tier and learn how to create stored procedures – and by the end of it we'll finally have something dynamically generated on our web page.

The main topics we'll touch in this chapter are:

❑   Thinking about what we want our catalog to look like and what functionality it should support

❑   Creating the database structures for the catalog and the data tier of the catalog

❑   Implementing the business objects required to make the catalog run

❑   Implementing an attractive user interface for the product catalog

Showing the Visitor What we Have

One of the essential features required in any electronic store is to allow the visitor to easily browse through its products. Just imagine what Amazon would be like without its excellent product catalog!

Whether our visitor is looking for something specific or is just browsing, it is important to make sure their experience with our site is a pleasant one. When looking for a specific product or product type, we want the visitor to find it as easily as possible. This is why we'll want to add search functionality to our site, and also find a clever way of structuring products into categories so they can be quickly and intuitively accessed.

Depending on the size of the store, it may be enough to group products under a number of categories, but if the number of products is quite high, we need to find even more ways to categorize and structure the product catalog.

Deciding the structure of the catalog is one of the first tasks we'll need to accomplish in this chapter. Once this is done, we will move to the technical details that will finally make the catalog work.

What Does a Product Catalog Look Like?

This is something that we need to think about for any kind of store, not just an e-commerce site. Separate from the visual part of the product catalog, which of course is very important, in this section we are more interested in the way we should structure the catalog in order to make it as intuitive and helpful as possible.

Today's web surfers are more demanding than they used to be. They expect to find out information quickly on whatever product or service they have in mind, and if they don't find it, they are likely to go to the competition before giving the site a second chance. Of course, we don't want this to happen to *our* visitors.

Besides, if we *do* have the product in our catalog, wouldn't it be a shame if our visitor didn't buy it because they couldn't find it? We need to place our products exactly where our visitor expects them to be and we want to make them easily accessible with an easy-to-use interface.

Because our electronic store will start with around one hundred products and will probably have much more in the future, we decide it's not enough to just group them in categories. We will also have a number of departments and each department will contain a number of categories. Each category can then have any number of products attached to it. After long hours of discussions with the client for whom we are creating the site, we come up with this schema of structuring the products:

> *Even if we have a pretty clear idea of the categories and departments, our client wants these to be configurable from the administrative part of the web site. This requirement is not unusual, because it is quite likely that categories and even departments will change in time. Of course, one solution would be for us to manually change these whenever needed, but this solution would be extremely complicated and highly unprofessional; in other words, something that we want to avoid. We'll create the administrative part of the product catalog, which will allow our client to manage the departments, categories, and products, in Chapter 7.*

Another particularly important detail that we need to think about is whether a category can exist in more than one department, and whether a product can exist in more than one category. As you already suspect, this is the kind of decision that can have implications on the way we code the product catalog, so this is why we need to consult our client and hear their opinion in this matter.

For the WroxJokeShop product catalog, each category can exist in only one department, but a product can exist in more than one category. For example, we may want a product named X to be found in both Y and Z categories. This decision will have some implications in the way we design the database, and we'll highlight them when we get there.

Finally, apart from having the products grouped in categories, we also want to have featured products. For this web site, a product can be featured either on the front page or in the department pages. Let's look at a few screenshots that will explain this by themselves.

Previewing the Product Catalog

Although we'll have the fully functional product catalog finished by the end of the next chapter, taking a look at it right now will help us have a better idea about we're heading. In the following screenshot, you can see the WroxJokeShop front page that has three featured products:

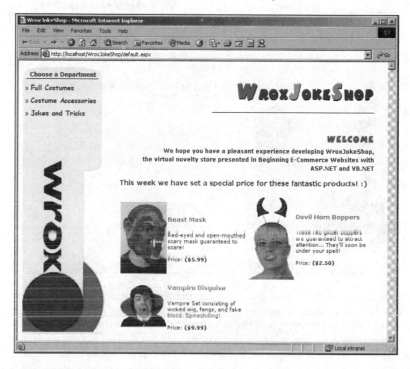

Note the departments list located in the upper left corner of the page. The list of departments is dynamically generated with data gathered from the database, and we'll create it in this chapter. Remember from the previous chapter when we saw the general schema of WroxJokeShop pages that the department list will be there on every page we visit.

When a department is clicked in the departments list, we get to the main page of the specified department. This will replace the store's list of promotional products with a page containing information specific to the selected department – including the list of featured products for that department. In the screenshot overleaf, we can see the page that will appear when the Jokes and Tricks department is selected:

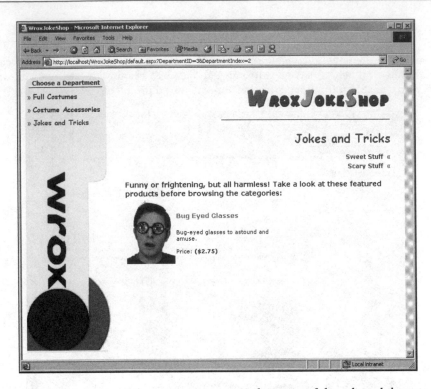

In the upper right-hand corner of the screen we can see the name of the selected department and the list of categories that belong to that department. We decided that in the department page only the featured products are listed because the complete list would be too long. The text above the list of featured products is the description for the selected department, which is read from the database. This tells us that we'll need to store in the database both a name and a description for each department.

In this page, when a particular category is selected, all its products are listed, along with an updated description text:

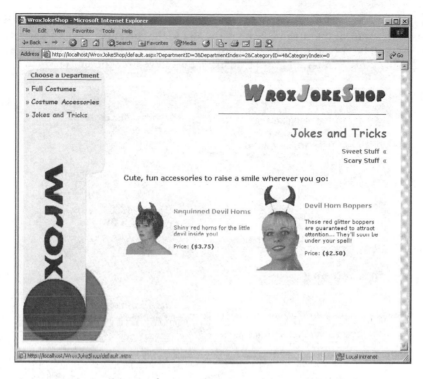

When a category is selected, all its products get listed – we no longer see featured products. Note that the description text also changes. This time, this is the description of the selected category.

What we'll Do in This Chapter

As you can see, our nice product catalog, although not very complicated, has more parts that need to be covered. In this chapter we'll only create the departments list, located in the upper left of the page:

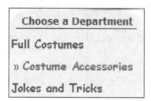

This will be very exciting, since it's the first time we'll see some dynamically generated data in our site – the names of the departments will be extracted from the database!

We cover just the creation of the department list in this chapter, which is in fact a user control, because we will also take a closer look at the mechanism that makes the control work. After we understand what happens behind the nice looking list of departments, we'll quickly implement the other components in the following chapter.

In Chapter 2, we discussed the three-tiered architecture that we'll use to implement the web application. The product catalog part of the site makes no exception to the rule, and its components (including the departments list) will be spread over the three logical layers. The following diagram previews what we'll create at each tier in this chapter, in order to achieve the desired functionality:

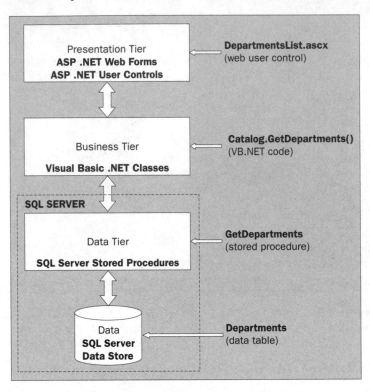

So far we have only played a bit with the presentation tier, in Chapter 2. Now, when building the catalog we'll finally meet the other two tiers and work further with the WroxJokeShop database. The database backend itself is not considered as being an integral part of the three-tiered architecture.

These are the main steps we will make towards having our own dynamically generated department list:

❑ Create the Department table in the database. In order to accomplish this we'll first learn the basic concepts of working with relational databases.

❑ Add the GetDepartments stored procedure to the database, which (like all the other stored procedures we'll write) is logically located in the data tier part of the application. For this we'll learn how to speak with the database using the SQL language.

❑ For the business tier element we'll first learn how to communicate with the database and call the stored procedure.

❑ Finally we'll implement the DepartmentsList.ascx control, which represents the goal of this chapter.

A Place to Store the Data

Although this is not a book about databases or relational database design, we will learn here all we need to know in order to make the product catalog work and understand how it works. For more information about database programming using SQL Server, we recommend reading *Professional SQL Server 2000 Programming* (ISBN 1-86100-448-6) or *Professional SQL Server 2000 Database Design* (ISBN 1-86100-476-1), both published by Wrox Press.

Essentially, a database is made up of *data tables* and the *relationships* that exist between them. Because in this chapter we'll work with a single data table, we'll study here only the database theory that applies to the table as a separate, individual database item. In the next chapter when we'll add the other tables to the picture we'll take a look at the theory behind *relational databases* by analyzing how the tables relate to each other.

After covering the necessary theory, we'll proceed to building the database table required to make the departments list work. Once the database is in place, we'll continue by creating the data tier that interacts with the table.

The Theory: What Makes up a Data Table

This section is a quick database lesson that covers the essential information you need to know, in order to be able to design simple data tables. We'll briefly discuss the main parts that make up a database table by taking a closer look at the Department table which we'll create later. More specifically, we'll cover:

❑   Primary Keys and why we need them

❑   SQL Server data types

❑   Unique columns

❑   Nullable columns and default values

❑   Identity columns

❑   Indexes

If you have enough experience with relational databases you might want to skip this section and go directly to the *Creating the Table* section.

This book assumes you know the basic database concepts. Still, let us make sure we use the same terms. The following data is extracted from the pubs database that comes with SQL Server:

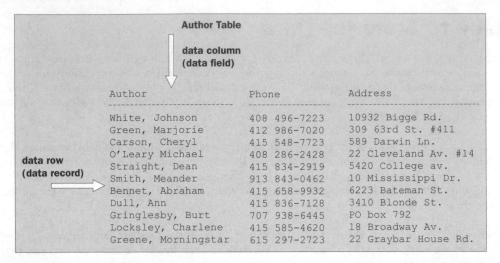

A data table is made up of columns and rows. Columns are also referred to as fields, and rows are sometimes also called records. Note that the image only shows a few of the columns from the original table.

Still, in a relational database, behind a simple list of data rows there is a good deal of hidden logic. Here we take a closer look only at the logic that applies to the table as an individual item, and in the following chapter we'll see how individual tables relate to each other, creating as a whole a relational database. For the purposes of our database lesson we'll use the Department table, which we'll create later in this chapter.

Previewing the Department Table

The database element of the product catalog is composed of tables, table relationships, and stored procedures. Because in this chapter we only cover the departments list, we'll only need to create one data table – the Department table. This is the table that will store our departments' data, and is one of the simplest tables we will work with.

With the help of modern tools like the SQL Server Enterprise Manager or Visual Studio .NET, it is very simple to create a data table in the database, *if* we know for sure what kind of data it will store. When designing a table there are two main things we need to think of: *what fields* should it contain, and *what data types* to use for these fields. Besides its data type, for a table field there are a few more properties that we will look at.

So, what fields do we need for the Department table? This can be easily answered by writing on paper a few examples of records that would be stored in that table. Remember from the previous screenshots that there isn't much information to store about a department: for each department we want to store its *name* and its *description*. The table containing departments' data might look like this one:

Name	Description
Full Costumes	We have the best costumes on the internet! Check out a few samples from our collection:
Costume Accessories	Accessories and fun items to jazz up that special costume. These products are on promotion:
Jokes and Tricks	Funny or frightening, but all harmless! Take a look at these featured products before browsing the categories:

From a table like this the names would be extracted to populate the list in the upper-left part of the web site, and the descriptions would be used as headers for the featured products list.

Primary Keys

The way we work with data tables in a relational database is a bit different from the way we usually work on paper. A fundamental requirement in relational databases is that each data row in a table must be *uniquely identifiable*. This makes sense – we usually save records into the database because at some point in time we'll need them back. But we can't do that if each row doesn't have something that guarantees its uniqueness. Let us explain this better with an example. Suppose that in the departments table presented above we add another record, making it look like this:

Name	Description
Full Costumes	We have the best costumes on the internet! Check out a few samples from our collection:
Costume Accessories	Accessories and fun items to jazz up that special costume. These products are on promotion:
Jokes and Tricks	Funny or frightening, but all harmless! Take a look at these featured products before browsing the categories:
Jokes and Tricks	This is the Jokes and Tricks department in Wrox JokeShop. Here are its products:

Look at this table, and then tell us the description of the Jokes and Tricks department. Yep, we have a problem – now you see our point. The question can't be answered because there are two departments with the name Jokes and Tricks; if we queried the table using the Name column then we would get two results. We weren't supposed to have more than one department with the same name!

The problem arises in situations where we expect to receive a single result. If we asked for the categories that belong to a specific department we would expect to receive more results, but not when we ask for the description or anything else about a *particular* department. Anyway, we couldn't list the categories that belong to a department if we can't uniquely identify the department we're looking for.

The solution of the problem consists in using a **primary key**, which allows us to uniquely identify a specific row out of the many. Technically, a *primary key* is a constraint applied on a table column that guarantees that the column will have unique values for all records in the table.

A table can have a single primary key constraint set, but that primary key can be composed of one or more columns. Note that the primary key is not a column itself – it is **a constraint** that applies to one or more of the existing columns. Constraints are rules that apply to data tables and make part of the **database integrity** rules of the database. The database itself takes care of its integrity and will make sure these rules aren't broken. If, for example, we try to add two identical values for a column that has a primary key constraint, the database will refuse the operation and will generate an error. We'll do some experiments later in this chapter to show this.

Although a primary key is not a column itself but a constraint that applies to that column, from now on when we say primary key we will be talking about the column that has the primary key constraint applied to it. Even if it's not 100% correct, it makes the text more readable.

Back to our example, setting the Name column to be the primary key of the Department table would solve the problem – we wouldn't be allowed to have two departments with the same name. If Name is the primary key of the Department table, searching for a row with a specific Name will always result with exactly one result if the name exists, or no results if there are no records with the specified name.

An alternative solution, and usually the preferred one, is to have an additional column in the table, named an ID column, to act as its primary key. With an ID column, our Department table would look like this:

DepartmentID	Name	Description
1	Full Costumes	We have the best costumes on the internet! Check out a few samples from our collection:
2	Costume Accessories	Accessories and fun items to jazz up that special costume. These products are on promotion:
3	Jokes and Tricks	Funny or frightening, but all harmless! Take a look at these featured products before browsing the categories:

Note the ID column named `DepartmentID`. We'll use the same naming convention for all ID columns in our data tables.

There are a few reasons for why it may be better to have a separate ID primary key column than to use the `Name` (or another existing column) as the primary key. One of them is that department names change in time – it's usually simpler to search for a specific ID (which doesn't change) than for a name. Second, SQL Server handles operations using numerical columns better than using text columns. Finally, there's a reason regarding the philosophy of primary keys – we set the primary key constraint on a column that actually *represents* that department. In our case, we consider that `Name` and `Description` are properties of a department and neither of them is representative enough for a department.

Here the primary key is composed of a single column, but as we said this is not a requirement. If the primary key is set on more than one column, the group of columns – taken as a unit – that are part of the primary key are guaranteed to be unique, even if the individual columns that form the primary key can have repeating values in the table. In the next chapter we'll have an example of a multi-valued primary key and we'll take a closer look there. For now it's enough to know that they exist.

Unique Columns

`Unique` is yet another kind of constraint that can be applied to table columns. This is similar to the primary key constraint because it doesn't allow having duplicate data for a column. Still there are differences. First, we are allowed to have multiple unique columns (as opposed to a single primary key, even if this can be composed of more than one column).

Unique columns are useful in cases where we already have a primary key, but we still have columns for which we want to have unique values. This might be the case for the `Name` column in the `Department` table, in the situation where the `DepartmentID` column is the primary key.

Another difference between primary keys and unique columns is that the unique column can be set to accept `NULL` values (in which case it can only accept *one* `NULL` value). This is not an important detail for this book but we have mentioned this difference for added information.

Columns and Data Types

Each column in a table has a particular data type. By looking at the previous screenshot with the `Department` table, `DepartmentID` has a numeric data type, while `Name` and `Description` contain text.

Since SQL Server supports many data types, it is important that we take a look at them, so we will be able to make correct decisions about how to create our tables. This is not an exhaustive list of SQL Server data types – instead we focus on the main types you might come across in your project. Please refer to *Professional SQL Server 2000 Programming*, MSDN, or SQL Server 2000 Books Online (http://www.microsoft.com/sql/techinfo/productdoc/2000/books.asp) for a more detailed list.

In order to keep the table short, under the *Data Type* heading we have listed only the most frequently used types, while similar data types are explained under the *Description and Notes* heading. We can also see a *Size in Bytes* heading – while it's not crucial to know these, especially nowadays when data storage is very cheap, many people like to know how much space various data types occupy. It is not important to memorize the list, but it is worth taking a look to get a idea what data types are available.

Data Type	Size in Bytes	Description and Notes
Int	4	Stores whole numbers from -2,147,483,648 to 2,147,483,647. Related types are SmallInt and TinyInt. There is also a Bit data type, which is able to store values of 0 and 1.
Money	8	Used to store monetary data with values from -2^{63} to $2^{63}-1$ with a precision of four decimal places. SQL Server supports the Float data type, which holds floating point data, but it is not recommended to store monetary information because of its lack of precision. A variation of Money is SmallMoney that has a smaller range but the same precision.
DateTime	8	Supports date and time data from January 1, 1753, through to December 31, 9999, with an accuracy of three hundreds of a second. There is also a SmallDateTime type with a range from January 1, 1900 to June 6, 2079, with an accuracy of one minute.
UniqueIdentifier	16	Stores a numerical Globally Unique Identifier (GUID). A GUID is guaranteed to be unique this property makes it very useful in certain situations.
VarChar, NVarChar	Variable	These data types are used to store variable-length character data. NVarChar stores Unicode data with a maximum length of 4,000 characters, and VarChar non-Unicode data with a maximum length of 8,000 characters.
Char, NChar	Fixed	These data types store fixed length character data. Values shorter than the declared size are padded with spaces. NChar is the Unicode version and goes to a maximum 4,000 characters, while Char can store 8,000 characters.
Text, NText	Fixed	These are used to store large sized fixed length character data. NText is the Unicode version and has a maximum size of 1,073,741,823 characters. Text has double this maximum size. Using these data types can slow down the database, and it's highly recommended to use Char, VarChar, NChar, or NVarChar instead.
Binary, VarBinary	Fixed/Variable	These data types store binary data with a maximum length of 8,000 bytes.
Image	Variable	Stores binary data of maximum $2^{31}-1$ bytes. Do not think that only pictures can be stored in this field – it can store any kind of binary data. For performance reasons, if there are alternatives, it is not recommended to store binary data directly in the database. For our products' pictures, for example, we will store just a path in the Product table that points to an image file on the hard disk.

Note that the table was written with SQL Server 2000 in mind. SQL Server 7 comes quite close, but there are a few different details, like the maximum size for character data.

Now let's get back to our `Department` table and see what data types we use in it. Please don't worry that you don't have the table yet in your database – we will create it a bit later. For now, we just want to get an idea about how data types work with SQL Server.

	Column Name	Data Type	Length	Allow Nulls
🔑	DepartmentID	int	4	
	Name	varchar	50	
	Description	varchar	200	✓

Department

If we know what these data types mean, the image is pretty self-describing. `ProductID` is an `int`, data type and `Name` and `Description` are `varchar` data types. The little golden key at the left of `ProductID` specifies that the column is the primary key of `Department` table.

We can also see the length of each field. Note that **Length** means different things for different data types. For numerical data types **Length** specifies the number of bytes, while for text data it specifies the number of characters. This is a subtle but important difference, because for Unicode text data (`nchar`, `nvarchar`, `ntext`), the actual space needed is two bytes per character.

Also, in case of numerical data (like `int`) this value is not configurable, but for `varchar` we can set different values depending on our requirements. We choose to have 50 characters available for the name and 200 for the description.

Some prefer to use `nvarchar` instead of `varchar` – this is in fact a requirement when you need to store extended Unicode characters. Otherwise, the non-Unicode versions are usually preferred because they occupy half of the size their Unicode pairs need. With large databases the difference becomes noticeable.

Nullable Columns and Default Values

Observe the **Allow Nulls** option in the design window of the `Department` table – some fields have this option checked, while others don't. If the option is checked the column will be allowed to store the `NULL` value.

The best and shortest definition for `NULL` is "undefined". In our `Department` table only `DepartmentID` and `Name` are really required, while `Description` is optional – meaning that we are allowed to add a new department without supplying a description for it. If we add a new row of data without supplying a value for columns that allow nulls, the `NULL` value will be automatically supplied for them.

Especially for character data, there is a subtle difference between a `NULL` value and an "empty" value. If we add a product with an empty string for its description, this means that we actually set a value for its description – it is an empty string, not an undefined (`NULL`) value.

The primary key field will never allow `NULL` values. For the other columns it is up to us (and our client) which fields are really required and which are not.

In some cases instead of allowing NULL values we'll prefer to specify default values. This way, if the value is unspecified when creating a new row, it will be supplied with the default value. The default value can be a literal value (like zero for a Salary column or "Unknown" a Description column), or it can be a system value such as GETDATE(), which returns the current date. In a later chapter we'll have a DateCreated column, which can be set to have the default value supplied by the GETDATE() function. We'll learn later how to set default column values.

Identity Columns

This might be a bit confusing. We already know that primary keys are used on columns that uniquely identify each row of a table. If we set a primary key column to also be an identity column, SQL Server will automatically fill that column with values when adding new rows, ensuring that the values are unique. This behavior is similar to AutoNumber columns in Microsoft Access.

When a column is set as an identity column we are not allowed to specify a value for it when inserting new data rows. We only set values for the other columns, and SQL Server or MSDE automatically sets the identity column. SQL Server can guarantee this column will contain a unique value, but only if we don't interfere with it.

When we set an identity column, we need to specify an **identity seed**, which is the first value that will be provided by SQL Server for that column, and an **identity increment value**, which specifies the number of units to increase between two consecutive records.

By default, identity seed and identity increment value are both set to 1, meaning that the first value will be 1 and the following ones will be generated by adding 1 to the last created value. DepartmentID in our Department table is an identity column, but this is not shown in the screenshot previously presented. We'll learn how to set identity columns a bit later, when creating the Department table.

Indexes

Indexes represent a topic that has to do with SQL Server performance tuning, so we'll mention them very briefly. Even if we don't need to learn about them in order to create an e-commerce store, it is very important for you to know that they exist and what they do. For more information about indexes, we recommend to you Rob Vieira's *Professional SQL Server 2000 Programming* book, which has a great coverage about these issues.

Indexes are database objects meant to increase the overall speed of database operations. Their way of work is based of the presumption that the vast majority of database operations are read operations. Having an index in a table makes searches and read operations very fast, but adding, modifying or deleting rows take a bit more time. Usually, the gains of having an index considerably outweigh the drawbacks.

On a table we can create one or more indexes, each index working on one column or on a set of columns. When a table is indexed on a specific column, its rows are either indexed or physically arranged based on the values of that column and of the type of index. This makes search operations using that column very fast. If, say, an index exists on DepartmentID and then we do a search for the department 934, the search would be performed very quickly.

The drawback of having indexes is that they can slow down database operations that add new rows or update existing ones. This happens because the index must be actualized (or the table rows rearranged) each time when these operations occur.

Before finishing this topic let me highlight a few main ideas to keep in mind about indexes:

❑ Indexes greatly increase search operations on the database, but they slow down operations that change the database (delete, update, and insert operations).

❑ Having too many indexes can slow down the general performance of the database. The general rule of thumb is to set indexes on columns frequently used in WHERE or ORDER BY clauses, used in table joins, or having foreign key relationships with other tables.

❑ By default, indexes are automatically created on primary key and unique table columns.

There are dedicated tools that we can use to test the performance of a database under stress conditions with and without particular indexes, and a serious database administrator might want to make some of these tests before deciding on a wining combination for indexes. Two popular tools are the Index Tuning Wizard that can be accessed through SQL Server's Enterprise Manager, and the Query Analyzer, which has the capability to show the execution plan of a particular SQL command.

In our application, we'll rely on the indexes that are automatically created for the primary keys.

Creating the Table

Remember from the diagram we saw at the beginning of this chapter that for the data tier part of our departments list we need first to create the Department table, and then we'll write a stored procedure (named GetDepartments) that reads this table. The stored procedure will then be called from the middle tier.

We created the WroxJokeShop database in Chapter 2. In the following *Try It Out* exercise we add the Department table to it.

Try It Out – Creating the Department Table

The complete database can be downloaded from http://www.wrox.com. Remember that Visual Studio .NET Professional Edition will allow you to create and add information to MSDE databases, but will only allow you to add information to previously created databases and tables in SQL Server 2000.

1. Using the Server Explorer in Visual Studio .NET, navigate to your SQL Server instance, and then to the WroxJokeShop database that we created in Chapter 2. Remember, if Server Explorer is not visible, press *Ctrl+Alt+S* to activate it.

2. First expand the **WroxJokeShop** database node – this will make sure Visual Studio .NET connects to the database. Then you can go to the **Database** menu and select the **New Table** item. Alternatively, you can expand the **WroxJokeShop** database, right-click on **Tables** and select **New Table**:

3. After clicking the **New Table** menu item, you'll be shown a form where you can add columns to the new table:

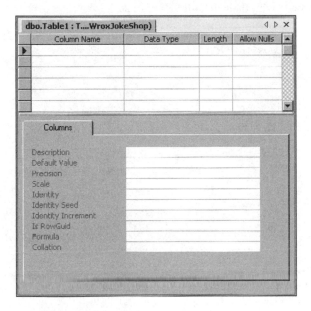

4. Using this form, add three columns, as shown below:

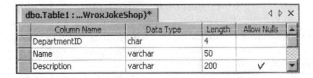

5. Now that we have the columns in place, we need to play a little bit with the DepartmentID column. First of all, right-click on it and select **Set Primary Key**, as in the following screenshot.

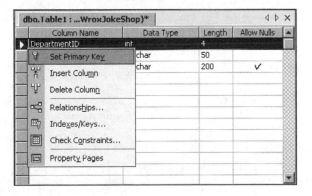

6. The last thing we need to do is to make the `DepartmentID` an identity column. Select the `DepartmentID` column, and set its Identity property to Yes. Leave Identity Seed and Identity Increment with their default values of 1.

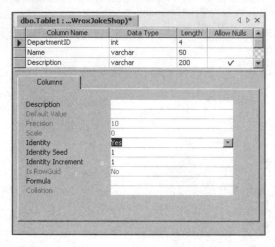

7. Now that everything is in place, we need to save the newly created table. Press *Ctrl+S* or go to File | Save Table 1. When asked, type `Department` for the table name.

8. Having the table structure saved in the database, we can open it to add some data. To open the `Department` table for editing, just double-click on its name in the Server Explorer. Using the editor integrated with Visual Studio, we can simply start adding rows. Because `DepartmentID` has been set as an `Identity` column, we cannot manually edit its data – SQL Server will automatically fill this field using the `Identity Seed` and `Identity Increment` we set up when we designed the table. The numbering will start with 1 and will be incremented with one unit each time.

Add three departments, as shown in the following table:

DepartmentID	Name	Description
1 (autonumbered)	Full Costumes	We have the best costumes on the internet! Check out a few samples from our collection:
2 (autonumbered)	Costume Accessories	Accessories and fun items to jazz up that special costume. These products are on promotion:
3 (autonumbered)	Jokes and Tricks	Funny or frightening, but all harmless! Take a look at these featured products before browsing the categories:

After adding these records the table should look like this in edit mode:

DepartmentID	Name	Description
1	Full Costumes	We have the best costumes on the internet! Check out a few samples from our collection:
2	Costume Accessories	Accessories and fun items to jazz up that special costume. These products are on promotion:
3	Jokes and Tricks	Funny or frightening, but all harmless! Take a look at these featured products before browsing the categories:

How It Works

We have just created our first database table! Not only have we created it, but we also set a primary key, set an identity column, and filled it with some data!

We could see that as soon as we have a clear idea about the structure of a table, Visual Studio .NET and MSDE or SQL Server make it very easy to implement it.

The Data Tier

Now that we have a table filled with data we should try to make something useful with it. Our ultimate goal with this table is to get the list of department names from a Visual Basic .NET program and populate the user control with that list.

In order to get data from a database we first need to know how to speak with it. SQL Server understands a language named Transact-SQL, or T-SQL. The usual way of communicating with SQL Server is to write a T-SQL command, send it to SQL Server and get the results back. However, these commands can be sent either directly from the business tier to SQL Server (without having an intermediary data tier), or can be centralized and saved as stored procedures. In a three-tier application, we always save the logic that interacts with the database in stored procedures.

Stored procedures are database objects that store programs written in the T-SQL language. These are much like normal functions; they accept input and output parameters and they have a return value. Using stored procedures for common data operations, apart from being a good programming practice, usually translates into better performance because they are precompiled and SQL Server knows how to execute them for best performance.

Our goal for this section is to write the GetDepartments stored procedure, but we'll first take a look at the language that makes them run.

The Theory: Speaking with the Database

SQL, or Structured Query Language, is the language used to communicate with modern relational database management systems. Most database systems support a particular dialect of SQL, such as T-SQL for SQL Server and PL*SQL for Oracle.

Because when it is analyzed in detail T-SQL can be a pretty big subject, we will have a very brief introduction to it. Once again, we advise you to study the SQL Server Books Online or other specific documentation for more information. We will cover just enough so you'll understand the code in our stored procedures.

The basic and most important SQL commands are SELECT, INSERT, UPDATE, and DELETE. Their names are pretty self-describing, and they allow us to perform basic operations on the database.

If you have SQL Server, you can use a program named Query Analyzer to play with these SQL statements. Unfortunately Query Analyzer is not included with MSDE or with Visual Studio .NET, so you may not have the means to actually test your T-SQL skills right now. If this is the case, don't worry because we'll do a lot of testing later, when we create the stored procedure.

Please be aware that each of these commands has more optional arguments and they can become more complex than those we have presented here. Still, in order to keep the presentation short and simple, we'll learn the most important and frequently used parameters.

SELECT

This is the most frequently used SQL statement. It is used to query the database for information. Its basic structure is:

```
SELECT <column list>
FROM <table name(s)>
[WHERE <restrictive condition>]
```

In SQL it is allowable to split a long statement like this, but you may prefer to write the whole command in a single line. The WHERE clause is written in square brackets because it is optional. SQL is not case sensitive, so it's not required to write SQL commands and clauses in upper case, or to use proper casing with table and columns. Still, for consistency and clarity we have decided to use these notations.

The following command returns the name of the department that has the DepartmentID of 1. In our case the returned value is Full Costumes, but we may have received no results if there was not a department with an ID of 1.

```
SELECT Name FROM Department WHERE DepartmentID = 1
```

If we want more columns to be returned, we simply list them, separated by commas. Alternatively, we can use *, which means "all columns". However, for performance reasons, if we need only some specific columns, it is wise to list them separately instead of asking for all of them. With our current Department table, the following two statements return the same results:

```
SELECT DepartmentID, Name, Description FROM Department
WHERE DepartmentID = 1
```

```
SELECT * FROM Department WHERE DepartmentID = 1
```

If we don't want to place any condition on the query, we simply remove the WHERE clause. The following SELECT statement returns all rows and all columns from the Product table:

```
SELECT * FROM Product
```

INSERT

It is probably no surprise to you that INSERT is used to add records to a table. Let's see its general syntax:

```
INSERT INTO <table name> (column list) VALUES (column values)
```

The following INSERT statement adds a department named 'Mysterious Department' to the Department table:

```
INSERT INTO Department (Name) VALUES ('Mysterious Department')
```

Notice that we didn't specify any value for the `Description` field, but since it was marked as nullable when we created the table, we are allowed to leave it blank (NULL). However, the `Name` field is required, so if we tried to specify a description without specifying a name we would have got an error:

```
INSERT INTO Department (Description) VALUES ('Some Description Here')
```

The error message specifies:

```
Cannot insert the value NULL into column ' Name ', table
'WroxJokeShop.dbo.Department'; column does not allow NULLs. INSERT fails.
```

Also please note that we didn't specify a `DepartmentID`. In fact, because `DepartmentID` has been set as an identity column, we're not allowed to manually add values in this column. SQL Server can guarantee that this column contains a unique value, but only if we don't interfere with it.

So, if we can't specify a value for `DepartmentID`, how can we find out what value was automatically supplied by SQL Server? For this, we have a special variable named `@@IDENTITY`. We can type its value by using the `SELECT` statement. The following two lines add a new record to `Department`, and return the `DepartmentID` of the row just added:

```
INSERT INTO Department (Name) VALUES ('Some New Department')
SELECT @@IDENTITY
```

UPDATE

The `UPDATE` statement is used to modify existing data, and has the following syntax:

```
UPDATE <table name>
SET <column name> = <new value> [, <column name> = <new value> ...]
[WHERE <restrictive condition>]
```

To change the name of a department with an ID of 43 to `Cool Department`, we would need a statement like this:

```
UPDATE Department SET Name='Cool Department' WHERE DepartmentID = 43
```

Be very careful with the `UPDATE` statement, because it makes it very easy to mess up an entire table. If the `WHERE` clause is omitted the change is applied to every record of the table – and this is something we don't want to happen. SQL Server will be happy to change all our records – even if all departments in the table would have the same name and description, they would still be perceived as different entities since they have `DepartmentID`s.

DELETE

The syntax of the `DELETE` command is actually very simple:

```
DELETE FROM <table name>
[WHERE <restrictive condition>]
```

The FROM keyword is optional and can be omitted. We generally use it because it makes the query sound more like normal English. Be careful, because a simple command like DELETE Department would erase all the rows in the Department table. The table itself isn't deleted by the DELETE command.

Most times we'll want to use the WHERE clause to delete a single row. Once again, be careful with this command, because if you forget to specify a WHERE clause you will end up deleting all of the rows in the specified table:

```
DELETE FROM Department
WHERE DeparmentID = 43
```

Creating the Stored Procedure

Here we create the GetDepartments stored procedure, this will read the departments' information from the Department table. This stored procedure is part of the data tier and will be accessed from the business tier. The final goal is to have this data displayed in the user control.

Before writing the stored procedure we first need to know the SQL code that does the necessary action. As we learned earlier, it's not even necessary to have a stored procedure. It is perfectly possible to save the SQL query in the business tier and use it directly to query the database.

While we'll not explain again the benefits of having the data-access logic in a separate tier – the data tier – it's still true that we first need to see the SQL code before saving it into a stored procedure.

How to Ask for a List of Department Names

Well this is quite straightforward – we need to query the database using a SELECT statement. The command could look like this:

```
SELECT * FROM Department
```

This would return all the department info to us. Asking for *all* the columns is useful when the columns might change in time and we want to be sure we get all of them. But when we know exactly what info we want from a table, it's always better to be specific about this. Asking for more data than necessary will not make the program stop working, but it can slow down its performance.

For our departments list we will need to know the name and ID for each department. Why the ID, you might wonder? Well, we know that the ID and not the name is what makes a department unique. When the visitor wants more information about a specific department, we'll search for that information based on its ID, not on its name.

The SELECT statement that works best for our situation is:

```
SELECT DepartmentID, Name
FROM Department
```

Saving the Query as a Stored Procedure

This is just like with data tables – once we know the structure, implementing it is a piece of cake. Now that we know the SQL code, the tools will help us save it as a stored procedure very easily.

The general form of a stored procedure, which has no input or output parameters, is as follows:

```
CREATE PROCEDURE <procedure name>
AS
    <stored procedure body>
```

Since the GetDepartments stored procedure doesn't have any parameters we don't bother with them right now. We'll see how to use input and output parameters in the following chapter.

Let's add the GetDepartments stored procedure to our database.

Try It Out – Writing the GetDepartments Stored Procedure

1. First, make sure the WroxJokeShop database is selected in Server Explorer. Then go to the Database menu, and select New Stored Procedure.

2. We are provided here with a skeleton for a new stored procedure:

```
CREATE PROCEDURE dbo.StoredProcedure1
/*
    (
        @parameter1 datatype = default value,
        @parameter2 datatype OUTPUT
    )
*/
AS
    /* SET NOCOUNT ON */
    RETURN
```

Here we can see the T-SQL statement used to create a stored procedure:

```
CREATE PROCEDURE <procedure name> AS <stored procedure body>
```

3. Please replace the default text with our GetDepartments stored procedure:

```
CREATE PROCEDURE GetDepartments AS

SELECT DepartmentID, Name
FROM Department

RETURN
```

4. Now press *Ctrl+S* to save the stored procedure. Unlike the tables, you won't be asked for a name, because the database already knows that we're talking about the GetDepartments stored procedure.

Note that after saving the procedure the CREATE keyword becomes ALTER. This happens because ALTER is used when we want to change an existing procedure.

5. Let's now test our first stored procedure to see that it is actually working. In Server Explorer, under our WroxJokeShop database, please open the **Stored Procedures** link.

6. Here, please right-click on GetDepartments and select **Run Stored Procedure**:

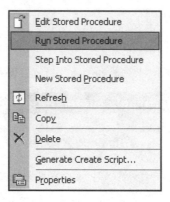

7. After running the stored procedure, we can see the results in the Output window:

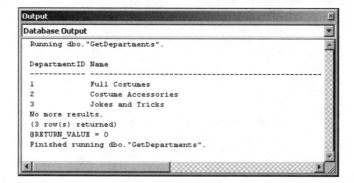

Great, our stored procedure works. In the screenshot you can see the departments that exist in the Department table at the moment.

The Business Tier

In this section we will learn how to access the database and call a stored procedure from Visual Basic .NET code. Then we'll create the middle-tier code that gets department data by calling the GetDepartments stored procedure.

The business layer part of the product catalog will consist of a `Catalog` class written in Visual Basic .NET, which will contain the necessary logic to get the catalog's data from the database and send it to the user interface layer, when it is requested. For our departments list we'll only need to add a single method to the `Catalog` class, named `GetDepartments`.

The Theory: How to Access SQL Server from VB.NET

The technology that permits accessing a database from Visual Basic .NET code is named **ADO.NET**. All .NET classes that are related to database access are collectively known as ADO.NET. This is the most modern Microsoft data-access technology, and it can be used from any .NET language, not only with Visual Basic .NET.

ADO.NET is a complex subject that requires a separate book by itself, and we will cover here just enough to help you understand how our business tier works. For more information about ADO.NET please refer to a specialized ADO.NET book.

You will notice that we make use of classes like `SqlConnection`, `SqlCommand`, and `SqlDataReader`. These objects and all the others whose names start with `Sql` are specifically created for SQL Server, and are part of the SQL Server Managed Data Provider. The SQL Server Managed Data Provider is the low-level interface between the database itself and our program. The ADO.NET objects that use this provider are grouped in the `System.Data.SqlClient` namespace, so we will need to import this namespace when we want to access SQL Server.

Since in this book we use SQL Server we will only work with the objects that are part of the SQL Server provider; however, keep in mind that if we needed to, it would have been very simple to update our program to use other database systems.

Each *database operation* always consists of three steps:

- ❏ *Open* a connection to the database
- ❏ *Perform* the needed operations with the database and get back the results
- ❏ *Close* the connection to the database

We always try to make the second step (executing the commands) as fast as possible. As we'll learn, keeping a data connection open for too long or having too many database connections open at the same time is expensive for our application's performance. The golden rule is to open the connection as late as possible, perform the necessary operations, and then close it immediately. We'll take a look at how to do each of these steps in the following sections.

Opening a Database Connection

The class used to connect to SQL Server is `SqlConnection`. When creating a connection we need to know at least the name of the SQL Server instance we're connecting to and authentication information that will permit us to access the server. Most of the time, we'll also want to specify a database that we want to work with.

So there are three important pieces of data we'll always specify when creating a new database connection. This connection data is grouped in what is called a **connection string**, which needs to be passed to the `SqlConnection` object. The following code snippet demonstrates how to create and open a database connection.

```
' Create the connection object
Dim connection As New SqlConnection()

' Set the connection string
connection.ConnectionString = _
  "Server=(local);" _
  & "User ID=sa; Password=;" _
  & "Initial Catalog=WroxJokeShop"

' Open the connection
connection.Open()
```

The code is pretty straightforward: we first create a `SqlConnection` object, then we set its `ConnectionString` property, and finally open the connection. A connection needs to be opened before using it for any operations.

Explaining the Connection String

If we take a look at the connection string, we can see it contains the three important parts we talked about earlier.

The first one is the SQL Server instance we're connecting to. For the MSDE version that comes with Visual Studio .NET, the instance name is `(local)\VSdotNET`. You will want to change this if your SQL Server instance has another name. In addition, you can use your computer name instead of `(local)`.

After specifying the server, we need to supply security information needed to login to the server. Security is a sensitive and important topic, but is large enough to deserve its own book, or at least a few chapters of a book. *Professional ASP.NET 1.0*, from Wrox Press (ISBN 1-86100-703-5), is a recommended read after you finish this book since it covers in detail security and more advanced topics not covered in this book.

We can log in to SQL Server by either using Windows Integrated Security or by supplying a SQL Server username and password. With Windows Integrated Security we don't have to supply a username and password because SQL Server will make use of our Windows login information. Because using Windows Integrated Security with ASP.NET can sometimes be tricky to configure, we will log in by supplying a SQL Server username and password.

By default there is a System Administrator (`sa`) account with a blank password. You need to be very careful with this account, and should never use it in a production system because it has full access to all database resources. If you don't have access to the `sa` account you'll need to ask for permission from the system administrator for an account that has access to `WroxJokeShop` database.

The final part of the connection string specifies the database we will be working with.

Note that usually we'll want to provide the connection string right when creating the connection, instead of setting the `ConnectionString` separately:

```
' Create the connection object
Dim connection As New SqlConnection(" ... connection string here ...
");

' Open the connection
connection.Open()
```

A final note about the connection string is that there are several synonyms that can be used inside it: for example, instead of `Server` we can use `Data Source`, or `Data Server`, or instead of `Initial Catalog` we can use `Database`. The list is much longer, and the complete version can be found in MSDN.

Issuing Commands Using the Connection

After we have an open connection, we usually want to do something interesting with it before closing it. When it comes to performing operations using a connection, we usually need to create a `SqlCommand` object. Since there are more tricks we can do with it, we'll take them one at a time.

Creating a SqlCommand object

`SqlCommand` will be our best friend when implementing the business tier. It is capable of storing information about what we want to do with the database – it can store a SQL query or the name of a stored procedure that needs to be executed. A `SqlCommand` is also aware of stored procedure parameters, which is a very useful feature for us, since many of our stored procedures have input and output parameters. Since our `GetDepartments` stored procedure doesn't have any parameters we won't learn how to play with them until the next chapter, when we'll create more stored procedures.

Here's the standard way of creating and initializing a `SqlCommand` object:

```
' Create the command object
Dim command As SqlCommand = New SqlCommand()
command.Connection = connection
command.CommandText = "GetDepartments"
command.CommandType = CommandType.StoredProcedure
```

Once again, there's no big mystery about the code. We first create a `SqlCommand` object, and then set some of its properties. The most important property that needs to be set is `Connection`, because each command needs to be executed on a specific connection. The other important property is `CommandText`, which specifies the command that needs to be executed. This can be a SQL query like `SELECT * FROM Departments`, but in our application this will always be the name of a stored procedure.

If we're setting the name of a stored procedure using `CommandText`, we will need to inform the `Command` object about this, because, by default, `CommandText` contains SQL queries. This is why we needed to manually set the `CommandType` property to `CommandType.StoredProcedure`.

While the previous code snippet shows a very nice and structured way to create a `SqlCommand` object, it is a bit long, and you might want to use one of the other ways of achieving the same result. Here is an example where we supply the `CommandText` and `Connection` when creating the object:

```
' Create the command object
Dim command As New SqlCommand("GetDepartments", connection)
command.CommandType = CommandType.StoredProcedure
```

Executing the Command

This is our moment of glory – finally, after creating a connection, a `SqlCommand` object and setting various parameters here and there, we have got to the stage we have been aiming for from the start: executing the command.

There are many ways we can execute the command, depending on the specifics. Does it return any information? If so, what kind of information, and in which format? We'll analyze the various scenarios later on, when we actually put the theory we're learning into practice, but for now let's take a look at the three `Execute` methods of the `SqlCommand` class: `ExecuteNonQuery()`, `ExecuteScalar()`, and `ExecuteReader()`.

`ExecuteNonQuery()` is used to execute a SQL statement or stored procedure that doesn't return any records. We'll use this method when we execute operations that update, insert, or delete information in the database. `ExecuteNonQuery()` has an integer return value that specifies the number of rows affected by the query – this proves useful if we want to know, for example, how many rows were deleted by the last delete operation, or if any rows have been added.

`ExecuteScalar()` is like `ExecuteNonQuery()` in that it returns a single value, although it returns a value that has been read from the database instead of the number of affected rows. It is used in conjunction with `SELECT` statements that select a single value. If the `SELECT` returns more rows and/or more columns, only the first column in the first row is returned.

`ExecuteReader()` is used with `SELECT` statements that return multiple records. This returns a `SqlDataReader` object, which contains the results of the query. A `SqlDataReader` is a forward-only and read-only cursor that reads the results one by one. It is particularly useful because it is very quick, and there are many objects that work with `SqlDataReader` objects. For example, for displaying the departments in the web user control we create, we'll use a `DataList` control that will take as a parameter a `SqlDataReader` object.

Note. The `SqlDataReader` object *requires an open connection* when it is used to read values from the data source. In other words, it doesn't store any information locally: it reads records from the database one by one, and only when finished can we close the connection. Because we'll need to read information from the `SqlDataReader` in the presentation tier, we'll not be able to close the connection in the business tier.

This is a bit against our *open connection – perform action – close connection* strategy, because the presentation tier (the `DataList` control that will list the departments) needs to receive an open `SqlDataReader`, which means an open database connection. However, the `SqlDataReader` can be instructed to automatically close the connection after all the rows have been retrieved.

Because the user control in the presentation tier will simply read all the rows from the `SqlDataReader` without processing them, the operation will be performed very quickly and the database connection will stay open for only a short period of time. In fact, the `SqlDataReader` is the ideal choice when we need to quickly retrieve a list of information without needing to do further processing on it.

If we want to do more processing on the retrieved data the data reader is not a good choice, because it is only aware of the current row read from the database – it doesn't store any other rows in memory. In this case we may want to have an in-memory copy of the selected data – this is done using other objects such as `SqlDataAdapter`, `DataSet`, and `DataTable`. We will not work with these objects in this book.

If all this theory about the way `SqlDataReader` works is a bit too much for now, don't worry because we'll take a closer look at it when we build the middle tier a bit later in this chapter.

Closing the Connection

It is important always to close the connection because open connections consume server resources, finally resulting in poor performance if not managed carefully.

For this reason, it is recommended to open the connection as late as possible, just before executing the command. After the command is executed, close it immediately. Here's an example from one of the methods we'll implement in the next chapter:

```
connection.Open()
command.ExecuteNonQuery()
command.Close ()
```

When we execute the command with `ExecuteReader()`, we pass the returned `SqlDataReader` to the calling method of the presentation tier. In this situation the connection can't be closed in the business tier. Instead, we rely on the `SqlDataReader` to close the connection itself after all its records have been read:

```
connection.Open()
Return command.ExecuteReader(CommandBehavior.CloseConnection)
```

Implementing the Business-Tier Functionality

The business layer part of the product catalog will consist of a file named `Catalog.vb`, which holds the `Catalog` class.

In this section, after creating the `Catalog` class, we implement the `GetDepartments()` method which will be called to populate the user control. In the next chapter we'll keep adding methods to this class to support the new pieces of functionality.

Adding the Catalog Class to the Solution

Let's start building the business layer by creating the `Catalog.vb` file, which will hold our `Catalog` class. For now you can close the **Server Explorer** window, if it is still present on your development environment.

Try It Out – Creating the Catalog Class

1. Make sure the Solution Explorer is visible in Visual Studio .NET. If it is not, press *Ctrl+Alt+L*. Here, right-click on WroxJokeShop and select Add | New Folder.

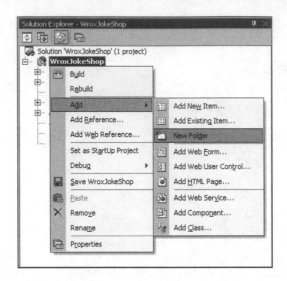

2. Choose BusinessObjects as the name of our new folder.

3. Now right-click on the BusinessObjects folder, and select Add | Add New Item.

4. In the dialog that appears, select **Class** from the **Templates** window, and call it Catalog.vb in the **Name** textbox. Then click **Open**.

We created a new folder named BusinessObjects, which will hold the classes of our business tier. There's yet one more step we want to make before writing the code.

Storing the Connection String in a Central Location

We learned that in every database operation there are three steps that always happen: opening the connection, issuing commands on it, and then closing it. Because we will create a new connection for every method of the business tier that performs database operations, it is a good programming practice to have the connection string saved in a central location. That way, if, for example, the password or the server name changes, we only need to change the connection string in one place rather than modifying many methods.

A common place to store configuration settings in web applications is their Web.config file. This is an external configuration file managed by ASP, written in the XML format. Web.config is a complex and powerful file and it can include many options regarding application's security, performance, behavior, and so on. Studying this file is beyond the scope of this book, but we'll take a look at its features that are directly related to our task. Right now we'll see how we can save our own configuration settings and how we can retrieve them from Visual Basic .NET code.

Try It Out – Storing the Connection String in Web.config

1. Make sure the Solution Explorer is visible, by pressing *Ctrl+Alt+L*. Then double-click on the Web.config file.

2. In `Web.config`, just below the `<configuration>` line, add the following:

```
<configuration>

  <appSettings>
    <add key="ConnectionString" value="Server=(local)\NetSDK;User
        ID=sa;Password=;Initial Catalog=WroxJokeShop" />
  </appSettings>

  <system.web>
```

You may need to modify the stored connection string depending on your particular SQL Server configuration.

3. Congratulations, you have just saved the connection string to the application's configuration file. Now open the `Catalog.vb` file by double-clicking on it in Solution Explorer. There, add the `connectionString` property to the `Catalog` class:

```
Public Class Catalog
    Private ReadOnly Property connectionString() as String
    Get
        Return ConfigurationSettings.AppSettings("ConnectionString")
    End Get
    End Property
End Class
```

How It Works – The Web.config Configuration File

`Web.config` is an XML file that stores configuration data that applies to the whole application. Here we are allowed to store values that can be then read from any place within our web application.

After we have saved the `ConnectionString` key to `Web.Config`, we can create a new `SqlConnection` object like this:

```
Dim connectionString as String
    connectionString = ConfigurationSettings.AppSettings("ConnectionString")
Dim connection As New SqlConnection(connectionString)
```

Since we will need to perform these steps in each method, we created the `connectionString` property, making our job of creating a new connection a bit easier. Using this property, from now on we'll be able to create a new `SqlConnection` object with a single line of code:

```
Dim connection As New SqlConnection(connectionString)
```

Adding the GetDepartments() method to the Catalog Class

The `Catalog` class will store all the methods that carry out database operations regarding the product catalog. Almost all methods of the `Catalog` class have a one-to-one relationship with the stored procedures that reside in SQL Server, and their names are self-explanatory.

Here we implement the `GetDepartments()` method. This method is used to get the list of departments from the database. It calls the `GetDepartments` stored procedure, and returns the results as a `SqlDataReader`.

Try It Out – Implementing GetDepartments

1. First, add the following line at the beginning of `Catalog.vb`:

```
Imports System.Data.SqlClient
```

2. Add the `GetDepartments` function to the `Catalog` class:

```
Imports System.Data.SqlClient

Public Class Catalog
    Public Function GetDepartments() As SqlDataReader
        ' Create the connection object
        Dim connection As New SqlConnection(connectionString)

        ' Create and initialize the command object
        Dim command As New SqlCommand("GetDepartments", connection)
        command.CommandType = CommandType.StoredProcedure

        ' Open the connection
        connection.Open()

        ' Return a SqlDataReader to the calling function
        Return command.ExecuteReader(CommandBehavior.CloseConnection)
    End Function

    Private ReadOnly Property connectionString() As String
      Get
        Return ConfigurationSettings.AppSettings("ConnectionString")
      End Get
    End Property
End Class
```

How It Works – The GetDepartments() Method

```
Imports System.Data.SqlClient
```

This line specifies that we're going to use objects from the `SqlClient` namespace. Remember, this namespace groups the objects that belong to the SQL Server managed data provider (the classes whose names start with `Sql`).

The `GetDepartments()` method employs the main steps of working with a database that we studied earlier. First, it creates a database connection and passes the connection string using the `connectionString` property:

```
' Create the connection object
Dim connection As New SqlConnection(connectionString)
```

Next, we create a `SqlCommand` object and set its `CommandText`, `Connection`, and `CommandType` properties. We supply the values for the first two of these when creating the object:

```
' Create and initialize the command object
Dim command As New SqlCommand("GetDepartments", connection)
command.CommandType = CommandType.StoredProcedure
```

Just before executing the command, we open the connection:

```
' Open the connection
connection.Open()
```

Finally, we execute the command using the `ExecuteReader()` method. The return type of the `ExecuteReader()` method is a `SqlDataReader` object, which is returned to the calling function:

```
' Return a SqlDataReader to the calling function
Return command.ExecuteReader(CommandBehavior.CloseConnection)
```

The Presentation Tier

Now that everything is in place in the other tiers, all we have to do is create the presentation tier part – this is the final goal we've been working towards from the beginning. As we could see in the screenshots at the beginning of this chapter, the departments list needs to look something like this, when the site is loaded in the web browser:

We implement this as a separate web user control named `DepartmentsList`, just as we did with the `Header` control in Chapter 2. Then we will add the user control to `default.aspx`.

The Choose a Department part is a simple image we store in the Images folder, the same folder that contains the WroxJokeShop logo used in Chapter 2. However, the list of departments needs to be dynamically generated based on what we have in the database. Fortunately, the .NET Framework provides us with a few very useful web controls that can help us solve this problem without entering too much code. One of them is `DataList`, which can be set to simply take a `SqlDataReader` object as input and generate a list based on its data.

Before actually writing the user control there's a little detail we need to take care of.

Preparing the Field: Setting the Styles

We want to set up a CSS (Cascading Style Sheets) file for our web site. CSS files are used to store font and formatting information that can be easily applied to various parts of the site. Instead of setting fonts, colors, and dimensions for a Label control we can simply set its CssClass to one of the existing styles.

In the following *Try It Out* exercise we set up a new CSS file for our site, and then add three styles to it that will be used the DepartmentsList user control.

Try It Out – Preparing the Styles

1. Let's delete the Styles.css file from the project. In Solution Explorer, right-click on the Styles.css file and click **Delete** on the menu that appears. Click **OK** when asked for confirmation.

2. Right-click on WroxJokeShop in Solution Explorer, then choose **Add | Add New Item**. From the **Templates** window choose **Style Sheet** and call it WroxJokeShop.css.

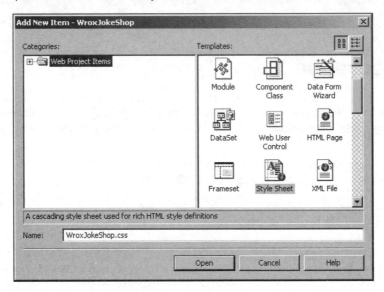

3. Open default.aspx in HTML View and modify it like this:

```html
<HTML>
  <HEAD>
    <title>WroxJokeShop</title>
    <meta content="Microsoft Visual Studio.NET 7.0" name="GENERATOR">
    <meta content="Visual Basic 7.0" name="CODE_LANGUAGE" >
    <meta content="JavaScript" name="vs_defaultClientScript" >
    <meta content="http://schemas.microsoft.com/intellisense/ie5"
          name="vs_targetSchema">
    <link href="WroxJokeShop.css" type="text/css" rel="stylesheet">
  </HEAD>
```

4. Open WroxJokeShop.css by double-clicking on it in Solution Explorer. Delete its contents and add these three styles to it:

```
A.DepartmentUnselected
{
  color: Blue;
  font-family: Comic Sans MS;
  text-decoration: none;
  font-size:  14px;
  font-weight: bold;
  line-height: 25px;
  padding-left: 0px
}

A.DepartmentUnselected:hover
{
  color: red;
  padding-left: 0px
}

A.DepartmentSelected
{
  color: green;
  font-family: Comic Sans MS;
  text-decoration: none;
  font-size:  14px;
  font-weight: bold;
  line-height: 25px;
  padding-left: 0px
}
```

How It Works – WroxJokeShop.css

Having a central place to store style information is very helpful and helps us easily change the look of the site in certain situations without changing a line of code.

We have deleted the automatically created file Styles.css and created a new one named WroxJokeShop.css. Another way, perhaps a simpler one, would have been to simply rename the existing Styles.css file and then delete its contents (its default contents are not appropriate for WroxJokeShop).

We then modified the default.aspx file to be aware of the newly created CSS file. This enables us to apply the styles that exist in WroxJokeShop.css in any component that exists in default.aspx, or in the web user controls it includes.

We finally added three styles that will be used in DepartmentsList. These refer to the way names should look when they are either unselected, unselected but with the mouse hovering over them, or selected.

Before moving on we want to highlight the built-in features in Visual Studio .NET for CSS files. While WroxJokeShop.css is open in edit mode, right-click on one of its styles and take a look at the menu that appears:

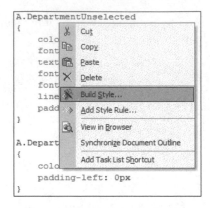

Clicking on the Build Style link opens a window where the selected style can be seen.

Creating the DepartmentsList Web User Control

Right now everything is in place, the only missing part being the user control itself. Let's implement DepartmentsList.ascx in the following *Try It Out* exercise.

Try It Out – Creating DepartmentsList.ascx

1. First let's create a new web user control in the UserControls folder. Right-click on UserControls folder, and then choose Add | Add Web User Control.

2. You'll be asked for the name of the new user control. Type DepartmentsList.ascx. Optionally you can type only DepartmentsList, and Visual Studio .NET will add the extension for you.

3. We are presented with the design window of our new DepartmentsList control. Make sure the toolbox is visible (*Ctrl+Alt+X*).

4. In the toolbox, double-click on the DataList entry to add one DataList object to the user control.

5. Change the name of our DataList from DataList1 to list. For this, click on the DataList control to select it, make sure the Properties windows is open (*F4*), and change the (ID) to list:

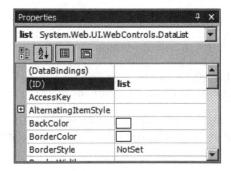

6. Now we need to enter the DataList in edit mode. For this, right-click on it, go to Edit Template and then select the Item Templates option. You should be presented with a form like this:

7. We need to add two HyperLink controls, one to the Item template and the other one to the SelectedItem template. Do this by dragging and dropping two HyperLink controls to the mentioned template locations.

8. For the first hyperlink, set the CssClass property to DepartmentUnselected. For the second, set the CssClass property to DepartmentSelected. Then set the Text property of both controls to an empty string (with other words, clear the Text property). The list control should then look like the screenshot below:

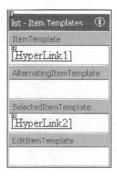

9. Enter the HTML view by clicking on the HTML tab at the bottom of the designer window. Here we need to make a few changes to the `HyperLink` controls. This is the full code, with the changes highlighted; take particular care about the `NavigateUrl` and `Text` fields of the `HyperLink` objects. Ensure that the code in each `asp:Hyperlink` section is on a single line rather than split over multiple lines as shown:

```
<%@ Control Language="vb" AutoEventWireup="false"
Codebehind="DepartmentsList.ascx.vb" Inherits="WroxJokeShop.DepartmentsList"
TargetSchema="http://schemas.microsoft.com/intellisense/ie5" %>

<img src="Images/DeptHeader.gif" border="0">

<asp:DataList id="list" runat="server">
  <SelectedItemTemplate>
     &raquo;
    <asp:HyperLink id="HyperLink2" runat="server"
        CssClass="DepartmentSelected"
        NavigateUrl='<%# "../default.aspx?DepartmentID=" &amp;
        DataBinder.Eval(Container.DataItem, "departmentID") &amp;
        "&amp;DepartmentIndex=" &amp; Container.ItemIndex %>'
        Text='<%# DataBinder.Eval(Container.DataItem, "Name") %>'>
    </asp:HyperLink>
  </SelectedItemTemplate>
  <ItemTemplate>
     &raquo;
    <asp:HyperLink id="HyperLink1" runat="server"
        CssClass="DepartmentUnselected"
        NavigateUrl='<%# "../default.aspx?DepartmentID=" &amp;
        DataBinder.Eval(Container.DataItem, "departmentID") &amp;
        "&amp;DepartmentIndex=" &amp; Container.ItemIndex %>'
        Text='<%# DataBinder.Eval(Container.DataItem, "Name") %>'>
    </asp:HyperLink>
  </ItemTemplate>
</asp:DataList>
```

10. Now let's open the code-behind file for the user control. Please select it in Solution Explorer and then either click on the **View Code** button or right-click the `DepartmentList.ascx` file and select **View Code**.

11. After we press the **View Code** button, Visual Studio .NET opens the code-behind file named `DepartmentsList.ascx.vb`. Among the automatically generated code, you can see a blank `Page_Load` method. Modify this method like this:

```
Private Sub Page_Load(ByVal sender As System.Object, _
                    ByVal e As System.EventArgs) Handles MyBase.Load
    ' The departmentIndex parameter is added to the query string when
    ' a department link is clicked. We need this because when the
    ' page is reloaded the DataList forgets which link was clicked.
    Dim listIndex As String = Request.Params("departmentIndex")
```

```
' If listIndex has a value, this tells us that the visitor
' has clicked on a department, and we inform the DataList about that
' (so it can apply the correct template for the selected item)
If Not listIndex Is Nothing Then
  list.SelectedIndex = CInt(listIndex)
End If


' Create a new Catalog object
Dim catalog As New Catalog()


' GetDepartments returns a SqlDataReader object that has
' two fields: DepartmentID and Name. These fields are read in
' the SelectedItemTemplate and ItemTemplate of the DataList
list.DataSource = catalog.GetDepartments()


' Needed to bind the child controls (the HyperLink controls)
' to the data source
list.DataBind()
```
```
End Sub
```

12. Press *Ctrl+Shift+B* to compile the project.

13. Open default.aspx in Design View. Here, please drag DepartmentsList.ascx from the Solution Explorer and drop it over the cell that reads "Place List of Departments Here". Delete the text from the cell, so that only the user control should be there:

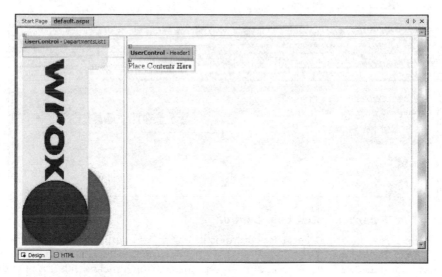

14. Make sure default.aspx is set as the start page for the project. If it is not, right-click on it and select **Set As Start Page**.

15. Press *F5* to execute the project.

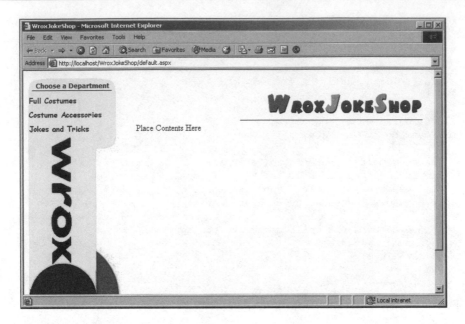

16. Let's see what happens when we click on a department. The following screenshot is taken after I clicked on the **Costume Accessories** link. Note that `default.aspx` got reloaded but with a different query string, and the **Costume Accessories** link is now listed using the `DepartmentSelected` style.

How It Works – The DepartmentsList User Control

The heart of the `DepartmentsList` user control is its `DataList` control, which generates the list of departments. In order to make a `DataList` work we need to edit its `ItemTemplate` property at the least. We also edited its `SelectedItemTemplate` property, which means that it is able to display a different look for a selected item.

The templates can be edited either in Design View mode or in HTML View mode. It is easier to work with the designer, but editing the HTML directly is more powerful and allows some tweaks that are not possible with the designer. For our `DataList` we knew that we wanted to have links – the reader needs to be able to click on a department. For this reason we added `HyperLink` controls to `ItemTemplate` and `SelectedItemTemplate` boxes in the designer. This created a part of the HTML code for us, which we built upon later on.

The `DataList` control is very flexible and configurable. The most basic steps that are generally made when implementing a data list are setting its `Item` and `SelectedItem` templates. The `ItemTemplate` applies to 'normal' list items, while the `SelectedItemTemplate` applies to the currently selected item.

It is very simple to create a `DataList` and its templates directly in HTML – we just need to implement the templates in a schema like the following:

```
<asp:DataList id="list" runat="server">
  <SelectedItemTemplate>
    <!- contents -->
  </SelectedItemTemplate>
  <ItemTemplate>
    <!- contents -->
  </ItemTemplate>
  <AlternatingItemTemplate>
    <!- contents -->
  </AlternatingItemTemplate>
</asp:DataList>
```

Now let's see what the templates of our `DataList` control contain. We basically want these to be links to different pages within our web site.

Because of the way we implement the presentation layer, `default.aspx` is the only page that gets called, but each time we add different parameters to the query string depending on what has been selected. When a department is clicked in the department list, `default.aspx` is reloaded but with a query string similar to the one in the following picture:

Address   http://localhost/WroxJokeShop/default.aspx?DepartmentID=2&DepartmentIndex=1

In the next chapter we will learn how `default.aspx` can update its contents depending on the supplied parameters. Right now, apart from having a different style for the selected item, the page doesn't change much.

We have added the links to where the `HyperLink` controls link to by directly editing the `ItemTemplate` and `SelectedItemTemplate`. Apart from the different `CssClass` property, these two styles have much the same definition:

```
<asp:HyperLink id="HyperLink2" runat="server"
    NavigateUrl='<%# "../default.aspx?DepartmentID=" &amp;
    DataBinder.Eval(Container.DataItem, "departmentID") &amp;
    "&amp;DepartmentIndex=" &amp; Container.ItemIndex %>'
    Text='<%# DataBinder.Eval(Container.DataItem, "Name") %>'>
```

Here we use the `DataBinder.Eval()` function that extracts data from the data source – in our case this is the `SqlDataReader` object that we get from the business tier. Basically, the HTML code above specifies that each department link should link to a page with the following form:

```
http://webservername/default.aspx?DepartmentID=XXX&DepartmentIndex=YYY
```

So, each time a department is clicked, we pass the `DepartmentID` in the query string, which will be read when a user control needs to know the ID of the department in the database (the `DepartmentID` field). We also send a `DepartmentIndex` parameter, which specifies the number of the department in the list. We need this because we need to tell the `DataList` which is the selected item, so it will be able to use the `SelectedItemTemplate` for that item. `DepartmentID` and `DepartmentIndex` are not related in any way. A department can have the `DepartmentID` of 123 in the database, but if it is the first department displayed in the list, the `DepartmentIndex` will be 0 (it is a zero-based list).

In the `Page_Load` method of `DepartmentsList`, we search for the `DepartmentIndex` parameter – if it has been passed, we inform the list which is the selected item:

```
' The departmentIndex parameter is added to the query string when
' a department link is clicked. We need this because when the
' page is reloaded the DataList forgets which link was clicked.
Dim listIndex As String = Request.Params("departmentIndex")

' If listIndex has a value, this tells us that the visitor
' has clicked on a department, and we inform the DataList about that
' (so it can apply the correct template for the selected item)
If Not listIndex Is Nothing Then
  list.SelectedIndex = CInt(listIndex)
End If
```

The `DataList` is loaded with data in its `Page_Load` method. This method is called every time the page is loaded, including after the visitor clicks on any of the links that exist on the page. In particular, every time the reader clicks on one of the departments `Page_Load` is called again where the `DataList` is filled again with data. In `Page_Load` we create a `Catalog` object (which is part of the business layer), and ask it politely for the list of departments.

```
' Create a new Catalog object
Dim catalog As New Catalog()

' GetDepartments returns a SqlDataReader object that has
' two fields: DepartmentID and Name. These fields are read in
' the SelectedItemTemplate and ItemTemplate of the DataList
list.DataSource = catalog.GetDepartments()

' Needed to bind the child controls (the HyperLink controls)
' to the data source
list.DataBind()
```

Keep in mind that we're working on the presentation tier right now. We don't care how the `Catalog` class or the `GetDepartments` method are implemented. We just need to know that `GetDepartments` returns a list of (`DepartmentID`, `Name`) pairs. While we are on the presentation tier we don't really care how `Catalog.GetDepartments()` does what it is supposed to do.

Code Download

The code you have just written is available in the download for this book from www.wrox.com. It should be easy for you to read through this book and build your solution as you go; however, if you want to check something from our working version, you can do. Instructions on loading the chapters are available in the README.TXT document in the download.

Summary

We have now reached the end of the chapter having built the web site to a slightly more advanced stage and dealt with the following:

❑   We have created the Department table and populated it with data

❑   We have added a stored procedure to the database and added code to access this stored procedure from the middle tier

❑   We have added the database connection string to the project to allow simple access to the database

❑   We have added the DepartmentList web user control to the site

In the next chapter we will continue building the site to include further tables and web user controls.

The Product Catalog: Adding Content

In the previous chapter we created a selectable list of departments for our web site. However, there is much more to a product catalog than that list of departments. In this chapter we continue by adding the rest of the product catalog features.

In this chapter we will:

❑   Learn about relational data and the types of relationships that occur between tables. We will them implement the necessary relationships between the tables in our database.

❑   Learn about database diagrams, and why they can be useful, and create one for our database.

❑   Write our stored procedures in the Data Tier, and see:

   ❑   How to use WHERE and JOIN clauses

   ❑   How to use input and output parameters

❑   Finally, see how to create a custom error page

That's a lot of material to get through, so let's get started!

What is the New Functionality?

In Chapter 2, we established the general structure of our future web site. We decided that each page would have the WroxJokeShop logo in the lower left part, the header in the upper right part and the list of departments in the upper left side of the page. We achieved this part in Chapters 2 and 3, and right now WroxJokeShop looks like this:

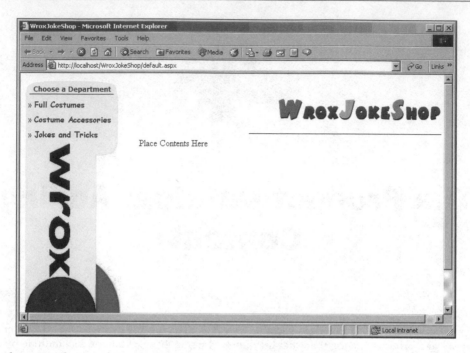

So, until now, we have only created the static parts of the site. Well, the list of departments is not really static, as it is generated from the database, but there is always the same `DepartmentsList.ascx` user control sitting in that part of the site and generating the list.

The part of the site that provides the actual content has a different structure depending on the page being visited. In order to better understand how to implement it, let's look once again at what we want to achieve. At the beginning of Chapter 3, we previewed how the full product catalog will look; let's take another look at how the dynamically generated part of the page looks for the parts of the site that we can browse.

For the main web page, the dynamically generated part should look like the following:

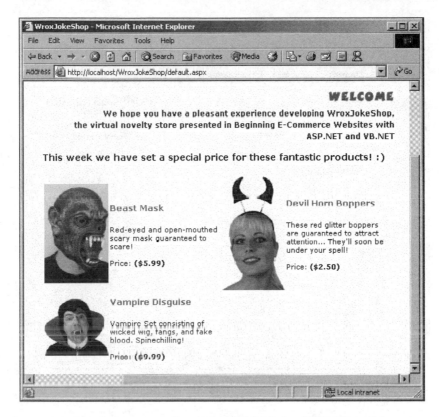

When we then visit a department, apart from it being highlighted in the list of departments, we will be presented with a page like this:

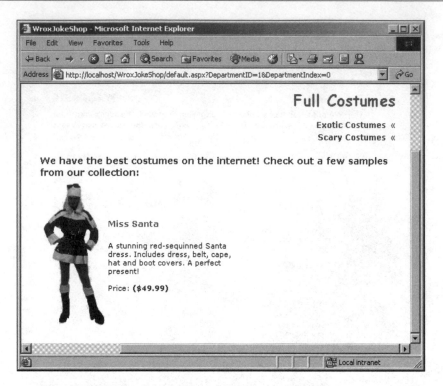

Finally, when we select a category, the page will look like the following:

These are the three main parts that we need implement. Notice that each page contains a list of products, but the text above it changes slightly from case to case.

As we know how we created the list of departments, it is pretty clear that the rest of the site will also be created in a similar way using custom web user controls. We will discuss the technical details of creating the user interface later in this chapter, when we implement the presentation tier. However, it is good to have an overview of what we are aiming to achieve.

We will create all of this functionality using the same techniques as in the previous chapter. First we'll create the data structures to hold the necessary data. As you can see from the screenshots, there's a lot more information to store than just the list of departments that is currently in the database. We'll also touch on some new theory issues, such as table relationships, which I'm sure you'll find very interesting. The business tier will come with some new tricks of its own – remember I warned you in Chapter 3 that we would play with stored procedure parameters here.

OK, enough talking. Here we go…

A New Place to Store the Data

Given the new functionality we need for this chapter, it's not surprising that we need to add more data tables to our database. However, this isn't just about adding new data tables. We also need to learn about relational data and the relationships that we can build between these data tables such that we can obtain more significant information from our database.

The Theory: What Makes a Relational Database

It is no mystery that a database is something that stores data – probably even school kids could confirm this. However, today's modern **Relational Database Management Systems (RDBMS)** such as SQL Server, Oracle, DB2, and others, have extended this basic role by adding the ability to store and manage **relational data**. This is a concept that needs some attention.

So what does *relational data* mean? It's easy to see that every piece of data ever written in a database is somehow related to some already existing information. Products are related to categories and departments, orders are related to products and customers, and so on. A relational database keeps its information stored in data tables, but is also aware of the relations between them.

These related tables form the *relational database*, which becomes an object with a significance of its own, rather than simply being a group of unrelated data tables. It is said that *data* becomes *information* only when we give significance to it, and establishing relations with other pieces of data is a good means of doing that.

Let's look at our product catalog and see what pieces of data it needs, and how we can transform this data into information.

For the product catalog, we'll need at least three data tables: one for departments, one for categories, and one for products. It is important to note that physically each data table is an independent database object, even if logically it is part of a larger entity – in other words, even though we say that a category *contains* products, the table that contains the products is not inside the table that contains categories. This is not in contradiction with the relational character of the database. The following figure shows a simple representation of three data tables including some selected sample data.

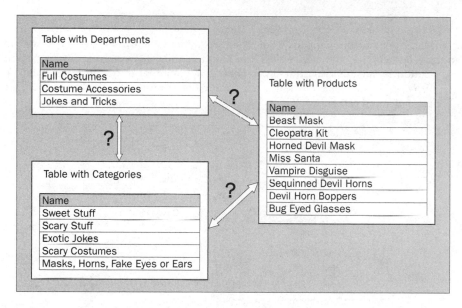

Note that when we say the two tables are related, we in fact mean that the records of those tables are related. So, if the products table is related to the categories table, this translates into each product record being somehow related to one of the records in the categories table.

The diagram doesn't show the physical representation of the database. For that reason we didn't list the table names there. Diagrams like this are used to decide *what* needs to be stored in the database. After we clearly know *what* to store, the next step is to decide *how* the listed data is related, which will lead us to the physical structure for the database. In the diagram, we can see three kinds of data that we want to store, but as we'll learn later, to implement this structure in the database we will make use of four tables, not three.

So, now that we know what data we want to store, let's think about how the three parts relate to each other. Apart from knowing that the records of two tables are related *somehow*, we also need to know *the kind of relationship* between them. Let's now take a closer look at the different ways in which two tables can be related.

Relational Data and Table Relationships

We continue our discovery into the world of relational databases by further analyzing the three logical tables we've been looking at so far. To make our lives easier, let's give them names now: the table containing products is Product, the table containing categories is Category, and the last one is our old friend, Department. No surprises there then! We're lucky that these tables implement the most common kinds of relationships that exist between tables, the **One-to-Many** and **Many-to-Many** relationships, so we have the chance to learn about them.

Some variations of these two primary relationship types exist, as well as the *One-to-One* relationship, which we will not cover in this book. This kind of relationship is not very popular and is not directly supported by the database system. Please consult SQL Server Books Online or *Professional SQL Server 2000 Programming* (ISBN: 1-86100-448-6) for more details about the One-to-One relationship.

One-to-Many

The One-to-Many relationship happens when one record in a table can be associated with multiple records in the related table, but not vice-versa. In our case, this happens for the `Department – Category` relation. A specific department can contain any number of categories, but each category belongs to *exactly one* department. The following picture better represents the One-to-Many relationship between departments and categories:

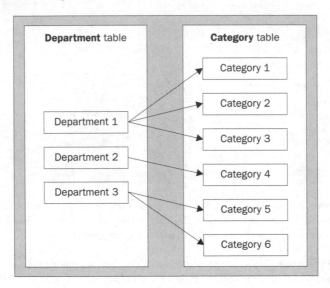

Another common scenario where we see the One-to-Many relationship is with the `Order – Order Details` tables. It makes sense that for every order we will have a number of order details that belong to that particular order.

We'll see a bit later how to implement the `Category` table and the relationship between `Category` and `Department`.

Many-to-Many

The other common type of relationship is the Many-to-Many relationship. This kind of relationship is implemented when records in both the tables in the relationship can have multiple matching records in the other. In our scenario, this happens for the `Product` and `Category` tables, because we know that a product can exist in more than one category (*one* product – *many* categories), and also a category can have more than one product (*one* category – *many* products).

This happens because we decided earlier on that a product could be in more than one category. If a product could only belong to a single category, we would have another One-to-Many relationship, just like that between departments and categories (where a category can't belong to more than one department).

If we represent this relationship with a picture like the one above, we get something like:

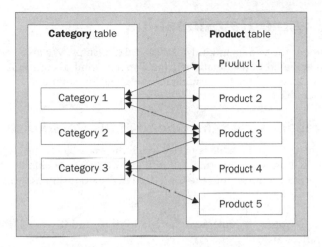

There are a few more details we need to know about the Many-to-Many relationship, but we'll discuss them later when we implement it in the WroxJokeShop database. For now it is only important to know what it is.

The Foreign Key Constraint

Relationships between tables are physically implemented in the database using **foreign key constraints**, or simply *foreign keys*.

We learned in the previous chapter about the *primary key* and *unique* constraints. We covered them there because they apply to the table as an individual entity. Foreign keys, on the other hand, always occur between two tables: the table in which the foreign key is defined (the *referencing table*) and the table the foreign key references (the *referenced table*).

SQL Server Books Online (BOL) defines a foreign key as being a column or combination of columns used to establish or enforce a link between data in two tables. Foreign keys are used both as a method of ensuring data integrity and to establish a relationship between tables.

Foreign keys, like the other types of constraints, apply certain restrictions in order to enforce database integrity. Unlike primary key and unique constraints that apply to a single table, the foreign key constraint applies restrictions on both the referencing and referenced tables. When establishing a One-to-Many relationship between the Department table and the Category table by using a foreign key constraint, the database will include this relationship as part of its integrity. It will not allow us to add a category to a nonexistent department, and it will not allow deleting a department if there are categories that belong to it.

We have learned the general theory of foreign keys here. We'll implement them in the following *Try It Out* exercise, where we have the chance to discuss in more detail how primary keys work. Then a bit later, in the database diagrams *Try It Out*, we'll learn how to visualize and implement them using the integrated diagramming feature in Visual Studio .NET.

Implementing Table Relationships

So we have an idea about the two main kinds of table relationships. We also know that these relationships are implemented in the database using a special kind of constraint – foreign keys. In the following exercises, we'll add all the tables and table relationships required for the product catalog to the WroxJokeShop database.

Departments, Categories, and the One-to-Many Relationship

Essentially, creating the Category table is pretty much the same as for the Department table we have already created, so we will move pretty quickly. Still, we will have our share of fun in this *Try It Out* as well, because this is where we implement the One-to-Many relationship between the Category and Department tables.

Let's first create the new table and implement the relationship, and then we'll explain the details in the *How It Works* section afterwards.

Try It Out – Creating the Category Table and Relating it to Department

1. There are two ways of creating the Category table. Either run the Category script from the code download or follow the steps below.

2. Using the Server Explorer (*Ctrl+Alt+S*), navigate to your SQL Server instance, and then to the WroxJokeShop database. Please also expand the database node to make sure Visual Studio establishes a connection with it. When the database is selected, go to the **Database** menu and click on **New Table**. Alternatively you can right-click on the **Tables** node under WroxJokeShop and select **New Table**.

3. Add the following columns using the form that appears:

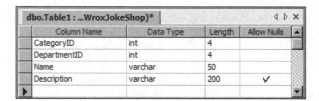

4. Right-click on the CategoryID field and select **Set Primary Key**. We also want CategoryID to be an identity column – set it as shown in the following screenshot:

5. Press *Ctrl+S* to save the table. When asked, type Category for the table's name.

6. While the Category table is still selected, go to the View menu, and then click on Relationships. Here is the place where we specify the details for the foreign key relationship. This works by relating a column of the referencing table (Category) to a column of the referenced table (Department). We want to relate the DepartmentID column in Category with the DepartmentID column of the Department table.

7. In the dialog that appears, press New.

8. In the Primary key table combo box, please select Department. Make sure that for the Foreign key table Category is selected.

9. Under Department, please select DepartmentID as the primary key column. Then do the same for Category – choose DepartmentID (not CategoryID!). Right now the Property Pages dialog should look like this:

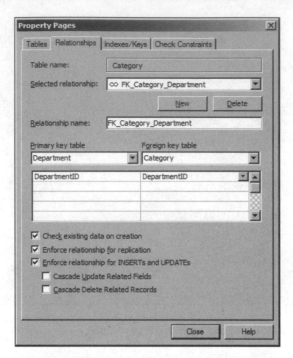

Keep in mind that if something goes wrong you can always get back to this page and click **Delete** to delete the relationship, and then create it again.

10. Press **Close** to save the relationship.

11. Press *Ctrl+S* to save the table again. You will be warned about the `Category` and `Department` tables being updated and asked for confirmation. This confirms once again that a foreign key relationship affects both tables that take part in the relationship. Click **Yes**.

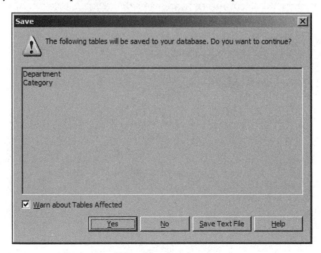

How It Works – The One-to-Many Relationship

OK, so we created a relationship between the `Category` and `Department` tables. But how does it work, and how does it affect our work and life? Let's study a bit the way we implemented this relationship.

In the `Category` table, apart from the primary key and the usual `Name` and `Description` columns, we added a `DepartmentID` column. This column is used to specify the department each category belongs to. This way, for each category, we can set one department. Moreover, because the `DepartmentID` field of `Category` doesn't allow `NULL` values, we will actually be required to supply a department for each category. Furthermore, because of the foreign key relationship we implemented, the database will not allow us to add categories to a non-existent department.

Actually, we can ask the database not to enforce the relationship. In the **Property Pages** dialog where we created the relationship there were a few checkboxes that are used to set some options for the foreign key. We left them with the default value, but let's see what they do:

- ❑ **Check existing data on creation.** This is enabled by default, and doesn't allow the creation of the relationship if the existing database records don't comply with it. In other words, the relationship can't be created if there are *orphaned categories* in the database (categories with a `DepartmentID` that references a department that doesn't exist in the `Department` table).

- ❑ **Enforce relationship for replication.** This option applies to database replication, which is beyond the scope of this book. Replication is a technology that allows the synchronization of data between multiple SQL Servers situated in different locations.

- ❑ **Enforce relationship for INSERTs and DELETEs.** This is probably the most important of the options. It tells SQL Server to make sure that database operations on the tables involved in the relationship don't break the relationship. When this option is selected, SQL Server won't allow us to add categories to non-existent departments or delete departments that have related categories.

- ❑ **Cascade Update Related Fields.** This option allows SQL Server to update existing data if this is required for database integrity. If the `DepartmentID` field of an existing department is changed, SQL Server will also change the `DepartmentID` fields of the categories that belong to that department – this way, even after we change the ID of the department, the categories will still belong to it. We don't check this option because we won't need to change departments IDs.

- ❑ **Cascade Delete Related Records.** This is a radical solution for keeping database integrity. If this is selected and we delete a department from the database, all its related categories would be automatically deleted by SQL Server. This is a sensitive option and you should be very careful with it.

In the One-to-Many relationship (and implicitly the foreign key constraint), we link two columns from two different tables. One of these columns is the primary key, and it defines the *One* part of the relationship. In our case, `DepartmentID` is the primary key of `Department`, so `Department` is the *one* that connects to *many* categories. We need to have a primary key on the *One* part as we need to ensure it is unique – we can't link a category to a department if we can't be sure that the department is unique – we must ensure that no two departments have the same ID; otherwise the relationship wouldn't make much sense.

Adding Categories Linked to Existing Departments

Since we have created a new table, let's populate it with some data. We'll also try to add data that would break the relationship that we established between the Department and Category tables.

1. Again, there are two ways to do this. Either run the PopulateCategory script from the code download or follow Steps 2 and 3 below.

2. Let's open the Category table for editing. For this, just double-click the table in Server Explorer.

3. Using the editor integrated with Visual Studio, we can simply start adding rows. Because CategoryID has been set as an Identity column, we cannot manually edit its data – SQL Server will automatically fill this field for us, using the Identity Seed and Identity Increment we set up when we designed the table. However, we will need to manually fill the DepartmentID field with ID values of existing departments. Please add categories as shown in the following screenshot:

CategoryID	DepartmentID	Name	Description
1	1	Exotic Costumes	Sweet costumes for the party girl:
2	1	Scary Costumes	Scary costumes for maximum chills:
3	2	Masks, Horns, Fake	Items for the master of disguise:
4	3	Sweet Stuff	Cute, fun accessories to raise a smile wherever you go:
5	3	Scary Stuff	Scary, funny accessories for the practical joker:

4. Now let's try to break the database integrity by adding a category to a non-existent department (for example, set the DepartmentID at 500). After filling the new category data, press *Tab* or click on the next row. This is the time when Visual Studio will submit the newly written data to SQL Server. If you have created the relationship properly, an error should occur. For more detailed information about the error, please click on the Help button.

Microsoft Development Environment

INSERT statement conflicted with COLUMN FOREIGN KEY constraint 'FK__Category__Depart__1B0907CE'. The conflict occurred in database 'WroxJokeShop', table 'Department', column 'DepartmentID'.
The statement has been terminated.

OK   Help

Categories, Products, and the Many-to-Many Relationship

Having added categories and departments to the database, the next logical step is to add products. This is a bit more complicated than just creating a Product table and adding data to it, as we did for Category. This is because between Product and Category we have a different kind of relationship from the one we have seen between categories and departments.

For the relationship between `Product` and `Category` we will implement a Many-to-Many relationship. Although logically the Many-to-Many relationship happens between two tables, SQL Server doesn't have the means to physically enforce this kind of relationship, so we cheat by adding a third table to the mix. This third table, named a **junction table** (also known as a *linking table* or *associate table*) and two One-to-Many relationships (two foreign key constraints) will help us achieve the Many-to-Many relationship. Let's see what we mean.

The junction table is used to associate products and categories, with no restriction on how many products can exist for a category, or how many categories a product can be added to. The following diagram explains the role of the junction table:

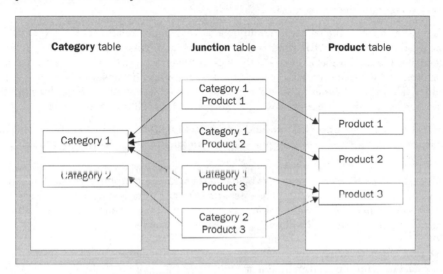

Note that each record in the junction table links one category with one product. We can have as many records as we like in the junction table, linking any category to any product. The linking table contains two fields, each one being a foreign key to the primary key of one of the two linked tables. In our case, the junction table will contain two fields: a `CategoryID` field and a `ProductID` field.

Each record in the junction table will consist of a (`ProductID`, `CategoryID`) pair, which will be used to associate a particular product with a particular category. By adding more records to the `ProductCategory` table we can associate a product with more categories or a category with more products, effectively implementing the Many-to-Many relationship.

I can't give a definitive recommendation for a naming convention to use for the junction table. Most of the time it will be OK to just join the names of the two linked tables – in our case, the junction table will be named `ProductCategory`. However, there are times when the junction table has a "meaning" of its own and can be named otherwise. For example, in the Northwind database that is supplied with Access and SQL Server we see the [`Order Details`] junction table, which links orders with products.

> *Because the Many-to-Many relationship is implemented using a third table that makes the connection between the linked tables, there is no need to add additional fields to the related tables in the way that we added the `DepartmentID` to the `Category` table.*

The Product Table: What Information Does It Store?

The `Product` table contains a few more fields than the usual ProductID, Name, and Description. Most of them are pretty self-describing but for completeness, let us look at a short description of each of them before creating the table:

❏ `ProductID` stores the unique ID of each product. This is the primary key.

❏ `Name` contains the product's name.

❏ `Description` contains the product's description.

❏ `Price` contains the product price.

❏ `ImagePath` stores the name (or could be a more complex relative path) of the file that contains the product's picture. SQL Server is able to store binary data, including pictures, directly into the database, but this results in poor database performance. It is much wiser to have only a picture location and file name stored into the database, and store the actual picture files in a separate folder. This also allows us to have the images saved on a separate physical location (for example, another hard disk), further improving performance for high-traffic web sites.

❏ `OnCatalogPromotion` is a bit field (can be set to either 0 or 1) that specifies if the product is featured on the web site front page. When initially loading the site, the first page will always list the products that have this bit set to 1.

❏ `OnDepartmentPromotion` is a bit field that specifies if the product is featured on the department pages. Remember that when visiting a department, the visitor is shown only the featured products of that department. If a product belongs to more than one department (remember it can belong to more than one category), it will be listed as featured on all those departments.

Using those bit fields allows us to let the site administrators highlight a set of products that are of particular importance for a department at a specific time (for example, before Christmas they will surely want to add Santa costumes and accessories, and so on).

OK, enough words, let's add the `Product` table to the database.

Try It Out – Creating the Product Table and Relating it to Category

1. Again we have two options for creating our `Product` table. Either run the `Product` script from our code download or follow steps two to four below.

2. Using the steps that we already know, create a new `Product` table that looks like this:

3. Don't forget to set ProductID as the primary key, and also make it an Identity column with the default values for Identity Seed and Identity Increment, as shown in the screenshot.

4. Press *Ctrl+S* to save the table, and type Product for its name. Great! Now we have a brand new Product table.

5. We now need to populate this table by running the PopulateProduct script from the code download.

6. Now let's implement the One-to-Many relationship with Category by creating the junction table. Again, we can do this either by running the ProductCategory script or following the steps below.

7. Create a new table with two fields, as in the screenshot below:

Column Name	Data Type	Length	Allow Nulls
ProductID	int	4	✓
CategoryID	int	4	✓

8. Now select both fields, ProductID and CategoryID, go to the **Diagram** menu and select **Set Primary Key**. Two golden keys will appear on the left side, and the **Allow Nulls** checkboxes will be automatically unchecked:

Column Name	Data Type	Length	Allow Nulls
ProductID	int	4	
CategoryID	int	4	

9. Press *Ctrl-S* to save the newly created table. Its name is `ProductCategory`.

10. We can now populate this new table by running the `PopulateProductCategory` script from the code download.

11. Open `ProductCategory` again in design mode, Click View | Relationships.

12. In the Property Pages dialog that appears, press New to create a new relationship.

13. For the Primary key table choose `Category`, and for the Foreign key table choose `ProductCategory`. For both tables choose `CategoryID` as the field used for the relationship. The relationship will automatically be named `FK_ProductCategory_Category`.

14. Press the New button again, because we now want to create the relationship between `Product` and `ProductCategory`.

15. Select `Product` for the Primary key table and `ProductCategory` for the Foreign key table. Then select `ProductID` as the field to implement the relationship, for both of them. This relationship will be automatically named `FK_ProductCategory_Product`.

16. Press Close to close the Property Pages dialog.

17. Press *Ctrl+S* to save the changes we have made by adding the relationships. You will be warned that `Product`, `Category`, and `ProductCategory` will be saved to the database. Press Yes to confirm.

How It Works – The Many-to-Many Relationship

In this *Try It Out* we created the `Product` table, and we implemented a Many-to-Many relationship with `Category`.

Many-to-Many relationships are created by adding a third table, called a junction table, which, in our case, is named `ProductCategory`. This table contains (`ProductID`, `CategoryID`) pairs, and each record in it associates a particular product with a particular category. So, if we see a record such as (1,4) in `ProductCategory`, we know that the `Product` with `ProductID` 1 belongs to the `Category` with `CategoryID` 4.

The Many-to-Many relationship is enforced by having two One-to-Many relationships – one between `Product` and `ProductCategory`, the other between `ProductCategory` and `Category`. In English, this can be translated as "*one* product can be associated with *many* product-category entries, each one of those being associated with *one* category". The relationship ensures that the products and categories that appear in the `ProductCategory` table actually exist in the database, and that we can't delete a product if we have a category associated with it and vice-versa.

Here is also the first time that we set a primary key consisting of more than one column. In `ProductCategory`, the primary key is formed from both the `ProductID` and `CategoryID` columns. This means that we'll not be allowed to have two identical (`ProductID`, `CategoryID`) pairs in the table. It is perfectly legal to have a `ProductID` or `CategoryID` more than once, as long as it is part of a unique (`ProductID`, `CategoryID`) pair. This makes sense, because we wouldn't want to have two identical records in this table. Each product can be associated with a category or not associated with a category; it cannot be associated with a particular category multiple times.

I agree that at first all the theory about table relationships can be a bit confusing, until you get used to them. However, in order to understand the relationship more clearly, we have a very useful tool: database diagrams.

Database Diagrams

Database diagrams are very useful because they provide us with the means to visualize not only the data tables, but also the relationships between them. Diagrams can also be used to create tables, and they allow us to create table relationship using drag and drop.

So far we have created four tables and we have three relationships, so our diagram will be pretty interesting already.

Try It Out – Creating a Database Diagram

1. Make sure our WroxJokeShop database is selected in Server Explorer. Then go to Database | New Diagram. Alternatively, you can right-click on the **Database Diagrams** node under WroxJokeShop and select **New Diagram**.

2. In the dialog that appears, we are invited to select which tables we want to add to the diagram. Since we want all of them, click **Add** four times, so all of our tables will be added. Then press **Close**.

3. After closing the dialog, we can see the tables and their relationships in the newly created diagram. You should see something like this:

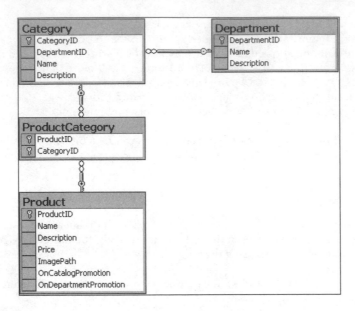

4. Press *Ctrl+S* to save the diagram. Select `WroxJokeShop` for the name.

How It Works – Database Diagrams

As you can see, database diagrams are useful things. If, until now, you could only imagine the relationships between the different tables, the diagram allows you to see what actually happens.

We can see in the diagram the three one-to-many relationships we created: one between `Department` and `Category`, one between `Category` and `ProductCategory`, and one between `ProductCategory` and `Product`. Here we can see, once again, that the many-to-many relationship between `Product` and `Category` is not implemented physically as such, but instead it is composed of two one-to-many relationships.

The diagram also shows us the type and direction of the relationships. Note that each relationship has a key symbol at the one part of each relationship, and an infinity symbol at the many side of the relationship. The table whose primary key is involved in the relationship is at the one side of the relationship and is marked with the little golden key.

One of the most useful things about diagrams is that we can edit database objects directly from the diagram. If you right-click on a table or on a relationship you'll see that we have a lot of features there. Feel free to experiment a bit to get a general idea of the features available. Although we won't use this feature here, keep in mind that it's possible to create foreign key relationships by simply dragging one column from a table to a different column of another (or even the same) table. This automatically opens the Create Relationship dialog.

We can also design a table directly within the diagram. For this, we need to switch the table to normal view, by right clicking on it, going to Table View and then selecting Standard:

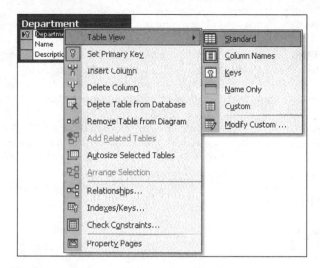

After we have the table in normal mode, we can edit it directly in the diagram. The following screenshot should explain how:

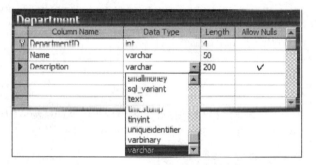

The Data Tier

So we have a database with a wealth of information just waiting to be read by somebody. As usual, we'll implement the data-access logic in stored procedures.

For this chapter, the data-tier logic is a bit more complicated than in the previous chapter. Here our presentation tier will perform queries like "give me the list of categories for a specific department" or "give me the details for this specific department or category". As you can see, the new requirements need to get data from multiple data tables and/or using input (and output) parameters.

The Theory: WHERE to JOIN?

Remember the SQL Query we used in the previous chapter? It was pretty simple, wasn't it? In that case we wanted to get the whole list of departments and the query looked like this:

```
SELECT DepartmentID, Name FROM Department
```

Of course, we placed this query into a stored procedure, but that's another story. The main thing to notice here is the extreme simplicity of the query. There is a single table involved, and we don't even filter the records with the WHERE clause (which we will discuss shortly). Things get a bit more complicated in this chapter, but don't worry; we still don't talk about rocket science!

Before continuing, there is a detail you should be aware of. Almost every SQL query, except maybe for the simplest ones, can be written in a number of alternative ways. Advanced database programming books have entire chapters explaining how we can get the same result using different interrogation techniques, the performance implications of each of them, and so on. In this book, we employ techniques that are generally recommended as good programming practices, and which I have found to work best for our joke shop.

Where to Use WHERE

The first new element we introduce in this chapter's stored procedures, which is also the most common one, is the WHERE clause. This is used to filter the records acted on by SELECT, UPDATE, and DELETE SQL statements.

We want to get the Name and Description of a particular department – so we specify that we need the details for only that one department. The SQL query that returns the Name and Description of the department with an ID of 3 is:

```
SELECT Name, Description FROM Department
WHERE DepartmentID = 3
```

Pretty basic. The same WHERE clause can be used to get the list of categories that belong to a particular department. Let's see the query, again using the department with an ID of 3:

```
SELECT Name, Description FROM Category
WHERE DepartmentID = 3
```

This query is still simple enough as we use a single table. The DepartmentID column is part of the Category table, so we filtered the records in Category based on that criterion.

Where to Use JOIN

Because we have our data stored in several tables, we frequently run into situations where not all of the information we want is in one table. Take a look at the following list that contains an example where data needs to be extracted from both the Department and Category tables:

	Department Name	Category Name	Category Description
1	Full Costumes	Exotic Costumes	Sweet costumes for the party girl:
2	Full Costumes	Scary Costumes	Scary costumes for maximum chills:
3	Costume Accessories	Masks, Horns, Fake Eyes or Ears	Items for the master of disguise:
4	Jokes and Tricks	Sweet Stuff	Cute, fun accessories to raise a smile wherever you go:
5	Jokes and Tricks	Scary Stuff	Scary, funny accessories for the practical joker:

In other cases, all the information we need is in just one table, but we need to place conditions on it, based on the information in another table. This happens, for example, when we need to extract the list of products that belong to a certain category. The following is a list of products that belong to the Masks, Horns, Fake Eyes or Ears category:

	ProductID	Name	Description	Price
1	1	Beast Mask	Red-eyed and open-mouthed scary...	5.9900
2	2	Cleopatra Kit	Full of Eastern promise. Includ...	14.9900
3	3	Horned Devil Mask	Full devil mask with horns. The...	5.9900
4	6	Sequinned Devil Horns	Shiny red horns for the little ...	3.7500

When extracting the products that belong to a category, the SQL query isn't the same as when extracting the categories that belong to a department. This is because of the Many-to-Many relationship that exists between Product and Category. We can't just filter the records in Product based on a certain CategoryID simply because, in this case, there is no CategoryID field in Product.

In order to get the list of products in a category, we first need to look in the ProductCategory table and get all the (ProductID, CategoryID) pairs where the CategoryID is the ID of the category we're looking for. When we get that list, we'll have the IDs of the all products in that category. Using these IDs we'll be able to generate the required product list.

Although this sounds pretty complicated to do, it can be done using a single SQL query. In fact, the real power of SQL lies in its ability to perform complex operations on large amounts of data using simple queries.

How to Use JOIN

As I hinted at earlier, the results shown in the previous screenshots are the result of table joins. Where we need to get a result set that is based on the data from multiple tables, this is a good indication that we might need to join these tables.

We will learn how to use this by analyzing the Product and ProductCategory tables, and the way we can get a list of products that belong to a certain category. Suppose we want to get all the products in the category where CategoryID = 5. The following screenshot shows the records that we want returned:

(selection from ProductCategory table)

	CategoryID	ProductID
1	1	2
2	1	4
3	2	5
4	3	1
5	3	2
6	3	3
7	3	6
8	4	6
9	4	7
10	5	8

(selection from the Product table)

	ProductID	Name	Description
1	1	Beast Mask	Red-eyed and open-mouthed...
2	2	Cleopatra Kit	Full of Eastern promise. ...
3	3	Horned Devil Mask	Full devil mask with horn...
4	6	Sequinned Devil Horns	Shiny red horns for the l...

Tables are joined in SQL using the JOIN clause. Joining one table with another results in the columns (not the rows) of those tables being joined. When joining two tables, there always needs to be a common column on which the join will be made. The query that joins the Product and ProductCategory tables is as follows:

```
SELECT *
FROM ProductCategory INNER JOIN Product
ON Product.ProductID = ProductCategory.ProductID
```

The result will look something like the following screenshot:

	ProductID	CategoryID	ProductID	Name	Description	Price
1	1	3	1	Beast Mask	Red-eyed and open-mout...	5.9900
2	2	1	2	Cleopatra Kit	Full of Eastern promis...	14.9900
3	2	3	2	Cleopatra Kit	Full of Eastern promis...	14.9900
4	3	3	3	Horned Devil Mask	Full devil mask with h...	5.9900
5	4	1	4	Miss Santa	A stunning red-sequinn...	49.9900
6	5	2	5	Vampire Disguise	Vampire Set consisting...	9.9900
7	6	3	6	Sequinned Devil Horns	Shiny red horns for th...	3.7500
8	6	4	6	Sequinned Devil Horns	Shiny red horns for th...	3.7500
9	7	4	7	Devil Horn Boppers	These red glitter bopp...	2.5000
10	8	5	8	Bug Eyed Glasses	Bug-eyed glasses to as...	2.7500

Note that the resultant table is composed of the fields from the joined tables, and they are synchronized on the ProductID column, which was specified as the column to make the join on. Now if we take a look at the resultant table, it's quite easy to see that we need a WHERE clause to provide just the records that have a CategoryID of 3. The new query would look like this:

```
SELECT *
FROM ProductCategory INNER JOIN Product
ON Product.ProductID = ProductCategory.ProductID
WHERE ProductCategory.CategoryID = 3
```

Note that when we work with multiple tables in the same query, we sometimes need to prefix the column name with the table name so that SQL Server will know for sure which column we are talking about. This is a requirement in the case of columns that exist in both tables (like ProductID); for the other columns SQL Server doesn't require us to specify the table, but this is considered good practice anyway. The previous query can also be written as:

```
SELECT *
FROM ProductCategory INNER JOIN Product
ON Product.ProductID = ProductCategory.ProductID
WHERE CategoryID = 3
```

OK, let's see the results:

	ProductID	CategoryID	ProductID	Name	Description
1	1	3	1	Beast Mask	Red-eyed and open-mouthed scary...
2	2	3	2	Cleopatra Kit	Full of Eastern promise. Includ...
3	3	3	3	Horned Devil Mask	Full devil mask with horns. The...
4	6	3	6	Sequinned Devil Horns	Shiny red horns for the little ...

Except that the list of columns is too long (they didn't all fit in this screenshot), this table has all that we need. The last step to get the results we want is to specify the columns we're interested in. Remember that we aren't required to prefix all columns with the table name, but in this case I recommend you to use the longer form because it results in clearer and more maintainable code:

```
SELECT Product.Name, Product.Description
FROM ProductCategory INNER JOIN Product
ON Product.ProductID = ProductCategory.ProductID
WHERE ProductCategory.CategoryID = 3
```

This finally gives us the results we were looking for:

	Name	Description
1	Beast Mask	Red-eyed and open-mouthed scary...
2	Cleopatra Kit	Full of Eastern promise. Includ...
3	Horned Devil Mask	Full devil mask with horns. The...
4	Sequinned Devil Horns	Shiny red horns for the little ...

The Stored Procedures

We're pretty close now to starting to write the stored procedures required for WroxJokeShop. Before doing that there's still another little thing (this time, it is really is little, honest) we need to learn about: stored procedure parameters.

In the previous example with table joins, we used a hard-coded CategoryID. In the stored procedures we write here we'll need to receive various data as input parameters, and sometimes return values as output parameters. Let's look at these in more detail.

Input and Output Stored Procedure Parameters

The syntax used to create a stored procedure with parameters is:

```
CREATE PROCEDURE <procedure name>
[(
    <parameter name> <parameter type> [=<default value>] [INPUT|OUTPUT],
    <parameter name> <parameter type> [=<default value>] [INPUT|OUTPUT],
    ...
    ...
)]
AS
        <stored procedure body>
```

Remember that the portions between the square brackets are optional. We can see that specifying parameters is optional, but if we specify them, they must be within parenthesis. For each parameter it is necessary to supply at least its name and its data type.

We can optionally supply a default value for the parameter. In this case, if the calling function doesn't supply a value for this parameter, the default value will be used instead. Also we can specify if the parameter is an input parameter or output parameter. By default, all parameters are input parameters. The value of output parameters can be set in the stored procedure and read by the calling function.

Stored procedure parameters are treated just like any other SQL variables, and their names start with @. Usually stored procedure parameters are called @DepartmentID, @CategoryID and so on, but that doesn't mean that we're limited to passing ID values or even numeric values as parameters.

121

The simplest syntax for setting the value of an output parameter is as follows:

```
SELECT @DepartmentID = 5
```

Implementing the Stored Procedures

Now let's add the stored procedures to the WroxJokeShop database, and then we'll have the chance to see them in action. Because we already know the steps for creating a stored procedure, we won't use *Try It Out* exercises here.

For each stored procedure, we will need its functionality somewhere in the presentation tier. In order for their purpose to be even clearer, please refer to the beginning of the chapter where we show some screenshots of the product catalog in action.

Please add the following stored procedures to the database:

GetDepartmentDetails

This stored procedure is needed when the user selects a particular department in the product catalog. When this happens, we need to query the database again to find out the name and the description of the particular department.

The stored procedure receives the ID of the selected department as a parameter and returns its name and description in the form of output parameters. We'll see a bit later, when we create the business tier, how to extract these parameters after executing the stored procedure.

The code for `GetDepartmentDetails` is as follows:

```
CREATE PROCEDURE GetDepartmentDetails
      (@DepartmentID int,
       @DepartmentName varchar(50) OUTPUT,
       @DepartmentDescription varchar(200) OUTPUT)
AS

SELECT @DepartmentName=[Name], @DepartmentDescription=[Description]
FROM Department
WHERE DepartmentID = @DepartmentID

RETURN
```

The `SELECT` statement is used to store the information in the `Name` and `Description` fields of the specified `DepartmentID` (which is an `INPUT` parameter here) to the `@DepartmentName` and `@DepartmentDescription` `OUTPUT` parameters. These are the output parameters that will be read by the business tier when calling the `GetDepartmentDetails` stored procedure.

When applying the database query, we specifically request the department that was selected by the visitor, using the `WHERE` clause:

```
WHERE DepartmentID = @DepartmentID
```

GetCategoriesInDepartment

When the visitor selects a particular department, not only do we want to show the department details, but we also want to display the categories that belong to that department. This will be done using the GetCategories procedure, which returns the list of categories in a specific department.

We only ask for the ID and the name for each category (but this time we don't return all the categories, only the ones that belong to the selected department). We will get the other details of a category (meaning its description) when the visitor clicks on it. Here is the code for GetCategories:

```
CREATE PROCEDURE GetCategoriesInDepartment
      (@DepartmentID int)
AS

SELECT CategoryID, [Name]
FROM Category
WHERE DepartmentID = @DepartmentID

RETURN
```

This time we don't use OUTPUT parameters – the list will get to the presentation tier in the form of a SqlDataReader which will be used to populate a DataList, as seen when we populated the list of departments in the previous chapter.

GetCategoryDetails

This stored procedure will be called when the reader clicks on a particular category, and we want to find out more information about it, namely its name and description. Here's the code:

```
CREATE PROCEDURE GetCategoryDetails
      (@CategoryID int,
       @CategoryName varchar(50) OUTPUT,
       @CategoryDescription varchar(200) OUTPUT)
AS

SELECT
       @CategoryName = [Name],
       @CategoryDescription = [Description]
FROM Category
WHERE CategoryID = @CategoryID

RETURN
```

GetProductsInCategory

When a visitor selects a particular category from a department, we will want to list all the products that belong to that category. For this, we will use the GetProductsInCategory stored procedure. We saw how this procedure works earlier when we learned about table joins. The single difference is that here we return more data about each product to the calling function than just its name and description. We'll see later in this chapter how to use the returned information to create a nice looking list of products.

```
CREATE PROCEDURE GetProductsInCategory
     (@CategoryID int)
AS

SELECT Product.ProductID, Product.[Name], Product.[Description],
     Product.Price, Product.ImagePath, Product.OnDepartmentPromotion,
     Product.OnCatalogPromotion
FROM Product INNER JOIN ProductCategory
ON Product.ProductID = ProductCategory.ProductID
WHERE ProductCategory.CategoryID = @CategoryID

RETURN
```

GetProductsOnDepartmentPromotion

When the visitor selects a particular department, apart from needing to list its name, description, and list of categories (we've written the necessary stored procedures for these tasks earlier), we also want to display the list of featured products for that department.

GetProductsOnDepartmentPromotion needs to return all the products that belong to a specific department and have the OnDepartmentPromotion bit set to 1. In GetProductsInCategory we needed to make a table join in order to find out the products that belong to a specific category. Now that we need to do this for departments the task is a bit more complicated because we can't directly know what products belong to what departments.

We know how to find categories that belong to a specific department (we did this in GetCategoriesInDepartment), and we know how to get the products that belong to a specific category (we did that in GetProductsInCategory). By combining this information, we can find out the list of products in a department. For this we need two table joins. We also filter the final result to get only the products that have the OnDepartmentPromotion bit set to 1.

We also use the DISTINCT clause. This filters the results to make sure we don't get the same record multiple times. This would happen when a product belongs to more than one category, and these categories are in the same department. In this situation we would get the same product returned for each of the matching categories, unless we filtered the results using DISTINCT.

```
CREATE PROCEDURE GetProductsOnDepartmentPromotion
   (@DepartmentID int)
AS

SELECT DISTINCT Product.ProductID, Product.[Name], Product.[Description],
                Product.Price, Product.ImagePath
FROM Product
INNER JOIN ProductCategory
ON Product.ProductID = ProductCategory.ProductID
INNER JOIN Category
ON ProductCategory.CategoryID = Category.CategoryID
WHERE Product.OnDepartmentPromotion = 1
      AND Category.DepartmentID=@DepartmentID

RETURN
```

GetProductsOnCatalogPromotion

This returns all the products that have the `OnCatalogPromotion` bit field set to 1. The value of this field, and also the rest of the information regarding the catalog, will be configurable from the administration part of the web site.

```
CREATE PROCEDURE GetProductsOnCatalogPromotion
AS

SELECT Product.ProductID,Product.[Name], Product.[Description],
       Product.Price, Product.ImagePath
FROM Product
WHERE Product.OnCatalogPromotion = 1


RETURN
```

Well, that's about it. Right now our data store is ready to hold and process our product catalog information. It's time to move to the next step: implementing the business tier of the product catalog.

The Business Tier

So we got to the business tier. Here we'll learn a few more tricks for ADO.NET. Let's first start with the usual theory part, after which we'll start writing the code.

The Theory: Working with Stored Procedure Parameters

Working with stored procedure parameters provides the major interest in this part of the chapter.

The ADO.NET class that deals with input and output stored procedure parameters is `SqlCommand`. This shouldn't come as a big surprise – we know that `SqlCommand` is responsible for executing commands on the database, so it makes sense that it should also deal with their parameters. In the following code snippets `command` is a `SqlCommand` object.

The Input Parameter

Here is the code that you'll need when adding input parameters to `SqlCommand` objects. In the code snippet `departmentId` is the parameter received by the VB.NET method, whose value is passed to the stored procedure.

```
' Add an input parameter and supply a value for it
command.Parameters.Add("@DepartmentID", SqlDbType.Int, 4)
command.Parameters("@DepartmentID").Value = departmentId
```

The first line adds a new stored procedure parameter named `@DepartmentID`, of type `SqlDbType.Int` and a size of 4, to the `Parameters` collection of the `SqlCommand` object. Note that to specify the data type we use the `SqlDbType` class, which can be used to specify any SQL Server data type.

The second line specifies a value for the parameter. Since `@DepartmentID` is a required input parameter (it doesn't have a default value defined in the stored procedure), we need to specify a value for it.

If the stored procedure has more than one parameter, the order we define them in here has no importance.

Note the naming conventions we employ here. The stored procedure parameter is named `@DepartmentID`, while its associated parameter in the VB.NET function is named `departmentId`. For variable names (including parameters) Microsoft recommends using camel casing (the first letter of each word except the first is capitalized). For database objects, including stored procedure parameters, we follow guidelines better suited for this task (you'll rarely see database columns, stored procedures, or parameters written using camel casing).

Two in One

Just a hint here: the previous two lines of code that add a stored procedure parameter and set its value can be written as a single line:

```
' Add an input parameter and supply a value for it
command.Parameters.Add("@DepartmentID", SqlDbType.Int, 4).Value = _
                                                departmentId
```

The syntax is a bit more complicated, but the result is identical.

Stored Procedure Parameters are Not Strongly Typed

When adding stored procedure parameters, we should use exactly the same name, type, and size as in the stored procedure. I say *we should* because actually we can break this rule, although this isn't recommended. For example, we could add `@DepartmentID` as a `varchar` or even `nvarchar` – as long as the value we set it to is a string containing a number, the database doesn't complain, and automatically makes the conversion. If you don't want to supply the data type of the parameter, you can use the shortened version of adding a parameter and its value at the same time:

```
command.Parameters.Add("@DepartmentID", departmentId)
```

This isn't a recommended programming practice, but it's good to know that it exists!

There are two main reasons why it's good to handle the data type in the business tier: first, this allows the business tier to have control over the validity of the data types that pass through it. Second, sending bogus information to a stored procedure can make it corrupt our data.

Note that our business tier procedures and functions always take their parameters as strings. We chose this approach for our architecture because we don't want the presentation tier to be bothered with the data types. The presentation tier, as you'll see, gets and receives the parameters as strings – in fact, the presentation tier doesn't mind what kind of product IDs we have (the format 123 is just as welcome as the KSJ222 format). It's the role of the business tier to interpret the data received from both the presentation tier and the business tier. Moreover, if at some time, a change occurs in the database and suddenly we have character based product IDs, we would only need to make the change in the data tier and the business tier, leaving the presentation tier untouched.

The Output Parameter

The code that creates an output parameter is as follows:

```
' Add an output parameter
command.Parameters.Add("@DepartmentDescription", SqlDbType.VarChar, 200)
command.Parameters("@DepartmentDescription").Direction = _
                                          ParameterDirection.Output
```

This is almost the same as the code for the input parameter, except instead of supplying a value for the parameter, we set its `Direction` property to `ParameterDirection.Output`. This tells our command that `@DepartmentDescription` is an output parameter.

Parameters are Independent Objects

Stored procedure parameters are represented in VB.NET code by a specialized class named `SqlParameter`. In order keep the code compact we don't create our procedures this way, but we could create `SqlParameter` objects, set their properties, and then add them to the `Parameters` collection of the `SqlCommand`, as in the following example:

```
Dim param As New SqlParameter("@MyBit", SqlDbType.Bit, 1)
param.Direction = ParameterDirection.Output
' or:
' param.Value = 5
command.Parameters.Add(param)
```

Getting the Results Back from Output Parameters

After executing the command, it is likely that we want to read the value of the output parameters. This is very simple to do. The usual way of doing this is to execute the command, close the connection if it is no longer required (and it usually isn't, at least in our application), and then read the value of the parameter from the `Command` object (or from a separate `SqlParameter` object, if it has been created as shown earlier). Here's an example:

```
' Open the connection, execute the command, and close the connection
connection.Open()
command.ExecuteNonQuery()
connection.Close()

' Get the results back
Dim name As String
name = command.Parameters("@DepartmentName").Value.ToString
```

Note that in this example, we call `ToString` to convert the returned value to a string. This is a recommended practice, even if the type of the parameter is `VarChar` or another string character type. This is important because the stored procedure has the option of not supplying values for its output parameters, in which case their value is set to `NULL`. This translates to `Nothing` in Visual Basic, and trying to save this value to a string variable would generate a runtime exception.

Calling `ToString` on the `Value` of the output parameter ensures that this is transformed to a string. `NULL` values sent from the database are transformed to empty strings instead of breaking our code.

If we are expecting a numerical value, using `ToString` is no longer the best solution. Instead, `IsNumeric` can be used, as in the following example:

```
' Get the results back
Dim iValue As Integer
Dim oValue As Object
iValue = command.Parameters("@DepartmentId").Value

If IsNumeric(oValue) Then
    iValue = CType(oValue, Integer)
Else
    iValue = 0
End If
```

Completing the Catalog Class

Let's now implement the business-tier methods. Each of them calls exactly one stored procedure, and they are named exactly like the stored procedures they are calling. Please open in Visual Studio the `Catalog.vb` file we created in the previous chapter, and prepare to fill it with business logic.

GetDepartmentDetails

This will be called from the presentation tier when a department is clicked and we want to display its name and description. The presentation tier will want to pass us the ID of the selected department, and we need to send it back the name and the description of the selected department. Remember that the `GetDepartmentDetails` stored procedure has exactly two output parameters, `Name` and `Description` – we extract them here and wrap them into a separate object.

What object you say? This is a nice technique: create a separate class for the particular purpose of storing data that we want to pass around. This class is named `DepartmentDetails` and looks like this:

```
Public Class DepartmentDetails
    Public Name As String
    Public Description As String
End Class
```

We wrap the department's name and description into one `DepartmentDetails` object and send it back to the presentation tier. The `DepartmentDetails` class can be either added in a separate file in the `BusinessObjects` folder, or added to one of the existing files. Most of the time, we'll want to create a separate file for each class, but because in this case `DepartmentDetails` is more like a tool for the `Catalog` class, I chose to add it to the `Catalog.vb` file.

Please add the `DepartmentDetails` class at the beginning of `Catalog.vb` (but not inside the `Catalog` class) like this:

```
Imports System.Data.SqlClient

Public Class DepartmentDetails
    Public Name As String
    Public Description As String
End Class

Public Class Catalog
    // ... code here
```

Next, add the `GetDepartmentDetails` function to the `Catalog` class. It doesn't matter where you place this function – for example, it doesn't need to be placed after the `connectionString` property, even if it uses that property.

```
Public Function GetDepartmentDetails(ByVal departmentId As String) _
                                 As DepartmentDetails
  ' Create the connection object
  Dim connection As New SqlConnection(connectionString)

  ' Create and initialize the command object
  Dim command As New SqlCommand("GetDepartmentDetails", connection)
  command.CommandType = CommandType.StoredProcedure

  ' Add an input parameter and supply a value for it
  command.Parameters.Add("@DepartmentID", SqlDbType.Int, 4)
  command.Parameters("@DepartmentID").Value = departmentId

  ' Add an output parameter
  command.Parameters.Add("@DepartmentName", SqlDbType.VarChar, 50)
  command.Parameters("@DepartmentName").Direction = _
                                   ParameterDirection.Output

  ' Add an output parameter
  command.Parameters.Add("@DepartmentDescription", _
                                   SqlDbType.VarChar, 200)
  command.Parameters("@DepartmentDescription").Direction = _
                                   ParameterDirection.Output

  ' Open the connection, execute the command, and close the connection
  connection.Open()
  command.ExecuteNonQuery()
  connection.Close()

  ' Populate a DepartmentDetails object with data from output parameters
  Dim details As New DepartmentDetails()
  details.Name = command.Parameters("@DepartmentName").Value.ToString
  details.Description = _
        command.Parameters("@DepartmentDescription").Value.ToString

  ' Return the DepartmentDetails object to the calling function
  Return details
End Function
```

We know what happens in this function pretty well because we analyzed it while learning about stored procedure parameters. Its main purpose in life is to send back the name and description of the relevant department. To do this, it calls the `GetDepartmentDetails` stored procedure, supplying it with a department ID. After execution, it reads the `@DepartmentName` and `@DepartmentDescription` output parameters, saves them into a `DepartmentDetails` object, and sends this object back to the calling function.

GetCategoriesInDepartment

This function is called when we need to display a department's details in the product catalog. Apart from adding the department name and description (returned by the previous function), we also need a list of categories that belong to that department. Please add this function to the `Catalog` class:

```
Public Function GetCategoriesInDepartment(ByVal _
                            departmentId As String) As SqlDataReader
    ' Create the connection object
    Dim connection As New SqlConnection(connectionString)

    ' Create and initialize the command object
    Dim command As New SqlCommand("GetCategoriesInDepartment", connection)
    command.CommandType = CommandType.StoredProcedure

    ' Add an input parameter and supply a value for it
    command.Parameters.Add("@DepartmentID", SqlDbType.Int, 4)
    command.Parameters("@DepartmentID").Value = departmentId

    ' Open the connection
    connection.Open()

    ' Return a SqlDataReader to the calling function
    Return command.ExecuteReader(CommandBehavior.CloseConnection)
End Function
```

GetCategoryDetails

Here, history repeats itself. Just as we needed to return a name and description for the selected department, we need to do the same thing for the categories. We'll use the same technique here, and wrap the data into a separate class.

Add the `CategoryDetails` class at the beginning of `Catalog.vb`. Don't place it inside the `Catalog` class!

```
Imports System.Data.SqlClient

Public Class DepartmentDetails
    Public Name As String
    Public Description As String
End Class

Public Class CategoryDetails
    Public Name As String
    Public Description As String
End Class

Public Class Catalog
        // ... class code here ...
```

Then add the `GetCategoryDetails` method to the `Catalog` class. Except for the fact that it calls another stored procedure and uses another class to wrap the return information, it is identical to `GetDepartmentDetails`:

```
Public Function GetCategoryDetails(ByVal categoryId As String) As _
                                                    CategoryDetails
    ' Create the connection object
    Dim connection As New SqlConnection(connectionString)

    ' Create and initialize the command object
    Dim command As New SqlCommand("GetCategoryDetails", connection)
    command.CommandType = CommandType.StoredProcedure

    ' Add an input parameter and supply a value for it
    command.Parameters.Add("@CategoryID", SqlDbType.Int, 4)
    command.Parameters("@CategoryID").Value = categoryId

    ' Add an output parameter
    command.Parameters.Add("@CategoryName", SqlDbType.VarChar, 50)
    command.Parameters("@CategoryName").Direction = _
                                    ParameterDirection.Output

    ' Add an output parameter
    command.Parameters.Add("@CategoryDescription", SqlDbType.VarChar, 200)
    command.Parameters("@CategoryDescription").Direction = _
                                    ParameterDirection.Output

    ' Open the connection, execute the command, and close the connection
    connection.Open()
    command.ExecuteNonQuery()
    connection.Close()

    ' Populate a CategoryDetails object with data from output parameters
    Dim details As New CategoryDetails()
    details.Name = _
            command.Parameters("@CategoryName").Value.ToString()
    details.Description = _
            command.Parameters("@CategoryDescription").Value.ToString()

    ' Return the CategoryDetails object to the calling function
    Return details
End Function
```

GetProductsInCategory

This returns the list of products that belong to a particular category. We return the list using a `SqlDataReader`, which will feed a `DataList` object to display the products list in a similar way to that used in Chapter 3 to fill in the list of departments:

```
Public Function GetProductsInCategory(ByVal categoryId As String) As _
                                                    SqlDataReader
    ' Create the connection object
    Dim connection As New SqlConnection(connectionString)

    ' Create and initialize the command object
    Dim command As New SqlCommand("GetProductsInCategory", connection)
```

```
    command.CommandType = CommandType.StoredProcedure

    ' Add an input parameter and supply a value for it
    command.Parameters.Add("@CategoryID", SqlDbType.Int, 4)
    command.Parameters("@CategoryID").Value = categoryId

    ' Open the connection
    connection.Open()

    ' Return a SqlDataReader to the calling function
    Return command.ExecuteReader(CommandBehavior.CloseConnection)
End Function
```

GetProductsOnDepartmentPromotion

This function returns the list of products featured for a particular department. It is needed to display the department's featured products when the customer visits the home page of a department.

```
Public Function GetProductsOnDepartmentPromotion(ByVal departmentId _
                                        As String) As SqlDataReader
    ' Create the connection object
    Dim connection As New SqlConnection(connectionString)

    ' Create and initialize the command object
    Dim command As New SqlCommand("GetProductsOnDepartmentPromotion", _
                                                        connection)
    command.CommandType = CommandType.StoredProcedure

    ' Add an input parameter and supply a value for it
    command.Parameters.Add("@DepartmentID", SqlDbType.Int, 4)
    command.Parameters("@DepartmentID").Value = departmentId

    ' Open the connection
    connection.Open()

    ' Return a SqlDataReader to the calling function
    Return command.ExecuteReader(CommandBehavior.CloseConnection)
End Function
```

GetProductsOnCatalogPromotion

This method is needed to get the list of products featured on the main page of the site.

```
Public Function GetProductsOnCatalogPromotion() As SqlDataReader
    ' Create the connection object
    Dim connection As New SqlConnection(connectionString)

    ' Create and initialize the command object
    Dim command As New SqlCommand("GetProductsOnCatalogPromotion", _
                                                        connection)
    command.CommandType = CommandType.StoredProcedure
```

```
    ' Open the connection
    connection.Open()

    ' Return a SqlDataReader to the calling function
    Return command.ExecuteReader(CommandBehavior.CloseConnection)
End Function
```

The Presentation Tier

Believe it or not, but right now the data and business tiers of the product catalog are complete for this chapter. All we have to do to utilize them is to implement their functionality in the presentation tier.

In this final section, we will create a few web user controls and integrate them into the existing project.

Displaying Data about the Selected Department

Execute the WroxJokeShop project (or load http://localhost/WroxJokeShop in your favorite web browser) to see once again what happens when the visitor clicks on a department. The main page, default.aspx, is reloaded, but this time with a query string at the end:

> http://localhost/WroxJokeShop/default.aspx?DepartmentID=2&DepartmentIndex=1

This happens because of the way we designed the departments' links in Chapter 3. We learned then that DepartmentIndex is used to select the department that was clicked on, so that it would be displayed using a different style.

Now we'll make use of the other parameter that appears when someone clicks on a department: if we know the DepartmentID, we can obtain any data about the selected department. We'll want to read the value of DepartmentID each time default.aspx is reloaded (this happens every time the visitor clicks on another department). This can be done by modifying the Page_Load event handler in the code-behind file of default.aspx.

Having a value supplied for DepartmentID is an indication that the visitor clicked on a department, and we want to do something about it. When we created default.aspx back in Chapter 2, we marked its lower-right table cell to run on the server side, and we named it pageContentsCell. Because pageContentsCell runs on the server side, we can manually populate it in code.

The user control responsible for showing the contents of a particular department is named Department.ascx and it is presented in the following *Try It Out*. We first create the control, and then we modify default.aspx to load it in pageContentsCell when DepartmentID is present in the query string.

Try It Out – Creating the Department Web User Control

1. Create a new web user control named Department.ascx in the **UserControls** folder. In case you don't remember, you will need to right-click on **UserControls** folder, and then choose **Add | Add Web User Control**.

133

2. The form can be created pretty easily using Visual Studio, but since it's pretty short, let's look at the HTML directly. Select **HTML** View and make sure the file looks like this:

```
<%@ Control Language="vb" AutoEventWireup="false" Codebehind="Department.ascx.vb"
Inherits="WroxJokeShop.Department"
TargetSchema="http://schemas.microsoft.com/intellisense/ie5" %>
```

```
<table cellspacing="0" width="100%">
  <tr>
    <td>
      <P align="right">
        <asp:Label id="departmentNameLabel" runat="server"
                                    CssClass="DepartmentTitle">
        </asp:Label>
      </P>
      <P align="right"><EM>[Place List of Categories Here]</EM></P>
      <P align="left">
        <asp:Label id="descriptionLabel" CssClass="ListDescription"
                                    runat="server">
        </asp:Label>
      </P>
    </td>
  </tr>
  <tr>
    <td vAlign="top" id="productsListCell" runat="server">
      <P align="left"><EM>[Place List of Products Here]</EM> </P>
    </td>
  </tr>
</table>
```

3. Open the form in **Design** View mode. The newly created control should look like this:

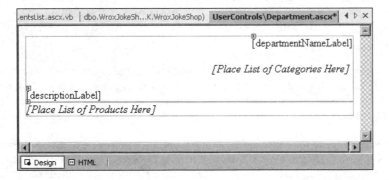

4. Now let's add the CSS styles that are used by the labels. Add the following to `WroxJokeShop.css`:

```
.DepartmentTitle
{
    color: green;
```

```
        font-family: Comic Sans MS;
        text-decoration: none;
        font-size:  24px;
        font-weight: bold;
        line-height: 15px;
        padding-left: 10px
    }


    .ListDescription
    {
        color: Black;
        font-family: Verdana, Helvetica, sans-serif;
        font-weight: bold;
        font size: 14px,
    }
```

In the HTML code, we set these styles to apply to the departmentNameLabel and descriptionLabel controls within the user control.

5. Open the code-behind file of the user control. First make sure the objects corresponding to the server-side components are declared at the beginning of the file, like this:

```
Public MustInherit Class Department
    Inherits System.Web.UI.UserControl
```

```
    Protected WithEvents departmentNameLabel As _
                                System.Web.UI.WebControls.Label
    Protected WithEvents descriptionLabel As _
                                System.Web.UI.WebControls.Label
    Protected WithEvents productsListCell As _
                            System.Web.UI.HtmlControls.HtmlTableCell
```

Visual Studio should automatically create these when we declare them as server-side components in the HTML code. If for some reason Visual Studio forgot to declare these objects, please do it yourself.

6. Then modify Page_Load like this:

```
Private Sub Page_Load(ByVal sender As System.Object, _
    ByVal e As System.EventArgs) Handles MyBase.Load
        ' The business layer Catalog object
        Dim catalog As Catalog = New Catalog()

        ' Retrieve DepartmentID from the query string
        Dim departmentID As String = Request.Params("DepartmentID")

        ' If the visitor requested for a department or a category
        ' we populate the labels with information
        If Not departmentID Is Nothing Then
            ' create the DepartmentDetails object
```

```
            Dim departmentDetails As New DepartmentDetails()

            ' fill the DepartmentDetails object with data
            departmentDetails =
                catalog.GetDepartmentDetails(departmentID)

            ' set the retrieved department name to the label
            departmentNameLabel.Text = departmentDetails.Name

            ' set the retrieved department description to the label
            descriptionLabel.Text = departmentDetails.Description
        End If
    End Sub
```

7. Now let's modify `default.aspx` to load the newly created user control when `DepartmentID` appears in the query string. If the visitor is browsing a department (`DepartmentID` is not `Nothing`), we populate `pageContentsCell` with the control we have just created (`Department.ascx`). Open `default.aspx.vb` and modify its `Page_Load` method like this:

```
Private Sub Page_Load(ByVal sender As System.Object, _
                      ByVal e As System.EventArgs) Handles MyBase.Load
    ' Save DepartmentID from the query string to a variable
    Dim departmentId As String = Request.Params("departmentID")

    ' Are we on the main web page or browsing the catalog?
    If Not departmentId Is Nothing Then
        Dim control As Control
        control = Page.LoadControl("UserControls/Department.ascx")
        pageContentsCell.Controls.Add(control)
    End If
End Sub
```

8. Delete the **Place Contents Here** text from `pageContentsCell` in `default.aspx`, because we load the `Department.ascx` user control when one of the departments is selected instead of that text. Because the `Department` user control is added to `pageContentsCell` in code, we don't need to drag it onto `default.aspx` as we did in Chapter 3 with `DepartmentsList.ascx`.

9. Execute the project. On the main page, select one of the departments. You should get a page like this:

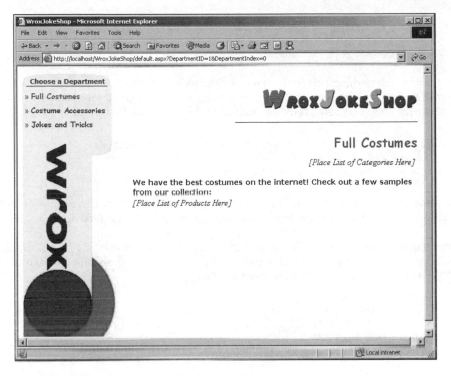

How It Works – The DepartmentsList Web User Control

The code isn't complicated, but since it's the first time we've done this, it's worth taking a closer look.

Every time default.aspx is reloaded, its Page_Load method gets called. We check to see if DepartmentID has been supplied in the query string:

```
' Save DepartmentID from the query string to a variable
Dim departmentId As String = Request.Params("departmentID")

' Are we on the main web page or browsing the catalog?
If Not departmentId Is Nothing Then
    ' ... do something useful with that departmentId ...
```

If indeed a department ID has been supplied (which means the visitor is browsing the catalog), we load Department.ascx:

```
' Save DepartmentID from the query string to a variable
Dim departmentId As String = Request.Params("departmentID")

' Are we on the main web page or browsing the catalog?
If Not departmentId Is Nothing Then
    Dim control As Control
    control = Page.LoadControl("UserControls/Department.ascx")
    pageContentsCell.Controls.Add(control)
End If
```

137

Please note that the three lines within this if statement could be replaced by the following line:

```
pageContentsCell.Controls.Add(Page.LoadControl("UserControls/Department.ascx"))
```

OK, so if there is a department ID in the query string, we load `Departments.ascx`. When this happens, the `Page_Load` method of `Department.ascx` gets executed too. Here we verify once again that a department is indeed being browsed (that is, we're not on the first page):

```
Dim departmentID As String = Request.Params("DepartmentID")
If Not departmentID Is Nothing Then
    ' we have a DepartmentID in the query string
```

This test is not really required because `default.aspx` loads `Department.ascx` only when the visitor clicks on a department, but it means our user control is better protected.

We get the required data using the `GetDepartmentDetails` method of the `Catalog` class, which returns a `DepartmentDetails` object populated with data about the specified department. Remember how the `DepartmentDetails` class has been defined:

```
Public Class DepartmentDetails
    Public Name As String
    Public Description As String
End Class
```

Because we have a method that returns our information packaged in a `DepartmentDetails` object, it is very easy to make use of the provided functionality:

```
    ' If the visitor requested for a department or a category
    ' we populate the labels with information
    If Not departmentID Is Nothing Then
        ' create the DepartmentDetails object
        Dim departmentDetails As New DepartmentDetails()

        ' fill the DepartmentDetails object with data
        departmentDetails = catalog.GetDepartmentDetails(departmentID)

        ' set the retrieved department name to the label
        departmentNameLabel.Text = departmentDetails.Name

        ' set the retrieved department description to the label
        descriptionLabel.Text = departmentDetails.Description
    End If
```

Displaying the List of Categories

Notice that in the last screenshot there are places that we left unfilled, like the [Place List of Categories Here] area. When the visitor clicks on a department, we want that area to be filled with the list of categories that belong to the selected department.

The CategoriesList web user control is very similar to the DepartmentsList web control. It will basically consist of a DataList control that will be populated with data from the Catalog class, just as we did for DepartmentsList. The DataList will also contain links to default.aspx, but this time the query string will also contain a CategoryID.

The steps in the following *Try It Out* are very like the ones in the DepartmentsList user control, so we will move a bit more quickly this time.

Try It Out – Creating the CategoriesList Web User Control

1. Add a new web user control to the UserControls folder, named CategoriesList.ascx.

2. Add a DataList object to the user control, and change its name to list.

3. Enter the DataList in edit mode by right-clicking on it, going to Edit Template, and then selecting the Item Templates option.

4. Add a HyperLink control to the Item Template, and a Label control to the SelectedItem Template.

5. For the hyperlink, set the CssClass property to CategoryUnselected. For the Label control, please set the CssClass property to CategorySelected.

6. Add the following styles to WroxJokeShop.css:

```
A.CategoryUnselected
{
    color:Blue;
    font-family: Verdana, Helvetica, sans-serif;
    text-decoration: none;
    font-size:  12px;
    font-weight: bold;
    line-height: 10px;
    padding-left: 15px
}

A.CategoryUnselected:hover
{
    color:Red;
    font-family: Verdana, Helvetica, sans-serif;
    text-decoration: none;
    font-size:  12px;
    font-weight: bold;
    line-height: 16px;
    padding-left: 15px
}

.CategorySelected
{
    color:Green;
    font-family: Verdana, Helvetica, sans-serif;
```

```
    text-decoration: none;
    font-size:  12px;
    font-weight: bold;
    line-height: 16px;
    padding-left: 15px
}
```

7. Go back to `CategoriesList.ascx` now. Enter the HTML View by clicking on the HTML tab at the bottom of the designer window. Here we need to make a few changes to the `HyperLink` controls. This is the full code, with the changes highlighted:

```
<%@ Control Language="vb" AutoEventWireup="false"
Codebehind="CategoriesList.ascx.vb" Inherits="WroxJokeShop.CategoriesList"
TargetSchema="http://schemas.microsoft.com/intellisense/ie5" %>
```

```
<asp:DataList CellPadding="0" CellSpacing="0" id="list" runat="server">
  <SelectedItemTemplate>
    <table border="0" width="550" cellspacing="0" cellpadding="0">
      <tr>
        <td align="right">
          <asp:Label id="Label1" runat="server"
            Text='<%# DataBinder.Eval(Container.DataItem, "Name") %>'
            CssClass="CategorySelected">Label
          </asp:Label> &laquo;
        </td>
      </tr>
    </table>
  </SelectedItemTemplate>
  <ItemTemplate>
    <table border="0" width="550" cellspacing="0" cellpadding="0">
      <tr>
        <td align="right">
          <asp:HyperLink id="HyperLink1" runat="server"
            NavigateUrl='<%# "../default.aspx?DepartmentID=" &amp;
             Request.Params("DepartmentID") &amp;
            "&amp;DepartmentIndex=" &amp;
             Request.Params("DepartmentIndex") &amp;
            "&amp;CategoryID=" &amp;
             DataBinder.Eval(Container.DataItem, "categoryID") &amp;
            "&amp;CategoryIndex=" &amp; Container.ItemIndex  %>'
             Text='<%# DataBinder.Eval(Container.DataItem, "Name") %>'
             CssClass="CategoryUnselected">HyperLink
          </asp:HyperLink> &laquo;
        </td>
      </tr>
    </table>
  </ItemTemplate>
</asp:DataList>
```

*With this section of code, please ensure that the sections of code emphasized in bold text appears on **one line only**. They appear on separate lines above for appearance, but will generate a runtime error if entered like this.*

8. Now let's open the code-behind file of the `CategoriesList` user control. We need to populate the `DataList` and mark the selected item when the user control loads. Please modify `Page_Load` like this:

```
Private Sub Page_Load(ByVal sender As System.Object, _
                      ByVal e As System.EventArgs) Handles MyBase.Load
    ' The department for which we are loading the categories
    Dim departmentId As String = Request.Params("DepartmentID")

    ' The index of the selected DataList item.
    Dim listIndex As String = Request.Params("CategoryIndex")

    ' The DataList item that was clicked is set as the selected item
    If Not listIndex Is Nothing Then
        list.SelectedIndex = CInt(listIndex)
    End If

    ' Create a new Catalog object
    Dim catalog As New Catalog()

    ' GetCategoriesInDepartment returns a SqlDataReader object that has
    ' two fields: CategoryID and Name. These fields are read in
    ' the SelectedItemTemplate and ItemTemplate of the DataList
    list.DataSource = catalog.GetCategoriesInDepartment(departmentID)

    ' Needed to bind the child controls (the HyperLink controls)
    ' to the data source
    list.DataBind()
End Sub
```

9. Open the code-behind file for `Department.ascx`, and modify `Page_Load` like this:

```
Private Sub Page_Load(ByVal sender As System.Object, _
    ByVal e As System.EventArgs) Handles MyBase.Load

    ' The business layer Catalog object
    Dim catalog As Catalog = New Catalog()

    ' Retrieve DepartmentID from the query string
    Dim departmentId As String = Request.Params("DepartmentID")

    ' Retrieve CategoryID from the query string
    Dim categoryId As String = Request.Params("CategoryID")

    ' If the visitor requested for a department or a category
    ' we populate the labels with information
    If Not departmentId Is Nothing Then
        ' create the DepartmentDetails object
        Dim departmentDetails As New DepartmentDetails()

        ' fill the DepartmentDetails object with data
        departmentDetails = catalog.GetDepartmentDetails(departmentID)
```

```
        ' set the retrieved department name to the label
        departmentNameLabel.Text = departmentDetails.Name

        ' If we're browsing a department we take its description
        ' and place it in descriptionLabel. If we're browsing a
        ' category we use the category's description instead
        If categoryId Is Nothing Then
            descriptionLabel.Text = departmentDetails.Description
        Else
            Dim categoryDetails As New CategoryDetails()
            categoryDetails = Catalog.GetCategoryDetails(categoryID)
            descriptionLabel.Text = categoryDetails.Description
        End If
    End If
End Sub
```

10. Press *Ctrl+Shift+B* to compile the project.

11. Let's now add the CategoriesList control to the Department control. Open the Department control in **Design** view. Drag the **CategoriesList** user control from Solution Explorer and drop it near the **[Place List of Categories Here]** text. Then remove the text. The design of Department.ascx should now look like this:

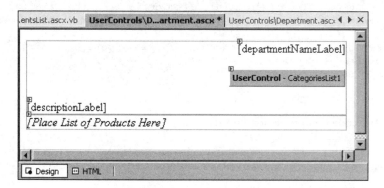

12. Press *F5* to execute the project. When the page loads, click on one of the departments. You'll see the categories list appear in the chosen place, and the selected department's description below it:

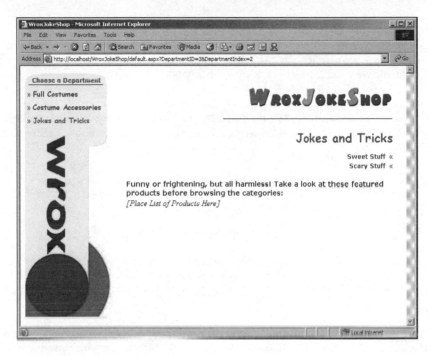

13. Now click on one of the categories. You'll see that it gets selected, and we see the category description instead of the department description:

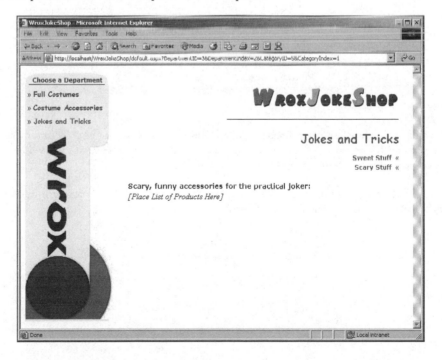

How It Works – The CategoriesList User Control

What is important to see here is what happens when we click on a category: default.aspx is reloaded, but this time we also have a CategoryID and CategoryIndex in the query string. In some of the other controls we create, we check for CategoryID.

If DepartmentID is present in the query string, this means we're either browsing a department, or a category of a particular department. We modified Department.ascx so that it displays the department description if the visitor is browsing a department, or the category description if the visitor has selected a category:

```
' If we're browsing a department we take its description
' and place it in descriptionLabel. If we're browsing a
' category we use the category's description instead
If categoryId Is Nothing Then
    descriptionLabel.Text = departmentDetails.Description
Else
    Dim categoryDetails As New CategoryDetails()
    categoryDetails = Catalog.GetCategoryDetails(categoryID)
    descriptionLabel.Text = categoryDetails.Description
End If
```

The CategoriesList appears on the department's web page whether a category is selected or not. Because CategoriesList is very similar to DepartmentsList, we won't study it again in detail here. Its Page_Load event handler checks if there is a CategoryIndex parameter present, which specifies the currently selected category (if any):

```
' The index of the selected DataList item.
Dim listIndex As String = Request.Params("CategoryIndex")

' The DataList item that was clicked is set as the selected item
If Not listIndex Is Nothing Then
    list.SelectedIndex = CInt(listIndex)
End If
```

This will result in the selected category being displayed using the SelectedItem template, which contains a label with CategorySelected style applied to it. Because we use a label here, the selected category can't be clicked again (we no longer have a link there).

We fill the DataList by calling the Catalog.GetCategoriesInDepartment method and supplying the value of the selected DepartmentID:

```
' The department for which we are loading the categories
Dim departmentID As String = Request.Params("DepartmentID")

' ...
' ...
' ...
```

```
' Create a new Catalog object
Dim catalog As New Catalog()

' GetCategoriesInDepartment returns a SqlDataReader object that has
' two fields: CategoryID and Name. These fields are read in
' the SelectedItemTemplate and ItemTemplate of the DataList
list.DataSource = catalog.GetCategoriesInDepartment(departmentID)

' Needed to bind the child controls (the HyperLink controls)
' to the data source
list.DataBind()
```

Displaying the Products

Whether we're on the main web page or we're browsing a department or a category, we want some products to appear instead of the [Place List of Products Here] text.

Here we create the ProductsList web user control, which is capable of displaying a list containing detailed information about the products. When executed, this control will look like this:

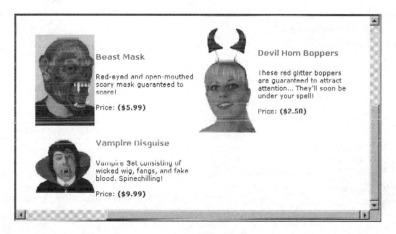

This user control will be used in multiple places within the web site. On the main page, it will display the products on catalog promotion (remember, the ones that have the OnCatalogPromotion bit set to 1). When the visitor selects a particular department, the ProductsList control will display the products featured for the selected department. Finally, when the visitor clicks on a category, the control will display all the products that belong to that category. Due to the way we implemented the database, we can have a product featured in the departments it belongs to, but not on the main page, or vice-versa. If a product belongs to more than one department, it will appear on the main page of each of these departments.

The ProductsList user control will only be displayed on the main web page and on the pages that appear when the visitor is browsing a department or a category. The control will choose what products to display after analyzing the query string. If both DepartmentID and CategoryID are present, this means that we should list the products of that category. If only DepartmentID is present, this tells us that we're visiting a department, so it should display its featured products. If DepartmentID is not present, this means we're on the main page, so we should see the catalog featured products.

In order to integrate the `ProductsList` control with the first page, we'll need to create an additional user control, which we will implement later. After creating `ProductsList` in the following *Try It Out* we'll be able to browse the products by `Department` and by `Category`. Afterwards we'll see how to add products to the main web page.

Try It Out – Creating the ProductsList Web User Control

1. Add a new web user control named `ProductsList` to the **UserControls** folder.

2. Open the control in **Design** View, and drag a **DataList** control from the toolbox on to it.

3. Rename the ID of the **DataList** to `list`.

4. Modify the HTML code of `ProductsList` like this:

```
<%@ Control Language="vb" AutoEventWireup="false"
Codebehind="ProductsList.ascx.vb" Inherits="WroxJokeShop.ProductsList"
TargetSchema="http://schemas.microsoft.com/intellisense/ie5" %>
<asp:DataList id="list" runat="server" RepeatColumns="2"
                                      HorizontalAlign="Left">
 <ItemTemplate>
  <table cellPadding="0" align="left">
   <tr>
    <td align="right">
     <img src='ProductImages/<%# DataBinder.Eval(Container.DataItem,
"ImagePath") %>'
           border="0" width="100"></a>
    </td>
    <td vAlign="middle" width="200">
     <span class="ProductName">
       <%# DataBinder.Eval(Container.DataItem, "Name") %>
     </span>
    <br><br>
    <span class="ProductDescription">
     <%# DataBinder.Eval(Container.DataItem, "Description", "{0:c}") %>
    <br><br>Price:
    </span>
    <span class="ProductPrice">
     <%# DataBinder.Eval(Container.DataItem, "Price", "({0:c})") %>
    </span>
   </tr>
  </table>
 </ItemTemplate>
</asp:DataList>
```

5. Right now, the way the product price is written depends on the culture of the computer running the site, because of the `{0:C}` parameter sent to `DataBinder.Eval`. For example, if the default culture were set to `fr-FR`, instead of $1.23 we would see 1,23 €. For more information on internationalization issues please consult an advanced ASP.NET book. For now, because we want to make sure our prices are expressed in the same currency (we choose US dollars for this example), please double-click on `Web.config` in Solution Explorer and find the following line:

```
<globalization requestEncoding="utf-8" responseEncoding="utf-8" />
```

Please modify this line like this:

```
<globalization
  requestEncoding="utf-8"
  responseEncoding="utf-8"
  culture="en-US"/>
```

This ensures that no matter how the development (or production) machine is set up, our prices will always be expressed in the same currency.

6. Modify the `Page_Load` event handler of `ProductsList` to look like this:

```
Private Sub Page_Load(ByVal sender As System.Object, _
                      ByVal e As System.EventArgs) Handles MyBase.Load

    ' Retrieve DepartmentID from the query string
    Dim departmentId As String = Request.Params("DepartmentID")

    ' Retrieve CategoryID from the query string
    Dim categoryId As String = Request.Params("CategoryID")

    ' Are we retrieving products for a Category, for a Department
    ' or for the main page?
    If Not categoryId Is Nothing Then

        ' category
        Dim catalog As Catalog = New Catalog()
        list.DataSource = catalog.GetProductsInCategory(categoryId)
        list.DataBind()

    ElseIf Not departmentId Is Nothing Then

        ' department
        Dim catalog As Catalog = New Catalog()
list.DataSource=catalog.GetProductsOnDepartmentPromotion(departmentId)
        list.DataBind()

    Else

        ' main page
        Dim catalog As Catalog = New Catalog()
        list.DataSource = catalog.GetProductsOnCatalogPromotion()
        list.DataBind()

    End If
End Sub
```

7. Add these styles to the `WroxJokeShop.css` file:

```
.ProductName
{
    color: Red;
    font-family: Verdana, Helvetica, sans-serif;
    font-weight: bold;
    font-size: 13px;
}

.ProductDescription
{
    color: Black;
    font-family: Verdana, Helvetica, sans-serif;
    font-size: 11px;
}

.ProductPrice
{
    color: Black;
    font-family: Verdana, Helvetica, sans-serif;
    font-weight: bold;
    font-size: 11px;
}
```

8. Build the solution by pressing *Ctrl+Shift+B*.

9. Open `Department.ascx` in **Design** View. Drag the **ProductsList.ascx** user control from Solution Explorer and drop it in the cell containing **[Place List of Products Here]**. Then delete the text, so that only the user control occupies the cell, as in the following screenshot:

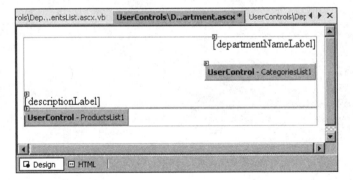

10. Press *F5* to execute the project, and navigate to one of the departments.

To see the product images, ensure you have the `ProductImages` folder from the code download located in your project folder.

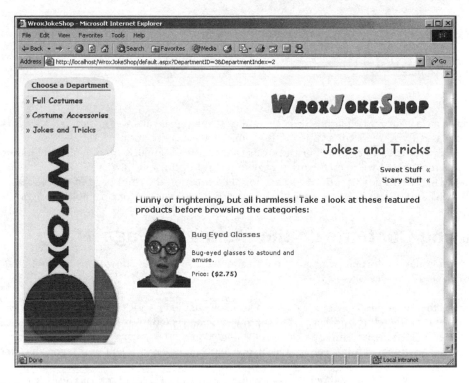

How It Works – The ProductsList User Control

The `ProductsList` control is very similar to `CategoriesList` and `DepartmentsList`, but the `ItemTemplate` contains a bit more HTML.

Its `Page_Load` event handler decides which method of the `Catalog` class to use in order to get the products list.

```
' Are we retrieving products for a Category, for a Department
' or for the main page?
If Not categoryId Is Nothing Then

    ' category
    Dim catalog As Catalog = New Catalog()
    list.DataSource = catalog.GetProductsInCategory(categoryId)
    list.DataBind()

ElseIf Not departmentId Is Nothing Then

    ' department
    Dim catalog As Catalog = New Catalog()
    list.DataSource = catalog.GetProductsOnDepartmentPromotion(departmentId)
    list.DataBind()

Else
```

```
                ' main page
                Dim catalog As Catalog = New Catalog()
                list.DataSource = catalog.GetProductsOnCatalogPromotion()
                list.DataBind()

        End If
```

If we have a `CategoryID` parameter in the query string this means we're visiting a category, so we call `catalog.GetProductsInCategory`. If we only have a `DepartmentID`, `GetProductsOnDepartmentPromotion` is called instead. Finally, if none of these parameters are found, this means that we're on the main page and `GetProductsOnCatalogPromotion` is called to give us the list. Right now `ProductsList` doesn't appear on the front page of the web site, but as soon as we add it (in the next exercise), it will work perfectly without needing a single change.

Displaying Contents on the Main Web Page

Apart from general information about the web site, we also want to show some promotional products on the first page of our web site.

Remember that in `default.aspx` we have a table cell named `pageContentsCell` that we fill with different details depending on what part of the site is being visited? When a department or a category is being visited, the `Department.ascx` control is loaded and it takes care of filling that space. We still haven't done anything with that cell for the first page, when no department or category has been selected.

In the following *Try It Out* we'll write a user control that contains some information about our web site, and shows the products that have been set up to be on promotion on the first page. Remember that the `Product` table contains a bit field named `OnCatalogPromotion`. Site administrators will set this bit to 1 for products that need to be featured in the first page.

Try It Out – Creating the FirstPageContents Web User Control

1. Let's start by creating the FirstPageContents.ascx web user control in the UserControls folder.

2. The page should look like this, when seen in HTML View:

```
<%@ Control Language="vb" AutoEventWireup="false"
Codebehind="FirstPageContents.ascx.vb" Inherits="WroxJokeShop.FirstPageContents"
TargetSchema="http://schemas.microsoft.com/intellisense/ie5" %>
<%@ Register TagPrefix="uc1" TagName="ProductsList" Src="ProductsList.ascx" %>
<p align="right">
  <img src="Images/welcome.gif" border="0" width="102" height="18">
  <br>
  <span class="FirstPageText">
    <br>
    We hope you have a pleasant experience developing WroxJokeShop,
    <br><br>
the virtual novelty store presented in Beginning E-Commerce Websites with
    <br><br>
    ASP.NET and VB.NET </span>
```

```
</p>
<span class="ListDescription">
  This week we have set a special price for these fantastic products! :)
</span>
<br>
<uc1:ProductsList id="ProductsList1" runat="server">
</uc1:ProductsList>
```

3. Enter the following style in `WroxJokeShop.css`:

```
.FirstPageText
{
    color. Navy;
    font-family: Verdana, Helvetica, sans-serif;
    text-decoration: none;
    font-size:  12px;
    font-weight: bold;
    line-height: 9px;
    padding-left: 10px
}
```

4. Right now, `FirstPageContents` should look like this when seen in Design View:

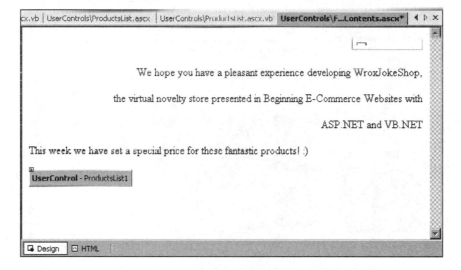

5. Open the code-behind file of `default.aspx` and make the following changes:

```
Private Sub Page_Load(ByVal sender As System.Object, _
                      ByVal e As System.EventArgs) Handles MyBase.Load

    ' Save DepartmentID from the query string to a variable
    Dim departmentId As String = Request.Params("departmentID")
```

```
' Are we on the main web page or browsing the catalog?
If Not departmentId Is Nothing Then
    Dim control As Control
    control = Page.LoadControl("UserControls/Department.ascx")
    pageContentsCell.Controls.Add(control)
Else
    Dim control As Control
    control = Page.LoadControl("UserControls/FirstPageContents.ascx")
    pageContentsCell.Controls.Add(control)
End If

End Sub
```

6. Execute the project. The first page should look like this:

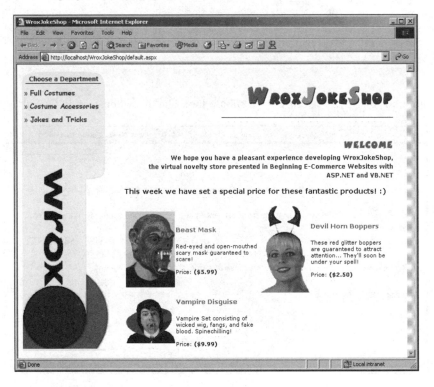

How It Works – FirstPageContents

We display the products list on the first page of the site by adding the `ProductsList` control to it. Remember that when we created the `ProductsList` user control, we made it smart enough to handle the products on catalog promotion.

Because we also want to have some other information on the front page, we created a separate control named `FirstPageContents`, which includes the `ProductsList` control.

Custom Error Page

The product catalog works quite nicely. Before we finish this chapter, we'll make another step towards improving the quality of our web site.

A serious web site will always want to provide a custom error page, which is shown to the visitor if an unexpected error happens. I say *unexpected error*, because there are some types of error that we might want to handle directly in the code (usually in the business tier) – say, if the visitor tries to load this page in the web browser:

http://*WroxJokeShop*/default.aspx?DepartmentID=999999999999&DepartmentIndex=0

If the visitor tries to load this page, the DepartmentID is interpreted as a string by the presentation tier. We have learned that we don't usually check the data type within the presentation tier, so the value 999999999999 is sent directly as a string to the business tier. In the business tier, we might want to check to see if the value is valid. The current code doesn't check this and will go on to try to get information about the selected department from the database.

The fact that there is no department with an ID of 999999999999 wouldn't bother us – we would simply get a void list of categories, an empty name and an empty description – *except* for the fact that 999999999999 is not a valid Int32 value. When the business tier tries to convert this to an integer to send it the database, an error is generated and we get an ugly error page:

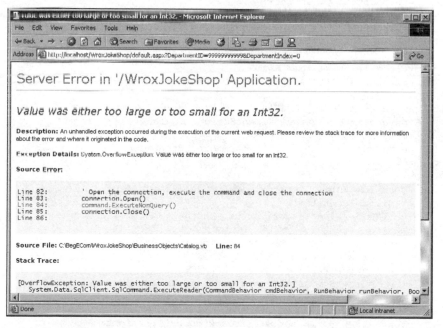

OK, we don't want the visitor to see this, do we? Apart from the fact that it looks ugly, we certainly don't want the visitor to see this kind of debugging info. Luckily, by default, this type of error detail is only available to requests on the local machine (http://localhost/WroxJokeShop/...). Requests from other domains will display a helpful error page without the debugging details.

In a production application, we'll want to have a custom error page displayed instead of the ones ASP.NET provides for us. Let's do this in the following *Try It Out*:

Try It Out – Adding a Custom Error Page to WroxJokeShop

1. In Solution Explorer, double-click on `Web.config`.

2. In this file, find this line:

```
<customErrors mode="RemoteOnly" />
```

Modify the line like this:

```
<customErrors defaultRedirect="/WroxJokeShop/error.aspx" />
```

3. Right-click on **WroxJokeShop** in Solution Explorer and select **Add | Add Web Form**. Type `error.aspx` when asked for the name of the new form.

4. Set the form to `gridLayout` mode, open it in **HTML View**, and modify it like this:

```
<%@ Page Language="vb" AutoEventWireup="false" Codebehind="error.aspx.vb"
Inherits="WroxJokeShop._error"%>
<%@ Register TagPrefix="uc1" TagName="Header" Src="UserControls/Header.ascx" %>
<!DOCTYPE HTML PUBLIC "-//W3C//Dtd HTML 4.0 Transitional//EN">
<html>
    <head>
        <title>error</title>
        <meta name="GENERATOR" content="Microsoft Visual Studio.NET
            7.0">
        <meta name="CODE_LANGUAGE" content="Visual Basic 7.0">
        <meta name="vs_defaultClientScript" content="JavaScript">
        <meta name="vs_targetSchema"
            content="http://schemas.microsoft.com/intellisense/ie5">
    </head>
    <body>
        <form id="Form1" method="post" runat="server">
        <P align="center">
        <uc1:Header id="Header1" runat="server"> </uc1:Header></P>
        <P align="center">
        <font size="5">Our website is experiencing temporary
            problems.</font></P>
        <P align="center">
        <font size="5">Thanks for visiting us - we hope we'll be
            seeing you again</font></P>
        <P align="center">
        <font size="5">in better circumstances. :)</font></P>

        </form>
    </body>
</html>
```

5. Press *Ctrl+Shift+B* to build the solution. Right now, remote clients trying to load http://*WroxJokeShop*/default.aspx?DepartmentID=999999999999&DepartmentIndex =0 would get the following page:

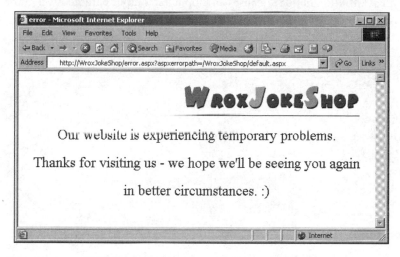

How It Works – The Custom Error Page

We have enabled the custom error page by modifying the `Web.config` configuration file. We'll meet this file again in the following chapters and will learn a few more tricks. However, this is a very powerful file and you can find out much more information about it in MSDN or an advanced ASP.NET book.

Note that after the modification, only the remote clients are presented with the new, nice error page. You, the developer working on the machine that hosts the site, would still receive the detailed error message showing debugging information.

Note that this error page implementation is a step away from being production quality. In a production environment we would want to warn the site administrator that something bad happened to the site – this action would be triggered in the `Form_Load` method of `error.aspx`.

In *Beginning ASP.NET 1.0 with VB.NET* (ISBN: 1-86100-733-7) and *Professional ASP.NET 1.0 Special Edition* (ISBN: 1-86100-703-5) you can find code samples on how to e-mail the administrator with the error code details, or how to save the error in the Windows Event log.

Summary

In this chapter, we finished creating our product catalog by building three new tables and defining the relationships between them. We created this functionality using the same techniques as in the previous chapter (using custom web user controls).

We also covered some new theory issues, including:

❑   Relational data and the types of relationships that can occur between tables

❑   Database diagrams, and why they can be useful

❑   How to use `WHERE` and `JOIN` clauses and input and output parameters in our SQL
    stored procedures

Searching the Catalog

In the previous chapters we implemented a functional product catalog for our site. However, it lacks an important feature: it cannot be searched. Our goal in this chapter is to allow the visitor to search the site for products by entering one or more keywords.

We will see how easy it is to add new functionality to a working site, and that this is in part due to the three-tier architecture we implemented. We will implement the search functionality by adding the necessary components to each of the three tiers.

What Kind of Search do we Want?

As always, there are a few things we need to think about before starting to code. We have learned that when analyzing the technical requirements of a new feature we want to add, it's good to look at that feature from the visitor's perspective.

So what kind of search would be most useful for the visitor? Most of the time, the answer to this comes from the customer for whom we are building the site. For the visual part, the answer is pretty simple – all types of searches require a textbox where the visitor can enter one or more words to search for.

In our site, since we're searching for products, the words entered by the visitor will be searched for in the products' names and descriptions. There are a few ways the text entered by the visitor can be treated. First, there is the *exact match* search – if the visitor enters an entire phrase, this would be searched in the database as it is, without splitting the words and searching for them separately.

There is the *all words* search, where the phrase entered by the visitor is split into words, and we search for products that contain every word entered by the visitor. This is like the *exact match* in that we still search for all the entered words, but this time the order is no longer important.

Finally, there is the *any words* search, where products that contain at least one of the entered words are found.

This simple classification isn't by any means complete. The search engine can be as complex as the one offered by www.google.com, which provides many options and features, and shows a ranked list of results; or as simple as searching the database for the exact string provided by the visitor.

Our web site will support the *any words* and *all words* search modes. This decision pretty much leads to the visual design of the search feature:

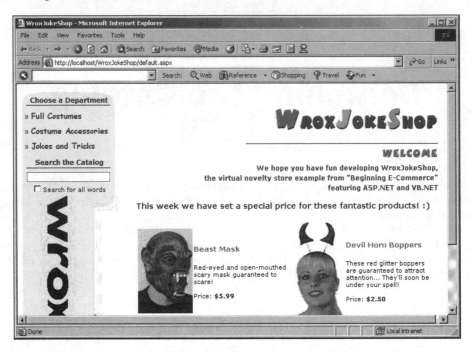

The textbox is there, as expected, along with a checkbox that allows the visitor to choose between an *all words* search and an *any words* search.

Another decision we need to make here is the way in which the search results should be displayed. How should the search results page look? We want to display, after all, a list of products that match the search criteria.

For WroxJokeShop we decided to display the list of products using the already existing ProductsList web user control. This makes our life easier because we can reuse its layout. A sample search page will look like this:

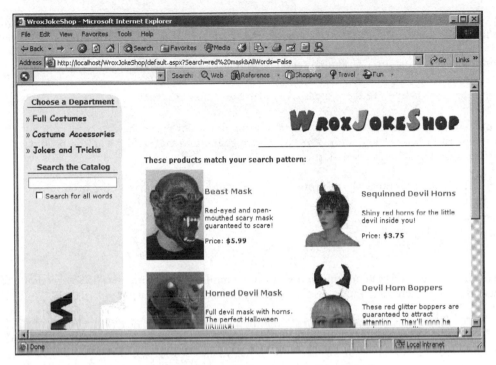

Let's start implementing this in the usual *data-business-presentation tier* style.

The Data Tier

Here we study the different ways that we can implement the search functionality in the database.

The Theory: Teaching the Database to Search Itself

From the database point of view, there are two main ways of searching the catalog.

One way is to use SQL Server's Full Text Search feature. This is an advanced feature of SQL Server Standard and Enterprise editions, which allows advanced keyword searches. These include searching for inflected forms of words such as plurals and various verb tenses, or words located in close proximity; and also the use of the Boolean operators (AND, AND NOT, OR). Additionally, it can also sort the results based on the rank, placing the most likely matches at the top.

The Full Text search engine runs as a service named Microsoft Search, which is only available with Server versions of Windows. Also, it isn't available with MSDE (the free version of SQL Server that we're using for this book). For these reasons we will not use Full Text searching for WroxJokeShop. However, if our client decides to make a software upgrade, we would only need to change the `SearchCatalog` stored procedure. For more detailed information about SQL Server's Full Text Search feature, please refer to *Professional SQL Server 2000 Programming* (ISBN: 1-86100-448-6) or *Professional SQL Server 7.0 Programming* (ISBN: 1-86100-231-9) from Wrox Press, or MSDN.

So how can we do searches without using that service? The answer is the standard, straightforward way of searching using the SELECT SQL command in conjunction with the WHERE and LIKE clauses. Since this is the first time that we have met the LIKE clause, let's look at a simple example. This will return all the products that have the word mask somewhere in their Description:

```
SELECT Name FROM Product WHERE Description LIKE '%mask%'
```

The percent (%) wildcard is used to specify any string of zero or more characters. Placing it before and after the word to be searched for in a WHERE clause guarantees that we'll get all the products whose description contains the word mask somewhere in it.

The following query returns all the products that contain the word mask in the product's Name or Description:

```
SELECT Name FROM Product
WHERE Description LIKE '%mask%' OR Name LIKE '%mask%'
```

This technique has the great advantage that it can be implemented using the MSDE version of SQL Server. However it has two important drawbacks that you need to be aware of:

❑ **Speed**. Because we're searching for text somewhere *inside* the Description and Name fields, the entire database needs to be searched on each query. Placing indexes on Description and Name would help if we searched for names and descriptions that started with a certain word, by using 'mask%' instead of '%mask%', but this is not what we need.

❑ **Implementation**. Because the number of words we search for is not constant, the SELECT query needs to be very flexible. I have found no *best* way to implement this – there are three main techniques frequently used by developers, but each has its own disadvantages.

Let's see what I mean by looking at each of these three techniques.

Dynamically Creating the Query in the Business Tier

First, we could generate the SQL query dynamically with VB.NET code in the business tier. So, if we search for the words red mask with an all-words search, the VB.NET code would create this SQL string:

```
SELECT Name FROM Product WHERE (Description LIKE '%red%' OR Name LIKE '%red%') AND
(Description LIKE '%mask%' OR Name LIKE '%mask%')
```

If we did an any-words search, the query would be:

```
SELECT Name FROM Product WHERE (Description LIKE '%red%' OR Name LIKE '%red%') OR
(Description LIKE '%mask%' OR Name LIKE '%mask%')
```

After creating these commands in the business tier, they are sent to the database for execution, without using an intermediary stored procedure, so the data tier is bypassed.

Generating this string in the business tier is a frequent solution, but it breaks the rules of three-tier programming. It places data tier logic (the way the query is created) in the business tier. When updating the database, instead of updating only the data tier, we would also need to update the business tier. Joining strings in the business tier in order to create a SQL query looks pretty ugly. Having the SQL query stored in the business tier can be practical in development environments when we want to quickly test functionality, but it is not recommended in a production environment.

Dynamically Creating the Query in the Data Tier

This is a less common approach, but it needs to be mentioned. An alternative to dynamically creating the query string in the business tier is to send the entire search string (in this case "red mask") to a stored procedure. OK, so this doesn't break the rules of three-tier architecture, but it is still an ugly thing to do, especially when the SQL code that dynamically generates the query becomes quite messy. Another drawback of dynamically generated queries in general (so this applies to the previous case as well) is that SQL Server can't pre-compile them and/or cache their results, although SQL Server 2000 is better at this than SQL Server 7.

I'll not expand on this too much, as we won't use this approach, but here are the main steps that would need to be taken:

❑ First, the whole search string is received as a string-type input parameter.

❑ This is then split into separate words – this can be done using the WHILE statement (by the way, there's no FOR LOOP statement).

❑ We might also need to use some string manipulation functions, such as CHARINDEX (which returns the position of a certain character in a string) and SUBSTRING (which returns a substring from a string). The whole list of string functions is available in SQL Server's Books Online.

❑ Using the extracted list of words, the query is created into a string variable.

If you are curious to see how to dynamically create a query and execute it, let's look at a working example. This kind of code can be used for our product catalog, but for simplicity, we'll only create a search using a single keyword. Here's the complete SQL query that will return all of the products that contain the word mask in their name or description:

```
/* This will contain the dynamically generated query */
DECLARE @query nvarchar(4000)

/* This is the keyword used for this sample search */
DECLARE @Word1 nvarchar(20)

/* We search for the word "mask" */
SET @Word1 = 'mask'

/* Here we create the query*/
SET @query = N'SELECT Product.ProductID,Product.Name, Product.Description,
Product.Price, Product.ImagePath' + CHAR(13)
SET @query = @query + N'FROM Product' + CHAR(13)
SET @query = @query + N'WHERE (Name LIKE ''%' + @Word1 + '%'' OR Description LIKE
''%' + @Word1 + '%'')' + CHAR(13)

/* Execute the query using the SQL Server's sp_executesql stored procedure*/
EXEC sp_executesql @query
```

There are a few points in this code that need explaining further. CHAR(13) represents a carriage return and is not really necessary, but is useful for debugging.

@query is finally created using the sp_executesql extended stored procedure (an internal SQL Server stored procedure). sp_executesql expects an nvarchar or nchar parameter, so @query needs to be of a Unicode type (this explains the N prefix applied to the strings in the previous lines of code).

Not Using Dynamically Generated Queries

This is the solution presented in this chapter. Here we use the plain old-style queries, which include the query SQL code directly in the stored procedure, instead of generating it dynamically and executing it with sp_executesql.

This solution is possible if we have the search keywords as parameters for the stored procedure. But wait, how do we know how many keywords the search string will contain? Well, we don't, and the workaround is to assume a maximum number of keywords. The stored procedure would be defined like this:

```
CREATE PROCEDURE SearchCatalog
(@AllWords bit,
@Word1 varchar(15) = NULL,
@Word2 varchar(15) = NULL,
@Word3 varchar(15) = NULL,
@Word4 varchar(15) = NULL,
@Word5 varchar(15) = NULL)
AS
     /* the query here */
```

Get the idea? We have a number of parameters with a default value of NULL. The business tier will send the keywords as parameters. If it sends less than maximum, there's not a problem because the others will have a default value, so they are not required.

The obvious disadvantage is that we'll always have a maximum number of keywords that can be accepted. However, if we set the maximum number to be large enough, the visitors will not feel this limitation. If a visitor ever introduces more that the maximum allowed number of words, the additional words are simply not sent to the data tier by the business tier.

The second drawback is that the business tier needs to know about the data-tier logic (regarding the maximum number of allowed words) – this is a data-tier limitation that has to be handled by the business tier. However, as we said previously, if we set the maximum number of words high enough, then we're not likely to have problems.

> *Even Google has a maximum number of allowed search words (ten), so it's not that bad to have this kind of limitation in our WroxJokeShop site.*

In this chapter, our code handles five input words, but it will be very simple to increase the maximum number, should you need to do this.

OK, to recap, we receive the input words as parameters. The business tier can send less parameters if required, but that's fine because they all have NULL for the default value. But how do we create the query that gets the products based on the values of these parameters? Here's what we will do for an "any words" search (note that we'll implement the entire stored procedure later, we are just previewing parts of it here).

```
SELECT Product.ProductID,Product.[Name], Product.[Description],
     Product.Price, Product.ImagePath
FROM Product
WHERE (Name LIKE '%'+@Word1+'%' OR Description LIKE '%'+@Word1+'%')
   OR (Name LIKE '%'+@Word2+'%' OR Description LIKE '%'+@Word2+'%')
   OR (Name LIKE '%'+@Word3+'%' OR Description LIKE '%'+@Word3+'%')
   OR (Name LIKE '%'+@Word4+'%' OR Description LIKE '%'+@Word4+'%')
   OR (Name LIKE '%'+@Word5+'%' OR Description LIKE '%'+@Word5+'%')
```

The logical expression where the @Word variable is NULL (Name LIKE '%'+@Word5+'%') returns
False; therefore this query returns exactly the needed products. For an "all words" search, the query
changes slightly:

```
SELECT Product.ProductID,Product.[Name], Product.[Description],
     Product.Price, Product.ImagePath
FROM Product
WHERE (Name LIKE '%'+@Word1+'%' OR Description LIKE '%'+@Word1+'%')
   AND (Name LIKE '%'+@Word2+'%' OR Description LIKE '%'+@Word2+'%'
                                          or @Word2 is NULL)
   AND (Name LIKE '%'+@Word3+'%' OR Description LIKE '%'+@Word3+'%'
                                          or @Word3 is NULL)
   AND (Name LIKE '%'+@Word4+'%' OR Description LIKE '%'+@Word4+'%'
                                          or @Word4 is NULL)
   AND (Name LIKE '%'+@Word5+'%' OR Description LIKE '%'+@Word5+'%'
                                          or @Word5 is NULL)
```

Here the logic changes a bit. We use AND instead of OR to tie the individual logical expressions together;
and the logical expressions should return True for NULL words, except for the first one. So, if all the
words are NULL we get no results, instead of the entire product catalog.

Implementing the SearchCatalog Stored Procedure

We have studied the major parts of this stored procedure earlier, and it's time to implement it. Using the
well-known steps, please add this stored procedure to your WroxJokeShop database:

```
CREATE PROCEDURE SearchCatalog
(@AllWords bit,
@Word1 varchar(15) = NULL,
@Word2 varchar(15) = NULL,
@Word3 varchar(15) = NULL,
@Word4 varchar(15) = NULL,
@Word5 varchar(15) = NULL)
AS

IF @AllWords = 0
    SELECT Product.ProductID,Product.[Name], Product.[Description], Product.Price,
Product.ImagePath
    FROM Product
    WHERE (Name LIKE '%'+@Word1+'%' OR Description LIKE '%'+@Word1+'%')
          OR (Name LIKE '%'+@Word2+'%' OR Description LIKE '%'+@Word2+'%')
```

```
              OR (Name LIKE '%'+@Word3+'%' OR Description LIKE '%'+@Word3+'%')
              OR (Name LIKE '%'+@Word4+'%' OR Description LIKE '%'+@Word4+'%')
              OR (Name LIKE '%'+@Word5+'%' OR Description LIKE '%'+@Word5+'%')

IF @AllWords = 1
    SELECT Product.ProductID,Product.[Name], Product.[Description], Product.Price,
Product.ImagePath
    FROM Product
    WHERE (Name LIKE '%'+@Word1+'%' OR Description LIKE '%'+@Word1+'%')
          AND (Name LIKE '%'+@Word2+'%' OR Description LIKE '%'+@Word2+'%' or
@Word2 is NULL)
          AND (Name LIKE '%'+@Word3+'%' OR Description LIKE '%'+@Word3+'%' or
@Word3 is NULL)
          AND (Name LIKE '%'+@Word4+'%' OR Description LIKE '%'+@Word4+'%' or
@Word4 is NULL)
          AND (Name LIKE '%'+@Word5+'%' OR Description LIKE '%'+@Word5+'%' or
@Word5 is NULL)

RETURN
```

The stored procedure reads the `@AllWords` bit parameter and decides what kind of search to do based on its value. The rest of the code was described earlier, in the *Theory* section.

The Business Tier

This part consists of the `SearchCatalog` method, which calls the `SearchCatalog` stored procedure. First add it to the `Catalog` class (its exact location within the class is not important), and then we'll comment on it:

```
Public Function SearchCatalog(ByVal searchString As String, _
                        ByVal allWords As String) As SqlDataReader
    ' Create the connection object
    Dim connection As New SqlConnection(connectionString)

    ' Create and initialize the command object
    Dim command As New SqlCommand("SearchCatalog", connection)
    command.CommandType = CommandType.StoredProcedure

    ' We guard agains bogus values here - if we receive anything
    ' different than "TRUE" we assume it's "FALSE"
    If allWords.ToUpper = "TRUE" Then
        ' we only do an "all words" search
        command.Parameters.Add("@AllWords", SqlDbType.Bit, 1)
        command.Parameters("@AllWords").Value = 1
    Else
        ' we only do an "any words" search
        command.Parameters.Add("@AllWords", SqlDbType.Bit, 1)
        command.Parameters("@AllWords").Value = 0
    End If
```

```
      ' We eliminate separation characters
      searchString = searchString.Replace(",", " ")
      searchString = searchString.Replace(";", " ")
      searchString = searchString.Replace(".", " ")

      ' We create an array which contains the words
      Dim words() As String = Split(searchString, " ")

      ' wordsCount contains the total number of words
      Dim wordsCount As Integer = words.Length
      ' index is used to parse the list of words
      Dim index As Integer = 0
      ' this will store the total number of added words
      Dim addedWords As Integer = 0

      ' We allow a maximum of 5 words
      While addedWords < 5 And index < wordsCount
          ' We add the @WordN parameters here
          If Len(words(index)) > 2 Then
              addedWords += 1
              ' Add an input parameter and supply a value for it
            command.Parameters.Add("@Word" + addedWords.ToString, words(index))
          End If
          index += 1
      End While
        ' Open the connection
      connection.Open()

      ' Return a SqlDataReader to the calling function
      Return command.ExecuteReader(CommandBehavior.CloseConnection)
  End Function
```

What we do here isn't very complicated. We've already used the steps involved in calling a SQL Server stored procedure from VB.NET code. Let's take a closer look at the bits that are unique to this method.

First, although this is almost common sense, it's worth noting how we handle the allWords parameter:

```
      ' We guard against bogus values here - if we receive anything
      ' different than "TRUE" we assume it's "FALSE"
      If allWords.ToUpper = "TRUE" Then
          ' we only do an "all words" search
          command.Parameters.Add("@AllWords", SqlDbType.Bit, 1)
          command.Parameters("@AllWords").Value = 1
      Else
          ' we only do an "any words" search
          command.Parameters.Add("@AllWords", SqlDbType.Bit, 1)
          command.Parameters("@AllWords").Value = 0
      End If
```

We expect allWords to contain "TRUE" or "FALSE" – this will be the value of the checkbox that can be set for each search. However, guarding against receiving other values is a good thing – if we send this value directly to the data tier, and expect it to do the conversion, it would generate an error if the value was not True or False.

167

This check makes the business tier better protected. At some point in the presentation tier, the value of `allWords` is read from the query string; the visitor could change it to any value – without proper handling, this has the potential to generate an application exception, which we want to avoid.

Then we have a code block where we eliminate unnecessary elements from the search string, such as punctuation elements:

```
' We eliminate separation characters
searchString = searchString.Replace(",", " ")
searchString = searchString.Replace(";", " ")
searchString = searchString.Replace(".", " ")
```

This is necessary because we later split the search string where we have spaces to get the individual words, so a search for "red,mask" wouldn't have give us any results. Although not present here, a common practice is also to eliminate the so-called "noise" words that are not relevant to a search, like "a", "or", "and", "on" and so on. You may want to add these too.

We also filter all the words that are one or two characters long. Simply typing a vowel into the search string would return the entire product catalog, and we certainly don't want that!

We split the search string into individual words using the `Split` Visual Basic function. This gives us an array of words. We split the string using the space character:

```
' We create an array which contains the words
Dim words() As String = Split(searchString, " ")
```

Finally, having the words listed, we add them as parameters for the stored procedure. We send a maximum of five words, while filtering out the words of one or two characters:

```
' wordsCount contains the total number of words
Dim wordsCount As Integer = words.Length
' index is used to parse the list of words
Dim index As Integer = 0
' this will store the total number of added words
Dim addedWords As Integer = 0

' We allow a maximum of 5 words
While addedWords < 5 And index < wordsCount
    ' We add the @WordN parameters here
    If Len(words(index)) > 2 Then
        addedWords += 1
        ' Add an input parameter and supply a value for it
        command.Parameters.Add("@Word" + addedWords.ToString, words(index))
    End If
    index += 1
End While
```

The Presentation Tier

It's time to see some colors in front of our eyes.

The Search Catalog feature has two basic interface elements that we need to implement. The first, most obvious one, is the place where the visitor enters the search string. As you have already seen in the previous screenshots, it looks like this:

This part of the user interface will be implemented as a separate user control named `SearchBox`, whose role is to provide a textbox and a checkbox for the visitor.

The other part of the user interface consists of the search results page, which displays the products matching the search criteria. Here's an example:

This will be implemented as a user control named `SearchResults`. We'll see that this incorporates the `ProductsList` user control, which will handle displaying the products.

The SearchBox User Control

Let us create the first user control, `SearchBox.ascx`, in the following *Try it Out*:

1. First we need to create the `SearchBox.ascx` file in our **UserControls** folder. Right-click on **UserControls**, then select **Add | Add Web User Control**, and type `SearchBox.ascx` when asked for the name.

2. We know that we can create the control either by using the **Design** View window, or by directly modifying the HTML. In this case, let's simply write the HTML for this file using HTML View:

```
<%@ Control Language="vb" AutoEventWireup="false" Codebehind="SearchBox.ascx.vb"
Inherits="WroxJokeShop.SearchBox"
TargetSchema="http://schemas.microsoft.com/intellisense/ie5" %>
<IMG src="Images/SearchBoxHeader.gif" border="0">
<table border="0" width="170" cellspacing="0" cellpadding="0">
  <tr>
    <td align="middle">
      <asp:TextBox id="searchTextBox" runat="server" Width="90%"
CssClass="SearchBox" BorderStyle="Groove" MaxLength="100" >
      </asp:TextBox>
    </td>
  </tr>
  <tr>
    <td align="middle">
      <asp:CheckBox id="allWordsCheckBox" CssClass="SearchBox" runat="server"
Text="Search for all words">
      </asp:CheckBox>
    </td>
  </tr>
</table>
```

3. Switch to **Design** View. The control should look like this:

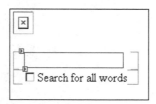

Remember that the header picture isn't visible right now, because the control will be executed in `default.aspx`, not in `UserControls`. Because of this, the picture's image does not point to the correct location when designing the control, but it will do when it is executed.

Note the `CssClass` used for both controls, and the fact that we set a maximum size of 100 characters for the textbox.

4. While in **Design** view, double-click on the textbox control (named **searchTextBox**). A `searchTextBox_TextChanged` method is automatically generated. This will be called when the visitor writes something in the textbox and presses the *Enter* key. Modify the event handler like so:

```
Private Sub searchTextBox_TextChanged(ByVal sender As System.Object, _
    ByVal e As System.EventArgs) Handles searchTextBox.TextChanged
  Response.Redirect("default.aspx?Search=" + searchTextBox.Text + _
    "&AllWords=" + allWordsCheckBox.Checked.ToString())
End Sub
```

5. Add the following style to `WroxJokeShop.css`. This style is used for the text in the `searchTextBox` and `allWordsCheckBox` controls:

```
.SearchBox
{
    font-family: Verdana, Helvetica, sans-serif;
    font-size: 11px;
    color: Black;
}
```

6. Add the newly created user control to `default.aspx`, by dragging it from the Solution Explorer and dropping it just below the **DepartmentsList** user control, like this:

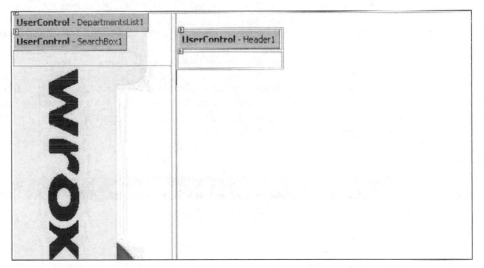

7. Press *F5* to execute the project. The search box should rest nicely in its place. Enter the words **red mask** and press *Enter*. You'll notice the page doesn't change a bit, except for the query string that appears:

http://localhost/WroxJokeShop/default.aspx?Search=red%20mask&AllWords=False

We'll deal with this a bit later. For now, let's see what we have just achieved.

How It Works – The SearchBox Web User Control

This user control isn't very complicated. When the visitor enters a new search string and presses *Enter*, `default.aspx` is reloaded with a `Search` parameter in the query string. We apply the same technique that we used for browsing departments, categories, and so on.

This means two things: that we'll want to create the `SearchResults` user control, and then modify `default.aspx` to recognize the search string in the query string. In the case that it is found, we'll load the `SearchResults` control in the `pageContentsCell` table cell in `default.aspx`.

The SearchResults User Control

Now we need to create the control that displays the search results. To simplify our work, we'll reuse the `ProductsList` user control. This is the control that we have used so far to list products for the main page, for departments, and for categories. Note that if we want to have the products displayed in another format for the catalog search, we need to create another user control.

Remember that `ProductsList` decides what products to list depending on the parameters received in the query string. Right now `ProductsList` searches for `DepartmentID` and for `CategoryID`, and makes a decision about what products to list depending on these parameters. If no parameter is found, it assumes we're on the main page and it displays the products that are on catalog promotion.

We need to modify `ProductsList` to recognize yet another parameter in the query string – the `Search` parameter. If this is found, we want to display the products that match the pattern specified by the `Search` parameter. Since we have already created the `SearchCatalog` method and stored procedure at the beginning of this chapter, our task is easy here – if `Search` is found, we simply send its value to the `SearchCatalog` method, which returns the results in the usual format.

In order to customize the search page (at least by adding a **These are your search results** message), we'll not place the `ProductsList` control directly on the main page (on `pageContentsCell` of `default.aspx`). Instead, we will create a `SearchResults` web user control; this allows us to easily change the search results page, should we ever want to do that.

OK, enough talk; let's write some code!

Try It Out – Creating The SearchResults Web User Control

1. Create a new user control in the **UserControls** folder, named `SearchResults.ascx`.

2. Add this to the HTML View:

```
<%@ Control Language="vb" AutoEventWireup="false"
Codebehind="SearchResults.ascx.vb" Inherits="WroxJokeShop.SearchResults"
TargetSchema="http://schemas.microsoft.com/intellisense/ie5" %>
<span class="FirstPageText">
    <br>
```

```
         These products match your search pattern:
         <br>
         <br>
</span>
```

3. In **Design** View, drag a `ProductsList` user control from the Solution Explorer onto the `SearchResults` user control. The user control should look like this:

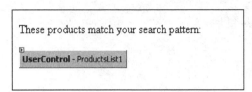

4. Modify the code-behind file of `ProductsList.ascx` like this:

```
Private Sub Page_Load(ByVal sender As System.Object, ByVal e As _
                      System.EventArgs) Handles MyBase.Load
    ' Retrieve DepartmentID from the query string
    Dim departmentId As String = Request.Params("DepartmentID")

    ' Retrieve CategoryID from the query string
    Dim categoryId As String = Request.Params("CategoryID")

    ' Retrieve CategoryID from the query string
    Dim searchString As String = Request.Params("Search")

    If Not searchString Is Nothing Then
        ' search results
        Dim allWords As String = Request.Params("AllWords")
        Dim catalog As Catalog = New Catalog()
        list.DataSource = catalog.SearchCatalog(searchString, allWords)
        list.DataBind()
    ElseIf Not categoryId Is Nothing Then
        ' category
        Dim catalog As Catalog = New Catalog()
        list.DataSource = catalog.GetProductsInCategory(categoryId)
        list.DataBind()
    ElseIf Not departmentId Is Nothing Then
        ' department
        Dim catalog As Catalog = New Catalog()
        list.DataSource = _
          catalog.GetProductsOnDepartmentPromotion(departmentId)
        list.DataBind()
    Else
        ' main page
        Dim catalog As Catalog = New Catalog()
        list.DataSource = catalog.GetProductsOnCatalogPromotion()
        list.DataBind()
    End If
End Sub
```

5. Now modify the code-behind file of `default.aspx`:

```
Private Sub Page_Load(ByVal sender As System.Object, ByVal e As _
                      System.EventArgs) Handles MyBase.Load
    ' Save DepartmentID from the query string to a variable
    Dim departmentId As String = Request.Params("departmentID")

    ' Save the search string from the query string to a variable
    Dim searchString As String = Request.Params("Search")

    ' Are we on the main web page, searching or browsing the catalog?
    If Not searchString Is Nothing Then
        ' if we're searching the catalog ...
        Dim control As Control
        control = Page.LoadControl("UserControls/SearchResults.ascx")
        pageContentsCell.Controls.Add(control)
    ElseIf Not departmentId Is Nothing Then
        ' if we're browsing a department or category ...
        Dim control As Control
        control = Page.LoadControl("UserControls/Department.ascx")
        pageContentsCell.Controls.Add(control)
    Else
        ' if we're on the main page ...
        Dim control As Control
        control = Page.LoadControl("UserControls/FirstPageContents.ascx")
        pageContentsCell.Controls.Add(control)
    End If
End Sub
```

6. Press *F5* to execute the project. Type **red mask** in the search textbox to get an output similar to this:

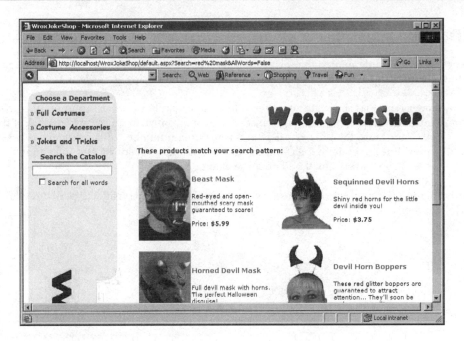

How It Works

We have just finished implementing the search functionality of the catalog. It was pretty easy, wasn't it?
We basically needed to change `default.aspx` and `ProductsList.ascx` to recognize the Search
parameter in the query string, which is set by the `SearchBox` control.

`ProductsList.ascx` calls the `catalog.SearchCatalog` method if the Search parameter is
found. This is our business tier method that returns the list of matching records:

```
If Not searchString Is Nothing Then
    ' search results
    Dim allWords As String = Request.Params("AllWords")
    Dim catalog As Catalog = New Catalog()
    list.DataSource = catalog.SearchCatalog(searchString, allWords)
    list.DataBind()
```

We modified `default.aspx` to load the `ProductsList` control if the Search parameter is found in
the query string:

```
If Not searchString Is Nothing Then
    ' if we're searching the catalog ...
    Dim control As Control
    control = Page.LoadControl("UserControls/SearchResults.ascx")
    pageContentsCell.Controls.Add(control)
```

Summary

In this chapter we implemented the search functionality of WroxJokeShop. This was the first time we have had a variable number of parameters, so we learned a few tips about how to handle this.

We saw, once again, that there are situations when there simply is no best solution to a problem, and that sometimes we need to make compromises. The compromise in our case consisted of the fact that we can't search for more than five words, but this maximum number of words can easily be increased by adding a few lines of code to the `CatalogSearch` stored procedure, and informing the `Catalog.CatalogSearch` method about the change.

The presentation tier consists of two user controls, which allow the visitor to perform searches in WroxJokeShop.

Receiving Payments using PayPal

Any e-commerce web site needs a way of receiving payments from customers. While the preferred solution for established companies is to open a merchant account, many small businesses choose to start with a simpler solution to implement, where they don't have to process credit card or payment information themselves.

There are a number of companies and web sites that can help individuals or small businesses that don't have the resources to process credit card and wire transactions, and can be used to intermediate the payment between companies and their customers. Many of these are relatively new and the handling of any individual's financial details is very sensitive. Additionally, a quick search on the Internet will find reports from both satisfied and unsatisfied customers for almost all of these companies. For these reasons we are not going to recommend any third party company.

We will simply list some of the companies currently providing these services, and we will demonstrate some of the functionality they provide with PayPal, as we use it on our web site in the first two stages of development:

❑   Learn how to create a new PayPal account

❑   Learn how to integrate PayPal in stage 1 of development, where we need a shopping cart and custom checkout mechanism

❑   Learn how to integrate PayPal in stage 2 of development where we have our own shopping cart, so we need to direct the visitor directly to a payment page

❑   Learn how to configure PayPal to automatically calculate shipping costs

It is worth noting that the contents of this chapter are not supposed to be a PayPal manual, but a quick guide to using PayPal. For any complex queries about the services provided, please contact PayPal, or the Internet Payment Service Provider you decide to use.

Internet Payment Service Providers

Here is a list of web sites you might want to take a look at. Their nature is very diverse, each of them having its advantages. Some of them transfer money person to person and payments need to be verified manually, others have sophisticated integration with your web site. Some work anywhere on the globe, while other work only for a single country.

The list is not a complete one. I also have found an even more complete list of payment systems at http://www.onlinepaymentsystems.com. While a major company does not endorse the site, it might prove to be helpful in your search for the service that best suits your needs.

- ❑ 2Checkout – www.2checkout.com
- ❑ AnyPay – www.anypay.com
- ❑ Billpoint – www.billpoint.com
- ❑ CCNow – www.ccnow.com
- ❑ Electronic Transfer – www.electronictransfer.com
- ❑ MultiCards – www.multicards.com
- ❑ Pay By Web – www.paybyweb.com
- ❑ Paymate – www.paymate.com.au
- ❑ PayPal – www.paypal.com
- ❑ PaySystems – www.paysystems.com
- ❑ ProPay – www.propay.com
- ❑ QuickPayPro – www.quickpaypro.com
- ❑ WorldPay – worldpay.com

For the demonstration in this chapter we chose to use PayPal. This company was recently bought by eBay, and apart from being quite popular nowadays (it claims that more than three million businesses use their services), it offers exactly the services that fit best into our web site for the first two stages of development. PayPal is available in a number of countries – the most up-to-date list can be found on its site.

For the first stage of development where we only have a searchable product catalog, PayPal allows us to add a shopping cart with checkout functionality with only a few lines of HTML code. Of course, a PayPal account is needed in order for this to work, and we'll see a bit later how to get one of these. I have searched for an alternative company to provide this feature but PayPal kept popping up at the top of the search results in my browser.

For the second stage of development where we need to manually record orders into the database, PayPal has a feature named **Single Item Purchases** that can be used to send the visitor directly to a payment page without the intermediate shopping cart.

For a summary of the features provided by PayPal point your browser to www.paypal.com and click on the **Businesses** link. That page contains a few other useful links that will show you the main features available.

Learning how to Use PayPal

Probably the best description of this service is the one found on its web site: "PayPal is an account-based system that lets anyone with an e-mail address securely send and receive online payments using their credit card or bank account".

PayPal is one of the companies that allow a small business like our electronic novelty store to receive payments from its customers. The visitor, instead of paying us directly, pays PayPal using a credit card or bank account. Then we use our PayPal account to get the money received from our customers. At the time of writing there is no cost involved in creating a new PayPal account, the service is free for the buyer, and costs a fee ranging between 0.7% and 2.9%, plus US 30 cents per transaction.

Please visit www.paypal.com to get updated and complete information, and of course pay a visit to its competitors before making a decision for your own e-commerce site. You will also want to check which of the services are available in your country, and what kind of credit cards are accepted by each company.

If you want to use PayPal beyond the exercises with our WroxJokeShop, you'll want to learn more about its service. On the main web page, at www.paypal.com, there is a Help link, which opens up their Help pages. These pages are very well structured and organized, and provide a very good search feature.

Also in the front page there is a Developers link (at the bottom of the page), which provides us with more technical information and allows us to join the PayPal Developer Network.

Let's see how to create a new PayPal account, and then how can this be integrated with WroxJokeShop.

Creating a New PayPal Account

The first step towards integrating PayPal into our web site is creating a new PayPal account. Let's do this in the following *Try It Out*.

Try It Out – Creating the PayPal Account

1. Browse to www.paypal.com using your favorite web browser.

2. Click on the Sign Up link.

3. If you live outside of the United States, click on the International Sign Up link, and then choose your country. There is an option on the next page of registration to select your primary currency from Pounds Sterling, Euros, or US Dollars.

4. PayPal supports three account types: Personal Account, Premier (personal) Account or Business Account. Please visit www.paypal.com for updated information about the exact differences between these types of accounts. For now it is important to know that in order to be able to integrate PayPal functionality into our web site (we'll see a bit later how), we need to open a Premier or Business account. Personal accounts cannot be used for web site integration.

   If you prefer a business account, click on the Business link at the top of the page. For the Premier account, make sure you to click the Yes radio button at the bottom of the Personal Account Sign Up, when prompted. If you choose not to make your account a premier account, you'll have the possibility to change this later, without being asked for any additional information.

5. Complete all of the requested information and you will receive an e-mail asking you to revisit the PayPal site to confirm the details you have entered.

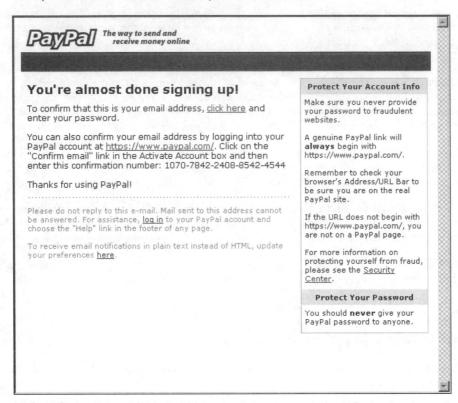

6. Click on the link, to complete your registration.

How It Works

After the PayPal account is set up, the e-mail address you provided will be your ID used by the customers to pay for the products and for you to log in.

There is a lot of functionality available within the PayPal service – it is a very usable site, and many of the functions are self-explanatory, hence we won't describe everything here. Remember that these sites are there for your business, so they're more than happy to assist with any of your queries.

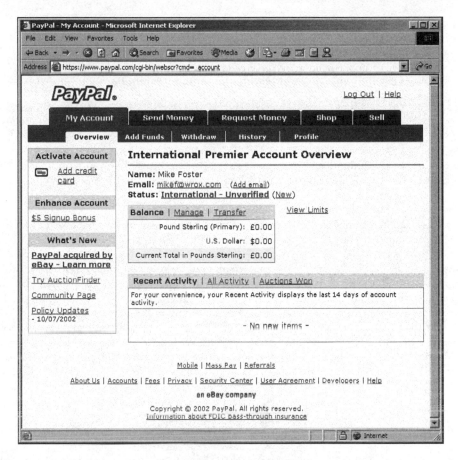

Now let's see now how we can actually use the new account for our web site.

Integrating PayPal into our Web Site

PayPal can be integrated into our web site at different stages of development. Remember that one of the reasons we chose it was because it offers shopping basket and checkout functionality without us needing to type a single line of code.

As PayPal provides us with shopping cart and checkout functionality we can integrate it into our web site as soon as we have created the product catalog. For this example I assume that you have just created the product catalog, and also implemented its search functionality (which is presented in Chapter 5).

In order to accept payments there are two important elements to be added on the user interface part of the site: **Add to Cart** buttons for each product, and a **View Cart** button somewhere else on the page. Provided we have a 'premier' or 'business' account, PayPal makes adding these buttons a piece of cake.

Take a look at the following HTML, which represents the **Add to Cart** button for a product named Beast Mask that costs $5.99.

```
<form target="paypal" action="https://www.paypal.com/cgi-bin/webscr"
      method="post">
  <input type="hidden" name="cmd" value="_cart">
  <input type="hidden" name="business" value="your_email_address">
  <input type="hidden" name="item_name" value="Beast Mask">
  <input type="hidden" name="amount" value="$5.99">
  <input type="image" src="Images/AddToCart.gif" name="submit">
  <input type="hidden" name="add" value="1">
</form>
```

The input fields are predefined, and their names are self-describing. The value of the business field needs to contain the e-mail address you used when you registered the PayPal account.

In our code we need to make sure this HTML code gets added to each product. What we need to do is modify the `DataList` control in the `ProductsList` user control by adding an **Add to Cart** button. The HTML code for the View Cart button is created in the same style.

PayPal also provides us with examples of how to integrate **Add to Cart** and **View Cart** buttons into our web site, and also button generators that based on certain data we provide (product name, product price), give us a HTML block similar to the one above. These are found by clicking on the **Developers** link at the bottom of the page, and then on **PayPal Solutions** in the menu on the left.

Since we want an **Add to Cart** button for every product, we'll need to modify the `ProductsList` user control. Then we'll add the **View Cart** button somewhere on the main web page, so it will be accessible at any time for the visitor. After the change, the `ProductsList` control will display products like this:

We'll place the **View Cart** button on `default.aspx` as shown in the following screenshot:

So, let us add PayPal integration in the next *Try It Out*:

Try It Out – Integrating with the PayPal Shopping Cart and Custom Checkout

1. Now let's add the PayPal HTML in *ProductsList.ascx*, just below the place we're displaying the product price:

```
<TD vAlign="middle" width="200">
  <span class="ProductName">
    <%# DataBinder.Eval(Container.DataItem, "Name") %>
  </span>
  <br>
  <br>
  <span class="ProductDescription">
    <%# DataBinder.Eval(Container.DataItem, "Description") %>
    <br>
    <br>
    Price: </span><span class="ProductPrice">
    <%# DataBinder.Eval(Container.DataItem, "Price",  "{0:c}") %>
  </span>
  <form target="paypal" action="https://www.paypal.com/cgi-bin/webscr"
      method="post">
    <input type="hidden" name="cmd" value="_cart">
    <input type="hidden" name="business" value="email@server.com">
    <input type="hidden" name="item_name" value='<%#
        DataBinder.Eval(Container.DataItem, "Name")%>'>
    <input type="hidden" name="amount"
        value='<%# DataBinder.Eval(Container.DataItem,
        "Price", "{0:c}")%>'>
    <input type="image" src="Images/AddToCart.gif" name="submit">
    <input type="hidden" name="add" value="1">
  </form>
</TD>
```

2. Now let's add the View Cart button. This will be placed in `default.aspx`, just below the SearchBox control, and above the Wrox logo. Open `default.aspx` in HTML View and modify it like this:

```
<td width="200" height="100%">
  <table height="100%" cellSpacing="0" cellPadding="0" width="100%"
background="Images/backgr.gif">
    <tr>
      <td vAlign="top" height="100%">
        <uc1:departmentslist id="DepartmentsList1" runat="server">
        </uc1:departmentslist>
        <uc1:searchbox id="SearchBox1" runat="server">
        </uc1:searchbox>
      </td>
    </tr>
    <tr>
      <td>
        <br>      
        <form method="post" action="https://www.paypal.com/cgi-bin/webscr"
                              target="paypal" name="_xclick">
          <input type="hidden" value="_cart" name="cmd">
          <input type="hidden" value="email@server.com" name="business">
          <input type="hidden" value="1" name="display">
          <input type="image" src="Images/ViewCart.gif" name="submit">
        </form>
      </td>
    </tr>
    <tr>
      <td>
        <IMG height="369" src="Images/Clown.jpg" width="197" border="0">
      </td>
    </tr>
  </table>
</td>
```

3. Please make sure you replace the `email@server.com` values with the e-mail address you submitted when you created your PayPal account.

> **Do this for both Add to Cart and View Cart buttons. You'll need to do that, if you want the money to get into your account!**

4. Press *F5* to execute the project. Your first page should look like this now:

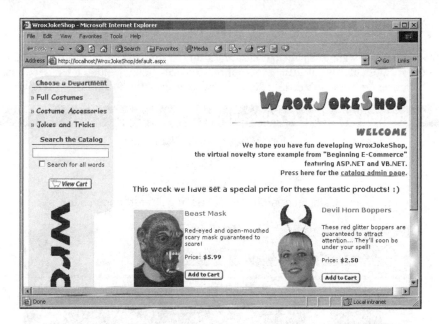

5. To see the PayPal shopping cart, click on one of the Add to Cart buttons to see what happens:

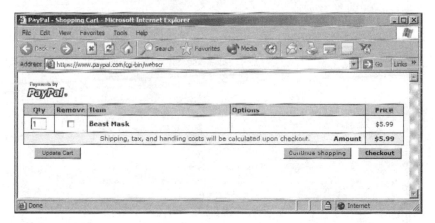

How It Works – PayPal Integration

Yes, it was just that simple. Right now all our visitors became potential customers! They can click on the Checkout button of the PayPal shopping cart, where they can buy the product!

After a customer makes a payment on our web site, an e-mail notification is sent to the e-mail address registered on PayPal, and also to the customer. Your PayPal account will reflect the payment, and you can view the transaction information in your account history or as a part of the history transaction log.

We touched a few of the details of the PayPal shopping cart, but for a complete description of its functionality you should take a look on the PayPal Shopping Cart manual, which is available for download at www.paypal.com.

Letting PayPal Calculate Shipping Costs

It is very likely that we'll want to charge our customers for the shipping costs of the products they buy. PayPal has the feature of automatically calculating the shipping costs, by adding either a fixed fee based on the subtotal, or a percentage of the subtotal. Let us see how to activate this feature in the following *Try It Out*.

Try It Out – Configuring PayPal to Add Shipping Costs

1. Go to www.paypal.com and log in into your PayPal Account.

2. Click on the Profile tab.

3. Click on Shipping Calculations link, in the Selling Preferences column.

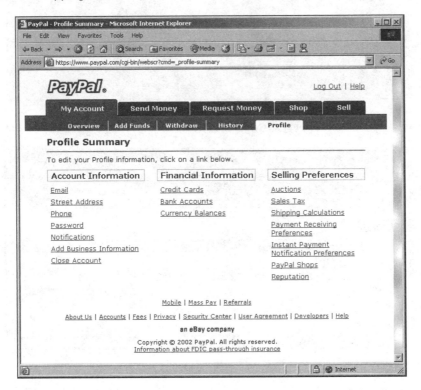

4. Click Edit.

Here we can choose to charge our customers with a flat fee depending on the total amount, or with a percentage of the total amount. With the flat fee, we can select, for example, to have a shipping fee of $5 for orders between $1 and $39.99, $10 for orders between $40 and $89.99, and so on. With a percentage fee, we can select to add a 5% fee for orders between $1 and $39.99, and a 10% fee for orders of at least $40. The percentage is calculated on the subtotal of the purchase.

5. Choose the Flat Amount ($) or Percentage (%) radio button, and enter the shipping amounts you would like to charge.

6. Click Save.

The PayPal Single Item Purchases

Single Item Purchases is a PayPal feature that allows us to redirect the visitor directly to a payment page instead of the PayPal shopping cart. This is useful for the second stage of development, where we handle our own shopping cart code.

In Chapter 9, when the visitor clicks on the Place Order button, apart from saving the order into the database, we need to redirect the customer to a page where they can give payment information. Remember that we create our own order processing system in the third phase of development (starting in Chapter 10), where we also handle our own credit card transactions.

If you want to implement the PayPal Single Item Purchases system for the second stage of development (more specifically, after creating the Place Order button), the following additional code to `placeOrderButton_Click` in the code behind of `ShoppingCart.ascx` should do the trick:

```
Private Sub placeOrderButton_Click(ByVal sender As System.Object,
        ByVal e As System.EventArgs) Handles placeOrderButton.Click
    ' The Shopping Cart object
    Dim cart As New ShoppingCart()

    ' We need to store the total amount because the shopping cart
    ' is emptied when creating the order
    Dim amount As Decimal = cart.GetTotalAmount()

    ' Create the order and store the order ID
    Dim orderId As String = cart.CreateOrder()

    ' This will contain the PayPal request string
    Dim redirect As String

    ' Create the redirect string
    redirect += "https://www.paypal.com/xclick/business=email@server.com"
    redirect += "&item_name=WroxJokeShop Order " & orderId
    redirect += "&item_number=" & orderId
    redirect += "&amount=" & String.Format("{0:c}", amount)
    redirect +=
        "&return=http://www.WroxJokeShop.com/PaymentSuccessful.aspx"
    redirect += "&cancel_return=http://www.WroxJokeShop.com"

    ' Load the PayPal payment page
    Response.Redirect(redirect)
End Sub
```

That's all we need to do to. Of course, don't forget to replace `email@server.com` with your registered PayPal e-mail address.

Note that because of the link we provided, the page is not redirected to the PayPal shopping cart but directly to a form where the customer can add payment information (the Single Item Purchases page). The following screenshot shows the payment page:

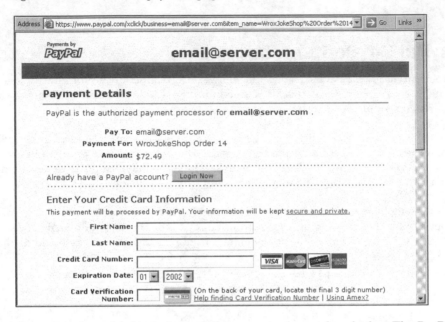

For more information about this kind of one-click payment, please take a look at The PayPal Single Item Purchases manual (a downloadable PDF file). You can also find information in the Seller Tools/Web Accept category in the PayPal Help page.

Summary

In this chapter we have seen how to integrate PayPal into our e-commerce site – a simple payment solution that many small businesses choose, so they don't have to process credit card or payment information themselves.

First we listed some of the alternatives to PayPal, before we guided you through the creation of a new PayPal account. We then covered how to integrate PayPal in stages 1 and 2 of development, first discussing a shopping cart, a custom checkout mechanism, and then how to direct the visitor directly to the payment page.

In the next chapter we will move on to look at a catalog administration page for the WroxJokeShop site.

Catalog Administration

In previous chapters we worked with catalog information that already existed in the database. You have probably inserted some records yourself, or maybe you downloaded the department, category, and product information from the Wrox web site. Obviously, for a realistic web site both ways are unacceptable, and we need to write some code to allow easy management of the information in the web store.

In this chapter we implement a Catalog Administration page. Since this can be done in many ways, generally a serious discussion with the client is required to get the specific list of features. In our case, the catalog administration page should allow our client to:

❑ Add or remove departments

❑ Modify existing departments' information (name, description)

❑ View the list of categories that belong to a department

❑ Add new categories to a department

❑ Edit existing categories' information (name, description)

❑ View the list of products in a specific category

❑ Edit product information (name, description, price, image path, department-based promotion, and catalog-based promotion)

❑ Assign an existing product to an additional category (a product can belong to multiple categories)

❑ Remove a product from a category; if after removal the product doesn't belong to any category, the product is completely removed from the catalog (so there won't be any orphan products)

❑ Select a product and see the categories it belongs to, and display its picture

The administration page also needs to ask for a user name and password.

So Where Do We Start?

Although the long list of objectives might look intimidating at first, it will be quite easy to implement it. We have already covered most of the theory in the previous chapters, but we still have a few bits of new information that we'll learn. For example, in this chapter we will learn how to update information in the database from the VB.NET code.

The first step we'll take towards our catalog administration page will be to create a simple login mechanism. This is a requirement, since only site administrators should be allowed to edit catalog information.

Next, we'll be building the site administration part of the site step by step by creating its main page and the constituent user controls. There is a single Web Form named `CatalogAdminPage.aspx` that has the following structure:

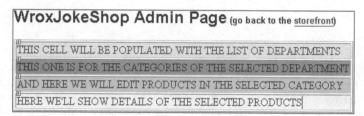

Each of the four cells of the table will be populated with user controls depending on the parameters sent in the query string. In the beginning there will be no parameters, so only the first cell will be shown, populated by the `DepartmentsAdmin.ascx` web user control, which will display a list of departments. The page will look like this:

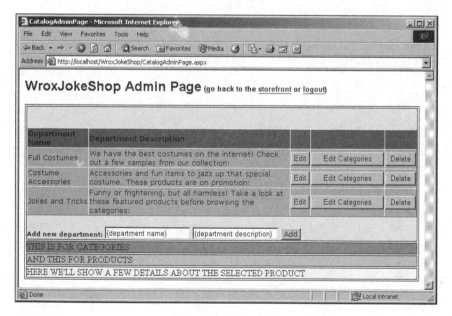

Although this looks like a `DataList` control, in fact it is a `DataGrid`. We'll learn more about this control later, when we create the `DepartmentsAdmin` web user control. For now it is important to know that it allows for easy integration of edit, select, and delete functionality. When the Edit, Edit Categories (Select), or Delete buttons are clicked, events are generated that can be handled in code.

When the Edit Categories button is selected, the page is reloaded but with an additional parameter in the query string: `DepartmentID`. This tells the `CatalogAdminPage` to fill the second table cell using the `CategoriesAdmin.ascx` control, which will display the categories that belong to the selected department. The `CatalogAdminPage` will look like this:

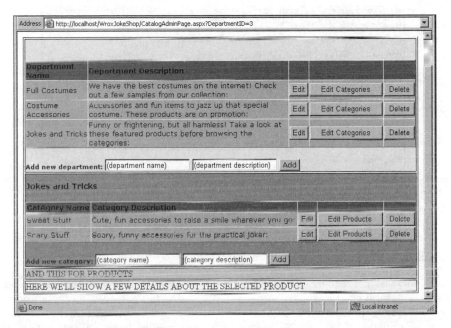

The process is the same for the following two table cells, for editing the products in the categories and the details of each product. Because of this amount of power that is available we need to ensure some kind of security precautions are in effect. Let's start with the construction of this in the next section.

Authenticating Administrators

Because we want only certain persons to access the catalog administration page, we need to implement some sort of security mechanism that controls access to the sensitive pages in our site.

Implementing security implies dealing with two important concepts: **authentication** and **authorization**. Authentication is the process where users are uniquely identified (most often by supplying a username and password), while authorization refers to what resources the authenticated user can access.

A user who wants to access the catalog administration page should first *authenticate* themselves. Once we know who the user is, we decide if they are authorized to access the administration page.

ASP.NET allows for more authorization and authentication methods. The three major ASP.NET authentication methods are: *basic authentication*, *integrated Windows authentication*, and *Forms authentication*.

Each authentication method has its advantages and disadvantages. We'll quickly analyze each of them.

From a user-interface perspective, Forms authentication is the most flexible and powerful – we are able to create our own forms and controls that request the user's credentials. On the other hand, neither basic nor Windows (integrated) authentication modes provide a flexible way of requesting authentication information. They both automatically raise a dialog similar to the one in the picture below:

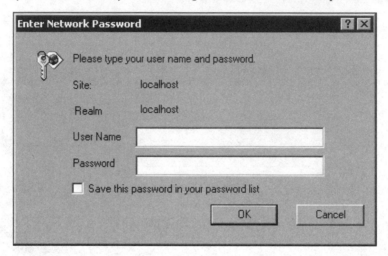

Differences also exist from a purely technical perspective.

Basic authentication isn't secure by itself; because the username-password combination is sent via the network in clear text, it can be read by someone intercepting the transmission. It can be made secure in conjunction with a technology like SSL (Secure Sockets Layer), which solves the problem by encrypting the information transferred between the participants. Basic authentication also has the disadvantage that the credentials are always compared against the Windows User Account Database, so every user needs to be registered on the server (we can't use a list of users stored in the database, for example). However its greatest advantage is ease of implementation, as it is supported by IIS and can be implemented without writing a single line of code.

Windows Integrated authentication security is more secure than basic authentication because the user's password is never sent over the network – instead its hash value is transmitted, so the privacy of the password is guaranteed. Simplifying the procedure (although this is not a complete definition), hashing is a process in which the original password is encrypted with a key in such a way that by having both the key and the hashed password someone can't calculate the initial password. It is also very easy to set up and, but can only work with the Windows User Account Database. Another disadvantage is that it only works with Internet Explorer.

Forms-based authentication is more flexible than the other two methods not only in the way it appears on the screen, but also in functionality. It can be used to use with username-password combinations taken from a database or even the `Web.config` configuration file, as we'll see later, and can be fine-tuned for an application's needs.

While basic authentication and Windows integrated authentication are the best fit for certain uses, in the context of securing a web site in general, and an e-commerce site in particular, forms-based authentication is the best choice because of the flexibility it provides.

For a more detailed explanation about ASP.NET Security please read Chapter 20 of *Beginning ASP.NET 1.0 with VB.NET*, from Wrox Press (ISBN 1-86100-733-7) or Chapter 14 of *Professional ASP.NET 1.0, Special Edition*, from Wrox Press (ISBN 1-86100-703-5). In this book we'll learn a bit more about security in Chapter 10 where we'll learn to work with hashed passwords.

For our example, we will use Forms authentication along with the `Web.config` configuration file. This file can contain various security options and also username-password combinations.

For this stage of the site we decided to use a very simple authentication mechanism. We use Forms authentication with a clear-text username and password, which are stored in the `Web.config` file. Because passwords are sent without any encryption or hashing mechanism, this isn't a really secure method. If the administration page is accessed from a remote location, user credentials can be intercepted by communication eavesdroppers. Also, in a serious scenario we would store username and password combinations in a database, but in order to ease our task we'll use the built-in ASP.NET feature of reading them directly from the configuration file. Let's implement this in our solution in the following exercise:

Try It Out – Implementing a Simple Security Check

1. Double-click on `Web.config` in Solution Explorer, and add the following sections to it. Be aware that the default authentication mode is Windows, and you'll need to change it to Forms:

```xml
<?xml version="1.0" encoding="utf-8" ?>
<configuration>
  <appSettings>
    <add key="ConnectionString" value="Server=localhost;User
ID=sa;Password=;Initial Catalog=WroxJokeShop" />
  </appSettings>

    <location path="CatalogAdminPage.aspx">
      <system.web>
        <authorization>
          <allow users="admin" />
          <deny users="*" />
        </authorization>
      </system.web>
    </location>

    <system.web>

      <!-- ... various settings here ... -->

      <authentication mode="Forms">
        <forms name="WroxJokeShop"
               loginUrl="Login.aspx" path="/" protection="All" timeout="60">
          <credentials passwordFormat="Clear">
            <user name="user" password="user"/>
            <user name="admin" password="admin"/>
          </credentials>
        </forms>
      </authentication>
```

We'll explain these additions in the *How It Works* section. For now it's enough to know that all users except admin will be denied access to CatalogAdminPage.aspx – the administration page we'll write a bit later.

Right now there are two users registered: admin (password: admin) and user (password: user), but only admin is authorized to access CatalogAdminPage.aspx.

2. Let's add the Login.aspx form now. Right-click on the **WroxJokeShop** project in Solution Explorer and select **Add | Add Web Form**. When asked for the form name, type Login or Login.aspx.

3. Change the pageLayout property of Login.aspx to FlowLayout. Then add controls to the form, as shown below:

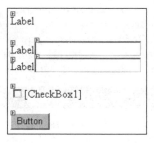

Note that after the Label control you should press *Enter*, and after the textboxes you should press *Shift+Enter*. When pressing *Shift+Enter*, instead of creating a new paragraph, Visual Studio simply adds a <BR> tag. Here's the HTML code that results just after adding the controls as shown in the previous screenshot:

```
<body>
  <form id="Form1" method="post" runat="server">
    <P>
      <asp:Label id="Label1" runat="server">Label</asp:Label></P>
    <P>
      <asp:Label id="Label2" runat="server">Label</asp:Label>
      <asp:TextBox id="TextBox1" runat="server"></asp:TextBox><BR>
      <asp:Label id="Label3" runat="server">Label</asp:Label>
      <asp:TextBox id="TextBox2" runat="server"></asp:TextBox></P>
    <P>
      <asp:CheckBox id="CheckBox1" runat="server"></asp:CheckBox></P>
    <P>
      <asp:Button id="Button1" runat="server" Text="Button"></asp:Button></P>
  </form>
</body>
```

4. Set the properties of each control to the values shown in the table:

Control Type	ID	Text
Label	loginMessageLabel	(Clear this property)
Label	userNameLabel	User Name:
TextBox	userNameTextBox	(Clear this property)
Label	passwordLabel	Password:
TextBox	passwordTextBox	(Clear this property)
CheckBox	persistCheckBox	Persist Security Info
Button	loginButton	Login

After setting these properties, the form will look like this:

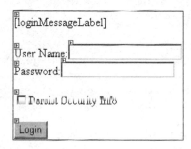

5. Now let's deal with the code. Please switch to the code-behind file, `Login.aspx.vb`, and add this as the first line:

```
Imports System.Web.Security
```

We'll use some classes from this namespace in the login mechanism, as we'll see a bit later.

6. Now let's modify `Page_Load` to set the welcome text in the first label:

```
Private Sub Page_Load(ByVal sender As System.Object, _
    ByVal e As System.EventArgs) Handles MyBase.Load
  loginMessageLabel.Text = "Hello! Please enter the magic formula:"
End Sub
```

7. Now let's add the code for the button's click event handler. To have Visual Studio .NET write the signature for you, switch back to Design View and double-click on the `Button` control. Then modify the event handler by adding this code:

```
Private Sub loginButton_Click(ByVal sender As System.Object, _
    ByVal e As System.EventArgs) Handles loginButton.Click
  ' Store the entered user name in a variable
  Dim user As String = userNameTextBox.Text
```

```
        ' Store the entered password in a variable
        Dim pass As String = passwordTextBox.Text

        ' This variable is True when persistCheckBox is checked
        Dim persist As Boolean = persistCheckBox.Checked

        ' Check if the (user, pass) combination exists
        If FormsAuthentication.Authenticate(user, pass) Then
          ' Attempt to load the originally solicited page using
          ' the supplied credentials
          FormsAuthentication.RedirectFromLoginPage(user, persist)
        End If
      End Sub
```

8. Now create the `CatalogAdminPage` Web Form in the existing solution by right-clicking on the project name in Solution Explorer and selecting **Add | Add Web Form**. Enter `CatalogAdminPage.aspx` for the name.

9. Compile the project with *Ctrl+Shift+B*, and then try to load `CatalogAdminPage` by browsing to http://localhost/WroxJokeShop/CatalogAdminPage.aspx using your favorite web browser. Because you aren't authenticated yet, you'll receive the `Login.aspx` page that we created earlier. After entering the correct username-password combination (`admin`/`admin`), you'll be forwarded to `CatalogAdminPage`, the page you initially requested.

How It Works – The Security Mechanism

The mechanism is pretty simple, and makes use of the `Web.config` configuration file. As pointed out in the previous chapters, there are lots of details about this file and it usually takes at least a chapter for this. For more details about using `Web.config` for securing ASP.NET applications we recommend an advanced book like *Professional ASP.NET 1.0, Special Edition*, from Wrox Press (ISBN 1-86100-703-5). This book has a chapter solely focused on ASP.NET security.

This being said, let's see what we did to make the mechanism work. First, we modified `Web.config`. The first addition consists of these lines:

```
<location path="CatalogAdminPage.aspx">
  <system.web>
    <authorization>
      <allow users="admin" />
      <deny users="*" />
    </authorization>
  </system.web>
</location>
```

This sets the authorization options for the `CatalogAdminPage.aspx` file. The user `admin` is granted access, while all the other users are denied using the `allow` and `deny` elements:

```
<allow users="admin" />
<deny users="*" />
```

Note that this list is read in sequential order. The following combination would reject all login attempts:

```
<deny users="*" />
<allow users="admin" />
```

The * wildcard is used for "all identities". There is a second wildcard character, ?, which means "anonymous users". If we wanted all anonymous users to be denied we would have used:

```
<location path="CatalogAdminPage.aspx">
  <system.web>
    <authorization>
      <deny users="?" />
    </authorization>
  </system.web>
</location>
```

This setting specifies that all anonymous users should be rejected. This means that both user and admin identities would be allowed access to CatalogAdminPage.

Note that by default all visitors are allowed access to all pages, so we need to explicitly deny access.

The other addition to Web.config specifies how to authenticate visitors that try to visit CatalogAdminPage. We specified the Forms authentication mode and the login page Login.aspx.

We can also see here the list of user/password combinations:

```
<authentication mode="Forms">
  <forms name="WroxJokeShop"
    loginUrl="Login.aspx" path="/" protection="All" timeout="60">
    <credentials passwordFormat="Clear">
      <user name="test" password="test"/>
      <user name="admin" password="admin"/>
    </credentials>
  </forms>
</authentication>
```

The passwordFormat attribute of the credentials element specifies the format in which the passwords are stored in the Web.config file. In this example we store them as clear text, which is a potential security risk, although note that Web.config is not accessible to visitors. We will learn how to use hashed passwords in Chapter 10 (*Customer Details*), where we will see how to encrypt our customers' passwords.

After adding the security bits to Web.config, unauthenticated visitors that access CatalogAdminPage.aspx will be automatically redirected to Login.aspx. The login form doesn't look extraordinary, but it doesn't matter too much because visitors won't see it anyway. When we browse to http://localhost/WroxJokeShop/CatalogAdminPage.aspx, we are shown the authentication page:

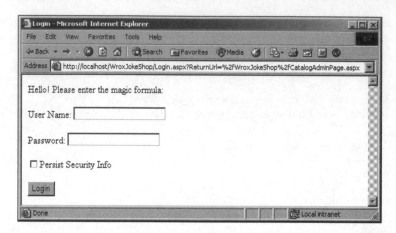

Notice the query string, which looks quite interesting although we didn't do anything about it. This is part of ASP.NET's security mechanism, and it is designed to make our life easy. If there are more pages that require authentication, the login form doesn't need to change – after the login is successful, we will be redirected to the correct page, the one we tried to access in the first place.

The code-behind file of Login.aspx consists mostly of the Button_Click event handler. This one uses the FormsAuthentication class from the System.Web.Security namespace to verify if the username and password combination is a valid one. As you can see, there are only two lines of code to do the trick:

```
' Store the entered user name in a variable
Dim user As String = userNameTextBox.Text

' Store the entered password in a variable
Dim pass As String = passwordTextBox.Text

' This variable is True when persistCheckBox is checked
Dim persist As Boolean = persistCheckBox.Checked

' Check if the (user, pass) combination exists
If FormsAuthentication.Authenticate(user, pass) Then
  ' Attempt to load the originally solicited page using
  ' the supplied credentials
  FormsAuthentication.RedirectFromLoginPage(user, persist)
End If
```

The FormsAuthentication.Authenticate() method simply returns True if the user is authenticated (the user exists and the password is correct), but it doesn't necessarily mean that they are authorized to accesses the solicited page. Remember that with our supplied Web.config data, the user account is not allowed to access the CatalogAdmin page.

Anyway, if the user is authenticated, we try to redirect them to the solicited page, using the FormsAuthentication.RedirectFromLoginPage() method. At this stage the *authorization* check is made – if the user isn't allowed to access the page, the login page gets loaded again. Otherwise, the user is redirected to the originally solicited page.

After the user has been authenticated and authorized, their credentials are stored in a cookie (if they selected to persist the information using the checkbox), and used on subsequent requests on the web page.

Note that the `RedirectFromLoginPage()` method has two parameters: the first one represents the user that has been authenticated, and the second is a Boolean value that specifies if the security cookie is durable. If that value is `True`, the authentication info is saved across browser sessions. If the value is `False`, if the browser is closed, on the next attempt to load a secured page the login page shows up again.

If the visitor accesses the `Login.aspx` page directly, and the authentication is successful they are then automatically redirected by default to the main page, `default.aspx`.

Setting up the Catalog Administration Page

The catalog administration part of the site will consist of a web form, `CatalogAdminPage.aspx`, and four user controls: `DepartmentsAdmin`, `CategoriesAdmin`, `ProductsAdmin`, and `ProductDetailsAdmin`. We will build each of these components one at a time. For each one we will implement the presentation layer, then write the business-tier sections, and finally we'll write the stored procedures in the database.

For now, let us lay down the basis in the following *Try It Out*:

Try It Out – Creating the Skeleton of the CatalogAdminPage

1. We created `CatalogAdminPage.aspx` in the previous Try It Out, when we implemented the security mechanism. Let's start now by adding a link to this page in the main web site. This wouldn't be a good idea for a production web site, but the link will come in handy in the development stage. Open the `FirstPageContents.ascx` web user control in HTML view and add this link to it:

```
<P align="right">
  <img src="Images/Welcome.gif" border="0" width="102" height="18">
  <br>
  <span class="FirstPageText">
    <br>
    We hope you have a pleasant experience developing WroxJokeShop,
    <br><br>
    the virtual novelty store presented in "Beginning E-Commerce"
    <br><br>
    Press here for the <a href="CatalogAdminPage.aspx">catalog admin page</a>.
  </span>
</P>
```

2. Open `CatalogAdminPage.aspx`, and make sure `pageLayout` property is set to `FlowLayout`.

3. Now open the file in HTML view, and add the following table to the automatically created code:

```
<body>
  <form id="Form1" method="post" runat="server">
    <strong>
    <font face="Arial" size="5">WroxJokeShop Admin Page</font>
    <font face="Arial" size="2" runat="server">
    (go back to the <a href="default.aspx">storefront</a> or
  <asp:LinkButton id="logoutButton" runat="server">logout</asp:LinkButton>)
    </font>
    </strong>
    <br><br>
      <table border="1" bordercolor="black" cellpadding="0">
        <tr>
          <td bgcolor="#ccff66" runat="server" id="departmentsCell">
            WE WILL EDIT DEPARMENTS IN THIS CELL
          </td>
        </tr>
        <tr>
          <td bgcolor="#9999ff" runat="server" id="categoriesCell">
            THIS IS FOR CATEGORIES
          </td>
        <tr>
          <td bgcolor="#ffcc66" runat="server" id="productsCell">
            AND THIS FOR PRODUCTS.
          </td>
        </tr>
        <tr>
          <td bgcolor="#edffff" runat="server" id="productDetailsCell">
            HERE WE'LL SHOW A FEW DETAILS ABOUT THE SELECTED PRODUCT
          </td>
        </tr>
      </table>
  </form>
</body>
```

4. Switch to Design view. The Form should look like the following screenshot:

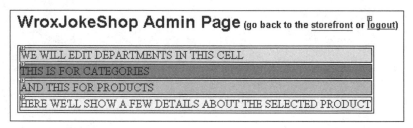

5. The text in each table cell is just an indication about what will be placed in that cell. You can keep the text for now, but remember to remove it after implementing the user controls that will fill the table cells.

6. Let's insert a reference now to `WroxJokeShop.css`. We'll add a few styles to this file to be used in the administration page. Add this line in the `<HEAD>` section of `CatalogAdminPage.aspx`:

```
<link href="WroxJokeShop.css" type="text/css" rel="stylesheet">
```

7. If these lines weren't automatically added by Visual Studio when editing the file in HTML View, add them to the code-behind file CatalogAdminPage.aspx.vb.

```
Public Class CatalogAdminPage
   Inherits System.Web.UI.Page
   Protected WithEvents departmentsCell As System.Web.UI.HtmlControls.HtmlTableCell
   Protected WithEvents categoriesCell As System.Web.UI.HtmlControls.HtmlTableCell
   Protected WithEvents productsCell As System.Web.UI.HtmlControls.HtmlTableCell
   Protected WithEvents productDetailsCell As
System.Web.UI.HtmlControls.HtmlTableCell
   Protected WithEvents logoutButton As System.Web.UI.WebControls.LinkButton
```

8. While in Design View please double-click on the logout button (which appears as a hyperlink), and modify its Click event handler like this:

```
Private Sub logoutButton_Click(ByVal sender As System.Object, _
     ByVal e As System.EventArgs) Handles logoutButton.Click
   System.Web.Security.FormsAuthentication.SignOut()
   Response.Redirect("default.aspx")
End Sub
```

9. Also in CatalogAdminPage.aspx.vb, modify Page_Load with the following code:

```
Private Sub Page_Load(ByVal sender As System.Object, _
     ByVal e As System.EventArgs) Handles MyBase.Load
   ' Save DepartmentID from the query string to a variable
   Dim departmentId As String = Request.Params("DepartmentID")

   ' Save CategoryID from the query string to a variable
   Dim categoryId As String = Request.Params ("CategoryID")

   ' Save ProductID from the query string to a variable
   Dim productId As String = Request.Params("ProductID")

   ' We always load the DepartmentsAdmin control in the first cell
   If True Then
     Dim control As Control
     control = Page.LoadControl("UserControls/DepartmentsAdmin.ascx")
     departmentsCell.Controls.Add(control)
   End If

   ' If a department is provided we load its categories
   If IsNumeric(departmentId) Then
     Dim control As Control
     control = Page.LoadControl("UserControls/CategoriesAdmin.ascx")
     categoriesCell.Controls.Add(control)
   End If
```

```
    ' If a category is selected we load its products
   If IsNumeric(categoryId) Then
     Dim control As Control
     control = Page.LoadControl("UserControls/ProductsAdmin.ascx")
     productsCell.Controls.Add(control)
   End If

    ' If a product is selected we display additional info about it
   If IsNumeric(productId) Then
     Dim control As Control
     control = Page.LoadControl("UserControls/ProductDetailsAdmin.ascx")
     productDetailsCell.Controls.Add(control)
   End If
 End Sub
```

10. We now want to add a new file to the BusinessObjects folder. We could have used Catalog.vb and the Catalog class, but that one was created specifically for the client functionality. For administering the catalog, apart from it being cleaner to have a separate class, we also get better flexibility and better performance (because the catalog administration code is only loaded when needed in CatalogAdminPage.aspx).

11. Right-click on BusinessObjects, then select Add | Add New Item. In the Templates window select Class and write CatalogAdmin.vb for the Name.

12. Modify CatalogAdmin.vb with the following code:

```
Imports System.Data.SqlClient

Public Class CatalogAdmin

   ' Add methods here

  Private ReadOnly Property connectionString() As String
    Get
      Return ConfigurationSettings.AppSettings("ConnectionString")
    End Get
  End Property
End Class
```

How It Works

We still don't have anything that we can actually test, except for the new link on the main page and the security mechanism that we built at the beginning of the chapter.

Still we put down the basic structure that we'll start filling throughout the rest of the chapter. We will need to create the four user controls that populate the table in CatalogAdminPage. By taking a look at the code-behind file of CatalogAdminPage, you can see we'll use the query string to decide what information we should present to the visitor. When the page is first loaded and no parameters have been sent, we only load DepartmentsAdmin.ascx:

```
' We always load the DepartmentsAdmin control in the first cell
If True Then
  Dim control As Control
  control = Page.LoadControl("UserControls/DepartmentsAdmin.ascx")
  departmentsCell.Controls.Add(control)
End If
```

When the visitor wants to see the categories of a department, a `DepartmentID` is attached to the query string, which results in `CategoriesAdmin` being loaded in the proper table cell:

```
' If a department is provided we load its categories
If IsNumeric(departmentId) Then
  Dim control As Control
  control = Page.LoadControl("UserControls/CategoriesAdmin.ascx")
  categoriesCell.Controls.Add(control)
End If
```

Remember that in the previous chapters we only checked if the specified parameter is supplied:

```
If Not departmentId Is Nothing Then
  ' ...
```

Here we use the `IsNumeric()` function that not only checks if the parameter exists, but if it is numeric. This is an example of business logic transferred from the business tier to the data tier – checking various data types. However, this practice is common for variables whose data types aren't going to change in time, and in this case sometimes it is better to check them as soon as possible.

For the visitors' area of our page, we attempt to transform the value taken from query string parameters to `Integer` in the business tier, and an exception is raised if the transformation is not possible. When the exception is raised, a nice looking error page is shown to the visitor. For the catalog administration page erroneous values are simply ignored with the `IsNumber()` function.

Both solutions can be best used in certain situations. Having the error handled in the business tier is a better idea if we want to react somehow other than having an error page sent to the visitor, or the error being ignored. For example, the site administrator can be told about the error. For more information on how to do this see either *Beginning ASP.NET 1.0 with VB.NET* or *Professional ASP.NET 1.0, Special Edition.*

Anyway, the general idea is that in normal conditions there shouldn't be any error. We can't have a value of `TryThis` for `DepartmentID` in the query string, except in the situation where a user types this on purpose. In this case receiving an error page or simply ignoring the value isn't going to hurt any legitimate visitor.

Let's get back to our code now. The same logic of loading user controls continues for the other two user controls: `ProductsAdmin` and `ProductDetailsAdmin`.

We have also created the `CatalogAdmin.vb` file, which will be our business object responsible for the catalog administration part of the site. For now we have only added the `connectionString` property that returns the connection string that is stored in the `Web.config` file. We have used the same property in `Catalog.vb` in Chapter 3, so we already know where and how we'll use it.

Administering Departments

The department administration sections will allow our customer to add, remove, or change department information. In order to implement this functionality we will, as usual, need to write the code for the presentation, business, and database layers. While so far we have always started with the database tier, in this chapter we reverse the order.

With the proper design work we would know exactly what to place in each tier, so the order of writing the code wouldn't matter. Actually, when the design is clearly established, a team of programmers can work at the same time and implement the three tiers concurrently, this being one of the benefits of having a tiered architecture.

However, this rarely happens in practice, except for the largest projects that really need very careful design and planning. In this case, usually the best way is to start with the lower levels (the database), to have the basics established before creating the user interface. For this to happen we need of course to analyze first what functionality is required for the user interface, otherwise we wouldn't know what to write in the data and business tiers.

In this chapter we will start with the presentation tier. This method has the advantage that it allows us to start implementing something faster, so as soon as we have the user interface ready we can see what we need to implement. However, this is only applicable if we have a very good overview of the architecture, and if we know beforehand how we will implement the other two tiers. This happens because in the presentation tier we call methods from the business tier (which we haven't created yet) and in the business tier we call methods from the data tier (which, again, we haven't yet created). If we don't have a clear idea how to implement these, this way of doing things can be tricky in the long run.

Since we already have a well-established architecture, it will be quite simple to write components as needed for each tier, without spending too much time on design. Of course, if we had to implement something new or more complicated we would have spent some time analyzing the full implications, but here we won't do anything more complicated than the code in the previous chapters.

One fundamental truth regarding most n-tiered applications (which also applies to our particular case) is that the business and database tiers are ultimately created to support the presentation tier. Drawing on paper and establishing exactly how we want our site to look (in other words, what functionality needs to be supported by the UI (User Interface)) is a good indication of what the database and business tier will contain.

In this chapter we'll do something similar to that: for each user control we'll first create the user interface, and then add the necessary pieces to the business and data layers. Because we're building on the already established architecture, using the same style, there won't be any surprises on any of these tiers.

The DepartmentsAdmin User Control

Let's take another look at what the DepartmentsAdmin web user control looks in action:

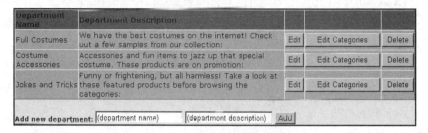

The control is formed of a list populated with the departments' information and with four additional controls (a label, two textboxes and a button) used to add new departments to the list.

The list control you see in the screenshot is not a DataList, but a DataGrid control. The DataGrid is more powerful than a DataList, and has many more features; in this chapter we will only use a few of DataGrid's possibilities, particularly the ones that allow for easy integration of Edit, Select, and Delete buttons, and database-bound column editing in design view. You can see the mentioned controls in the screenshot above, where the Select button is called Edit Categories.

All that we do here with the DataGrid is also possible to do with a DataList, but using the DataGrid eases our work considerably because of its rich set of built-in features. If there's a performance penalty for using a more complex control we aren't worried about it, because the administration page will not be frequently accessed, at least compared to the main web site.

Because of the flexibility provided by the 3-tier architecture, if we're worried about performance we can simply move the administration parts of the site to another server. This would require us to create another project on the other server that would contain the CatalogAdmin.aspx page, its related user controls (DepartmentsAdmin.ascx, CategoriesAdmin.ascx, ProductsAdmin.ascx, and ProductDetails.ascx), and its supporting business-tier class CatalogAdmin. The data tier wouldn't need to change because it is located in the database, which is the same for both visitors and administrators.

Try It Out – Implementing DepartmentsAdmin.ascx

1. Create a new web user control named DepartmentsAdmin in the **UserControls** folder.

2. From the toolbox add a new DataGrid control, a Label control, two TextBox controls and a Button control to the form, as shown below:

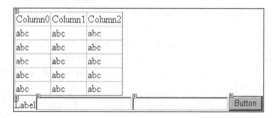

3. Let's start editing the controls' properties, starting with the DataGrid. Set the ID of the grid to departmentsGrid, and the Width property to 100%.

4. Now let's open the Property Builder of departmentsGrid. Right-click on the DataGrid and select the Property Builder item from the menu:

Alternatively, when the DataGrid is selected, we can click on the Property Builder link located at the bottom of the Properties window:

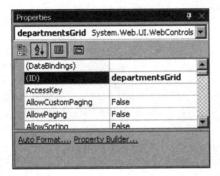

5. The Property Builder window has several tabs that allow us to customize almost anything about the data grid regarding both its functionality and appearance. Right now we're interested in specifying what columns it will contain after being connected to the data source. By default the DataGrid displays all the columns received from the data source, but we want to customize the information presented. In the Property Builder, click on the Columns tab in the left side of the window.

6. Here, please unselect the Create columns automatically at run time checkbox. This tells the DataGrid that we want to manually specify its columns. If we leave this checkbox checked, when we set a data source for the DataGrid (for example using a SqlDataReader object), it gets all its columns, and then appends the manually created ones. At the end of this exercise you might want to experiment with checking this checkbox, but for now please leave it unchecked.

7. We want to add two columns for **Department Name** and **Department Description**, and then three columns for editing, selecting, and deleting rows. **Department Name** and **Department Description** are bound columns (they get their values directly from database columns retrieved from the data source). Please select **Bound column** in the **Available columns** list, and then click the arrow button twice. This will add two **Bound Column** records to the **Selected columns** list.

8. Expand **Button Column** in the **Available columns** list, and add an **Edit, Update, Cancel** field, a **Select** field, and finally a **Delete** field. Right now we should have five columns in the **Selected columns** list. Let's set the properties for each of them.

9. Select the first bound column, and set the **Header Text** to `Department Name` and the **Data Field** to `Name`. Leave the other options at their default values. **Data Field** refers to the field from the database that will be used to populate this column. Since `departmentsGrid` will be populated with data from the `Department` table, we already know that the department name is stored in a field from that table called `Name`.

10. For the second bound column, set the **Header Text** to `Department Description` and the **Data Field** to `Description`.

11. For the **Edit, Update, Cancel** button please change **Button type** to `PushButton`, and leave the other options in place. Then please do the same for the **Delete** button.

12. For the **Select** field please change its **Text** (not **Header Text**) property to **Edit Categories**, and the **Button type** to `PushButton`.

13. In order to improve the look of the `DataGrid` a little bit, let's play with the colors. In the left tab of the window click on **Format**. Then from the **Objects** list select **Header** and set its **Back color** to **Teal**, its **font name** to **Verdana**, and its **font size** to **X-Small** and **Bold**. Then expand the **Items** category, select **Normal Items** and set its **Back color** to **Silver**, its **font name** to **Verdana**, and **font size** to **X-Small**. After these changes click **OK**; your data grid should look like this:

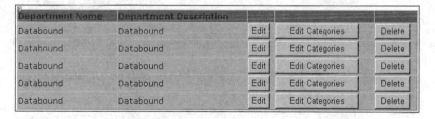

As you can see, you can also play with fonts, colors, styles, and alignments, and customize the look of the data grid in many ways.

14. Let's change the other controls now. For the label control, change its **Text** property to `Add new department:` For the first textbox, set the **ID** to `departmentNameTextBox`, and the **Text** to `(department name)`. For the second textbox, set the **ID** to `departmentDescriptionTextBox`, and the **Text** to `(department description)`. For the button set the **ID** to `addDepartmentButton`, and the **Text** to `Add`.

15. Open the `WroxJokeShop.css` file and add these two styles to the file:

```
.AdminPageText
{
  color: Navy;
  font-family: Verdana, Helvetica, sans-serif;
  text-decoration: none;
  font-size:  11px;
  font-weight: bold;
  line-height: 12px;
}

.AdminButtonText
{
  color: Black;
  font-family: Verdana, Helvetica, sans-serif;
  font-size: 12px;
}
```

16. Set the `CssStyle` of the label to `AdminPageText`. Set the `CssStyle` of the button to `AdminButtonText`.

17. After all the changes we have done, the user control should look like this in **Design** view:

Department Name	Department Description			
Databound	Databound	Edit	Edit Categories	Delete
Databound	Databound	Edit	Edit Categories	Delete
Databound	Databound	Edit	Edit Categories	Delete
Databound	Databound	Edit	Edit Categories	Delete
Databound	Databound	Edit	Edit Categories	Delete
Add new department:	(department name)	(department description)	Add	

The styles we applied for the label, textboxes, and button are applied when the page is executed. Right now the page doesn't have any functionality, but when we run it this control will look like this:

Department Name	Department Description			
Full Costumes	We have the best costumes on the internet! Check out a few samples from our collection:	Edit	Edit Categories	Delete
Costume Accessories	Accessories and fun items to jazz up that special costume. These products are on promotion:	Edit	Edit Categories	Delete
Jokes and Tricks	Funny or frightening, but all harmless! Take a look at these featured products before browsing the categories:	Edit	Edit Categories	Delete
Add new department:	(department name)	(department description)	Add	

18. The first step in order to make the data grid functional is to populate it with data in the `Page_Load` method:

```
Private Sub Page_Load(ByVal sender As System.Object,_
    ByVal e As System.EventArgs) Handles MyBase.Load
  If Not Page.IsPostBack Then
    ' Update the data grid
    BindDepartments()
  End If
End Sub
```

```
Private Sub BindDepartments()
  ' The business tier object
  Dim catalog As New CatalogAdmin()

  ' Supply the data grid with the list of departments
  departmentsGrid.DataSource = catalog.GetDepartmentsWithDescriptions

  ' The DataKey of each row is the department's ID. We will use this
  ' when we need to get the department ID of a selected data row
  departmentsGrid.DataKeyField = "DepartmentID"

  ' Bind the data grid to the data source
  departmentsGrid.DataBind()
End Sub
```

Note that in the BindDepartments() method we call a method of CatalogAdmin class,
GetDepartmentsWithDescriptions that hasn't been written yet. BindDepartments() is the
method that will be called by all the other methods that make changes to the database – it updates the
information in the DataGrid control.

Note that until we write the GetDepartmentsWithDescriptions() method in CatalogAdmin,
the line that calls it will be underlined by Visual Studio to mark the problem.

We'll see what these lines do in the *How It Works* section at the end of the exercise.

19. Next we need to write the event handlers for the Edit, Edit Categories (Select), and Delete
buttons. Visual Studio .NET helps us generate the method signatures for these event handlers.
First select the departmentsGrid from the first combo box as in the following picture:

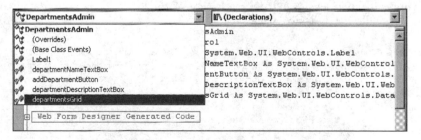

Then select the event you want to handle from the second combo box:

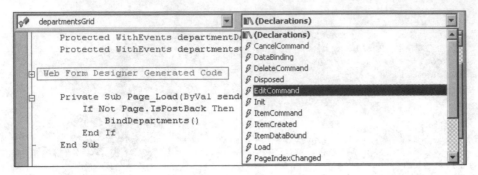

After clicking the `EditCommand` event, the method prototype is automatically added to the code. Now modify it like this:

```
Private Sub departmentsGrid_EditCommand(ByVal source As Object, _
    ByVal e As System.Web.UI.WebControls.DataGridCommandEventArgs) _
    Handles departmentsGrid.EditCommand
  ' We enter edit mode
  departmentsGrid.EditItemIndex = e.Item.ItemIndex

  ' Update the data grid
  BindDepartments()
End Sub
```

20. When the **Edit** button is clicked, the grid enters into edit mode (note that you can't test this yet, as the business and data tiers are not there yet):

Department Name	Department Description				
Full Costumes	We have the best costume	Update	Cancel	Edit Categories	Delete

Here, instead of the **Edit** button, the `DataGrid` places two buttons: **Update** and **Cancel**. In order to make editing functional, we need to supply code that reacts when these buttons are clicked. When the **Update** button is clicked, an `UpdateCommand` event is generated for the `DataGrid`, and clicking on **Cancel** generates a `CancelCommand` data grid event. Visual Studio .NET can help you generate the method signatures for these events in the same fashion as the `EditCommand` in the previous step. Now add the following code for these two events:

```
Private Sub departmentsGrid_UpdateCommand(ByVal source As System.Object, _
    ByVal e As System.Web.UI.WebControls.DataGridCommandEventArgs) _
    Handles departmentsGrid.UpdateCommand
  Dim departmentId As String
  Dim departmentName As String
  Dim departmentDescription As String

  ' DepartmentID is the DataKey field (set in BindDepartments)
  departmentId = departmentsGrid.DataKeys(e.Item.ItemIndex)
  ' We get the department name from the data grid
  departmentName = CType(e.Item.Cells(0).Controls(0), TextBox).Text
```

```
   ' We get the department description from the data grid
   departmentDescription = CType(e.Item.Cells(1).Controls(0), TextBox).Text

   ' Pass the values to the business tier to update department info
   Dim catalog As New CatalogAdmin()
   catalog.UpdateDepartment( _
     departmentId, departmentName, departmentDescription)

   ' Cancel edit mode
   departmentsGrid.EditItemIndex = -1

   ' Update the data grid
   BindDepartments()
End Sub

Private Sub departmentsGrid_CancelCommand(ByVal source As Object, _
    ByVal e As System.Web.UI.WebControls.DataGridCommandEventArgs) _
    Handles departmentsGrid.CancelCommand
   ' Cancel edit mode
   departmentsGrid.EditItemIndex = -1

   ' Update the data grid
   BindDepartments()
End Sub
```

21. Now let's add the code that reacts to the Edit Categories button. In fact, this is a Select button and when clicked it triggers the SelectedIndexChanged event. Use Visual Studio .NET to add the signature for this event handler, and then add the highlighted code:

```
Private Sub departmentsGrid_SelectedIndexChanged(ByVal sender As Object, _
    ByVal e As System.EventArgs) _
    Handles departmentsGrid.SelectedIndexChanged
   Dim departmentId As String

   ' DepartmentID is the DataKey field (set in BindDepartments)
   departmentId = departmentsGrid.DataKeys(departmentsGrid.SelectedIndex)

   ' We reload the page with a DepartmentID parameter in the query string
   Response.Redirect("CatalogAdminPage.aspx?DepartmentID=" & departmentId)
End Sub
```

22. Finally, here's the code for the DeleteCommand event handler:

```
Private Sub departmentsGrid_DeleteCommand(ByVal source As Object, _
    ByVal e As System.Web.UI.WebControls.DataGridCommandEventArgs) _
    Handles departmentsGrid.DeleteCommand
   Dim departmentId As String

   ' DepartmentId is the DataKey field (set in BindDepartments)
   departmentId = departmentsGrid.DataKeys(e.Item.ItemIndex)
```

```
  ' The business tier object
  Dim catalog As New CatalogAdmin()

  ' We try to delete the department, but if it has related categories the
  ' database will generate an exception because this would violate its
  ' integrity
  Try
    catalog.DeleteDepartment(departmentId)

    ' Update the data grid
    BindDepartments()
  Catch
    ' Here we can show an error message specifying that the department
    ' can't be deleted. At the moment we simply redisplay the grid

    ' Update the data grid
    BindDepartments()
  End Try
End Sub
```

23. The final step of this exercise represents adding the addDepartmentButton_Click event
handler method:

```
Private Sub addDepartmentButton_Click(ByVal sender As System.Object, _
    ByVal e As System.EventArgs) Handles addDepartmentButton.Click
  Dim catalog As New CatalogAdmin()

  ' Add the new department to the database
  catalog.AddDepartment(departmentNameTextBox.Text, _
    departmentDescriptionTextBox.Text)

  ' Update the data grid
  BindDepartments()
End Sub
```

How It Works – DepartmentsAdmin.ascx

We wrote a lot of code in this exercise, and we still can't test anything. This is the tough part of first
creating the user interface – in order to be able to see any results we need to implement the other tiers.

Still, the code is not that complicated if we take a closer look at it. It is mostly about working with the
DataGrid control. For example, to enter a row into edit mode, we just need to set the DataGrid's
EditItemIndex property to the index of the column we want to change. We do this in the
EditCommand event handler method:

```
Private Sub departmentsGrid_EditCommand(ByVal source As Object, _
    ByVal e As System.Web.UI.WebControls.DataGridCommandEventArgs) _
    Handles departmentsGrid.EditCommand
  ' We enter edit mode
  departmentsGrid.EditItemIndex = e.Item.ItemIndex
```

```
   ' Update the data grid
   BindDepartments()
End Sub
```

The `EditCommand` event handler receives a `DataGridCommandEventArgs` object named e, which we use to get the row on which the **Edit** button has been clicked (`e.Item.ItemIndex` returns this number). This is then set to the `EditItemIndex` property of the grid, which makes the grid enter into edit mode (when it shows **Update** and **Delete** buttons instead of **Edit**).

We take similar action in the `CancelCommand` event handler, except that there we want to stop editing columns. The way to do this is setting `EditItemIndex` to -1:

```
Private Sub departmentsGrid_CancelCommand(ByVal source As Object, _
    ByVal e As System.Web.UI.WebControls.DataGridCommandEventArgs) _
    Handles departmentsGrid.CancelCommand
    ' Cancel edit mode
    departmentsGrid.EditItemIndex = -1

    ' Update the data grid
    BindDepartments()
End Sub
```

These two event handlers have pretty standard implementations, and you'll see this code in the other user controls as well. The code is just a bit more complicated in the event handler methods that need to access the database and eventually update database information. For example, in order to update existing information we need to get the information from the editing textboxes:

Department Name	Department Description				
Full Costumes	We have the best costum	Update	Cancel	Edit Categories	Delete

So, we need to learn how to extract this information from the data grid. Luckily, this is a very simple task. The second issue that appears here is that we need to know the ID of the department! If we want to delete or edit an existing department we need to know the value of its `DepartmentID`, and this value can't be seen anywhere in the grid!

Actually, we didn't include this `DepartmentID` in the grid on purpose, because this is low-level detail and the site administrator doesn't care about the ID anyway. However, we need a way of storing the ID somewhere. The designers of the `DataGrid` control anticipated this would be a very common problem and they added a `DataKeys` property to the `DataGrid`, which holds a key for each row in the grid.

The mechanism works like this: when binding the `DataGrid` to the data source, we specify a `DataKeyField`. This is done in `BindDepartments`:

```
Private Sub BindDepartments()
    ' The business tier object
    Dim catalog As New CatalogAdmin()

    ' Supply the data grid with the list of departments
    departmentsGrid.DataSource = catalog.GetDepartmentsWithDescriptions
```

217

```
      ' The DataKey of each row is the department's ID.
      ' We will use this when we need to get the department ID of a selected data
      ' row
      departmentsGrid.DataKeyField = "DepartmentID"

    ' Bind the data grid to the data source
    departmentsGrid.DataBind()
  End Sub
```

The highlighted line tells the `DataGrid` that it should read the `DepartmentID` for each row and save it as the `DataKey` for the specified row. Then when we need the key for a specific row, we just need the row index. In order to see this in action, let's take a look at the `UpdateCommand` event handler. It starts like this:

```
Private Sub departmentsGrid_UpdateCommand(ByVal source As Object, _
    ByVal e As System.Web.UI.WebControls.DataGridCommandEventArgs) _
    Handles departmentsGrid.UpdateCommand
  Dim departmentId As String
  Dim departmentName As String
  Dim departmentDescription As String

    ' DepartmentID is the DataKey field (set in BindDepartments)
    departmentId = departmentsGrid.DataKeys(e.Item.ItemIndex)
    ' We get the department name from the data grid
    departmentName = CType(e.Item.Cells(0).Controls(0), TextBox).Text
    ' We get the department description from the data grid
    departmentDescription = CType(e.Item.Cells(1).Controls(0), TextBox).Text

    ' ...... other code here ......
  End Sub
```

Indeed, to get the department ID we just read the `DataKeys` by passing the index of the item being edited. To get `departmentName` and `departmentDescription` we need to do a little trick. The `DataGrid` has the ability to hold any kind of data in each of its cells. If we want, we can make a column being edited contain more controls, not just a `TextBox`.

For this reason, in order to read the text written in the textbox, we need to take a couple of additional steps. For example, to get `departmentName`, we read the first cell of the row, `e.Item.Cells(0)`, and we get the first control from the cell – `e.Item.Cells(0).Controls(0)`. We know for sure that the textbox is the first control, because it is the only control.

Note that the first control of that cell could be any kind of control, so before reading its `Text` property we need to manually convert it to a `TextBox`. This can be done using the `CType()` method, which takes two parameters: the object to be converted and the destination type, and returns the object converted to the desired type. We finally read the `Text` property on the converted `TextBox` object:

```
departmentName = CType(e.Item.Cells(0).Controls(0), TextBox).Text
```

After finding the department ID, name, and description we can call the `UpdateDepartment()` method of the `CatalogAdmin` class, which will take care of updating catalog information:

```
' Pass the values to the business tier to update department info
Dim catalog As New CatalogAdmin()
catalog.UpdateDepartment(departmentId, departmentName, departmentDescription)

' Cancel edit mode
departmentsGrid.EditItemIndex = -1

' Update the data grid
BindDepartments()
```

Of course, right now `CatalogAdmin` is empty and there is no `UpdateDepartment` class, but we are going to write it in the next exercise. We did know how to use the method even though it hasn't been written yet because it's pretty obvious that a method like this would require the three parameters we mentioned

Middle-Tier Methods for Departments Administration

We called many middle-tier methods in the code-behind file of `DepartmentsAdmin.ascx`. In the `BindDepartments()` method we call `GetDepartmentsWithDescriptions` to populate the data grid with a list of departments:

```
' Sub: BindDepartments
' Supply the data grid with the list of departments
departmentsGrid.DataSource = catalog.GetDepartmentsWithDescriptions
```

When updating a department's info, we call a method named `UpdateDepartment()`. We supply this method with the ID of the department we want to update, a name, and a description that needs to be set for that department:

```
' Sub: departmentsGrid_UpdateCommand
' Pass the values to the business tier to update department info
Dim catalog As New CatalogAdmin()
catalog.UpdateDepartment( _
   departmentId, departmentName, departmentDescription)
```

When deleting a department we simply need to supply a department ID to the `DeleteDepartment()` method of the business tier:

```
' Sub: departmentsGrid_DeleteCommand
catalog.DeleteDepartment(departmentId)
```

Finally, when adding a new department we call `AddDepartment()`. This needs only a name and description for the new department, because the ID will be automatically generated by the database – remember that its primary key, the `DepartmentID` column is also an Identity column. You might want to take another look at the identity columns section in Chapter 3.

```
' Sub: addDepartmentButton_Click
' Add the new department to the database
catalog.AddDepartment(departmentNameTextBox.Text, _
   departmentDescriptionTextBox.Text)
```

So, there are four methods that need to be implemented in the business tier, in the `CatalogAdmin` class: `GetDepartmentsWithDescriptions()`, `UpdateDepartment()`, `DeleteDepartments()`, and `AddDepartment()`. Note that we include all of them in a `#Region` section (which ends with `#End Region`). This isn't part of the Visual Basic language, but a feature of Visual Studio .NET that lets us group a number of methods. These can be then managed like any other method in Visual Studio .NET:

```
  Imports System.Data.SqlClient

⊟ Public Class CatalogAdmin

       ' Add methods here
⊞ │ Departments │

⊟     Private ReadOnly Property connectionString() As String
⊟       Get
            Return ConfigurationSettings.AppSettings("ConnectionString")
        End Get
      End Property
└ End Class
```

Adding the Methods

Now it's time to implement each one of them. Please add this code to the `CatalogAdmin` class in the `CatalogAdmin.vb` file:

```
Imports System.Data.SqlClient

Public Class CatalogAdmin

#Region " Departments "
  Public Function GetDepartmentsWithDescriptions() As SqlDataReader
    ' Create the connection object
    Dim connection As New SqlConnection(connectionString)

    ' Create and initialize the command object
    Dim command As New SqlCommand("GetDepartmentsWithDescriptions", _
      connection)
    command.CommandType = CommandType.StoredProcedure

    ' Open the connection
    connection.Open()

    ' Return a SqlDataReader to the calling function
    Return command.ExecuteReader(CommandBehavior.CloseConnection)
  End Function

  Public Function UpdateDepartment(ByVal departmentId As String, _
      ByVal departmentName As String, ByVal departmentDescription As String)
    ' Create the connection object
    Dim connection As New SqlConnection(connectionString)
```

```vb
        ' Create and initialize the command object
        Dim command As New SqlCommand("UpdateDepartment", connection)
        command.CommandType = CommandType.StoredProcedure

        ' Add an input parameter and supply a value for it
        command.Parameters.Add("@DepartmentID", SqlDbType.Int, 4)
        command.Parameters("@DepartmentID").Value = departmentId

        ' Add an input parameter and supply a value for it
        command.Parameters.Add("@DepartmentName", SqlDbType.VarChar, 50)
        command.Parameters("@DepartmentName").Value = departmentName

        ' Add an input parameter and supply a value for it
        command.Parameters.Add("@DepartmentDescription", SqlDbType.VarChar, 200)
        command.Parameters("@DepartmentDescription").Value = departmentDescription

        ' Open the connection, execute the command and close the connection
        connection.Open()
        command.ExecuteNonQuery()
        connection.Close()
    End Function

    Public Function DeleteDepartment(ByVal departmentId As String)
        ' Create the connection object
        Dim connection As New SqlConnection(connectionString)

        ' Create and initialize the command object
        Dim command As New SqlCommand("DeleteDepartment", connection)
        command.CommandType = CommandType.StoredProcedure

        ' Add an input parameter and supply a value for it
        command.Parameters.Add("@DepartmentID", SqlDbType.Int, 4)
        command.Parameters("@DepartmentID").Value = departmentId

        ' Open the connection, execute the command and close the connection
        connection.Open()
        command.ExecuteNonQuery()
        connection.Close()
    End Function

    Public Function AddDepartment(ByVal departmentName As String, _
        ByVal departmentDescription As String)
        ' Create the connection object
        Dim connection As New SqlConnection(connectionString)
        ' Create and initialize the command object
        Dim command As New SqlCommand("AddDepartment", connection)
        command.CommandType = CommandType.StoredProcedure

        ' Add an input parameter and supply a value for it
        command.Parameters.Add("@DepartmentName", SqlDbType.VarChar, 50)
        command.Parameters("@DepartmentName").Value = departmentName
```

```
      ' Add an input parameter and supply a value for it
      command.Parameters.Add("@DepartmentDescription", SqlDbType.VarChar, 200)
      command.Parameters("@DepartmentDescription").Value = departmentDescription

      ' Open the connection, execute the command and close the connection
      connection.Open()
      command.ExecuteNonQuery()
      connection.Close()
    End Function
  #End Region

    Private ReadOnly Property connectionString() As String
      Get
        Return ConfigurationSettings.AppSettings("ConnectionString")
      End Get
    End Property
  End Class
```

What these methods do is clear enough as we have already seen many similar methods in the previous chapters. It is more interesting to see how the data-tier logic is implemented in the stored procedures.

Stored Procedures for Departments Administration

Here we have four stored procedures that perform the four basic tasks for departments: retrieve departments, update departments, delete departments, and insert departments. These stored procedures are called from the business-tier methods we just added.

GetDepartmentsWithDescriptions

This is the simplest stored procedure we implement here. It returns the complete list of departments with their identities, names, and descriptions. This is similar to the `GetDepartments` stored procedure called to fill the departments list from the store front, but this one also returns the descriptions.

```
CREATE PROCEDURE GetDepartmentsWithDescriptions AS

SELECT DepartmentID, Name, Description FROM Department

RETURN
```

UpdateDepartment

This stored procedure updates the name and description of an existing department. This is done using the UPDATE SQL statement.

```
CREATE PROCEDURE UpdateDepartment
(@DepartmentID int,
@DepartmentName varchar(50),
@DepartmentDescription varchar(1000))

AS
UPDATE Department
```

```
SET [Name] = @DepartmentName, [Description] = @DepartmentDescription
WHERE DepartmentID = @DepartmentID

RETURN
```

DeleteDepartment

DeleteDepartment deletes an existing department from the database.

```
CREATE PROCEDURE DeleteDepartment
(@DepartmentID int)
AS

DELETE FROM Department
WHERE DepartmentID = @DepartmentID

RETURN
```

AddDepartment

AddDepartment inserts a new department into the database.

```
CREATE PROCEDURE AddDepartment
(@DepartmentName varchar(50),
@DepartmentDescription varchar(1000))
AS

INSERT INTO Department ([Name], [Description])
VALUES (@DepartmentName, @DepartmentDescription)

RETURN
```

Testing the DepartmentsAdmin Web User Control

We have added a lot of code, and now finally everything is put together and we can execute the page. There is just one thing left to do, to remove the text from the cell in CatalogAdminPage, as shown below:

```
<td bgcolor="#ccff66" runat="server" id="departmentsCell">
   WE WILL EDIT DEPARMENTS IN THIS CELL
</td>
```

Run the solution using either the Start button or *F5*.

After supplying the admin credentials (admin as both user and password in our case), we are allowed to see the catalog administration page:

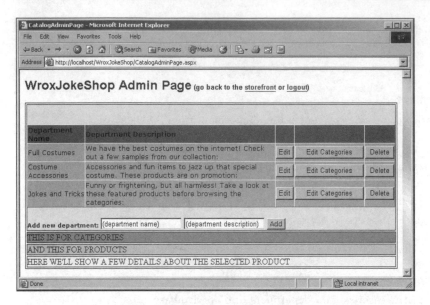

All the functionality regarding department administration works fine, with the exception of the **Edit Categories** link. When this is clicked, the page is reloaded with a `DepartmentID` parameter in the query string. When this parameter is present, `CatalogAdminPage` tries to load the `CategoriesAdmin.ascx` user control, which hasn't been written yet and a runtime exception is generated. This will get fixed as soon as we write the `CategoriesAdmin` user control in the next section.

Administering Categories

The category administration bits are quite similar to what we did for departments, so we won't have too much explanation this time.

The main player in the whole categories administration part is the `CategoriesAdmin` user control. This one is loaded when the administrator clicks on the **Edit Categories** button in the grid in the `DepartmentsAdmin` control. When we press **Edit Categories** on the Jokes and Tricks department, `CategoriesAdmin` will look like this:

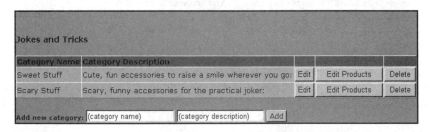

`CategoriesAdmin` is loaded on the page when there is a `DepartmentID` parameter in the query string. This is the piece of code in the `Form_Load` method of `CatalogAdminPage.aspx.vb` that takes care of this:

```
' If a department is provided we load its categories
If IsNumeric(departmentId) Then
  Dim control As Control
  control = Page.LoadControl("UserControls/CategoriesAdmin.ascx")
  categoriesCell.Controls.Add(control)
End If
```

DepartmentID is added to the query string in the SelectedIndexChanged event of the departmentsGrid (which is triggered when an **Edit Categories** button is clicked), in DepartmentsAdmin.ascx.vb:

```
Response.Redirect("CatalogAdminPage.aspx?DepartmentID=" & departmentId)
```

The CategoriesAdmin Web User Control

The steps here are pretty similar to what we know from the DepartmentsAdmin control.

Try It Out – Implementing CategoriesAdmin.ascx

1. Create a new web user control named CategoriesAdmin.ascx in the **UserControls** folder.

2. From the toolbox add a new Label, then another DataGrid control, then another Label control, two TextBox controls, and a Button control to the form, as shown below:

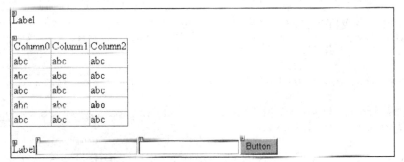

3. Please clear the **Text** property of the first label, set its **ID** to departmentNameLabel, and set its **CssClass** property to ListDescription.

4. Now let's set up the properties for the data grid. Set its **ID** to categoriesGrid, and its **Width** property to 100%.

5. Now open the **Property Builder** form of the data grid and select the **Columns** tab. There, make sure that the **Create columns automatically at runtime** checkbox is not checked. Then add two **Bound Column** fields, then an **Edit, Update, Cancel** field, a **Select** field, and a **Delete** field to the **Selected Columns** list.

6. For the first bound column, set the **Header Text** to Category Name and the **Data Field** to Name. Leave the other options with their default values.

7. For the second bound column, set **Header Text** to `Category Description` and the **Data Field** to `Description`.

8. For the **Edit, Update, Cancel,** and **Delete** fields please change **Button type** to `PushButton`, and leave the other options in place.

9. For the **Select** field please change its **Text** property to `Edit Products`, and the **Button type** to `PushButton`.

10. Finally, modify the colors for the data grid just as we did for the grid in `DepartmentsAdmin` user control. In the left tab of the window click on **Format**. Then from the **Objects** list select **Header** and set its **Back color** to **Teal**, its **Font name** to **Verdana**, and **Font size** to **X-Small** and bold. Then expand the **Items** record, select **Normal Items** and set its **Back color** to **Silver**, its **Font name** to **Verdana**, and **Font size** to **X-Small**. After clicking **OK**, the data grid should look like this:

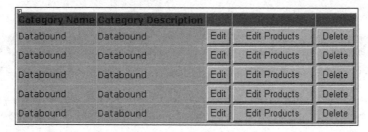

11. Let's now set the properties for the other controls. For the `Label` control, change its **Text** property to `Add new category:`, its **CssClass** property to `AdminPageText`, and its **ID** to `newCategoryLabel`.

12. For the first textbox, set the **ID** to `categoryNameTextBox`, and the **Text** to `(category name)`.

13. For the second textbox, set the **ID** to `categoryDescriptionTextBox`, and the **Text** to `(category description)`.

14. For the button set the **ID** to `addCategoryButton`, and the **Text** to `Add`. Then set its **CssClass** property to `AdminButtonText`.

After all the changes, the control should look like this, when viewed in Design View:

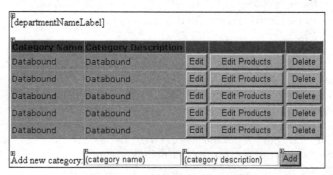

15. Let's now deal with the code behind a little bit. Double-click somewhere on the
CategoriesAdmin control, but not on one of its constituent controls. This should open the
Page_Load method. Please add the following code to it:

```
Private Sub Page_Load(ByVal sender As System.Object, _
    ByVal e As System.EventArgs) Handles MyBase.Load
    If Not Page.IsPostBack Then
        ' Update the data grid
        BindCategories()

        ' Save DepartmentID from the query string to a variable
        Dim departmentId As String
        departmentId = Request.Params("DepartmentID")

        ' Retrieve the name of the department
        Dim catalog As New Catalog()
        Dim departmentDetails As DepartmentDetails
        departmentDetails = catalog.GetDepartmentDetails(departmentId)

        ' The text of departmentNameLabel is set the name of the department
        departmentNameLabel.Text = departmentDetails.Name
    End If
End Sub
```

```
Private Sub BindCategories()
    ' Save DepartmentID from the query string to a variable
    Dim departmentId As String
    departmentId = Request.Params("DepartmentID")

    ' The business tier object
    Dim catalog As New CatalogAdmin()

    ' Supply the data grid with the list of departments
    categoriesGrid.DataSource = _
        catalog.GetCategoriesWithDescriptions(departmentId)

    ' The DataKey of each row is the category ID.
    ' We will use this when we need to get the category ID for a row that
    ' has been selected or is being edited
    categoriesGrid.DataKeyField = "CategoryID"

    ' Bind the data grid to the data source
    categoriesGrid.DataBind()
End Sub
```

16. Now we need to handle the EditCommand, UpdateCommand, CancelCommand,
SelectedIndexChanged, and DeleteCommand events of the data grid. This will make the
grid fully functional, and the code is pretty similar to what we had in the DepartmentsAdmin
user control. Remember that the signatures can be generated by Visual Studio .NET:

```
Private Sub categoriesGrid_EditCommand(ByVal source As Object, _
    ByVal e As System.Web.UI.WebControls.DataGridCommandEventArgs) _
    Handles categoriesGrid.EditCommand
  ' Enter the category into edit mode
  categoriesGrid.EditItemIndex = e.Item.ItemIndex

  ' Update the data grid
  BindCategories()
End Sub

Private Sub categoriesGrid_UpdateCommand(ByVal source As Object, _
    ByVal e As System.Web.UI.WebControls.DataGridCommandEventArgs) _
    Handles categoriesGrid.UpdateCommand
  Dim categoryId As String
  Dim categoryName As String
  Dim categoryDescription As String

  ' CategoryID is the DataKey field (set in BindDepartments)
  categoryId = categoriesGrid.DataKeys(e.Item.ItemIndex)
  ' We get the category name from the data grid
  categoryName = CType(e.Item.Cells(0).Controls(0), TextBox).Text
  ' We get the category description from the data grid
  categoryDescription = CType(e.Item.Cells(1).Controls(0), TextBox).Text

  ' Pass the values to the business tier to update department info
  Dim catalog As New CatalogAdmin()
  catalog.UpdateCategory(categoryId, categoryName, categoryDescription)

  ' Cancel edit mode
  categoriesGrid.EditItemIndex = -1

  ' Update the data grid
  BindCategories()
End Sub

Private Sub categoriesGrid_CancelCommand(ByVal source As Object, _
    ByVal e As System.Web.UI.WebControls.DataGridCommandEventArgs) _
    Handles categoriesGrid.CancelCommand
  ' Cancel edit mode
  categoriesGrid.EditItemIndex = -1

  ' Update the data grid
  BindCategories()
End Sub

Private Sub categoriesGrid_SelectedIndexChanged(ByVal sender As Object, _
    ByVal e As System.EventArgs) _
    Handles categoriesGrid.SelectedIndexChanged
  Dim departmentId As String
  Dim categoryId As String

  ' Get the department ID from the query string
  departmentId = Request.Params("DepartmentID")
```

```
' CategoryID is the DataKey field for categoriesGrid
categoryId = categoriesGrid.DataKeys(categoriesGrid.SelectedIndex)

' Reload CatalogAdminPage.aspx by specifying a DepartmentID
' and CategoryID
Response.Redirect("CatalogAdminPage.aspx?DepartmentID=" _
   & departmentId & "&CategoryID=" & categoryId)
End Sub


Private Sub categoriesGrid_DeleteCommand(ByVal source As Object, _
   ByVal e As System.Web.UI.WebControls.DataGridCommandEventArgs) _
   Handles categoriesGrid.DeleteCommand
Dim categoryId As String

' CategoryID is the DataKey field for categoriesGrid
categoryId = categoriesGrid.DataKeys(e.Item.ItemIndex)

' The business tier object
Dim catalog As New CatalogAdmin()

' We try to delete the category, but if it has related products the
' database will generate an exception because this would violate its
' integrity
Try
   catalog.DeleteCategory(categoryId)
   BindCategories()
Catch
   ' Here we can show an error message specifying that the category
   ' can't be deleted. At the moment we simply redisplay the grid

   ' Update the data grid
   BindCategories()
End Try
End Sub
```

17. Finally let's handle the Click event of the addCategoryButton. Double-click on the button in Design View to have the signature generated and add the following lines:

```
Private Sub addCategoryButton_Click(ByVal sender As System.Object, _
   ByVal e As System.EventArgs) Handles addCategoryButton.Click
' Get the department ID from the query string
Dim departmentId As String
departmentId = Request.Params("DepartmentID")

' Add the new category to the database. Apart from specifying its name
' and description, we also mention the department it belongs to
Dim catalog As New CatalogAdmin()
catalog.AddCategory(departmentId, categoryNameTextBox.Text, _
   categoryDescriptionTextBox.Text)

' Update the data grid
BindCategories()
End Sub
```

How It Works – CategoriesAdmin.ascx

Even though right now the project is not compilable yet, let's see how this user control will look when executed. This helps in understanding what happens there.

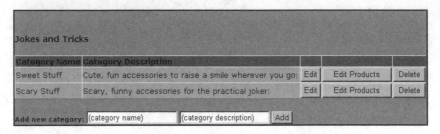

On the top of the control we can see the name of the department, and then the list of categories that belong to it. At the bottom we have the controls that allow us to add a new category to the selected department.

Most of the code is similar to what we did for the DepartmentsAdmin web user control. Still let's recap the main points to keep in mind about the code.

Let's first take a look at the Page_Load event. This event is similar to what we had in DepartmentsAdmin, but we didn't analyze it much at that point. The Page_Load event is fired when the control is loaded (or reloaded). There, we first check if the user control is being loaded in response to a client postback, or if it is being loaded for the first time:

```
If Not Page.IsPostBack Then
  ' Update the data grid
  BindCategories()

  ' ... other code here
```

But what does this mean? ASP.NET controls and forms have a great feature that allows them to remember their state between client requests. This is very useful because the ASP.NET form is reloaded each time something happens with its controls.

For example, if our data grid is filled with information and we change the state of a checkbox in the form (or if we click on a button, and so on), the form is reloaded but the data grid is still filled with data. This is something new in ASP.NET, because with regular ASP or with HTML we need to fill every control with data every time the page loads.

So, in ASP.NET we'll want to update the information in the data grid and in the other controls only when the page loads for the first time. If the page is reloaded for any reason (a button is clicked for example) we don't want to access the database again and update the data grid (and whichever other controls there are), because the data is still there. This is the reason why we first check the value of Page.PostBack in Page_Load before updating any information in the user control (but the same idea applies to web forms in exactly the same way):

```
If Not Page.IsPostBack Then
```

Page.IsPostBack returns True if the page is loaded because of a client postback (something happened on the form), and returns False when the form is loaded for the first time. When Page.IsPostBack is False, we populate the data grid and set the first label in the control to display the department name. For this we use the GetDepartmentDetails() method from the Catalog class and the DepartmentDetails class, which we wrote back in Chapter 4:

```
Private Sub Page_Load(ByVal sender As System.Object, _
    ByVal e As System.EventArgs) Handles MyBase.Load
  If Not Page.IsPostBack Then
    ' Update the data grid
    BindCategories()

    ' Save DepartmentID from the query string to a variable
    Dim departmentId As String
    departmentId = Request.Params("DepartmentID")

    ' Retrieve the name of the department
    Dim catalog As New Catalog()
    Dim departmentDetails As DepartmentDetails
    departmentDetails = catalog.GetDepartmentDetails(departmentId)

    ' The text of departmentNameLabel is set the name of the department
    departmentNameLabel.Text = departmentDetails.Name
  End If
End Sub
```

We have the BindCategories() method that populates the grid. Since the CategoriesAdmin web user control is displayed on the administration page, this means that we have a DepartmentID parameter in the query string, and we want to have the grid contain the categories that belong to the specified department:

```
Private Sub BindCategories()
  ' Save DepartmentID from the query string to a variable
  Dim departmentId As String
  departmentId = Request.Params("DepartmentID")

  ' The business tier object
  Dim catalog As New CatalogAdmin()

  ' Supply the data grid with the list of departments
  categoriesGrid.DataSource =
    catalog.GetCategoriesWithDescriptions(departmentId)
```

As you can see, we send the departmentId parameter to the GetCategoriesWithDescriptions() method, which will be written in the business tier. Then, also in BindCategories, we set the DataKey field for the grid:

```
  ' The DataKey of each row is the category ID.
  ' We will use this when we need to get the category ID for a row that
  ' has been selected or is being edited
  categoriesGrid.DataKeyField = "CategoryID"
```

This is very useful. When a row of the grid is selected for viewing its products, for deletion or update, we'll need to know the ID of the category displayed in that row. Since we set the `DataKeyField` to `CategoryID`, we'll just need to know the `DataKey` of the specified row of the DataGrid.

The `UpdateCommand` and `DeleteCommand` event handlers receive a `DataGridCommandEventArgs` object named e which we use to find out on what line of the data grid the **Update** or **Delete** button was clicked. By asking the `DataKey` of that line, we find out the `CategoryID` of the category that is being updated or deleted:

```
' CategoryID is the DataKey field for categoriesGrid
categoryId = categoriesGrid.DataKeys(e.Item.ItemIndex)
```

We also need to find out the `CategoryID` in the `SelectedIndexChanged` event (which is triggered when clicking the **Edit Products** button, since this is the **Select** button of the grid). Still, in this event handler we don't receive a `DataGridCommandEventArgs` object, so we can't find out the index of the selected row using the traditional `e.Item.ItemIndex`. However, here we have an even simpler method: when the **Select** button of a grid is clicked, we can get its index using the `DataGrid`'s `SelectedIndex` property. Once we know the index, again it's very simple to find out the category ID:

```
' CategoryID is the DataKey field for categoriesGrid
categoryId = categoriesGrid.DataKeys(categoriesGrid.SelectedIndex)
```

In the `SelectedIndexChanged` event handler we need to get a department ID (which we take from the query string) and a category ID. We then use them to reload the page, with both IDs being appended to the query string:

```
' Reload CatalogAdminPage.aspx by specifying a DepartmentID
' and CategoryID
Response.Redirect("CatalogAdminPage.aspx?DepartmentID=" _
  & departmentId & "&CategoryID=" & categoryId)
```

Remember from the way we implemented the `Form_Load` method in `CatalogAdminPage`, that when a `CategoryID` is present it will try to load the `ProductsAdmin` user control, which we'll build a bit later.

Another thing to notice is the way we enter the data grid in edit mode. This happens in the `EditCommand` event handler, and is done by setting the `EditItemIndex` property of the `DataGrid` to the row we want to edit. Once this is done, the `DataGrid` takes care of the details, and displays editable textboxes in the rows being edited.

We cancel edit mode in the `UpdateCommand` and `CancelCommand` event handlers. Remember that the **Delete** and **Cancel** buttons appear only when the grid is in edit mode (they replace the **Edit** button), and after they are clicked we need to exit edit mode:

```
' Cancel edit mode
categoriesGrid.EditItemIndex = -1
```

In the `DeleteCommand` we once again use a `Try...Catch...Finally` block:

```
Try
    catalog.DeleteCategory(categoryId)
    BindCategories()
Catch
    ' Here we can show an error message specifying that the category
    ' can't be deleted. At the moment we simply redisplay the grid

    ' Update the data grid
    BindCategories()
End Try
```

We have implemented this error-trapping mechanism because the database might raise an error if the category we attempt to delete has related products (this would break the database integrity because it would result in orphaned products). If an exception is caught in the code from the Try block, the execution is passed to the Catch block. Note that in the Catch block we simply ignore the error and update the information in the data grid, although this update isn't really necessary because the data grid doesn't get modified if no records are deleted.

Middle-Tier Methods for Categories Administration

Here we write the methods of the CatalogAdmin class that support the functionality required by the CategoriesAdmin user control. These methods support the basic administrative operations with categories, and are the following: GetCategoriesWithDescriptions, UpdateCategory, DeleteCategory, and AddCategory.

Please add these methods to CatalogAdmin.vb, just after the Departments region (which contains similar methods for departments):

```
#Region " Categories "
    Public Function GetCategoriesWithDescriptions( _
        ByVal departmentId As String) As SqlDataReader
        ' Create the connection object
        Dim connection As New SqlConnection(connectionString)

        ' Create and initialize the command object
        Dim command As New SqlCommand( _
            "GetCategoriesWithDescriptions", connection)
        command.CommandType = CommandType.StoredProcedure

        ' Add an input parameter and supply a value for it
        command.Parameters.Add("@DepartmentID", SqlDbType.Int, 4)
        command.Parameters("@DepartmentID").Value = departmentId

        ' Open the connection
        connection.Open()

        ' Return a SqlDataReader to the calling function
        Return command.ExecuteReader(CommandBehavior.CloseConnection)
    End Function
```

```
Public Function UpdateCategory(ByVal categoryId As String, _
    ByVal categoryName As String, ByVal categoryDescription As String)
  ' Create the connection object
  Dim connection As New SqlConnection(connectionString)

  ' Create and initialize the command object
  Dim command As New SqlCommand("UpdateCategory", connection)
  command.CommandType = CommandType.StoredProcedure

  ' Add an input parameter and supply a value for it
  command.Parameters.Add("@CategoryID", SqlDbType.Int, 4)
  command.Parameters("@CategoryID").Value = categoryId

  ' Add an input parameter and supply a value for it
  command.Parameters.Add("@CategoryName", SqlDbType.VarChar, 50)
  command.Parameters("@CategoryName").Value = categoryName

  ' Add an input parameter and supply a value for it
  command.Parameters.Add("@CategoryDescription", SqlDbType.VarChar, 200)
  command.Parameters("@CategoryDescription").Value = categoryDescription

  ' Open the connection, execute the command, and close the connection
  connection.Open()
  command.ExecuteNonQuery()
  connection.Close()
End Function

Public Function DeleteCategory(ByVal categoryId As String)
  ' Create the connection object
  Dim connection As New SqlConnection(connectionString)

  ' Create and initialize the command object
  Dim command As New SqlCommand("DeleteCategory", connection)
  command.CommandType = CommandType.StoredProcedure

  ' Add an input parameter and supply a value for it
  command.Parameters.Add("@CategoryID", SqlDbType.Int, 4)
  command.Parameters("@CategoryID").Value = categoryId

  ' Open the connection, execute the command, and close the connection
  connection.Open()
  command.ExecuteNonQuery()
  connection.Close()
End Function

Public Function AddCategory(ByVal departmentID As String, _
    ByVal categoryName As String, ByVal categoryDescription As String)
  ' Create the connection object
  Dim connection As New SqlConnection(connectionString)

  ' Create and initialize the command object
  Dim command As New SqlCommand("AddCategory", connection)
  command.CommandType = CommandType.StoredProcedure
```

```
      ' Add an input parameter and supply a value for it
      command.Parameters.Add("@DepartmentID", SqlDbType.Int, 4)
      command.Parameters("@DepartmentID").Value = departmentID

      ' Add an input parameter and supply a value for it
      command.Parameters.Add("@CategoryName", SqlDbType.VarChar, 50)
      command.Parameters("@CategoryName").Value = categoryName

      ' Add an input parameter and supply a value for it
      command.Parameters.Add("@CategoryDescription", SqlDbType.VarChar, 200)
      command.Parameters("@CategoryDescription").Value = categoryDescription

      ' Open the connection, execute the command, and close the connection
      connection.Open()
      command.ExecuteNonQuery()
      connection.Close()
    End Function
#End Region
```

After having written these four methods, it's time to implement the stored procedures that support their functionality.

Stored Procedures for Categories Administration

Here we have four stored procedures, each of them being called by one of the four methods we have previously written for the business tier. Please add each of the following stored procedures to the WroxJokeShop database:

GetCategoriesWithDescriptions

This is the stored procedure that takes the ID of a department as parameter and returns the categories that belong to that department. Unlike the GetCategories stored procedure, this one also returns their descriptions.

```
CREATE PROCEDURE GetCategoriesWithDescriptions
(@DepartmentID int)
AS

SELECT CategoryID, [Name], [Description]
FROM Category
WHERE DepartmentID = @DepartmentID

RETURN
```

UpdateCategory

The UpdateCategory stored procedure updates the name and description of a category.

```
CREATE PROCEDURE UpdateCategory
(@CategoryID int,
@CategoryName varchar(50),
```

```
@CategoryDescription varchar(1000))
AS


UPDATE Category
SET [Name] = @CategoryName, [Description] = @CategoryDescription
WHERE CategoryID = @CategoryID

RETURN
```

DeleteCategory

DeleteCategory deletes a certain category from the database. If the category has products that belong to it, the database will raise an error because the deletion would affect the database integrity – remember that we have implemented the One-to-Many relationship between Category and Product tables using a foreign key relationship back in Chapter 4. In this case the error is trapped in the presentation tier (the CategoriesAdmin user control) which simply ignores the error and refreshes the information in the data grid.

```
CREATE PROCEDURE DeleteCategory
(@CategoryID int)
AS

DELETE FROM Category
WHERE CategoryID = @CategoryID

RETURN
```

AddCategory

AddCategory adds a new category to the database. Apart from the name and description of the new category, we also need a DepartmentID, which specifies the department the category belongs to. Note that we don't need to (in fact, we can't) specify a CategoryID because CategoryID is an identity column in the Category table, and its value is automatically generated by the database when inserting a new record.

```
CREATE PROCEDURE AddCategory
(@DepartmentID int,
@CategoryName varchar(50),
@CategoryDescription varchar(50))
AS

INSERT INTO Category (DepartmentID, [Name], [Description])
VALUES (@DepartmentID, @CategoryName, @CategoryDescription)

RETURN
```

Testing the CategoriesAdmin Web User Control

The code is finally ready. Again, remove the text from the categories cell in CatalogAdmin.aspx. Build the project and then press *F5* to run the project. When you click on the **Edit Categories** for one of the departments, your administration page should look like the following screenshot:

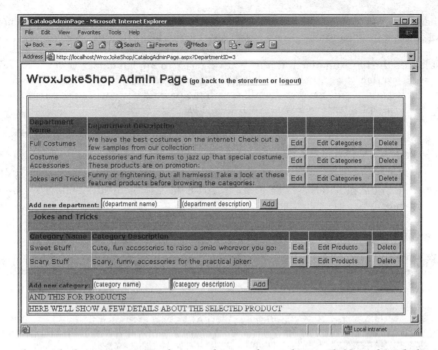

Feel free to play with the options, to make sure they work as advertised. Note that clicking on Edit Products generates an error because we didn't write the `ProductsAdmin` user control.

Administering Products

We have got to the last major part of the catalog administration page: the place where we edit the products that belong to the selected category. This one has a few more controls than the other ones:

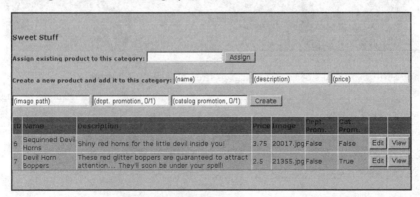

The interface is a bit more complex but there's nothing too complicated. We have a list with the products that belong to the selected category, and the means of adding new products to that category. To add a new product to the category we can either assign an already existing product to the category, or enter the complete data for a new product that will be added to the database and associated to the current category.

Note that here we need to know the product's ID – so the data grid now contains an ID column. In order to assign an existing product to the category, we enter the product's ID and click the Assign button.

This might not be the best solution, but it is relatively easy to implement. In order to have a good and easy-to-use user interface for the administration part of the catalog we would need to write a lot more code. Once you've got the idea and are familiar with the techniques, you'll know for sure the best way of applying the principles learned to your own web sites.

The ProductsAdmin Web User Control

We saw in the earlier screenshot what this user control is going to look like. Most of its functionality is similar to the one of the previous user controls, but with this user control we'll take a closer look at error handling techniques.

Let's implement it in the following *Try It Out*:

Try It Out – Implementing ProductsAdmin.ascx

1. Create a new web user control named `ProductsAdmin.ascx` in the **UserControls** folder.

2. Please add labels, textboxes, buttons and a `DataGrid` as shown below:

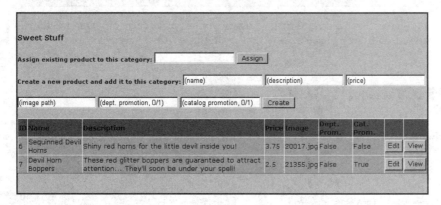

3. Change the properties of each control to the values in the following table:

Control Type	ID Property	Text Property
Label	categoryNameLabel	n/a
Label	errorMessageLabel	n/a
Label	assignProductLabel	Assign existing product to this category:
TextBox	productIdTextBox	(id)

Control Type	ID Property	Text Property
Button	assignProductButton	Assign
Label	newProductLabel	Create a new product and add it to this category:
TextBox	nameTextBox	(name)
TextBox	descriptionTextBox	(description)
TextBox	priceTextBox	(price)
TextBox	imageTextBox	(image path)
TextBox	departmentPromotionTextBox	(dept. promotion, 0/1)
TextBox	catalogPromotionTextBox	(catalog promotion, 0/1)
Button	createProductButton	Create
DataGrid	productsGrid	n/a

4. Set the CssClass property of the first Label control (categoryNameLabel) to ListDescription. Set the CssClass of the second Label control (errorMessageLabel) to AdminErrorText, and the CssClass of the other two labels to AdminPageText. Set the CssClass property of the two buttons to AdminButtonText.

5. Add the following style to WroxJokeShop.css:

```
.AdminErrorText
{
  font-weight: bold;
  font-size: 12px;
  color: red;
  font-style: italic;
  font-family: Verdana, Helvetica, sans-serif;
}
```

Right now, the control should look like this, when viewed in Design View. Remember that the CSS styles don't apply when designing the form, only when it is executed.

6. Now let's modify our `DataGrid`'s properties. Open the **Property Builder** and select the **Columns** page. Unselect the **Create columns automatically at runtime** checkbox, and add nine columns, according to the following table:

Column Type	Header Text	Data Field	Other Properties
Bound Column	ID	ProductID	Read Only
Bound Column	Name	Name	
Bound Column	Description	Description	
Bound Column	Price	Price	
Bound Column	Image	ImagePath	
Bound Column	Dept.prom.	OnDepartmentPromotion	
Bound Column	Cat.prom.	OnCatalogPromotion	
Edit, Update, Cancel			Button type: PushButton
Select			Button type: PushButton Text: View

7. Let's change the `DataGrid` colors as we did for the other grids. In the left tab of the window click on **Format**. Then from the **Objects** list select **Header** and set its **Back color** to Teal, its **Font name** to Verdana, and **Font size** to X-Small and bold. Then expand the **Items** record, select **Normal Items**, and set its **Back color** to Silver, its **Font name** to Verdana, and **Font size** to X-Small. Click **OK**.

8. After all the changes, the user control should look like this when viewed in Design View:

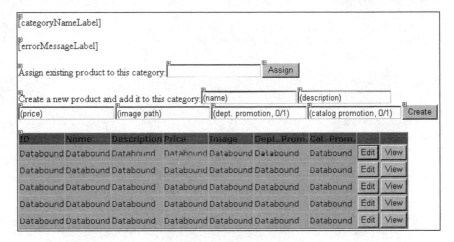

9. Now let's play with the code. Most of the code is pretty similar to that in the previous user controls, but there are a few bits we'll take a closer look at, after the code listing. Remember to use Visual Studio .NET to generate the event handler signatures for you. Here is the listing of the code-behind file ProductsAdmin.ascx.vb:

```
Private Sub Page_Load(ByVal sender As System.Object, _
    ByVal e As System.EventArgs) Handles MyBase.Load
  If Not Page.IsPostBack Then
    ' Populate the data grid with products
    BindProducts()

    ' Obtain the CategoryID from the query string
    Dim categoryId As String
    categoryId = Request.Params("CategoryID")

    ' Set categoryNameLabe.Text to the name of the selected category
    Dim catalog As New Catalog()
    Dim categoryDetails As CategoryDetails
    categoryDetails = catalog.GetCategoryDetails(categoryId)
    categoryNameLabel.Text = categoryDetails.Name
  End If
End Sub

Private Sub BindProducts()
  ' Obtain the CategoryID from the query string
  Dim categoryId As String
  categoryId = Request.Params("CategoryID")

  ' Create the business tier object
  Dim catalog As New Catalog()

  ' Populate the data grid with the list of products that belong to
```

```
        ' the selected category
        productsGrid.DataSource = catalog.GetProductsInCategory(categoryId)

        ' Set the DataKey field
        productsGrid.DataKeyField = "ProductID"

        ' Bind the grid to the data source
        productsGrid.DataBind()
    End Sub

    Private Sub assignProductButton_Click(ByVal sender As System.Object, _
        ByVal e As System.EventArgs) Handles assignProductButton.Click
        ' This sub assigns a product specified by its ProductID to the
        ' currently selected category. The ID of the product is read from its
        ' textbox, and the ID of the category is taken from the query string
        Dim productId As String, categoryId As String
        productId = productIdTextBox.Text
        categoryId = Request.Params("CategoryID")

        Try
            ' Attempt to assign the product to the category. If the operation
            ' is successful, the error message is cleared
            Dim catalog As New CatalogAdmin()
            catalog.AssignProductToCategory(productId, categoryId)

            ' If errorMessageLabel preserves its ViewState we need to
            ' manually clear it after successful actions
            errorMessageLabel.Text = ""
        Catch ex1 As FormatException
            ' If an FormatException error is thrown, probably the
            ' entered ID is not a number
            errorMessageLabel.Text = "Please enter a numeric ID."
        Catch ex2 As SqlClient.SqlException
            ' If a SqlException is thrown the error comes from the database.
            errorMessageLabel.Text = _
"The product doesn't exist or is already assigned to the specified category"
        Catch
            ' We display this message if we don't know the cause of the error
            errorMessageLabel.Text = _
"Unknown error: could not assign the product to the category"
        Finally
            ' Finally, no matter if an error occured or not, we update
            ' the products grid by calling BindProducts
            BindProducts()
        End Try
    End Sub

    Private Sub createProductButton_Click(ByVal sender As System.Object, _
        ByVal e As System.EventArgs) Handles createProductButton.Click
        Dim categoryId As String
        Dim productName As String
        Dim productDescription As String
        Dim productPrice As String
```

```
   Dim productImage As String
   Dim onDepartmentPromotion As String
   Dim onCatalogPromotion As String

   ' Gather the product details from the textboxes, except the category ID
   ' which is read from the query string
   categoryId = Request.Params("CategoryID")
   productName = nameTextBox.Text
   productDescription = descriptionTextBox.Text
   productPrice = priceTextBox.Text
   productImage = imageTextBox.Text
   onDepartmentPromotion = departmentPromotionTextBox.Text
   onCatalogPromotion = catalogPromotionTextBox.Text

   Try
      ' Attempt to create the product and assign it to the currect category.
      ' If the operation is successful, the error message is cleared.
      Dim catalog As New CatalogAdmin()
      catalog.CreateProductToCategory(categoryId, productName, _
         productDescription, productPrice, productImage, _
         onDepartmentPromotion, onCatalogPromotion)
      errorMessageLabel.Text = ""
   Catch
      ' We tell the admin if an error occurs when creating the product.
      ' The operation can fail if the input data is invalid (for example,
      ' price containing non-numerical data).
      errorMessageLabel.Text = _
         "Could not create product. Please verify the input values."
   Finally
      ' Finally, no matter if an error occured or not, we update
      ' the products grid by calling BindProducts
      BindProducts()
   End Try
End Sub

Private Sub productsGrid_CancelCommand(ByVal source As Object, _
   ByVal e As System.Web.UI.WebControls.DataGridCommandEventArgs) _
   Handles productsGrid.CancelCommand
   ' Exit edit mode
   productsGrid.EditItemIndex = -1
   BindProducts()
End Sub

Private Sub productsGrid_UpdateCommand(ByVal source As Object, _
   ByVal e As System.Web.UI.WebControls.DataGridCommandEventArgs) _
   Handles productsGrid.UpdateCommand
   Dim id As String
   Dim name As String
   Dim description As String
   Dim price As String
   Dim image As String
   Dim onDepartmentPromotion As String
   Dim onCatalogPromotion As String
```

243

```
    ' Gather product information
    id = productsGrid.DataKeys(e.Item.ItemIndex)
    name = CType(e.Item.Cells(1).Controls(0), TextBox).Text
    description = CType(e.Item.Cells(2).Controls(0), TextBox).Text
    price = CType(e.Item.Cells(3).Controls(0), TextBox).Text
    image = CType(e.Item.Cells(4).Controls(0), TextBox).Text
    onDepartmentPromotion = CType(e.Item.Cells(5).Controls(0), TextBox).Text
    onCatalogPromotion = CType(e.Item.Cells(6).Controls(0), TextBox).Text

    Try
      ' Try to update the product info. If everything is OK clear the
      ' error label.
      Dim catalog As New CatalogAdmin()
      catalog.UpdateProduct(id, name, description, price, image, _
        onDepartmentPromotion, onCatalogPromotion)
      errorMessageLabel.Text = ""
    Catch
      ' Let the reader know if the product's information could not be
      ' changed.
      ' This can happen because of invalid input data.
      errorMessageLabel.Text = _
"Could not update product info. Please verify the input values."
    Finally
      ' No matter if an error occurs or not we cancel edit mode and update
      ' the products grid information
      productsGrid.EditItemIndex = -1
      BindProducts()
    End Try
  End Sub

  Private Sub productsGrid_EditCommand(ByVal source As Object, _
      ByVal e As System.Web.UI.WebControls.DataGridCommandEventArgs) _
      Handles productsGrid.EditCommand
    ' Enter the grid into edit mode and rebind the data grid
    productsGrid.EditItemIndex = e.Item.ItemIndex
    BindProducts()
  End Sub

  Private Sub productsGrid_SelectedIndexChanged( _
      ByVal sender As System.Object, ByVal e As System.EventArgs) _
      Handles productsGrid.SelectedIndexChanged
    Dim departmentId As String
    Dim categoryId As String
    Dim productName As String
    Dim productId As String
    Dim imagePath As String

    ' Gather product information
    departmentId = Request.Params("DepartmentID")
    categoryId = Request.Params("CategoryID")
    productId = productsGrid.DataKeys(productsGrid.SelectedIndex)
    productName = productsGrid.Items(productsGrid.SelectedIndex).Cells(1).Text()
    imagePath = productsGrid.Items(productsGrid.SelectedIndex).Cells(4).Text
```

```
        ' Send product info in the query string
        ' This is used in the ProductDetailsAdmin user control
        Response.Redirect("CatalogAdminPage.aspx?DepartmentID=" & departmentId _
          & "&CategoryID=" & categoryId & "&ProductID=" & productId _
          & "&ProductName=" & productName & "&ImagePath=" & imagePath)
    End Sub
```

How It Works

Most methods are similar to the those we wrote for the previous controls. One of the less significant changes is what happens when a certain product is selected. As usually, we reload the form by adding something to the query string. In this case we add more details (ProductID, ProductName, and ImagePath) about the product so we won't have to read them again from the database in the ProductDetailsAdmin control, which we'll write in the next section:

```
        ' Send product info in the query string.
        ' This is used in the ProductDetailsAdmin user control.
        Response.Redirect("CatalogAdminPage.aspx?DepartmentID=" & departmentId _
          & "&CategoryID=" & categoryId & "&ProductID=" & productId _
          & "&ProductName=" & productName & "&ImagePath=" & imagePath)
```

What is new here is that we have a more involved error-handling mechanism. With the previous controls we took our time to see how the various event handlers for the data grid are implemented, and here we take a closer look at the error-handling mechanism.

The mechanism is similar in the three event handlers that use it (assignProductButton_Click(), createProductButton_Click(), and productsGrid_UpdateCommand()), but is a bit more involved with assignProductButton_Click(). We'll first look at how the other two event handlers handle errors, and then we'll get back to the assignProductButton_Click() method.

Note that all these are examples where the errors are handled on the presentation tier. This is a requirement since we want to give some feedback to the administrator directly in the web page. If we handled the error in the business tier (and didn't rethrow the exception so it can be received by the presentation tier), we probably would want to inform the administrator by other means (e-mail or recording error in the Windows Event log). *Beginning ASP.NET 1.0 with VB.NET* and *Professional ASP.NET 1.0, Special Edition*, both from Wrox Press, provide examples of how to do this.

Let's see what we did in createProductButton_Click() and productsGrid_UpdateCommand(). First, we placed the code that may generate an error in a Try block:

```
    Try
      ' Try to update the product info. If everything is OK clear the
      ' error label.
      Dim catalog As New CatalogAdmin()
      catalog.UpdateProduct(id, name, description, price, image, _
        onDepartmentPromotion, onCatalogPromotion)
      errorMessageLabel.Text = ""
```

In the Try block we first execute the business-tier method that performs the wanted functionality. If this doesn't generate any error, the text of the errorMessageLabel is reset. If an error occurs, the code in the Catch block is executed instead:

```
Catch
    ' Let the reader know if the product's information could not be
    ' changed.
    ' This can happen because of invalid input data.
    errorMessageLabel.Text = _
"Could not update product info. Please verify the input values."
```

Here we simply set the text of the errorMessageLabel to a text that should be clear enough to the person reading it. At the end we have the Finally block. This one is guaranteed to get executed no matter if an error occurs in the Try block or not, and this is the place used to add any cleanup procedures or logic that we want to be executed no matter what happens in the Try and Catch blocks:

```
Finally
    ' No matter if an error occurs or not we cancel edit mode and update
    ' the products grid information
    productsGrid.EditItemIndex = -1
    BindProducts()
End Try
```

As explained earlier when we talked about postback, ASP.NET by default retains the state of controls in the page. This means that once the errorMessageLabel is set to display an error message, it remains set until we explicitly reset it to another value (it isn't reset by default between page loads). In this case this default behavior doesn't work for us because after the page gets reloaded (due to other user actions), the error message is then obsolete. In the current code we manually reset the label in the Try blocks if no error occurs, but this isn't really the best solution.

In order to make the errorMessageLabel control "forget" its state between page loads we should set its EnableViewState property to False. This way its Text property is always reset between page loads, except the times when we specifically set it to display an error message. This solution has the advantages that we wouldn't need to reset the errorMessageLabel in every other place that doesn't generate an error; also the network traffic is reduced because the value of the user control is not passed between the browser and the server on each page request. Setting EnableViewState to False on the controls that don't require remembering their values between client requests is one of the optimizations that improve the site's performance, but this is regarded as an advanced topic and we will not cover more details about it in this book. For more details about ASP.NET optimization techniques we highly recommend you reading *Professional ASP.NET 1.0, Special Edition*, from Wrox Press (ISBN 186100-703-5).

After creating the middle tier and data tier logic to support the ProductsAdmin user control, an error message will look like this:

```
Sweet Stuff

Could not create product. Please verify the input values.

Assign existing product to this category: [            ]  Assign

Create a new product and add it to this category: [(name)        ] [(description)        ]
[(price)        ] [(image path)    ] [(dept. promotion, 0/1)] [(catalog promotion, 0/1)]  Create
```

Like noted earlier, in `assignProductButton_Click` the error-handling procedure is a bit more involved. Here we take advantage of the fact that we can have multiple `Catch` blocks associated with a single `Try` block. When a .NET method throws an error, the error is packaged in an error object, which is created from a class derived from `System.Exception`. We can have multiple `Catch` blocks that handle the error depending on the exact type of exception that has been thrown. If this sounds too complicated in theory, let's see it in practice.

First we have the usual operation in the `Try` block, which is susceptible to throwing exceptions:

```
Try
    ' Attempt to assign the product to the category. If the operation
    ' is successful, the error message is cleared
    Dim catalog As New CatalogAdmin()
    catalog.AssignProductToCategory(productId, categoryId)
```

Having multiple `Catch` blocks allows us to react differently depending on the kind of error that has been thrown. Here there are two kinds of errors we can meet: the first one happens if we type, for example, a string instead of a number for the `ProductID`. In this case a `FormatException` error will be generated in the business tier when it tries to convert the `ProductID` received as a string to an integer.

The second kind of error happens if the `ProductID` is in the correct format (so it's a number), but either the specified `ProductID` doesn't exist in the database, or the specified `ProductID` is already assigned to the category. In these situations we would receive a `SqlException` from the database.

We know there are two main types of errors that can happen. One of them results in a `FormatException` being thrown, while the other one throws a `SqlException`. In this case we added two `Catch` blocks that are thought to react only to these two specific kinds of errors:

```
Catch ex1 As FormatException
    ' If an FormatException error is thrown, probably the
    ' entered ID is not a number
    errorMessageLabel.Text = "Please enter a numeric ID."
Catch ex2 As SqlClient.SqlException
    ' If a SqlException is thrown the error comes from the database.
    errorMessageLabel.Text = _
"The product doesn't exist or is already assigned to the specified category"
```

Note that each of these `Catch` blocks can tell the administrator the reason for the error. Finally, we add a general-purpose `Catch` block that receives all other kinds of errors and displays a generic error message:

```
    Catch
      ' We display this message if we don't know the cause of the error
      errorMessageLabel.Text = _
   "Unknown error: could not assign the product to the category"
```

Note that in complex projects we can build our own kinds of errors that can be sent from the business tier when certain things happen. This would allow us to fine-tune the error-handling mechanism specifically for our needs. The flexibility goes even further as generated exceptions can also contain error codes and text that can be directly displayed to the visitor, and so on.

We'll want to create our own exceptions when the built-in system errors are not enough – the complete list of system-supplied exception classes can be found in MSDN. If you are familiar with the .NET base classes you might be interested to know that all the system-supplied exceptions derive from the `System.SystemException` class, which in turns derives from `System.Exception`. We can create our own exception classes by deriving them from `System.ApplicationException` (which also derives from `System.Exception`).

Too bad that right now we can't test any of the analyzed scenarios because the business and data tiers haven't been written yet (the drawback of coding the user interface first). Let's quickly implement them so we can get to test the code!

Middle-Tier Methods for Products Administration

These methods are similar to what we have done so far – they all access data-tier stored procedures we'll write afterwards. For now, please add the following methods to `CatalogAdmin.vb`:

Please add these methods to `CatalogAdmin.vb`, just after the `Categories` region:

```vb
#Region " Products "
  Public Function AssignProductToCategory(ByVal productId As String, _
      ByVal categoryId As String)
      ' Create the connection object
    Dim connection As New SqlConnection(connectionString)

      ' Create and initialize the command object
    Dim command As New SqlCommand("AssignProductToCategory", connection)
    command.CommandType = CommandType.StoredProcedure

      ' Add an input parameter and supply a value for it
    command.Parameters.Add("@ProductID", SqlDbType.Int, 4)
    command.Parameters("@ProductID").Value = productId

      ' Add an input parameter and supply a value for it
    command.Parameters.Add("@CategoryID", SqlDbType.Int, 4)
    command.Parameters("@CategoryID").Value = categoryId

      ' Open the connection, execute the command and close the connection
    connection.Open()
    command.ExecuteNonQuery()
    connection.Close()
```

```
End Function

Public Function CreateProductToCategory(ByVal categoryId As String, _
    ByVal productName As String, ByVal productDescription As String, _
    ByVal productPrice As String, ByVal productImage As String, _
    ByVal onDepartmentPromotion As String, _
    ByVal onCatalogPromotion As String)
  ' Create the connection object
  Dim connection As New SqlConnection(connectionString)

  ' Create and initialize the command object
  Dim command As New SqlCommand("CreateProductToCategory", connection)
  command.CommandType = CommandType.StoredProcedure

  ' Add an input parameter and supply a value for it
  command.Parameters.Add("@CategoryID", SqlDbType.Int, 4)
  command.Parameters("@CategoryID").Value = categoryId

  ' Add an input parameter and supply a value for it
  command.Parameters.Add("@ProductName", SqlDbType.VarChar, 50)
  command.Parameters("@ProductName").Value = productName

  ' Add an input parameter and supply a value for it
  command.Parameters.Add("@ProductDescription", SqlDbType.VarChar, 1000)
  command.Parameters("@ProductDescription").Value = productDescription

  ' Add an input parameter and supply a value for it
  command.Parameters.Add("@ProductPrice", SqlDbType.Money, 8)
  command.Parameters("@ProductPrice").Value = productPrice

  ' Add an input parameter and supply a value for it
  command.Parameters.Add("@ProductImage", SqlDbType.VarChar, 50)
  command.Parameters("@ProductImage").Value = productImage

  If onDepartmentPromotion.ToUpper = "TRUE" _
      Or onDepartmentPromotion = "1" Then
    ' If we receive "True" or "1" for onDepartmentPromotion ...
    command.Parameters.Add("@OnDepartmentPromotion", SqlDbType.Bit, 1)
    command.Parameters("@OnDepartmentPromotion").Value = 1
  Else
    ' For all the other values we assume the product is not on promotion
    command.Parameters.Add("@OnDepartmentPromotion", SqlDbType.Bit, 1)
    command.Parameters("@OnDepartmentPromotion").Value = 0
  End If

  If onCatalogPromotion.ToUpper = "TRUE" _
      Or onCatalogPromotion = "1" Then
    ' If we receive "True" or "1" for onCatalogPromotion ...
    command.Parameters.Add("@OnCatalogPromotion", SqlDbType.Bit, 1)
    command.Parameters("@OnCatalogPromotion").Value = 1
  Else
    ' For all the other values we assume the product is not on promotion
    command.Parameters.Add("@OnCatalogPromotion", SqlDbType.Bit, 1)
```

```
      command.Parameters("@OnCatalogPromotion").Value = 0
    End If

    ' Open the connection, execute the command and close the connection
    connection.Open()
    command.ExecuteNonQuery()
    connection.Close()
End Function

' This is identical to CreateProductToCategory, except that we call
' the UpdateProduct stored procedure instead of CreateProductToCategory
Public Function UpdateProduct(ByVal productId As String, _
    ByVal productName As String, ByVal productDescription As String, _
    ByVal productPrice As String, ByVal productImage As String, _
    ByVal onDepartmentPromotion As String, _
    ByVal onCatalogPromotion As String)

    ' Create the connection object
    Dim connection As New SqlConnection(connectionString)

    ' Create and initialize the command object
    Dim command As New SqlCommand("UpdateProduct", connection)
    command.CommandType = CommandType.StoredProcedure

    ' Add an input parameter and supply a value for it
    command.Parameters.Add("@ProductID", SqlDbType.Int, 4)
    command.Parameters("@ProductID").Value = productId

    ' Add an input parameter and supply a value for it
    command.Parameters.Add("@ProductName", SqlDbType.VarChar, 50)
    command.Parameters("@ProductName").Value = productName

    ' Add an input parameter and supply a value for it
    command.Parameters.Add("@ProductDescription", SqlDbType.VarChar, 1000)
    command.Parameters("@ProductDescription").Value = productDescription

    ' Add an input parameter and supply a value for it
    command.Parameters.Add("@ProductPrice", SqlDbType.Money, 8)
    command.Parameters("@ProductPrice").Value = productPrice

    ' Add an input parameter and supply a value for it
    command.Parameters.Add("@ProductImage", SqlDbType.VarChar, 50)
    command.Parameters("@ProductImage").Value = productImage

    If onDepartmentPromotion.ToUpper = "TRUE" Or onDepartmentPromotion = "1" Then
      ' If we receive "True" or "1" for onDepartmentPromotion ...
      command.Parameters.Add("@OnDepartmentPromotion", SqlDbType.Bit, 1)
      command.Parameters("@OnDepartmentPromotion").Value = 1
    Else
      ' For all the other values we assume the product is not on promotion
      command.Parameters.Add("@OnDepartmentPromotion", SqlDbType.Bit, 1)
      command.Parameters("@OnDepartmentPromotion").Value = 0
    End If
```

```
    If onCatalogPromotion.ToUpper = "TRUE" Or onCatalogPromotion = "1" Then
      ' If we receive "True" or "1" for onCatalogPromotion ...
      command.Parameters.Add("@OnCatalogPromotion", SqlDbType.Bit, 1)
      command.Parameters("@OnCatalogPromotion").Value = 1
    Else
      ' For all the other values we assume the product is not on promotion
      command.Parameters.Add("@OnCatalogPromotion", SqlDbType.Bit, 1)
      command.Parameters("@OnCatalogPromotion").Value = 0
    End If

    ' Open the connection, execute the command, and close the connection
    connection.Open()
    command.ExecuteNonQuery()
    connection.Close()
  End Function
#End Region
```

What is interesting to note about this code is the way we deal with the `OnCatalogPromotion` and `OnDepartmentPromotion` sections. In the user interface, the administrator can type anything for these fields. Here we test if their value is `True` or 1, in which cases we transform it to 1. For all the other values we assume the value is 0. This is yet another way of error handling, or better said a way to avoid error handling. If the administrator types some erroneous value, we just assume it's 0 and we avoid sending values to the database that would generate an exception.

Stored Procedures for Products Administration

These are the three stored procedures that support the user interface functionality. Let's take a look at each of them.

AssignProductToCategory

This is called when the administrator types a `ProductID` in the `CategoriesAdmin` user control and clicks on the **Assign** button. When that happens the entered product ID is associated with the category by adding a (`ProductID`, `CategoryID`) value pair into the `ProductCategory` table.

```
CREATE PROCEDURE AssignProductToCategory
(@ProductID int, @CategoryID int)
AS

INSERT INTO ProductCategory (ProductID, CategoryID)
VALUES (@ProductID, @CategoryID)

RETURN
```

Note that we don't do any verification here. If an error occurs (because the entered `ProductID` is not associated with any product or the `ProductID`, `CategoryID` pair already exists in the `ProductCategory` table), the error is trapped in the control and the administrator is notified.

Still, since we talked about the error-handling techniques, it's worth noting that we can make the stored procedure smart enough to do some validation before attempting to add the (ProductID, CategorID) pair to ProductCategory table. By including validation in the stored procedure then an error is not generated, the action is ignored, and the administrator is not notified. However this approach does not work in our scenario. Here is a bullet-proof version of the stored procedure, which attempts to insert the new record into ProductCategory only if the ProductID and CategoryID values exist and the pair doesn't already exist in the database:

```
CREATE PROCEDURE AssignProductToCategory
(@ProductID int, @CategoryID int)
AS

IF EXISTS
  (SELECT [Name]
   FROM Product
   WHERE ProductID=@ProductID)
  AND EXISTS
  (SELECT [Name]
   FROM Category
   WHERE CategoryID=@CategoryID)
  AND NOT EXISTS
  (SELECT *
   FROM ProductCategory
   WHERE CategoryID=@CategoryID AND ProductID=@ProductID)
INSERT INTO ProductCategory (ProductID, CategoryID)
VALUES (@ProductID, @CategoryID)

RETURN
```

CreateProductToCategory

This stored procedure is called when we create a new product. When creating the product it also assigns it to a category, so we don't end up having orphan products. Because the ProductID column is an identity column, we are assured the generated value is unique. A side effect is that we can be certain the (ProductID, CategoryID) pair doesn't exist in the ProductCategory table, since the newly created ProductID didn't exist in the database before.

```
CREATE PROCEDURE CreateProductToCategory
(@CategoryID int,
 @ProductName varchar(50),
 @ProductDescription varchar(1000),
 @ProductPrice Money,
 @ProductImage varchar(50),
 @OnDepartmentPromotion bit,
 @OnCatalogPromotion bit)
AS

DECLARE @ProductID int

INSERT INTO Product ([Name], [Description], Price, ImagePath,
OnDepartmentPromotion, OnCatalogPromotion )
```

```
VALUES (@ProductName, @ProductDescription, CONVERT(money,@ProductPrice),
@ProductImage, @OnDepartmentPromotion, @OnCatalogPromotion)

SELECT @ProductID = @@Identity

INSERT INTO ProductCategory (ProductID, CategoryID)
VALUES (@ProductID, @CategoryID)

RETURN
```

Here is a line of code of particular importance:

```
SELECT @ProductID = @@Identity
```

We know that identity columns are automatically generated by the database. If you ever wondered how you can find out what value has been generated, here's the answer: the @@Identity system value. This needs to be saved into a variable immediately, because its value can be rewritten after other SQL statements execute. After we find out what ID was generated for the new product, we assign it to the category that we receive as a parameter:

```
INSERT INTO ProductCategory (ProductID, CategoryID)
VALUES (@ProductID, @CategoryID)
```

UpdateProduct

This stored procedure updates the information of a product.

```
CREATE PROCEDURE UpdateProduct
(@ProductID int,
 @ProductName varchar(50),
 @ProductDescription varchar(1000),
 @ProductPrice money,
 @ProductImage varchar(50),
 @OnDepartmentPromotion bit,
 @OnCatalogPromotion bit)
AS

UPDATE Product
SET [Name] = @ProductName,
    [Description] = @ProductDescription,
    Price = CONVERT(money,@ProductPrice),
    ImagePath = @ProductImage,
    OnDepartmentPromotion = @OnDepartmentPromotion,
    OnCatalogPromotion = @OnCatalogPromotion
WHERE ProductID = @ProductID

RETURN
```

Testing the ProductsAdmin Web User Control

Remove the text from the products section of `CatalogAdminPage` and make sure the project is compiled by pressing *Ctrl+Shift+B* and then press *F5* in Visual Studio .NET. Make your way till you see the `ProductsAdmin` user control in action, and play with its functionality. Try to assign the product with the ID "ERROR" to a category and see what happens:

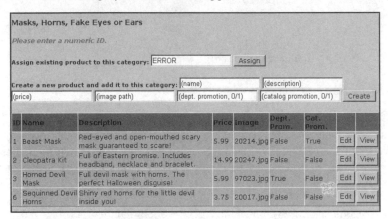

Viewing Product Details and Deleting Products

The products list we built earlier is wonderful, but it lacks two important features: first, it doesn't show us the products' images. It would have probably been a bit awkward to see the pictures in the data grid. Also, we don't have the possibility to delete the products.

When it comes to product removal, things aren't straightforward: we can either simply unassign the product from a category by removing the record from `ProductCatagory` table, or we can effectively remove the product from the `Product` table. Because of the way we access products in the catalog by selecting a category, we need to make sure there are no orphaned products, meaning products that belong to no category, because we couldn't access them using the current administration interface.

So, if we added a **Delete** button to the data grid, what kind of deletion would that button have to do? Delete the product from the database? This would work, but it's a bit awkward if we have a product assigned to more categories and we only want to remove it from a single category. On the other hand, if the **Delete** button removes the product from the current category, we can get to have orphaned products: they exist in the `Product` table, but they don't belong to any category so we can't access them.

The simple solution we'll implement sounds like that: if the product belongs to more than one category, the **Delete** button will simply unassign the product from the current category. If the product belongs to only one category, the product will first be unassigned from the current category, and then also removed from the `Product` table.

In order for this strategy to work, we need to let the administrator know which are the categories that the product belongs to (so they will know what the **Delete** button does to that product). To make this simple, we create yet another user control, which displays more information about the selected product. We can see its picture and the categories it belongs to, and we have a **Delete** button.

The ProductDetailsAdmin Web User Control

This is the control that allows us to see and delete a product. Note that we don't implement error handling in this part so we can focus better on the task at hand, although this isn't recommended for a production system.

This is the way the control will look for a product that belongs to a single category:

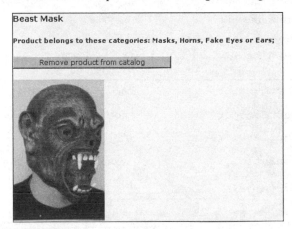

While this is what we'll see if the product belongs to more categories. The text on the Delete button also changes to reflect its new functionality:

So let's start implementing the control.

Try It Out – Implementing ProductDetailsAdmin.ascx

1. Create a new user control named ProductDetailsAdmin, in the **UserControls** folder.

2. Add three labels, a button, and an image control, as shown:

3. Set their properties like this:

Control Type	ID Property	Text Property
Label	productNameLabel	n/a
Label	productCategoryLabel	Product belongs to these categories:
Label	categoriesListLabel	n/a
Button	actionButton	(We will set this in code)
Image	productImage	n/a

4. Set the **CssClass** of `productNameLabel` to `ListDescription`. Set the **CssClass** of the other two labels to `AdminPageText`. Set the **CssClass** of the button to `AdminButtonText`.

5. After the changes, the control looks like this, when viewed in **Design** Mode:

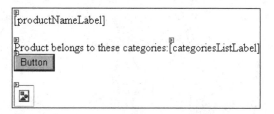

6. Now please double-click somewhere in the control, but not on one of its constituent controls, to open the `Page_Load` event handler. Modify it like this:

```
Private Sub Page_Load(ByVal sender As System.Object, _
    ByVal e As System.EventArgs) Handles MyBase.Load
  If Not Page.IsPostBack Then
    ' Set the product name in the top label
    ' The product name is attached to the query string
    ' when a product is selected in ProductsAdmin
    Dim productName As String
    productName = Request.Params("ProductName")
    productNameLabel.Text = productName
```

```
      ' Display the product's image. The ImagePath parameter
      ' is also received in the query string
      Dim productImagePath As String
      productImagePath = Request.Params("ImagePath")
      productImage.ImageUrl = "../ProductImages/" & productImagePath

      ' categoriesCount will contain the number of categories
      ' for the product
      Dim categoriesCount As Integer = 0

      ' The business tier object
      Dim catalog As New CatalogAdmin()

      ' Get the ProductID from the query string
      Dim productId As String
      productId = Request.Params("ProductID")

      ' Get the list of categories into a SqlDataReader object
      Dim categories As SqlClient.SqlDataReader
      categories = catalog.GetCategoriesForProduct(productId) '

      ' Read each category and add its name to the label
      While (categories.Read)
        categoriesListLabel.Text += categories.GetString(0) & "; "
        categoriesCount = categoriesCount + 1
      End While

      ' Always close the SqlDataReader. This allows the database
      ' connection to be closed too
      categories.Close()

      ' Set the text of the Delete button depending on
      ' the number of categories
      If categoriesCount = 1 Then
        actionButton.Text = "Remove product from catalog"
      Else
        actionButton.Text = "Remove product from current category"
      End If
    End If
  End Sub
End Sub
```

7. While in Design View, please double-click the button, then complete its event handler method like this:

```
Private Sub actionButton_Click(ByVal sender As System.Object, _
    ByVal e As System.EventArgs) Handles actionButton.Click
  Dim productId As String
  productId = Request.Params("ProductID")

  Dim categoryId As String
  categoryId = Request.Params("CategoryID")
```

```
        Dim departmentId As String
        departmentId = Request.Params("DepartmentID")

        Dim catalog As New CatalogAdmin()
        catalog.RemoveFromCategoryOrDeleteProduct(productId, categoryId)

        Response.Redirect("CatalogAdminPage.aspx?DepartmentID=" _
          & departmentId & "&CategoryID=" & categoryId)
    End Sub
```

How It Works

Here we first implemented the logic in Load_Form. This displays the name of the product and shows its picture.

So far when we received SqlDataReader objects we directly passed them to DataTables or DataGrids, and they took care of extracting the data from the data reader. This time we manually parse the reader and extract the name of each category from it. We add all the category names to the categoriesListLabel, and finally close the data reader:

```
        ' Get the list of categories into a SqlDataReader object
        Dim categories As SqlClient.SqlDataReader
        categories = catalog.GetCategoriesForProduct(productId) '

        ' Read each category and add its name to the label
        While (categories.Read)
          categoriesListLabel.Text += categories.GetString(0) & "; "
          categoriesCount = categoriesCount + 1
        End While

        ' Always close the SqlDataReader. This allows the database
        ' connection to be closed too
        categories.Close()
```

Finally we decide what text to place on the button:

```
        ' Set the text of the Delete button depending on
        ' the number of categories
        If categoriesCount = 1 Then
          actionButton.Text = "Remove product from catalog"
        Else
          actionButton.Text = "Remove product from current category"
        End If
```

The button seems to have a simpler purpose. When clicked, it first calls the RemoveFromCategoryOrDeleteProduct method of the business tier (which we'll implement soon), and then redirects to the category page for that product. This is necessary, since after removal the product might not exist in the database so we don't want the ProductDetailsAdmin web user control to attempt loading it.

Middle-Tier Methods for Product Details Admin

Please add the following methods to the `CatalogAdmin` class. The first one is called when the **Delete** button is clicked, and the other is used to get the list of categories that are related to the specified product. Since their functionality is better expressed by the stored procedures they call, we'll discuss more about them when we implement the data tier.

```
#Region " Product Details "
  Public Function RemoveFromCategoryOrDeleteProduct( _
    ByVal productId As String, ByVal categoryId As String)
    ' Create the connection object
    Dim connection As New SqlConnection(connectionString)

    ' Create and initialize the command object
    Dim command As New SqlCommand( _
      "RemoveFromCategoryOrDeleteProduct", connection)
    command.CommandType = CommandType.StoredProcedure

    ' Add an input parameter and supply a value for it
    command.Parameters.Add("@ProductID", SqlDbType.Int, 4)
    command.Parameters("@ProductID").Value = productId

    ' Add an input parameter and supply a value for it
    command.Parameters.Add("@CategoryID", SqlDbType.Int, 4)
    command.Parameters("@CategoryID").Value = categoryId

    ' Open the connection, execute the command and close the connection
    connection.Open()
    command.ExecuteNonQuery()
    connection.Close()
  End Function

  Public Function GetCategoriesForProduct( _
      ByVal productId As String) As SqlDataReader
    ' Create the connection object
    Dim connection As New SqlConnection(connectionString)

    ' Create and initialize the command object
    Dim command As New SqlCommand("GetCategoriesForProduct", connection)
    command.CommandType = CommandType.StoredProcedure

    ' Add an input parameter and supply a value for it
    command.Parameters.Add("@ProductID", SqlDbType.Int, 4)
    command.Parameters("@ProductID").Value = productId

    ' Open the connection
    connection.Open()

    ' Return a SqlDataReader to the calling function
    Return command.ExecuteReader(CommandBehavior.CloseConnection)
  End Function
#End Region
```

Stored Procedures for Product Details Admin

Add the following stored procedures to the WroxJokeShop database:

RemoveFromCategoryOrDeleteProduct

This stored procedure verifies how many categories the product exists in. If it exists in more than one category, it just removes it from the current category (ID received as a parameter). If the product is associated with a single category, it is first removed from the category and then effectively deleted from the database.

```
CREATE PROCEDURE RemoveFromCategoryOrDeleteProduct
(@ProductID int, @CategoryID int)
AS

IF (SELECT COUNT(*) FROM ProductCategory WHERE ProductID=@ProductID)>1
  DELETE FROM ProductCategory
  WHERE CategoryID=@CategoryID AND ProductID=@ProductID
ELSE
 BEGIN
   DELETE FROM ProductCategory WHERE ProductID=@ProductID
   DELETE FROM Product where ProductID=@ProductID
 END

RETURN
```

GetCategoriesForProduct

This stored procedure returns a list of the categories that belong to the specified product. Only their names are returned, since this is the only information we're interested in.

```
CREATE PROCEDURE GetCategoriesForProduct
(@ProductID int)
AS

SELECT Name
FROM Category INNER JOIN ProductCategory
ON Category.CategoryID = ProductCategory.CategoryID
WHERE ProductCategory.ProductID = @ProductID

RETURN
```

Testing the ProductDetailsAdmin Web User Control

Once again, remove the text from the products details section of `CatalogAdminPage` and build. To see if this works, let's just open the details page of a product by clicking on the View button for one product in the `ProductsAdmin` control. We should see something like this:

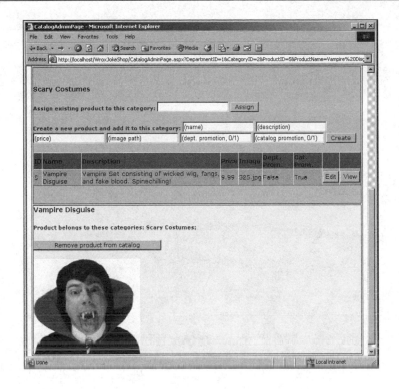

Summary

We've done quite a lot of coding in this chapter. We implemented four user controls, along with their middle-tier methods and stored procedures for the data tier. We learned how to implement a simple authentication scheme so only administrators are allowed to access the catalog administration page.

We made contact with the DataGrid, which is a probably the most powerful control that comes packaged with the .NET Framework. We learned how to use its built-in features for editing, selecting, updating, and deleting records.

We also learned a few techniques about error trapping and handling.

The Shopping Basket

Dear reader, welcome to the second stage of development! This is the stage where we start improving and adding new features to the already existing, fully functional e-commerce site. Because our site is working well and its customers are happy with it, there's no need to rush into changing anything before we know what we want to do.

So, what could we improve about it? Well, the answer to this question isn't that hard to find if we take a quick look at the popular e-commerce sites on the web. They have user personalization and product recommendations, they remember customers' preferences, and boast many other features that make the site easy to remember and hard to leave without first buying something.

Because in the first stage of development we extensively relied on a third party-payment processor (PayPal), and it supplied an integrated shopping basket, we didn't record any shopping cart or order info into the database. Right now, our site isn't capable of displaying a list of "most wanted" products, or any other information about the products that have been sold through the web site, because, at this stage, we don't keep track of the products that we have sold. This makes it impossible to implement any of the improvements listed earlier.

It's obvious that saving order information into the database is our first priority and most of the features we want to implement next rely on having a record of the products we have sold. In order to achieve this functionality, we'll implement a custom shopping basket and a custom checkout.

In this chapter we will implement the custom shopping basket, which will store its data into the local WroxJokeShop database. This will provide us with more flexibility, compared to the PayPal shopping basket over which we have no control and which cannot be saved into our database for further processing and analysis. With the custom shopping basket, when the visitor clicks on the Add to Cart button for a product, a new entry is created in the database and the visitor will be shown a page like this:

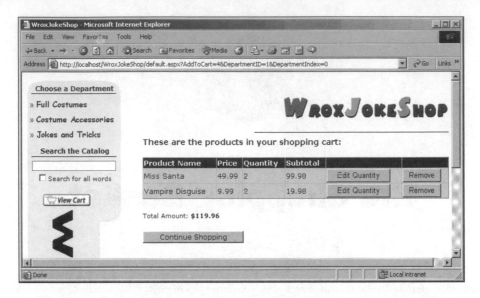

At the end of this chapter we will have a functional shopping basket, but the visitor will not yet have the ability to order the products contained in it. We will take care of this in the next chapter, when we will implement a custom checkout. Simply put, in the next chapter, we will add the Proceed to Checkout button. When the visitor clicks this button, the products in the shopping basket will be saved as a separate order into the database, and the visitor will be redirected to a page where they can pay for them. If you integrated the PayPal shopping cart for the first development stage, starting with the next chapter PayPal will only be used to handle payment, and we will not rely on its shopping cart any more.

Before moving to the details, let's review what we'll do in this chapter:

❑ Talk about how to design our shopping cart

❑ Add a new database table to store shopping cart records

❑ Create the stored procedures that work with the new table

❑ Implement the business layer procedures

❑ Implement the Add to Cart and View Cart buttons; if you implemented them to work with PayPal as explained in the PayPal chapter, here we'll make them work with the new shopping cart instead of the PayPal shopping cart

❑ Implement the custom shopping cart

Designing the Shopping Cart

Before starting to write the code for the shopping cart, let us have an overview of what we're going to do.

First, note that we won't have any personalization features at this stage of the site. We don't care who buys our products, we just want to know what products have been sold, and when. When we add user customization features in the later chapters, our task will be pretty simple: we'll only have to associate each order with one of our registered customers, and eventually ask the visitor to authenticate before proceeding to checkout.

If we required the visitor to log in before adding any products to their shopping cart, we could have associated each added product to the visitor's basket. But this is not an option, since we haven't implemented visitor personalization yet or the required authentication code. Moreover, even if we had that code in place, we wouldn't want to require the visitor to log in before adding products to the cart. For WroxJokeShop we prefer not to force the visitors to supply additional information earlier than necessary, so we'll work with temporary shopping carts.

Having that said, probably the best way to store shopping cart information is to generate a unique cart ID for each shopping cart and save it on the visitor's computer as a cookie. When the visitor clicks on the Add to Cart button, the server first verifies if the cookie exists on the client computer. If it does, we add the specified product to the existing cart. Otherwise, the server generates another cart ID, saves it to the client's cookie, and then adds the product to the newly generated shopping cart.

In the previous chapter, we created the user controls by starting with the presentation layer components. However, this strategy doesn't work here because now we need to do a bit more design work beforehand, so we'll take the more common approach, and start with the database tier.

The Database

Because we have already created tables and stored procedures in the previous chapters, we will not use the *Try it Out* approach again to explain how to create them.

A Place to Store Shopping Cart Items

Since we want to store shopping cart information in the database, we need to create the database structures that allow us to do so. Here we take a look at the database table that will store shopping cart information, and in the data tier section we'll implement the stored procedures that work with this table.

The ShoppingCart Table

We will store all the information from all the shopping carts in a single table named ShoppingCart. Please add this table to your WroxJokeShop database, and then we'll comment upon it:

	Column Name	Data Type	Length	Allow Nulls	
🔑	CartID	varchar	50		
🔑	ProductID	int	4		
	Quantity	int	4		
	DateProductAdded	datetime	8		
▶					

First we have a `CartID` field, which is the unique ID we'll generate for each shopping cart. Note that this is not an integer field like the other ID columns we have created so far. It is a `varchar` field, which will be filled with a GUID string. A GUID (Globally Unique Identifier) is a value guaranteed to be unique across time and space. Two generated GUIDs will never be the same.

We have another field that we expected here: `ProductID`. This one holds the ID of an existing product. Because we want to ensure we don't hold any non-existent products, we'll add a foreign key relationship between the `ShoppingCart` and `Product` tables, and the database will take care of its own integrity.

Note that the primary key is formed of both `CartID` and `ProductID` fields (we have a *composite primary key*). This makes sense, because a particular product can exist only once in a particular shopping cart, so a (`CartID`, `ProductID`) pair shouldn't appear more than once in the table. If the visitor adds a product more than once, we simply increase the `Quantity` value. The relationship is tied between the `ProductID` columns in the `ShoppingCart` and `Product` tables. In the diagram, the relationship will be represented like this:

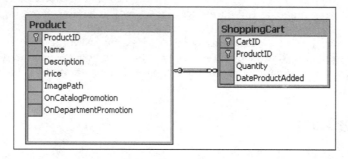

Note that each record in `ShoppingCart` also has a `DateProductAdded` field. This one will be automatically populated with the current date when a new product is added to the cart, and will be useful when we want to delete old records.

Before moving on, please create the `ShoppingCart` table as shown earlier, and then implement the one-to-many relationship (by adding a foreign key constraint) between the `Product` and `ShoppingCart` tables. The steps were explained in Chapter 4, and you might want to re-read some paragraphs in that chapter if you don't exactly remember the steps. Remember that you can also create this table and relationship by running the SQL script provided in the code download for this chapter (`ShoppingCart.sql`).

> *Feel free to use* `smalldatetime` *instead of* `datetime` *for the* `DataProductAdded` *column. This will store the date with less precision, down to minutes, and this is good enough for our purposes.*

The Stored Procedures

Now we'll add the necessary database stored procedures. These perform the basic shopping cart actions:

❑   `AddProductToCart` adds a product to a shopping cart

- ❑ UpdateCartItem modifies a shopping cart record

- ❑ RemoveProductFromCart deletes a record from the ShoppingCart table

- ❑ GetShoppingCartProduct gets the list of products in the specified shopping cart, and is called when we want to show the user their shopping cart

- ❑ GetTotalAmount returns the total cost of the products in the specified product cart

Let's create each of these methods one at a time:

AddProductToCart

AddProductToCart is called when the visitor clicks on the Add to Cart button while browsing the products.

If the specified product already exists in the shopping cart, its quantity should be increased by one; if the product doesn't exist, one unit is added to the shopping cart.

This stored procedure receives a CartID and a ProductID as parameters. This stored procedure needs to add a new record to the ShoppingCart table, or update an existing record if the product has already been added.

So we first search to see if we already have a record for the selected product in the cart. If we find a (CartID, ProductID) pair in the ShoppingCart table, we find out the current product quantity and update it by adding one unit. Otherwise a new record is created in the ShoppingCart table.

```
CREATE Procedure AddProductToCart
(@CartID varchar(50),
 @ProductID int)
As

IF EXISTS
   (SELECT CartID
    FROM ShoppingCart
    WHERE ProductID = @ProductID AND CartID = @CartID)

   BEGIN
      DECLARE @CountItems int

      SELECT @CountItems = ShoppingCart.Quantity
      FROM ShoppingCart
      WHERE ProductID = @ProductID AND CartID = @CartID

      UPDATE ShoppingCart
      SET Quantity = @CountItems + 1
      WHERE ProductID = @ProductID AND CartID = @CartID
   END
ELSE
    INSERT INTO ShoppingCart (CartID, ProductID, Quantity, DateProductAdded)
    VALUES (@CartID, @ProductID, 1, GETDATE())

RETURN
```

Note that we use the GETDATE() system function to retrieve the current date. Note that it's equally possible to set the GETDATE() function as the default value of the DateProductAdded field – this way we wouldn't need to supply a value when adding the new record.

UpdateCartItem

UpdateCartItem is used when we want to update the quantity of an existing shopping cart item. This will be called when editing the product quantity in the shopping cart:

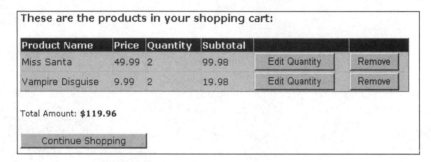

UpdateCartItem is pretty similar to AddProductToCart, except that it receives an additional Quantity parameter that specifies the exact quantity value that should exist in the shopping cart.

UpdateCartItem will mainly be called for products that exist in the database, so we could update the value without checking if there is an existing record. Still, the verification makes the stored procedure more robust and less likely to generate errors if it is accidentally called in a different way from how it was supposed to be.

Also, note that Quantity can be zero. If the visitor modifies the existing quantity of a product to zero, the product is not removed from the shopping cart. This might be helpful if the visitor decides to increase the quantity later. If the visitor wants to remove the product, there is a **Delete** button in the shopping cart, which calls the procedure we'll present next, RemoveProductFromCart.

```
CREATE Procedure UpdateCartItem
(@CartID varchar(50),
 @ProductID int,
 @Quantity int)
As

IF EXISTS
   (SELECT CartID
    FROM ShoppingCart
    WHERE ProductID = @ProductID AND CartID = @CartID)

   BEGIN
      DECLARE @CountItems int

      SELECT @CountItems = Count(ProductID)
      FROM ShoppingCart
      WHERE ProductID = @ProductID AND CartID = @CartID
```

```
        IF @CountItems > 0
            UPDATE ShoppingCart
            SET Quantity = @Quantity
            WHERE ProductID = @ProductID AND CartID = @CartID
    END
ELSE
    INSERT INTO ShoppingCart (CartID, ProductID, Quantity)
    VALUES (@CartID, @ProductID, @Quantity)

RETURN
```

RemoveProductFromCart

Here's the stored procedure that removes a product from the shopping cart. This will happen when the Remove button is clicked for one of the products in the shopping cart.

```
CREATE PROCEDURE RemoveProductFromCart
(@CartID varchar(50),
 @ProductID int)
AS

DELETE FROM ShoppingCart
WHERE CartID = @CartID and ProductID = @ProductID

RETURN
```

GetShoppingCartProducts

In this stored procedure we join the ShoppingCart and Product tables in order to get a list of detailed shopping cart information.

```
CREATE PROCEDURE GetShoppingCartProducts
(@CartID varchar(50))
AS

SELECT Product.ProductID, Product.[Name], Product.[Price], ShoppingCart.Quantity,
Product.[Price]*ShoppingCart.Quantity AS Subtotal
FROM ShoppingCart
INNER JOIN Product
ON ShoppingCart.ProductID = Product.ProductID
WHERE ShoppingCart.CartID = @CartID

RETURN
```

Note that here we use a calculated column, Subtotal, which is calculated as Price*Quantity (Product.[Price]*ShoppingCart.Quantity AS Subtotal). When sending back the results, Subtotal will be seen as a separate column.

GetTotalAmount

GetTotalAmount returns the total value of the products in the shopping cart. This is called when displaying the total amount when viewing the shopping cart.

We have an `@Amount` variable that stores the sum of each product's price times its quantity in the shopping cart. If the cart is empty `@Amount` isn't given any value and is left NULL. In the end, we test this and return 0 if `@Amount` is NULL to avoid a type mismatch error in the business tier.

```
CREATE PROCEDURE GetTotalAmount
(@CartID varchar(50))
AS

DECLARE @Amount money

SELECT @Amount = SUM(Product.[Price]*ShoppingCart.Quantity)
FROM ShoppingCart
INNER JOIN Product
ON ShoppingCart.ProductID = Product.ProductID
WHERE ShoppingCart.CartID = @CartID

IF @Amount IS NULL
     SELECT 0
ELSE
     SELECT @Amount

RETURN
```

This stored procedure returns a value for the business tier using the SELECT statement. As we learned, to get this single value we use the `SqlCommand.ExecuteScalar()` method in the business tier.

The Business Layer

Here we'll need to create the usual methods that call the stored procedures we've just written. For the shopping cart operations, we create a new file in the `BusinessObjects` folder.

Please right-click on the `BusinessObjects` folder and select **Add | Add new Item**. Select **Class** from the **Templates** window, and name it `ShoppingCart.vb`.

Generating Shopping Cart IDs

There are a couple of bits in the `ShoppingCart` class that will be called by all the other methods. One of these is the `connectionString` property, which we already know from the previous chapters. Here we have another property named `shoppingCartId`, which returns the cart ID of the current visitor. It is important to understand how this property works.

When the visitor changes their product cart by adding, removing or changing records, methods of the `ShoppingCart` class will be called. For example, when the visitor clicks on the **Add to Cart** button, a method of the `ShoppingCart` class named `AddProduct` will be called. All the methods of the `ShoppingCart` class receive either no parameters (such as `GetTotalAmount` or `GetProducts`), or one parameter, namely `productId` (`AddProduct`, `UpdateProductQuantity`, `RemoveProduct`). `UpdateProductQuantity` also has a `quantity` parameter.

What I want you to notice is that none of the methods receives a `CartID` parameter, and this might appear strange, since all the stored procedures we have written so far do require a `CartID` parameter. So, you might ask, how does the `AddProduct` method know which `CartID` to send to the `AddProductToCart` stored procedure?

The answer is that the `CartID` is taken care of here, at the business-layer level. We write a `shoppingCartId` read-only property which, when called, returns the `CartID` of the visitor for whom the call has been made. But how do we find out the unique `CartID` of the visitor? Well, the answer lies in the use of cookies. Cookies are client-side pieces of information that are managed by the visitor's browser; they are stored as name-value pairs. Cookies have the advantage of not consuming server resources (as they are managed at the client), and have configurable expiration. This is useful because we can set the shopping cart cookie to expire when the browser session ends (so a new shopping cart is created every time the visitor comes back to our site), or they can be set to exist indefinitely on the client computer.

> *A potential problem with using cookies is that they can be disabled at the client side. As a second choice, instead of using cookies we could use the ASP.NET session state through the* `Session` *object, although by default this uses cookies as part of its inner mechanism too.*

In the `shoppingCartId` property we check if a cookie named `WroxJokeShop_CartID` exists on the visitor's browser. If it does, this means that the visitor already has a shopping cart created, so the value of the cookie is read, and it is used as the `CartID`. If the cookie doesn't exist, we generate a new GUID value, which is stored in the `WroxJokeShop_CartID` cookie. This way, the same GUID is used for all the subsequent calls because it is read from the cookie.

This is the `ShoppingCart.vb` file:

```
Imports System.Data.SqlClient

Private ReadOnly Property shoppingCartId()
  Get
  Dim context As HttpContext = HttpContext.Current

Public Class ShoppingCart
  ' If the WroxJokeShop_CartID cookie doesn't exit
  ' on client machine we create it with a new GUID
  If context.Request.Cookies("WroxJokeShop_CartID") Is Nothing Then
    ' Generate a new GUID
    Dim cartId As Guid = Guid.NewGuid()
    ' Create the cookie and set its value
    Dim cookie As New HttpCookie("WroxJokeShop_CartID", cartId.ToString)
    ' Current Date
    Dim currentDate As DateTime = DateTime.Now()
    ' Set the time span to 10 days
    Dim ts As New TimeSpan(10, 0, 0, 0)
    ' Expiration Date
    Dim expirationDate As DateTime = currentDate.Add(ts)
    ' Set the Expiration Date to the cookie
```

```
      cookie.Expires = expirationDate
      ' Set the cookie on client's browser
      context.Response.Cookies.Add(cookie)
    End If
    ' the value stored in WroxJokeShop_CartID
    ' is returned, as it contains the visitor's cart ID
    Return context.Request.Cookies("WroxJokeShop_CartID").Value
    End Get
End Property

Private ReadOnly Property connectionString() As String
  Get
    Return ConfigurationSettings.AppSettings("ConnectionString")
  End Get
End Property

  '
  ' add the other methods here
  '

End Class
```

If we set an expiration time for the cookie, it becomes a persistent cookie and is saved as a file by the computer's browser. We set our cookie to expire in 10 days, so our visitor's shopping cart exists for ten days from the time it is created. If an expiration date is not specified, the cookie is stored only for the current browser session.

If we want our site to work even with browsers that have cookies disabled, we can store the cart ID in the Session object. The problem is that the ASP.NET session state, by default, works with cookies. In order to make the ASP.NET work without cookies, you first need to open Web.config and make this change:

```
<sessionState
    _ mode="InProc"
    _ stateConnectionString="tcpip=127.0.0.1:42424"
    _ sqlConnectionString="data source=127.0.0.1;use_u32 ?id=sa;password="
    _ cookieless="true"
    _ timeout="20" />
```

Note that by default the cookieless mode is "false", so ASP.NET does use cookies for storing session state. In cookieless mode, an ID for the session state is automatically saved by ASP.NET in the query string:

http://localhost/wroxjokeshop/(vcmq0tz22y2okxzdq1bo2w45)/default.aspx

This looks a bit ugly, but works without using cookies. Once we enable cookieless session state support, we need to replace the old shoppingCartId property with one that works with the Session object instead of cookies:

```
Private ReadOnly Property shoppingCartId()
  Get
    Dim context As HttpContext = HttpContext.Current
```

```
      ' Get the value of WroxJokeShop_CartID session variable
      ' (note that in might be void)
      Dim id As String
      id = context.Session("WroxJokeShop_CartID")
      ' Check to see if WroxJokeShop_CartID exists
      If id = "" Then
        ' Generate a new GUID
        Dim cartId As Guid = Guid.NewGuid()
        ' Store the generated GUID in the session state
        context.Session("WroxJokeShop_CartID") = cartId.ToString
        id = context.Session("WroxJokeShop_CartID")
      End If
      Return id
    End Get
  End Property
```

Implementing the Methods

Since we have the skeleton set up in the `ShoppingCart` class, we can implement the business logic. We'll have five methods, corresponding to the five stored procedures we wrote earlier. Please add the following methods to the `ShoppingCart` class:

```
    Public Function AddProduct(ByVal productId As String)
      ' Create the connection object
      Dim connection As New SqlConnection(connectionString)

      ' Create and initialize the command object
      Dim command As New SqlCommand("AddProductToCart", connection)
      command.CommandType = CommandType.StoredProcedure

      ' Add an input parameter and supply a value for it
      command.Parameters.Add("@CartID", SqlDbType.VarChar, 50)
      command.Parameters("@CartID").Value = shoppingCartId

      ' Add an input parameter and supply a value for it
      command.Parameters.Add("@ProductID", SqlDbType.Int, 4)
      command.Parameters("@ProductID").Value = productId

      ' Open the connection, execute the command and close the connection
      connection.Open()
      command.ExecuteNonQuery()
      connection.Close()
    End Function

    Public Function UpdateProductQuantity(ByVal productId As String, ByVal
        quantity As Integer)
      ' Create the connection object
      Dim connection As New SqlConnection(connectionString)

      ' Create and initialize the command object
      Dim command As New SqlCommand("UpdateCartItem", connection)
      command.CommandType = CommandType.StoredProcedure
```

```
        ' Add an input parameter and supply a value for it
        command.Parameters.Add("@CartID", SqlDbType.VarChar, 50)
        command.Parameters("@CartID").Value = shoppingCartId

        ' Add an input parameter and supply a value for it
        command.Parameters.Add("@ProductID", SqlDbType.Int, 4)
        command.Parameters("@ProductID").Value = productId

        ' Add an input parameter and supply a value for it
        command.Parameters.Add("@Quantity", SqlDbType.Int, 4)
        command.Parameters("@Quantity").Value = quantity

        ' Open the connection, execute the command, and close the connection
        connection.Open()
        command.ExecuteNonQuery()
        connection.Close()
End Function

Public Function RemoveProduct(ByVal productId As String)
        ' Create the connection object
        Dim connection As New SqlConnection(connectionString)

        ' Create and initialize the command object
        Dim command As New SqlCommand("RemoveProductFromCart", connection)
        command.CommandType = CommandType.StoredProcedure

        ' Add an input parameter and supply a value for it
        command.Parameters.Add("@CartID", SqlDbType.VarChar, 50)
        command.Parameters("@CartID").Value = shoppingCartId

        ' Add an input parameter and supply a value for it
        command.Parameters.Add("@ProductID", SqlDbType.Int, 4)
        command.Parameters("@ProductID").Value = productId

        ' Open the connection, execute the command, and close the connection
        connection.Open()
        command.ExecuteNonQuery()
        connection.Close()
End Function

Public Function GetProducts() As SqlDataReader
        ' Create the connection object
        Dim connection As New SqlConnection(connectionString)

        ' Create and initialize the command object
        Dim command As New SqlCommand("GetShoppingCartProducts", connection)
        command.CommandType = CommandType.StoredProcedure

        ' Add an input parameter and supply a value for it
        command.Parameters.Add("@CartID", SqlDbType.VarChar, 50)
        command.Parameters("@CartID").Value = shoppingCartId
```

```
    ' Return the results
    connection.Open()
    Return command.ExecuteReader(CommandBehavior.CloseConnection)
End Function

Public Function GetTotalAmount() As Decimal
    ' Create the connection object
    Dim connection As New SqlConnection(connectionString)

    ' Create and initialize the command object
    Dim command As SqlCommand = New SqlCommand("GetTotalAmount", _
        connection)
    command.CommandType = CommandType.StoredProcedure

    ' Add an input parameter and supply a value for it
    command.Parameters.Add("@CartID", SqlDbType.VarChar, 50)
    command.Parameters("@CartID").Value = shoppingCartId

    ' Save the total amount to a variable
    Dim amount As Decimal
    connection.Open()
    amount = command.ExecuteScalar()

    ' Close the connection
    connection.Close()

    ' Return the amount
    Return amount
End Function
```

We are already familiar with most of the code in each of these methods. The only new thing is the use of the `ExecuteScalar()` method, which is used here for the first time. This is used to get the value returned by the `GetTotalAmount` stored procedure.

Note that usually when using `ExecuteScalar()` we need to use an additional variable to store the resulting value if we want to send this value back to the calling function from the presentation tier. In our code we used the `amount` variable to store the returned amount, then we closed the connection and returned the value stored in the variable:

```
    ' Save the total amount to a variable
    Dim amount As Decimal
    connection.Open()
    amount = command.ExecuteScalar()

    ' Close the connection
    connection.Close()

    ' Return the amount
    Return amount
```

A common mistake is to use the `ExecuteScalar()` method in the same way as we would use `ExecuteNonQuery()`, like this:

```
' Don't try this at home
connection.Open()
Return command.ExecuteScalar()
connection.Close()
```

The problem with this code is that it returns before having the chance to close the database connection. When using `ExecuteScalar()`, always use an intermediary variable if the value needs to be returned to the client.

The User Interface

We'll deal in the rest of this chapter with building the user interface part of the shopping cart. After updating the storefront, we'll have **Add to Cart** buttons for each product, and a **View Cart** button in the left part of the page:

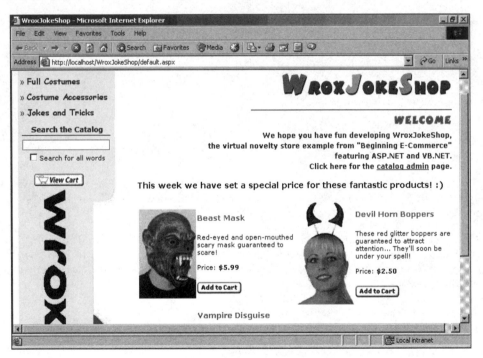

If you added PayPal integration as presented in Chapter 6, you will already have these buttons on your site, and we'll update their functionality here.

When clicking on either **Add to Cart** or **View Cart**, the `ShoppingCart.ascx` web user control (which we'll build a bit later) is loaded into the `pageContentsCell` cell of `default.aspx`. You can see this user control in action in the following screenshot:

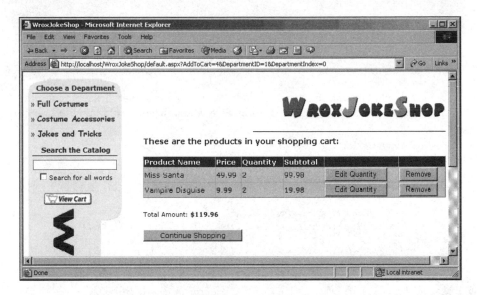

The mechanism for loading the `ShoppingCart.ascx` web control is the same one we have already used in `default.aspx` to load the other controls. When the **Add to Cart** button is clicked we reload `default.aspx` with an additional parameter (**AddToCart**) in the query string:

```
http://localhost/OldWroxJokeShop/default.aspx?AddToCart=10
```

When clicking on **View Cart**, the parameter added to the query string is `ViewCart`.

Before moving on, let's recap the main steps we'll make in order to implement the whole user interface of the shopping cart:

- ❑ Add **Add to Cart** buttons for products
- ❑ Add the **View Cart** button to `default.aspx`
- ❑ Modify the code behind of `default.aspx` to recognize the `AddToCart` and `ViewCart` query string parameters
- ❑ Implement the `ShoppingCart` user control

The Add to Cart Buttons

Here we want to change the code of `ProductsList.ascx`. We want each displayed product to include an **Add to Cart** button with a link like the ones shown a bit earlier (which is a link to `default.aspx` with an additional `AddToCart` parameter in the query string).

If you implemented the PayPal shopping cart, we'll want to change the **Add to Cart** buttons to link to our web site instead of PayPal. Open `ProductsList.ascx` in the **HTML View** and locate the following code, which you'll need to change.

277

```
<form target="PayPal" action="https://www.paypal.com/cgi-bin/webscr"
   method="post">
  <!-- the PayPal form here-->
</form>
```

Whether you used PayPal or not, the resulting code should be the same. Please update the HTML of your ProductsList.ascx as shown in the following. The new code is highlighted:

```
<TD vAlign="middle" width="200">
  <span class="ProductName">
    <%# DataBinder.Eval(Container.DataItem, "Name") %>
  </span>
  <br><br>
  <span class="ProductDescription">
    <%# DataBinder.Eval(Container.DataItem, "Description") %>
    <br><br>
    Price: </span><span class="ProductPrice">
    <%# DataBinder.Eval(Container.DataItem, "Price",  "{0:c}") %>
  </span>
  <br><br>
  <a href='default.aspx?AddToCart=<%# DataBinder.Eval(Container.DataItem,
      "ProductID") %>&amp;<%# Request.QueryString%>'>
  <img src="Images/AddToCart.gif" border="0"> </a>
</TD>
```

With this piece of code we create a link to default.aspx where we add the AddToCart parameter to the original query string. After making this change, please execute the page to make sure the buttons appear OK:

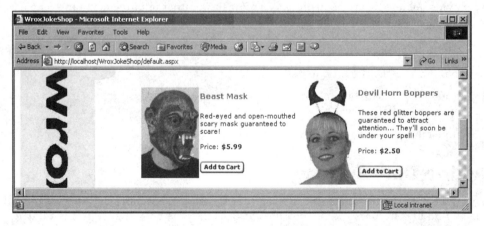

Now browse to your favorite department and click on the **Add to Cart** button. You'll see that default.aspx is reloaded with the additional AddToCart parameter appended at the beginning of the query string:

http://localhost/default.aspx?AddToCart=18&DepartmentID=2&DepartmentIndex=1

The value of the AddToCart parameter is the ID of the product that we want to add to the cart.

Note that we also keep the rest of the query string parameters. These will be useful when we implement the **Continue Shopping** button with the ShoppingCart.ascx control. When the **Continue Shopping** button is clicked, we simply need to remove the AddToCart parameter from the query string and the visitor will be forwarded to the page they were on before they pressed the **Add to Cart** button.

Note that right now clicking on the **Add to Cart** buttons has no effect. We'll change the Form_Load method in default.aspx.vb to recognize the AddToCart parameter a bit later, after we create (or update, if it is working with PayPal) the **View Cart** button.

The View Cart Button

Now we want to take care of the **View Cart** button.

When the ViewCart button is clicked, we'll want to add the ViewCart parameter to the query string, in the same style we did with for the **Add to Cart** buttons.

If you had a PayPal shopping cart, locate the following code in default.aspx, because we'll change it here:

```
<form name="_xclick" target="paypal"
    action="https://www.paypal.com/cgi-bin/webscr" method="post">
  <!-- the PayPal form here-->
</form>
```

Instead of this code, we want to have an ImageButton control. No matter if you used PayPal or not, the resulting HTML code in default.aspx should look like this:

```
<table height="100%" cellSpacing="0" cellPadding="0" width="100%"
    background="Images/backgr.gif">
  <tr>
  <td vAlign="top" height="100%">
    <uc1:departmentslist id="DepartmentsList1" runat="server">
    </uc1:departmentslist>
    <uc1:searchbox id="SearchBox1" runat="server">
    </uc1:searchbox>
  </td>
  </tr>
  <tr>
  <td><br>
            
    <asp:imagebutton id="viewCartButton" runat="server"
        ImageUrl="Images/ViewCart.gif">
    </asp:imagebutton>
  </td>
  </tr>
  <tr>
  <td>
    <IMG height="369" src="Images/wrox.jpg" width="197" border="0">
  </td>
  </tr>
</table>
```

Now switch to design view and double-click on the button to generate the `Click` event handler. Please add the following code to it:

```
Private Sub viewCartButton_Click(ByVal sender As System.Object, _
    ByVal e As System.Web.UI.ImageClickEventArgs) Handles
    viewCartButton.Click
    Response.Redirect("default.aspx?ViewCart=1&" &
        Request.QueryString.ToString)
End Sub
```

Here we simply add the `ViewCart` parameter to the existing query string with a predefined value. We actually don't care what that value is; the simple presence of the `ViewCart` parameter will instruct `default.aspx` to load the shopping cart without adding any additional products to it (in the same way that it does when the `AddToCart` parameter shows up).

Modifying default.aspx to Load ShoppingCart

We didn't create the `ShoppingCart.ascx` user control, but we know where it will be placed and the mechanism to load it. We'll create the control a bit later, but for now let's finish our work with `default.aspx`.

Please open the `Page_Load` method in `default.aspx.vb` now. We want it to load `ShoppingCart.ascx` in the `pageContentsCell` when the `AddToCart` or `ViewCart` parameters are found in the query string.

```
Private Sub Page_Load(ByVal sender As System.Object, ByVal e As
    System.EventArgs) Handles MyBase.Load
  ' Save DepartmentID from the query string to a variable
  Dim departmentId As String = Request.Params("DepartmentID")

  ' Save the search string from the query string to a variable
  Dim searchString As String = Request.Params("Search")

  ' Save the product id from the query string to a variable
  Dim addToCartProductID As String = Request.Params("AddToCart")

  ' We need to find out if the ViewCart parameter has been supplied
  Dim viewCart As String = Request.Params("ViewCart")

  If Not viewCart Is Nothing Or Not addToCartProductID Is Nothing Then
    ' we display the shopping cart
    Dim control As Control
    control = Page.LoadControl("UserControls/ShoppingCart.ascx")
    pageContentsCell.Controls.Add(control)
  ElseIf Not searchString Is Nothing Then
    ' if we're searching the catalog ...
    Dim control As Control
    control = Page.LoadControl("UserControls/SearchResults.ascx")
    pageContentsCell.Controls.Add(control)
  ElseIf Not departmentId Is Nothing Then
```

```
      ' if we're browsing a department or category ...
      Dim control As Control
      control = Page.LoadControl("UserControls/Department.ascx")
      pageContentsCell.Controls.Add(control)
   Else
      ' if we're on the main page ...
      Dim control As Control
      control = Page.LoadControl("UserControls/FirstPageContents.ascx")
      pageContentsCell.Controls.Add(control)
   End If
End Sub
```

Creating the ShoppingCart Web User Control

Right now, clicking on the View Cart or Add to Cart button will generate an exception because the ShoppingCart.ascx is the user control that displays the visitor's shopping cart. Since there are more steps required to create it, let's create this, step by step, in the following exercise.

Try It Out – Creating ShoppingCart.ascx

1. Create a new web user control named ShoppingCart.ascx in the UserControls folder.

2. Add three labels, one DataGrid, and one button to the control, as shown in the following screenshot:

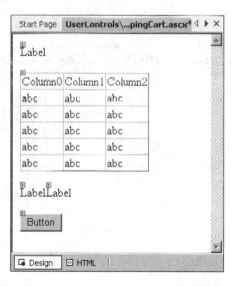

3. Now modify the properties for each control as shown in the following table:

Control Type	ID Property	Text Property	CssClass Property
Label	(doesn't matter)	These are the products in your shopping cart:	ListDescription
DataGrid	grid		
Label	(doesn't matter)	Total Amount:	ProductDescription
Label	totalAmountLabel	(should be void)	ProductPrice
Button	continueShoppingButton	Continue Shopping	AdminButtonText

Note that for this grid we reused some styles that we created in the previous chapters. This is not really professional since the styles' names aren't suited for these controls and changing the style for one page results in the look of this control being changed as well. For a product-quality solution we would prefer to create another set of styles. However, for the purpose of this chapter we prefer to focus on the more important aspects of the control.

4. Select the DataGrid and click on the Property Builder link, situated in the lower part of the Properties Window.

5. Select Columns from the menu on the left. There unselect the Create Columns automatically at runtime checkbox. Then add six fields and set their properties as shown in the following table:

Column Type	Header Text	Data Field	Other Properties
Bound Column	Product Name	Name	Read Only
Bound Column	Price	Price	Read Only
Bound Column	Quantity	Quantity	
Bound Column	Subtotal	Subtotal	Read Only
Edit, Update, Cancel			Change Button type to PushButton and Edit Text to Edit Quantity.
Delete			Change Button type to PushButton and Text to Remove

6. Let's play a bit with the colors now. Click Format on the left menu and Header in the Objects list. Then set its appearance properties as in the following picture:

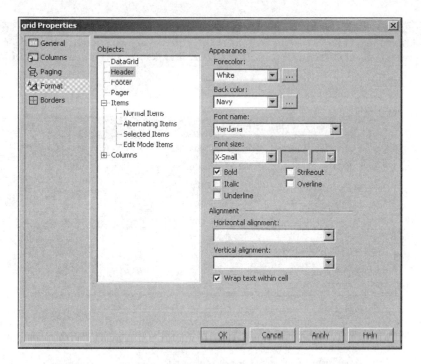

7. Now change the look for the Normal Items template:

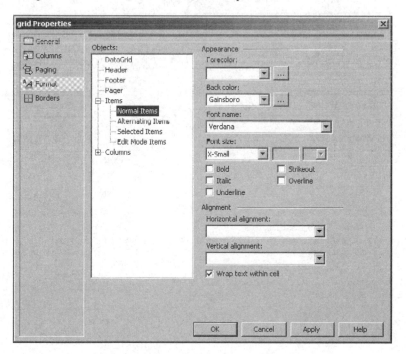

8. Right, now press **OK** to exit the **Property Builder** window. Select the `DataGrid` and set its **Width** property to 100%. This will make the grid fit very nicely onto the page, even when it is resized. Right now the `ShoppingCart` control looks like this when viewed in **Design** View:

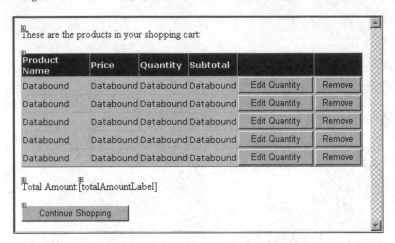

9. The visual part is now ready. Let's start writing the code behind with the `Page_Load` method and its two helper methods:

```vb
Private Sub Page_Load(ByVal sender As System.Object, ByVal e As
    System.EventArgs) Handles MyBase.Load
  If Not Page.IsPostBack Then
    Dim productID As String = Request.Params("AddToCart")

    ' If we receive an AddToCart parameter in the query string, this
    ' is the ID of the product for which the Add to Cart button
    ' was clicked
    If Not productID Is Nothing Then
      Dim cart As New ShoppingCart()
      cart.AddProduct(productID)
    End If

    ' Update the data grid
    BindShoppingCart()
  End If
End Sub

Private Sub BindShoppingCart()
  ' Populate the data grid and set its DataKey field
  Dim cart As New ShoppingCart()
  grid.DataSource = cart.GetProducts
  grid.DataKeyField = "ProductID"
  grid.DataBind()

  ' Set the total amount label using the Currency format
  totalAmountLabel.Text = String.Format("{0:c}", cart.GetTotalAmount())
End Sub
```

How It Works

You can now run the project and test the **Add to Cart** and **View Cart** buttons. The shopping cart is not yet fully functional, in that its **Continue Shopping** button doesn't work, and also the grid's **Remove** and **Edit Quantity** buttons don't work either.

Still, we have laid down the basis of the `ShoppingCart` user control. The user interface is in its final form. For the labels we have reused some styles we created earlier in this book, and we have played a little bit with the `DataGrid`'s colors.

In `Form_Load`, we first test if there is an `AddToCart` parameter in the query string. If there is, we use the `AddProduct` method of the `ShoppingCart` class to add the specified product to the cart:

```
If Not Page.IsPostBack Then
  Dim productID As String = Request.Params("AddToCart")

  ' If we receive an AddToCart parameter in the query string, this
  ' is the ID of the product for which the Add to Cart button
  ' was clicked
  If Not productID Is Nothing Then
    Dim cart As New ShoppingCart()
    cart.AddProduct(productID)
  End If
```

Then, there is a call to `BindShoppingCart`, which takes care of populating the `DataGrid` and the `totalAmountLabel`. In `BindShoppingCart`, we also set the `DataKeyField` to `ProductID`, which will instruct the grid to remember the `ProductID` for each row in the grid. This will help us later when we need to update grid information (remove products or edit quantities).

The text for `totalAmountLabel` is returned from the `ShoppingCart.GetTotalAmount` function, and is presented using the currency format.

```
' Set the total amount label using the Currency format
totalAmountLabel.Text = String.Format("{0:c}", cart.GetTotalAmount())
```

Remember, we used the same `{0:c}` string formatter in the `ProductsList.ascx` control to correctly show the product prices. The letter `c` is used to specify the display mode, and the `0` part specifies that we're applying the selected format for the first parameter – this being `cart.GetTotalAmount`.

Additionally, when we created `ProductsList.ascx`, we set the culture information to `en-US` in `Web.config`, to make sure the product prices are always written with the US format, no matter what the default computer configuration is.

Adding 'Continue Shopping' Functionality

We have the **Continue Shopping** button, but at this point it doesn't do much. While in **Design** View, double-click on the **Continue Shopping** button. This will automatically create the `continueShoppingButton_Click` event handler. Please modify it like this:

```vbnet
Private Sub continueShoppingButton_Click(ByVal sender As System.Object, _
    ByVal e As System.EventArgs) Handles continueShoppingButton.Click
  ' This will contain the original location but without
  ' the AddToCart and ViewCart parameters
  Dim redirectPage As String

  ' For a start we initialize it with the location of default.aspx
  redirectPage = Request.Url.AbsolutePath + "?"

  Try
    ' We redirect to the original page by removing the
    ' AddToCart or ViewCart bits from the query string
    Dim query As System.Collections.Specialized.NameValueCollection
    query = Request.QueryString

    ' Will hold the name of each query string parameter
    Dim paramName As String

    ' Will host the value of each query string parameter
    Dim paramValue As String

    ' Used to parse the query string
    Dim i As Integer

    For i = 0 To query.Count - 1
      ' We guard against null (Nothing) parameters
      If Not query.AllKeys(i) Is Nothing Then
        ' Get the parameter name
        paramName = query.AllKeys(i).ToString()

        ' Test to see if the parameter is not AddToCart or ViewCart
        If paramName.ToUpper <> "ADDTOCART" And paramName.ToUpper <>
            "VIEWCART" Then
          ' Get the value of the parameter
          paramValue = query.Item(i)

          ' Append the parameter to the page
          redirectPage = redirectPage + paramName + "=" + paramValue + "&"
        End If
      End If
    Next
  Catch ex As Exception
    ' If something goes wrong we redirect to the main page
    redirectPage = "default.aspx"
  End Try

  Response.Redirect(redirectPage)

End Sub
```

This method might seem a bit scary at first, but actually it's very simple, provided we know a couple of details about the how the query string is stored inside the Request object.

What this method does is remove the `AddToCart` and `ViewCart` parameters from the query string. The straightforward solution would be to take the query string and do textual searches for the elements we want to remove. Still, a much more powerful and flexible solution is to check the elements of the query string one by one from the parameters collection, and include only the ones different from `AddToCart` and `ViewCart`. Let's analyze the code and see how this is done.

Let's analyze the code from the beginning. First we declare the `redirectPage` variable that is initialized to contain a reference to the `default.aspx` page. This is done using the `Request.Url.AbsolutePath` property that returns the location of the original page, but without the query string. This is just what we need, because we want to separately add the query string parameters.

```
' This will contain the original location but without
' the AddToCart and ViewCart parameters
Dim redirectPage As String

' For a start we initialize it with the location of default.aspx
redirectPage = Request.Url.AbsolutePath + "?"
```

Then we make use of the `Request.QueryString` parameter, which is a `NameValueCollection`. Because we didn't import the `System.Collections.Specialized` namespace at the beginning of the file, we needed to specify the fully qualified name for the class when declaring the query object:

```
' We redirect to the original page by removing the
' AddToCart or ViewCart bits from the query string
Dim query As System.Collections.Specialized.NameValueCollection
query = Request.QueryString
```

`NameValueCollection` objects are built to contain a list of key value pairs. The `Request.QueryString` parameter returns exactly the collection of query string parameters we need to parse.

We parse the elements in the `query` object using a `For` loop:

```
For i = 0 To query.Count - 1
```

In the `For` loop there are a few things we need to do. First, we check that the current pair is not null (`Nothing`). This can happen when the query string ends with a `&` sign, resulting in a pair with no key and value:

```
For i = 0 To query.Count - 1
    ' We guard agains null (Nothing) parameters
    If Not query.AllKeys(i) Is Nothing Then
```

We obtain the key name (parameter name) of a specific element in the query object using `query.AllKeys(i)`, and the value of that key using `query.Item(i)`.

First we test if the parameter name is different from `AddToCart` and `ViewCart` (using `ToUpper`, so we avoid other forms of these words as well). If it's different, we add it to `redirectPage`:

```
    For i = 0 To query.Count - 1
      ' We guard agains null (Nothing) parameters
      If Not query.AllKeys(i) Is Nothing Then
        ' Get the parameter name
        paramName = query.AllKeys(i).ToString()

        ' Test to see if the parameter is not AddToCart or ViewCart
        If paramName.ToUpper <> "ADDTOCART" And paramName.ToUpper <>
           "VIEWCART" Then
          ' Get the value of the parameter
          paramValue = query.Item(i)

          ' Append the parameter to the page
          redirectPage = redirectPage + paramName + "=" + paramValue + "&"
        End If
      End If
    Next
```

We have put the logic into a `Try` block. If an error happens (although it shouldn't because we did proper checking), `redirectPage` is automatically reset to `default.aspx`.

```
    Catch ex As Exception
      ' If something goes wrong we redirect to the main page
      redirectPage = Request.Url.AbsolutePath
    End Try
```

At the end, we redirect to the page contained in `redirectPage`:

```
    Response.Redirect(redirectPage)
```

Allowing the Visitor to Change the Quantity

We have already touched on the edit features of the `DataGrid` when we created the administration part of the catalog in the previous chapter. We'll apply what we learned there for the shopping cart grid by adding event handlers for the events generated by the grid.

Remember that Visual Studio can help us by automatically generating the event handler signature. For this we need to select, in the first combo box situated at the top of the code editor (while we're in the code-behind file for `ShoppingCart.ascx`), the control for which we want the method signature generated:

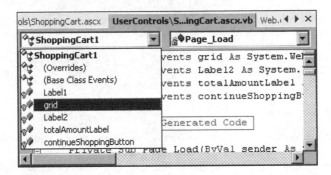

Then we open the second combo box and choose the event that we want to handle:

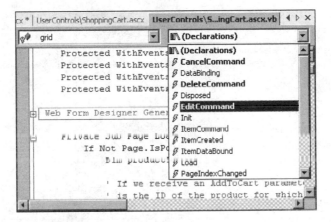

Please generate event handlers for `EditCommand`, `CancelCommand`, `UpdateCommand`, and `DeleteCommand`. Now let's fill each of them with code.

EditCommand

This one puts the grid into edit mode. Note that only the `DataGrid` fields that haven't been marked as read-only are editable.

```
Private Sub shoppingCartGrid_EditCommand(ByVal source As Object, ByVal e _
    As System.Web.UI.WebControls.DataGridCommandEventArgs) Handles _
    grid.EditCommand
    ' we enter edit mode, and then "select" the item and display
    ' its categories
    grid.EditItemIndex = e.Item.ItemIndex
    BindShoppingCart()
End Sub
```

CancelCommand

When the grid is in edit mode and the Cancel button is pressed, the `CancelCommand` event is generated. Here we set `EditItemIndex` to `-1`, which cancels the edit mode.

```
Private Sub shoppingCartGrid_CancelCommand(ByVal source As Object, ByVal e _
    As System.Web.UI.WebControls.DataGridCommandEventArgs) Handles _
    grid.CancelCommand
  grid.EditItemIndex = -1
  BindShoppingCart()
End Sub
```

UpdateCommand

UpdateCommand comes into action when the grid is in edit mode and the **Update** button is clicked. We update the shopping cart by sending the new product quantity to the UpdateProductQuantity method of the ShoppingCart class. We read the DataKeys property to find out the ProductID of the product being edited.

```
Private Sub shoppingCartGrid_UpdateCommand(ByVal source As Object, ByVal e _
    As System.Web.UI.WebControls.DataGridCommandEventArgs) Handles _
    grid.UpdateCommand
  Dim productId As String = grid.DataKeys(e.Item.ItemIndex)
  Dim quantity As String = CType(e.Item.Cells(2).Controls(0),
      TextBox).Text

  Try
    Dim cart As New ShoppingCart()
    cart.UpdateProductQuantity(productId, quantity)
  Catch
    ' If the update generates an error, here is the place
    ' we should warn the reader about it, eventually by
    ' setting the text of an error label
  Finally
    grid.EditItemIndex = -1
    BindShoppingCart()
  End Try
End Sub
```

Because the UpdateCommand is susceptible to generating errors (it's very easy to type a string instead of a number in the **Quantity** box, for example), we implement a simple error trapping mechanism. Here, in the case of an error, we simply update the grid with data, but as we saw in the previous chapter, we can use a label control to inform the visitor of the error.

DeleteCommand

This is triggered when the **Remove** button is clicked. We use the ShoppingCart.RemoveProduct method.

```
Private Sub shoppingCartGrid_DeleteCommand(ByVal source As Object, ByVal e _
    As System.Web.UI.WebControls.DataGridCommandEventArgs) Handles _
    grid.DeleteCommand
  Dim productId As String
  productId = grid.DataKeys(e.Item.ItemIndex)

  Dim cart As New ShoppingCart()
  cart.RemoveProduct(productId)
  BindShoppingCart()
End Sub
```

Testing the Shopping Cart

We just finished the code for this chapter, and it's time to play with it and make sure everything works as expected. You might especially want to test the new data grid functionality that we just implemented. When the grid enters into edit mode, only the quantity is editable, because we set the other fields as read-only when creating the grid.

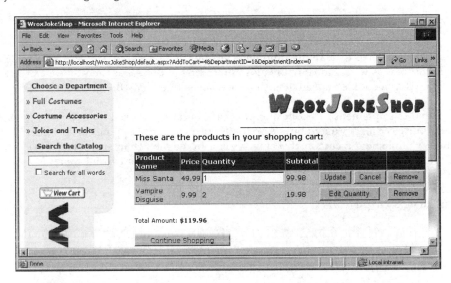

You can now play around with testing here – adding products to the shopping cart, changing the quantity, and removing items.

The Next Steps

There are two more things we need to take into account now that we have finished writing the shopping cart.

The first one is related to the catalog administration part. Remember that while administering the catalog we have the capability to delete products from the catalog. This is done using the `RemoveFromCategoryOrDeleteProduct` stored procedure.

In that procedure, the code which removes the product is as follows:

```
DELETE FROM ProductCategory WHERE ProductID=@ProductID
DELETE FROM Product where ProductID=@ProductID
```

If we wanted to delete a product, we first needed to remove all its instances in the `ProductCategory` table – otherwise the database wouldn't let us remove the product because it would break the referential integrity.

Now the problem reappears with the `ShoppingCart` table. Because we have placed a foreign key relationship on the `ProductID` column, between the `ShoppingCart` and `Product` tables, if the product exists in a shopping cart somewhere it can't be removed from the database. An attempt to do so will result in a runtime exception.

The solution is to update the `RemoveFromCategoryOrDeleteProduct` stored procedure to also remove all the references to the product from the `ShoppingCart` table before attempting to delete it from the database.

This task should be a piece of cake to you right now, so I'm leaving this to you as an exercise.

Summary

In this chapter we learned to store the shopping cart information in the database, and we learned a few things in the process as well. Probably the most interesting of these was the way we can store the shopping cart ID as a cookie on the client, since we haven't done anything similar so far in this book.

We also wanted to implement a custom shopping cart, because we need a way to control and analyze the products our customers want to buy. Also, building a custom shopping cart is a requirement if we want to further implement a custom checkout system. In the next chapter we'll add a "Place Order" button to the shopping cart, which will allow us to save the shopping cart information as a separate order in the database.

See you in the next chapter!

Dealing with Customer Orders

The good news is that our brand-new shopping cart looks good and is fully functional. The bad news is that it doesn't allow the visitor to actually place an order, making it totally useless in the context of a production system.

As you have probably already guessed, we'll deal with that problem in this chapter, in two separate stages. In the first part of the chapter we will implement the client-side part of the order placing mechanism. More precisely, we will add a Place Order button onto the shopping cart control, which will allow the visitor to order the products in the shopping cart.

In the second part of the chapter we'll implement a simple orders administration page where the site administrator can view and handle pending orders.

The code for each part of the site will be presented in the usual way, starting with the database layer, continuing with the business layer, and finishing with the user interface.

Implementing an Order Placing System

The whole order placing system is related to the Place Order button we mentioned earlier. Let's see how this button will look after we update the ShoppingCart control in this chapter:

Product Name	Price	Quantity	Subtotal		
Miss Santa	49.99	2	99.98	Edit Quantity	Remove
Vampire Disguise	9.99	2	19.98	Edit Quantity	Remove

These are the products in your shopping cart:

Total amount: **$119.96**   Place Order

Continue Shopping

Looking at the picture, the button looks quite boring for something that we can easily say is the centre of this chapter's universe. Still, there is a lot of logic hidden behind it, so let's talk about what we want to happen when that button is clicked by the customer. Remember that at this stage we don't care who places the order, but we do want to store information in the database about the products that have been sold.

Basically, two things need to happen when the customer clicks the Place Order button:

❑ First, the order must be stored somewhere in the database. This means that we must save the shopping cart's products to an order named WroxJokeShop Order *nnn* and clear the shopping cart.

❑ Secondly, we redirect the customer to a PayPal payment page where the customer pays the necessary amount for the order.

For the second development stage of the book we still don't process payments ourselves, but use a third-party payment processor instead. Note that at this stage we no longer need the PayPal shopping cart since we implemented our own in the previous chapter. Instead, as we'll see, we'll use the Single Item Purchases option of PayPal, which redirects the visitor directly to a payment page.

A problem that arises when using a third-party payment processor is that the customer can change their mind and cancel the order while at the checkout page. This can result in orders that are saved to the database (the order is saved *before* the page is redirected to the payment page), but for which payment wasn't completed.

This makes it obvious that we need a payment confirmation system, along with a database structure able to store status information about each order.

The confirmation system that we'll implement is quite simple. Every payment processor, including PayPal, can be instructed to send a confirmation message after a payment has been processed. We'll allow the site administrator to manually check, in the administration page, which orders have been paid for. These orders will be known as **verified orders**. We'll see later in this chapter how to manage them in the orders management part of the site.

Now that we have an idea of what we want to do with that Place Order button, the next major concerns are *what* order information to store in the database and *how* to store it. As we saw in the past, deciding how to store information helps us have a better idea of how the whole system works.

Storing Orders in the Database

So what is there about an order that needs to be stored? After some analysis we see that there are two kinds of information that need to be stored:

❑ Firstly, there are general details about the order: the date the order was created, whether and when the products have been shipped, whether the order is verified, completed, or canceled, and a few other details.

❑ Secondly, for each order we need to store the products that belong to that order and their quantities.

In the order administration page that we'll create later in this chapter, we'll be able to see the general order information in a table like this:

Order ID	Date Created	Date Shipped	Verified	Completed	Canceled	Customer	
6	11/4/2002 3:24:00 PM	11/4/2002 3:32:00 PM	True	True	False		View Details
5	11/4/2002 2:14:00 PM		True	False	False		View Details
4	11/4/2002 2:00:00 PM		True	False	True		View Details
3	11/3/2002 4:50:00 PM	11/4/2002 3:41:00 PM	True	True	False		View Details
2	11/2/2002 6:24:00 PM		True	False	False		View Details
1	11/2/2002 6:20:00 PM	11/4/2002 3:43:00 PM	True	True	False		View Details

When an order is selected we can see its details:

Product ID	Product Name	Quantity	Unit Cost	Subtotal
2	Cleopatra Kit	1	14.99	14.99
4	Miss Santa	1	49.99	49.99

We'll have two data tables in the database that will store our order information. The first one is Orders, which stores general order information, and the second one is OrderDetail, which stores the order's products. The tables in the screenshots above don't display all the information that is stored in the Orders and OrderDetail tables, so let's have a look at these tables.

The Tables

Due to the nature of the information we want to store, we need two data tables: Orders and OrderDetail. The Orders table will store information regarding the order as a whole, while OrderDetail contains the products that belong to each order.

So far we have been consistent about naming our tables in singular form (ShoppingCart, Department and so on). However, here we make an exception for the Orders table. Because ORDER is an SQL keyword, we can't use it as a name unless written with square brackets, like this: [Order]. For the purposes of this book, we prefer to break the naming convention to avoid any confusion while writing the SQL code, and generally speaking, it is not good practice to use keywords as names.

These tables have a one-to-many relationship between their OrderID fields. One-to-many is the usual relationship implemented between an Orders table and an OrderDetail table. The OrderDetail table contains *many* records that belong to *one* order. You might want to revisit Chapter 4 where the table relationships are explained in more detail.

Now let's implement the tables in the following *Try It Out* exercise.

Try It Out – Adding the Orders and the OrderDetail tables to the database

1. First add the Orders table to the database, as shown in the following figure.

Column Name	Data Type	Length	Allow Nulls
OrderID	int	4	
DateCreated	smalldatetime	4	
DateShipped	smalldatetime	4	✓
Verified	bit	1	
Completed	bit	1	
Canceled	bit	1	
Comments	varchar	200	✓
CustomerName	varchar	50	✓
ShippingAddress	varchar	200	✓
CustomerEmail	varchar	50	✓

2. Next, please add the `OrderDetail` table:

Column Name	Data Type	Length	Allow Nulls
OrderID	int	4	
ProductID	int	4	
ProductName	varchar	50	
Quantity	int	4	
UnitCost	money	8	

3. Please implement the one-to-many relationship between the tables by creating a foreign key relationship on the `OrderID` column. Remember that if you created the tables directly in the diagram, you can create the relationship by dragging the `OrderID` column from one of the tables to the other table. The table where `OrderID` is the whole primary key (`Orders` in this case) will be:

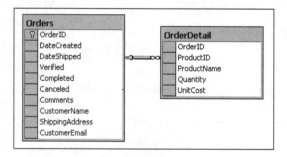

4. After adding the tables containing the shown fields, let's take care of a few details that are in the diagram diagrams. First, in the `Orders` table, please make the `OrderID` column an `Identity` column with both `Identity Seed` and `Identity Increment` set to **1**.

Remember that making a column an identity column tells the database to automatically generate value for it when new records are added to the table. We aren't allowed to supply our own values for that field when adding new records. As seen in a previous chapter, the ID generated value can be found by reading the `@@Identity` system value. We'll use this when creating the `CreateOrder` stored procedure a bit later.

5. Next, please set the default value for the three bit fields (`Verified`, `Completed`, and `Canceled`) in the `Orders` table to **0**.

How It Works – The Data Tables

Now that we have created the tables, let's take a closer look at they way they are designed.

The Orders Table

The Orders table basically contains two categories of information: data about the order itself (the first seven fields), and data about the customer that made the order (last three fields).

An alternative would be to store the customer information in a separate table named Customer and store only the customer ID in the Orders table. However, storing customer data is not one of the goals of this development stage. At this stage we prefer to keep things simple because we don't really care who made the order, we only want to know what products have been sold. This will allow us to focus better on the task at hand. We will seriously deal with creating a separate Customer table in Chapter 10.

Third-party payment processors like PayPal store and manage the complete customer information, so it doesn't need to be stored in our database as well. We have added the CustomerName, ShippingAddress, and CustomerEmail fields as optional fields that can be filled by the administrator if it makes their job easier to have this information at hand for certain (or all) orders.

Now let's take a look at the other fields. We have the necessary OrderID column, which is also the primary key of the table. The other required field (that doesn't allow null values) is DateCreated. We really want to know the date when each order was created. Note that in this implementation we'll have to manually supply a value for the DateCreated field, but keep in mind that we can supply a function as the default value for it (and that function would be getdate(), which returns the current date).

Apart from OrderID and DateCreated there are three bit fields that show the status of the order: Verified, Completed, and Canceled. These fields will store 0 for No and 1 for Yes. Note that instead of having more bit fields, we could have a single Status field, which would contain the order status coded as an integer value, for example 1 for Processing, 2 for Completed, 3 for Canceled, and so on.

The Verified field will be set to 1 after the payment has been confirmed by PayPal. The site administrator will do this, upon receipt of the payment confirmation mail. After the payment is confirmed (and the order is verified), the products are shipped, so the DateShipped field is populated and the Completed bit is set to 1.

The administrator may want to mark an order as canceled (by setting the Canceled bit to 1) if it hasn't been verified in a certain amount of time, or for other various reasons. The Comments field will be used to record whatever special information might show up about the order.

The OrderDetail Table

Let's see now what information the OrderDetail table contains. Take a look at the following screenshot to see what some typical OrderDetail records look like:

OrderID	ProductID	ProductName	Quantity	UnitCost
1	7	Devil Horn Boppers	1	2.5
2	4	Miss Santa	1	49.99
3	2	Cleopatra Kit	1	14.99
3	4	Miss Santa	1	49.99
4	4	Miss Santa	2	49.99
4	5	Vampire Disguise	2	9.99
5	5	Vampire Disguise	1	9.99
6	3	Horned Devil Mask	1	5.99

Each record in `OrderDetail` represents an ordered product that belongs to the order specified by `OrderID`. The primary key is formed by both `OrderID` and `ProductID` because a particular product can be ordered only once in one order. There is a `Quantity` field that contains the number of ordered items, so it wouldn't make any sense to have one `ProductID` recorded more than once for one order.

You might be wondering why we record both the product ID and the price and product name in the `OrderDetail` table. If we have the product ID, we can get the all of the product's details from the `Product` table without having any duplicated information, so the question is valid.

We chose to duplicate the product data in the `OrderDetail` table to guard against product information changes. The name of the product can be slightly modified by the site administrators, and also the price. We do store the `ProductID` because this is the only programmatic way to link back to the original product info, but we also make a copy of the product's price and name to have them just the way they were when the order was made.

The Stored Procedures

At this stage we only need two stored procedures. The most important is `CreateOrder`, which takes the products from a shopping cart and creates an order with them. The other procedure we create is `EmptyShoppingCart`, which empties the visitor's cart after the order has been placed.

We start with `EmptyShoppingCart`, since this is called from `CreateOrder`.

EmptyShoppingCart

This isn't the most interesting stored procedure we have ever written, but nevertheless it is quite important for our store. The customer expects the shopping cart to be empty after buying the products. Here's the stored procedure:

```
CREATE PROCEDURE EmptyShoppingCart
(@CartID varchar(50))
AS

DELETE FROM ShoppingCart
WHERE CartID = @CartID

RETURN
```

CreateOrder

The heart of the order placing mechanism consists of the `CreateOrder` stored procedure. This gets called when the customer decides that they want to buy the products in the shopping cart and presses the **Place Order** button.

The role of `CreateOrder` is to create a new order based on the products in the customer's shopping cart. This implies adding a new record to the `Orders` table and a number of records (one record for each product) in the `OrderDetail` table.

Please create the `CreateOrder` stored procedure in the WroxJokeShop database, and then we'll talk a bit more about it.

```
DECLARE @OrderID int
INSERT INTO Orders (DateCreated, Verified, Completed, Canceled)
VALUES (GETDATE(), 0, 0, 0)
SET @OrderID = @@IDENTITY

INSERT INTO OrderDetail
     (OrderID, ProductID, ProductName, Quantity, UnitCost)
SELECT
     @OrderID, Product.ProductID, Product.[Name],
     ShoppingCart.Quantity, Product.Price
FROM Product JOIN ShoppingCart
ON Product.ProductID = ShoppingCart.ProductID
WHERE ShoppingCart.CartID = @CartID

EXEC EmptyShoppingCart @CartID

SELECT @OrderID
GO
```

We named our table Orders *instead of* Order *because this conflicts with the* ORDER *SQL keyword. However, it is perfectly possible to have any name for a table, including names containing spaces, if we write their names between square brackets, like* [ORDER] *or* [Order Details]*.*

The first step we make in this procedure is to create the new record in the Orders table. We need to do this at the beginning because we need to find out what OrderID was generated for the new order. Remember that the OrderID field is an identity column and is automatically generated by the database.

```
DECLARE @OrderID int
INSERT INTO Orders (DateCreated, Verified, Completed, Canceled)
VALUES (GETDATE(), 0, 0, 0)
SET @OrderID = @@IDENTITY
```

What you see here is the basic mechanism of extracting the newly generated ID. After the INSERT statement we save the value of @@IDENTITY to a variable.

Using the @OrderID variable we add the OrderDetail records by gathering information from the Product and ShoppingCart tables. From ShoppingCart we need the list of the products and their quantities, and from Product we get their names and prices. We also get the ProductID from Product but we could also get it from ShoppingCart; the result would be the same, since the table join is made on the ProductID column.

After creating the order we empty the visitor's shopping cart. This is done with a simple stored procedure named EmptyShoppingCart, which we've already seen. A stored procedure is called from within another stored procedure using the EXEC command:

```
EXEC EmptyShoppingCart @CartID
```

The last step for the CreateOrder stored procedure is to return the OrderID to the calling function using the SELECT keyword. This will be required later when we tell the customer their order number.

```
SELECT @OrderID
```

Updating the Business Layer

Luckily, at this stage we only need a single method named `CreateOrder`, which we'll add in the `ShoppingCart` class.

CreateOrder

Please add this method to the `ShoppingCart` class:

```
Public Function CreateOrder() As String
  ' Create the connection object
  Dim connection As New SqlConnection(connectionString)

  ' Create and initialize the command object
  Dim command As New SqlCommand("CreateOrder", connection)
  command.CommandType = CommandType.StoredProcedure

  ' Add an input parameter and supply a value for it
  command.Parameters.Add("@CartID", SqlDbType.VarChar, 50)
  command.Parameters("@CartID").Value = shoppingCartId

  ' Save the value that needs to be returned to a variable
  Dim orderId As String
  connection.Open()
  orderId = command.ExecuteScalar()

  ' Close the connection
  connection.Close()

  ' Return the saved value
  Return orderId
End Function
```

The method calls the `CreateOrder` stored procedure in the usual way. Note that we return to the caller the stored procedure's return value, which will be the `OrderID` of the newly created order.

Remember that `ExecuteScalar` is the `SqlCommand` method used to execute stored procedures that return a single value.

Implementing the User Interface

We have finally got to the part where we'll see the code we wrote so far working for us. The user interface consists of our star, the **Place Order** button, which allows the visitor to become a customer.

The Place Order Button

This button is the only addition on the visitor side for the custom checkout. Let's first place the button on the `ShoppingCart` web user control, and then we'll implement the functionality by handling its `Click` event.

The `ShoppingCart` user control will look like this after we add the button:

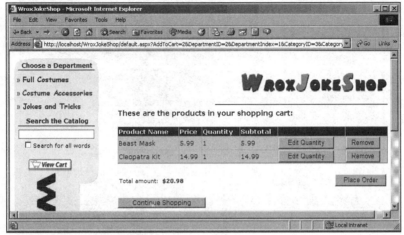

We get the desired functionality by following a few simple steps. The first one involves actually adding the button to the form.

Adding the Button to the Form

To add the Place Order button as seen in the picture we'll create a table with a single line containing two cells. The first cell contains the two `Label` controls, and the right cell contains the Place Order button. Please edit the HTML of the `ShoppingCart` web control and place this code in it instead of the original two labels, just between the `DataGrid` and the `continueShopping` button:

```
<table width="100%">
  <tr>
    <td width="100%">
      <asp:label id="Label1" runat="server" CssClass="ProductDescription">
        Total amount:</asp:label> 
      <asp:label id="totalAmountLabel" runat="server"
        CssClass="ProductPrice"></asp:label>
    </td>
    <td>
      <asp:Button id="placeOrderButton" runat="server"
                                 Text="Place Order">
      </asp:Button>
    </td>
  </tr>
</table>
<P>
```

After implementing this change, `ShoppingCart.ascx` should look like this when viewed in Design View:

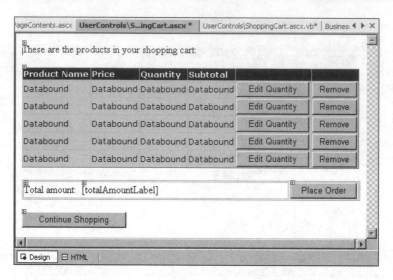

Having the Button Disabled if the Cart is Empty

Cool, now we have a **Place Order** button in the shopping cart. Note that this button should be enabled only when the shopping cart is not empty. In order to make sure of this, please modify `BindShoppingCart` in `ShoppingCart.ascx.vb`:

```
Private Sub BindShoppingCart()
  ' Populate the data grid and set its DataKey field
  Dim cart As New ShoppingCart()
  grid.DataSource = cart.GetProducts
  grid.DataKeyField = "ProductID"
  grid.DataBind()

    ' If the value of the shopping cart is 0 we assume it is empty
    If cart.GetTotalAmount = 0 Then
      placeOrderButton.Enabled = False
    Else
      placeOrderButton.Enabled = True
    End If

    ' Set the total amount label using the Currency format
    totalAmountLabel.Text = String.Format("{0:c}", cart.GetTotalAmount())
End Sub
```

You can run the project and test the new shopping cart. You'll see that the **Place Order** button gets enabled only when the shopping cart amount is greater than zero, which happens when there is at least one product in it.

Implementing the Place Order Functionality

Now it's time to implement the **Place Order** button's functionality. Make sure the project is not running, open `ShoppingCart.ascx` in **Design** View and double-click on the **Place Order** button. Then modify the automatically generated `placeOrderButton_Click` event handler like this:

```
Private Sub placeOrderButton_Click(ByVal sender As System.Object, ByVal e
    As System.EventArgs) Handles placeOrderButton.Click
  ' The Shopping Cart object
  Dim cart As New ShoppingCart()

  ' We need to store the total amount because the shopping cart
  ' is emptied when creating the order
  Dim amount As Decimal = cart.GetTotalAmount()

  ' Create the order and store the order ID
  Dim orderId As String = cart.CreateOrder()

  ' After saving the order into our database, we need to
  ' redirect to a page where the customer can pay for the
  ' order. Please take a look at the "Single Item Purcases"
  ' section of the PayPal appendix to see how you can
  ' integrate PayPal here

  ' Right now we redirect to default.aspx
  Response.Redirect("default.aspx")
End Sub
```

As you can also see in the code, the event handler method is not complete. Apart from saving the order into the database, we should also redirect to a payment page.

Administering Orders

Welcome to the second part of this chapter! You must be quite happy that finally the visitor has the option to *buy* our products. Well, actually, the customer has the option to *pay* for our products (if we integrated a payment system with our site), because we haven't yet implemented a system where we can see pending orders so we can ship the products for the orders that have been paid for.

Without a carefully designed administration page, where the administrator can quickly see the status of pending orders, our site wouldn't function very well when customers start buying our products.

Note that in this chapter we don't aim at creating a perfect order administration system, but rather something that is simple and functional enough to get you on the right track.

There are three main components we need to create here. First is the `OrdersAdminPage.aspx` Web Form, and then there are its two constituent user controls, `OrdersAdmin.ascx` and `OrderDetailsAdmin.ascx`. The main page is very simple, but the user controls are a bit more complex and we'll implement their functionality in the usual order, starting with the data layer.

The OrdersAdminPage Web Form

This page is very much like `CatalogAdminPage`. Just like `CatalogAdminPage`, we have a table with cells that are handled at the server side. The first cell of the table will be automatically filled with the `OrdersAdmin` web user control, which looks like this:

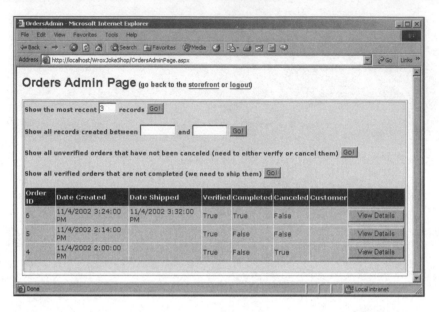

When the View Details button is clicked for any of the listed orders, the second table cell in `OrdersAdminPage` is filled with `OrderDetailsAdmin` web user control, which displays detailed information about the selected order.

We'll analyze these user controls more a bit later. For now, let's implement their container Web Form, `OrdersAdminPage`.

Creating the Form

We will implement this Web Form in a few easy steps, described in the following *Try It Out*.

Try It Out – Creating the OrdersAdminPage Web Form

1. The first step is to create the file in the WroxJokeShop project. Please add a new web form to the WroxJokeShop project and name it `OrdersAdminPage.aspx`. After creating it please change its `pageLayout` property to `FlowLayout`.

2. Now please open the file in HTML View. Let's first add a reference to the CSS file, `WroxJokeShop.css`:

```
<HEAD>
  <title>OrdersAdminPage</title>
  <meta name="GENERATOR" content="Microsoft Visual Studio.NET 7.0">
  <meta name="CODE_LANGUAGE" content="Visual Basic 7.0">
  <meta name="vs_defaultClientScript" content="JavaScript">
  <meta name="vs_targetSchema"
      content="http://schemas.microsoft.com/intellisense/ie5">
  <link href="WroxJokeShop.css" type="text/css" rel="stylesheet">
</HEAD>
```

3. Then modify the <body> area as shown in the listing below. This adds the table, with its two table cells, to the form.

```
<body>
  <form id="Form1" method="post" runat="server">
    <strong>
      <font face="Arial" size="5">Orders Admin Page</font>
      <font face="Arial" size="2">
        (go back to the <a href="default.aspx">storefront</a> or
        <asp:LinkButton id="logoutButton"
        runat="server">logout</asp:LinkButton>)
      </font>
    </strong>
    <br><br>
    <table border="1">
      <tr>
        <td bgcolor="#ccff66" runat="server" id="ordersCell"></td>
      </tr>
      <tr>
        <td bgcolor="#9999ff" runat="server" id="orderDetailsCell"></td>
      </tr>
    </table>
  </form>
</body>
```

When the page is switched to Design View, it should look like this:

4. Let's take care of the code-behind file now. Open `OrdersAdminPage.aspx.vb`. We will first check to make sure that Visual Studio has defined the table cell objects. If it hasn't, make sure to add them at the beginning of the file:

```
Public Class OrdersAdminPage
  Inherits System.Web.UI.Page
  Protected WithEvents ordersCell As _
      System.Web.UI.HtmlControls.HtmlTableCell
  Protected WithEvents orderDetailsCell As _
      System.Web.UI.HtmlControls.HtmlTableCell
```

5. Modify the `Page_Load` method:

```
Private Sub Page_Load(ByVal sender As System.Object, _
    ByVal e As System.EventArgs) Handles MyBase.Load
```

```
    ' Save OrderID from the query string to a variable
    Dim orderId As String = Request.Params("OrderID")

    ' Always load the OrdersAdmin.ascx web user control
    If True Then
      Dim control As Control
      control = Page.LoadControl("UserControls/OrdersAdmin.ascx")
      ordersCell.Controls.Add(control)
    End If

    ' Load OrderDetailsAdmin only if we have an Order ID in the query string
    If Not orderId Is Nothing Then
      Dim control As Control
      control = Page.LoadControl("UserControls/OrderDetailsAdmin.ascx")
      orderDetailsCell.Controls.Add(control)
    End If
  End Sub
```

6. Finally, let's add the `Click` event handler for the logout button:

```
Private Sub logoutButton_Click(ByVal sender As System.Object, ByVal e As
    System.EventArgs) Handles logoutButton.Click
  System.Web.Security.FormsAuthentication.SignOut()
  Response.Redirect("default.aspx")
End Sub
```

How It Works – OrdersAdminPage.aspx

There's nothing extraordinary about this page. It is important to take a quick look and see what happens in the `Page_Load` method. Note that we always load the `OrdersAdmin.ascx` control and add it to the first table cell:

```
    Dim control As Control
    control = Page.LoadControl("UserControls/OrdersAdmin.ascx")
    ordersCell.Controls.Add(control)
```

The `OrderDetailsAdmin.ascx` control is loaded in the second table cell, but only if we have an `OrderID` parameter supplied in the query string. This happens when the **View Details** button is clicked for a specific order:

```
    If Not orderId Is Nothing Then
      Dim control As Control
      control = Page.LoadControl("UserControls/OrderDetailsAdmin.ascx")
      orderDetailsCell.Controls.Add(control)
    End If
```

Finally we implemented the functionality for the logout button.

Implementing Security

Now let's extend the simple security mechanism for the page we created. Modify `Web.config` by adding the following lines just after the ones for `CatalogAdminPage.aspx`:

```
<location path="CatalogAdminPage.aspx">
  <system.web>
    <authorization>
      <allow users="admin" />
      <deny users="*" />
    </authorization>
  </system.web>
</location>

<location path="OrdersAdminPage.aspx">
  <system.web>
    <authorization>
      <allow users="admin" />
      <deny users="*" />
    </authorization>
  </system.web>
</location>

<system.web>
```

Having a Link to OrdersAdminPage on the First Page

Finally, before moving on, let's add a link to the `OrdersAdminPage` by updating the `FirstPageContents.ascx` user control, which should look like this when opened in Internet Explorer:

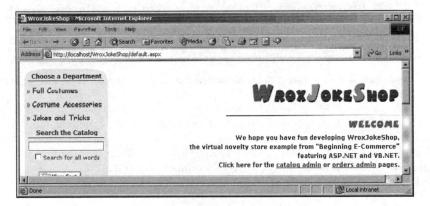

Open `FirstPageContents.ascx` in **HTML** View and add a link to `OrdersAdminPage.aspx` near the link to the catalog admin page, as in the following code snippet:

```
...
ASP.NET and VB.NET.
    <br>
    <br>
    Click here for the <a href="CatalogAdminPage.aspx">catalog
        admin</a> or <a href="OrdersAdminPage.aspx">
        orders admin</a> pages. </span>
    </P>
```

The OrdersAdmin Web User Control

This is the web control that fills the first table cell in the order administration page, and has the role of allowing the administrator to view the orders that have been placed on the web site. Because the orders list will become very long, it is important to have a few well-chosen filtering options.

The following screenshot shows how the control will look when first loaded in the orders administration page:

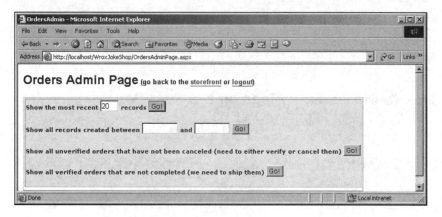

The options are pretty self-describing. Apart from the selection of the most recent records and selection by date, we have two additional selection modes.

The first shows the unverified and non-canceled orders. This will show the recent orders that have been placed and for which payment confirmation from PayPal is still pending (these orders have a pending status). If the payment is confirmed, the administrator will mark them as `Verified`. If the payment is not confirmed in a reasonable amount of time we'll want to cancel the order (marking it as `Canceled`), so that it will not be listed again when the button is clicked again at a later time.

The last selection mode is for the orders that have been verified but are not yet completed. These are the orders that have been paid for, but for which we haven't yet shipped the products. After the products are shipped, we'll mark the order as `Completed`.

When one of the buttons is clicked, a grid containing the requested orders appears below:

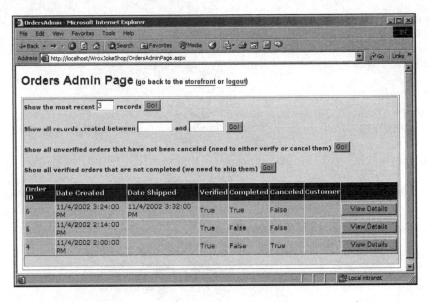

Even though we present the OrdersAdmin user control in this section, we first want to implement its supporting database and business-tier functionality. As the picture suggests, for this user control the database functionality will consist of four stored procedures that retrieve orders based on certain criteria. Let's look at them.

The Database Stored Procedures

Please add the following stored procedures to the WroxJokeShop database.

GetMostRecentOrders

In this stored procedure we use the SET ROWCOUNT statement to limit the number of rows returned by the SELECT statement. The parameter, @Count, specifies the number of records. The SELECT command simply returns the necessary rows, in descending order of the date they were created.

```
CREATE PROCEDURE GetMostRecentOrders
(@Count int)
AS

SET ROWCOUNT @Count

SELECT OrderID, DateCreated, DateShipped,
       Verified, Completed, Canceled, CustomerName
FROM Orders
ORDER BY DateCreated DESC

SET ROWCOUNT 0
```

Note that in the end we reset ROWCOUNT to 0, which means that we don't limit the number of returned rows. Also, here is the first time we see the ORDER BY clause.

ORDER BY is used to sort the returned results from the SELECT statement. The default sorting mode is ascending, but by adding DESC we set the descending sorting mode, which should show the most recent orders first. Remember that it was because of this ORDER clause that we called our order table Orders, in order to avoid possible confusion with the object names.

GetOrdersBetweenDates

This one simply returns all the records where the date matches the start and end dates, both of which are supplied as parameters. The returned results are sorted descending by date.

```
CREATE PROCEDURE GetOrdersBetweenDates
(@StartDate smalldatetime,
 @EndDate smalldatetime)
AS

SELECT OrderID, DateCreated, DateShipped,
       Verified, Completed, Canceled, CustomerName
FROM Orders
WHERE DateCreated BETWEEN @StartDate AND @EndDate
ORDER BY DateCreated DESC
```

GetUnverifiedUncanceledOrders

The criterion here is pretty simple. We want the orders that have not been verified yet, but have not been canceled either. In other words, we want to see the records that will be either verified (and then completed when the shipment is done), or canceled (if the payment isn't confirmed in a reasonable amount of time). The code is pretty straightforward:

```
CREATE PROCEDURE GetUnverifiedUncanceledOrders
AS

SELECT OrderID, DateCreated, DateShipped,
       Verified, Completed, Canceled, CustomerName
FROM Orders
WHERE Verified=0 AND Canceled=0
ORDER BY DateCreated DESC
```

GetVerifiedUncompletedOrders

Here we want to return all the orders that have been verified but not yet completed. The administrator will want to see these orders when a shipment has been done and the order needs to be marked as Completed. When an order is marked as completed, the DateShipped field will also be populated.

```
CREATE PROCEDURE GetVerifiedUncompletedOrders
AS

SELECT OrderID, DateCreated, DateShipped,
       Verified, Completed, Canceled, CustomerName
FROM Orders
WHERE Verified=1 AND Completed=0
ORDER BY DateCreated DESC
```

The Business Layer Methods

As usual, this is where we create the Visual Basic methods that access the stored procedures we have just created. But first, we want to create a new class in the `BusinessObjects` folder:

Creating the OrderManager Class

Create a new Visual Basic class file in the `BusinessObjects` folder named `OrderManager.vb`. Right-click on `BusinessObjects`, click on **Add New Item**, select **Class** from the Templates window and select `OrderManager.vb` (or simply `OrderManager`) for the file name.

Open the newly created file and add the usual `connectionString` property and import the `SqlClient` namespace:

```
Imports System.Data.SqlClient

Public Class OrderManager
  Private ReadOnly Property connectionString() As String
    Get
      Return ConfigurationSettings.AppSettings("ConnectionString")
    End Get
  End Property


  '
  ' Add methods here
  '
End Class
```

GetMostRecentOrders

Now please add the `GetMostRecentOrders` method to the `OrderManager` class. This one calls the `GetMostRecentOrders` stored procedure and returns a list of most recent orders to the calling function, in the form of a `SqlDataReader`.

```
    Public Function GetMostRecentOrders(ByVal count As Integer) As
        SqlDataReader
      ' Create the connection object
      Dim connection As New SqlConnection(connectionString)

      ' Create and initialize the command object
      Dim command As New SqlCommand("GetMostRecentOrders", connection)
      command.CommandType = CommandType.StoredProcedure

      ' Add an input parameter and supply a value for it
      command.Parameters.Add("@Count", SqlDbType.Int, 4)
      command.Parameters("@Count").Value = count

      ' Return the results
      connection.Open()
      Return command.ExecuteReader(CommandBehavior.CloseConnection)
    End Function
```

GetOrdersBetweenDates

This method returns all the orders that have been placed in a certain period of time, specified by a start date and an end date.

```
Public Function GetOrdersBetweenDates(ByVal startDate As String, ByVal
    endDate As String) As SqlDataReader
  ' Create the connection object
  Dim connection As New SqlConnection(connectionString)

  ' Create and initialize the command object
  Dim command As New SqlCommand("GetOrdersBetweenDates", connection)
  command.CommandType = CommandType.StoredProcedure

  ' Add an input parameter and supply a value for it
  command.Parameters.Add("@StartDate", SqlDbType.SmallDateTime)
  command.Parameters("@StartDate").Value = startDate

  ' Add an input parameter and supply a value for it
  command.Parameters.Add("@EndDate", SqlDbType.SmallDateTime)
  command.Parameters("@EndDate").Value = endDate

  ' Return the results
  connection.Open()
  Return command.ExecuteReader(CommandBehavior.CloseConnection)
End Function
```

GetUnverifiedUncanceledOrders

The method returns a list of orders that have not been verified yet, but were not canceled either. These are the records that need to be either verified (and then set to completed when the shipment is done), or canceled (if the payment isn't confirmed in a reasonable amount of time).

```
Public Function GetUnverifiedUncanceledOrders() As SqlDataReader
  ' Create the connection object
  Dim connection As New SqlConnection(connectionString)

  ' Create and initialize the command object
  Dim command As New SqlCommand("GetUnverifiedUncanceledOrders",
      connection)
  command.CommandType = CommandType.StoredProcedure

  ' Return the results
  connection.Open()
  Return command.ExecuteReader(CommandBehavior.CloseConnection)
End Function
```

GetVerifiedUncompletedOrders

This method returns all the orders that have been verified but not yet completed. The administrator will want to see these orders when a shipment has been done and the order needs to be marked as Completed. When an order is marked as completed, the DateShipped field will also be populated.

```
Public Function GetVerifiedUncompletedOrders() As SqlDataReader
  ' Create the connection object
  Dim connection As New SqlConnection(connectionString)

  ' Create and initialize the command object
  Dim command As New SqlCommand("GetVerifiedUncompletedOrders",
     connection)
    command.CommandType = CommandType.StoredProcedure

  ' Return the results
  connection.Open()
  Return command.ExecuteReader(CommandBehavior.CloseConnection)
End Function
```

The Presentation Tier: OrdersAdmin.ascx

Here we'll implement the OrdersAdmin control. First we'll create the control and add the constituent controls on the form using Visual Studio's Design view mode, and then we'll write the code-behind file.

Try It Out – Creating the Interface of OrdersAdmin

1. Create a new web user control in the **UserControls** folders named OrdersAdmin.ascx

2. Add the controls, as shown below:

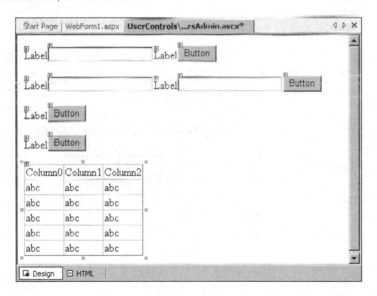

3. Set the properties for each control as described in the following tables.

The controls for the first line should have their properties set as shown below:

Control Type	ID	Text	CssClass	Width
Label	(doesn't matter)	Show the most recent	AdminPageText	
TextBox	recordCountTextBox	20		35px
Label	(doesn't matter)	records	AdminPageText	
Button	mostRecentButton	Go!	AdminButtonText	

These are the property settings for the second line:

Control Type	ID	Text	CssClass	Width
Label	(doesn't matter)	Show all records created between	AdminPageText	
TextBox	startDateTextBox	(empty)		70px
Label	(doesn't matter)	and	AdminPageText	
TextBox	endDateTextBox	(empty)		70px
Button	betweenDatesButton	Go!	AdminButtonText	

The controls for the third line should be set as these:

Control Type	ID	Text	CssClass
Label	(doesn't matter)	Show all unverified orders that have not been canceled (need to either verify or cancel them)	AdminPageText
Button	unverifiedOrdersButton	Go!	AdminButtonText

The controls for the fourth and final lines should be set thus:

Control Type	ID	Text	CssClass	Width
Label	(doesn't matter)	Show all verified orders that are not completed (we need to ship them)	AdminPageText	
Button	verifiedOrdersButton	Go!	AdminButtonText	
DataGrid	grid			100%

4. Open the DataGrid's Property Builder page and select the Columns tab. There, please unselect the **Create columns automatically at runtime** checkbox. Set the data grid's columns like this:

Column Type	Header Text	Data Field	Other Properties
Bound Column	Order ID	OrderID	
Bound Column	Date Created	DateCreated	
Bound Column	Date Shipped	DateShipped	
Bound Column	Verified	Verified	
Bound Column	Completed	Completed	
Bound Column	Canceled	Canceled	
Bound Column	Customer	CustomerName	
Select			Set **Text** property to **View Details** and **Button type** to PushButton

5. In the Property Builder window, click on the **Format** link on the left and select the **Header** tab. Set its properties as shown in the screenshot overleaf:

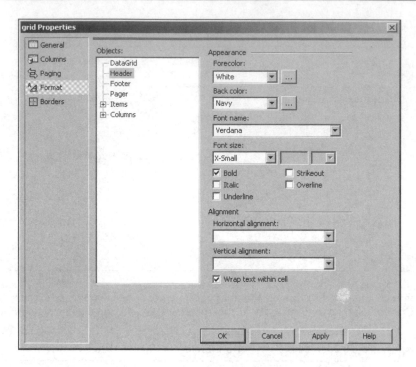

6. Then open the Normal Items template and set its properties like this:

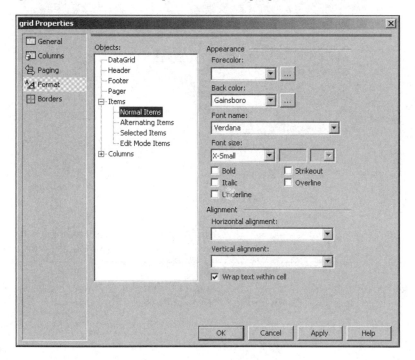

7. So far we have only added objects we are already familiar with from the previous chapters. For this exercise, however, we are going to introduce the **validator controls** provided by the .NET Framework. These provide a quick and easy means to do some validation of the input values at the presentation tier level. In our form we need to test to see if the values entered into the textboxes are valid before querying the business tier with them. Please add, just above the data grid, a `Label` control, two `RangeValidator` controls, a `CompareValidator` control, and a `ValidationSummary` control, as shown in the screenshot:

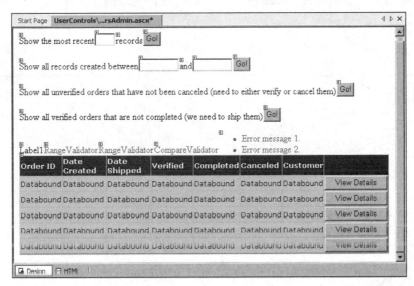

8. Let's now set the properties for each of the newly added controls. We'll take a closer look at them in the How it Works section, afterwards.

Control	Property Name	Property Value
Label	(ID)	errorLabel
	Text	(should be empty)
	CssClass	AdminErrorText
RangeValidator	(ID)	startDateValidator
	ControlToValidate	startDateTextBox
	Display	None
	ErrorMessage	Invalid start date.
	MaximumValue	1/1/2005
	MinimumValue	1/1/1999
	Type	Date

Table continued on following page

Control	Property Name	Property Value
RangeValidator	(ID)	EndDateValidator
	ControlToValidate	endDateTextBox
	Display	None
	ErrorMessage	Invalid end date.
	MaximumValue	1/1/2005
	MinimumValue	1/1/1999
	Type	Date
CompareValidator	(ID)	compareDatesValidator
	ControlToCompare	endDateTextBox
	ControlToValidate	startDateTextBox
	Display	None
	ErrorMessage	End date should be more recent than start date.
	Operator	LessThan
	Type	Date
ValidationSummary	(ID)	validationSummary
	CssClass	AdminErrorText
	HeaderText	Validation errors:

9. Press *F5* to execute the project. Browse to the OrdersAdminPage, add some invalid values in the textboxes and click one of the Go! buttons. You should receive an error message similar to the ones in the following screenshot:

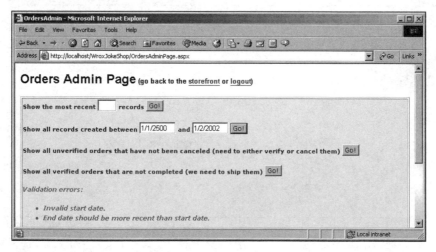

How It Works

This is the first example in this book where we played with the validator controls. A validator control is a control that validates the value of other controls. It can be associated only with input controls – like the textboxes in our example.

For our page we had the following requirements regarding the input textboxes:

- ❑ The values in `startDateTextBox` and `endDateTextBox` need to be correct formatted dates between 1/1/1999 and 1/1/2005

- ❑ The end date needs to be more recent than the start date

> Note that the validation controls have the power to prevent the page from being submitted to the server – if any of the validator controls signal an error, none of the **Go!** Buttons will work, ensuring that the business tier is only called with valid values.

The first requirement is implemented using `RangeValidator` controls, and the second using a `CompareValidator`. We also have a `ValidationSummary` control that gets the errors from the validator controls and displays them into a single, easy-to-read list.

The .NET Framework provides more validator controls, each being specialized in a certain type of validation: `RequiredFieldValidator`, `CompareValidator`, `RangeValidator`, `RegularExpressionValidator` and `CustomValidator`.

Here we will only briefly analyze the way `CompareValidator` and `RangeValidator` work, since these are the ones we have used for our example. Still, the way all the validation controls work is similar, with the exception of `CustomValidator`, which is more powerful, and its validation logic can be programmed manually. We also work with the `ValidationSummary` control, which gathers all the error messages from the validation controls in the page and presents them in a separate list, as we could see in the screenshot.

Please take a look in MSDN or *Professional ASP.NET 1.0* for detailed information about the validator controls.

So let's see how we made our three validator controls work. We have three `RangeValidator` controls, which test if the data type of each textbox is correct and its value is in a specified range of values. When adding a new `RangeValidator` control, we usually want to set these properties:

- ❑ ControlToValidate: we must set this property to the control that we want to validate.

- ❑ Display: if we don't use a `ValidationSummary` control, we leave this as **Dynamic** or **Static**, which results in the error message being displayed right in the place where the validator is placed. But since in our example we are using the `ValidationSummary` control, we set the **Display** to **None**, so that the error messages aren't displayed twice.

- ❑ ErrorMessage: this property contains the message to be displayed if the control is not validated.

❑ **Type**: this property specifies the data type that should exist in the control being validated. We set this property to **Date** for the two textboxes.

❑ **MinimumValue, MaximumValue**: these specify the maximum and minimum value that should exist in the control being validated.

The `CompareValidator` compares the values of two input controls, and has a few properties that are specific to it:

❑ **ControlToCompare, ControlToValidate**: the two controls that need to be compared. The one specified by **ControlToValidate** is the reference control.

❑ **Operator**: specifies what kind of comparison should be done between the two controls. Possible values are **Equal**, **NotEqual**, **GreaterThan**, **GreaterThanEqual**, **LessThan**, **LessThanEqual**, and **DataTypeCheck**. When **Operator** is selected, only the data type of the **ControlToValidate** is verified, and the control specified by **ControlToCompare** is ignored.

For the `ValidationSummary` control we set the **CssClass** property to the style we used for errors in the catalog administration page back in Chapter 7. We also set a **HeaderText** property which represents the header to be displayed before the list of errors.

Note that the layout of this control can be changed by setting the **DisplayMode** property. It can also be set up to raise a dialog box by setting the **ShowMessageBox** property to **True**.

Before moving to the next step, note that we also have a `Label` control. This will be used to display the errors that come from the database or the business tier. Note that the user will never see the error from either the `Label` control or the `ValidationSummary` control, simply because the form can't be submitted if there are validation problems.

Let's now implement the code behind of the `OrdersAdmin` control.

Try It Out – Implementing the Logic in the Code Behind File

1. There are five steps we need to make here: we need to implement the `Click` event handler for each of the Go! buttons, and then for the `SelectedIndexChanged` event of the data grid.

While in design view, please double-click on the first Go! button, then modify its `Click` event handler like this:

```
Private Sub mostRecentButton_Click(ByVal sender As System.Object, _
    ByVal e As System.EventArgs) Handles mostRecentButton.Click
    Dim om As New OrderManager()
    Dim recordCount As Integer

    Try
        recordCount = Int32.Parse(recordCountTextBox.Text)

        grid.DataSource = om.GetMostRecentOrders(recordCount)
        grid.DataKeyField = "OrderID"
        grid.DataBind()
    Catch
        errorLabel.Text = "Could not get the requested data!"
    End Try
End Sub
```

This method populates the data grid with the familiar routine. It calls the GetMostRecentOrders method from the middle tier, which in turn calls the GetMostRecentOrders stored procedure. Any error that occurs, results in the data grid being emptied. This guards against any kinds of errors, including bogus data being entered into the recordCountTextBox.

2. Switch to Design View and double-click on the second **Go!** button, then modify its Click event handler like this:

```
Private Sub betweenDatesButton_Click(ByVal sender As System.Object, _
    ByVal e As System.EventArgs) Handles betweenDatesButton.Click
    Dim om As New OrderManager()
    Dim startDate As String
    Dim endDate As String

    Try
        startDate = startDateTextBox.Text
        endDate = endDateTextBox.Text

        grid.DataSource = om.GetOrdersBetweenDates(startDate, endDate)
        grid.DataKeyField = "OrderID"
        grid.DataBind()
    Catch
        errorLabel.Text = "Could not get the requested data!"
    End Try
End Sub
```

This method is very similar to the preceding one. One difference is that here we send the input data from the textboxes (the two dates) as strings to the middle tier. The data type casting is done in the middle tier in this case, when the two dates are sent as SqlDbType.SmallDateTime parameters to the GetOrdersBetweenDates stored procedure.

3. Switch to Design View and double-click on the third **Go!** button, and then modify its Click event handler like this:

```
Private Sub unverifiedOrdersButton_Click(ByVal sender As System.Object, _
    ByVal e As System.EventArgs) Handles unverifiedOrdersButton.Click
    Dim om As New OrderManager()

    Try
        grid.DataSource = om.GetUnverifiedUncanceledOrders()
        grid.DataKeyField = "OrderID"
        grid.DataBind()
    Catch
        errorLabel.Text = "Could not get the requested data!"
    End Try
End Sub
```

4. Switch to Design View and double-click on the fourth **Go!** button, and then modify its Click event handler like this:

```
Private Sub verifiedOrdersButton_Click(ByVal sender As System.Object, _
    ByVal e As System.EventArgs) Handles verifiedOrdersButton.Click
  Dim om As New OrderManager()

  Try
    grid.DataSource = om.GetVerifiedUncompletedOrders()
    grid.DataKeyField = "OrderID"
    grid.DataBind()
  Catch
    errorLabel.Text = "Could not get the requested data!"
  End Try
End Sub
```

5. Finally, switch again to Design View and double-click on the data grid to generate the signature for the `SelectedIndexChanged` event handler. Then add these lines to it:

```
Private Sub grid_SelectedIndexChanged(ByVal sender As System.Object, _
    ByVal e As System.EventArgs) Handles grid.SelectedIndexChanged
  Dim orderId As String
  orderId = grid.DataKeys(grid.SelectedIndex)
  Response.Redirect("OrdersAdminPage.aspx?OrderID=" & orderId)
End Sub
```

Here we simply obtain the ID of the order of we clicked the **View Details** button for – remember that **View Details** is the **Select** button of the grid, so clicking it triggers the `SelectedIndexChanged` event. Then we reload `OrdersAdminPage.aspx` by adding the `OrderID` parameter to it. This will make `OrdersAdminPage` load the `OrderDetailsAdmin` user control (which we'll create later) in the second cell of the administration page.

How It Works

Each of the buttons' `Click` event handlers calls one of the methods we have written in the `OrderManager` class and populates the data grid with the returned `SqlDataReader`.

Since we took care of the basic validation for the input data, we shouldn't get any errors from the business tier or database. Anyway, we included the code that might generate errors in `Try` blocks, and if something bad happens we let the user know by setting a simple error message in the `errorLabel` control. This could happen, for example, if the SQL Server instance is paused or stopped. Remember that it's possible to even further fine-tune the error messages by implementing multiple `Catch` blocks to differently deal with each kind of error.

The `SelectedIndexChanged` event of the data grid is generated when we click on its **Select** buttons, which have the **View Details** text. When one of these buttons is clicked, the page is reloaded with the `OrderID` parameter appended in the query string. Remember that `OrdersAdminPage` loads the `OrderDetailsAdmin` user control in the second table cell when an order ID is supplied.

The OrderDetailsAdmin Web User Control

This user control allows the administrator to edit the details of a particular order. The most common tasks will be to mark an unverified order as either Verified or Canceled (it can't be directly marked as Completed if it is not verified yet), and to mark a verified order as Completed when the shipment is dispatched.

Take a look at the following image to see what OrderDetailsAdmin looks like in action:

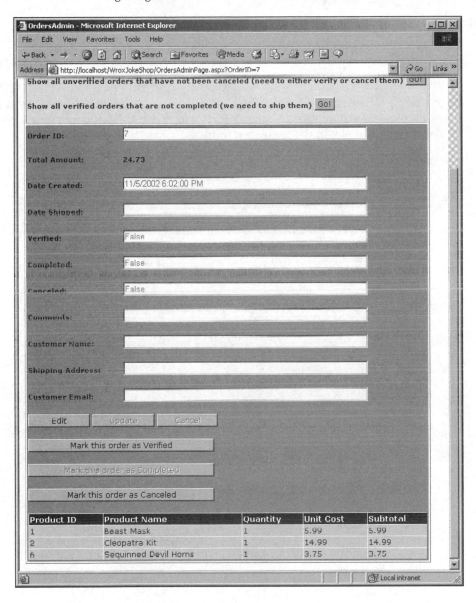

You can see that we provide the administrator with three very useful buttons: **Mark this order as Verified**, **Mark this order as Completed**, and **Mark this order as Canceled**. These will be enabled or disabled, depending on the status of the order. We also have the **Edit**, **Update**, and **Cancel** buttons, which allow the administrator to manually edit any of the details of an order. When the **Edit** button is pressed all of the textboxes (except for the one holding the order ID) become editable.

We have an overview idea about what we're aiming to do with this control. We'll implement it in the usual style starting with the data tier.

The Database Stored Procedures

Here we implement the data tier logic that will support the functionality required by the UI (User Interface). There are six operations that we'll allow the administrator to do, and we implement them with the following stored procedures:

- ❑ GetOrderInfo will get back the data needed to populate the textboxes of the form with general order information, like the total amount, date created, date shipped, and so on. You can see the complete list in the previous screenshot.

- ❑ GetOrderDetails returns all the products that belong to the selected order, and its return data is used to fill the grid at the bottom of the form.

- ❑ UpdateOrder is called when the form was in edit mode, and we submit new data to update the selected order.

- ❑ MarkOrderAsVerified is called to set the Verified bit of the selected order to 1.

- ❑ MarkOrderAsCompleted sets the Completed bit of the order to 1.

- ❑ MarkOrderAsCanceled sets the Canceled bit of the order to 1.

Let's now implement each of these stored procedures.

GetOrderInfo

This stored procedure returns the information necessary to fill the long list of textboxes in the OrderDetailsAdmin control.

```
CREATE PROCEDURE GetOrderInfo
(@OrderID int)
AS

SELECT OrderID, (SELECT SUM(UnitCost*Quantity) FROM OrderDetail WHERE OrderID =
@OrderID) as TotalAmount, DateCreated, DateShipped, Verified, Completed, Canceled,
Comments, CustomerName, ShippingAddress, CustomerEmail
FROM Orders
WHERE OrderID = @OrderID
```

Note that here we use a subquery to generate the TotalAmount field. All the required data we need is read from the Orders table, but in order to get the total amount of an order we need to take a look at the OrderDetail table as well.

The query that returns the total amount of a particular order uses the SUM function to sum up the subtotal of each product in the order, and is as follows:

```
SELECT SUM(UnitCost*Quantity) FROM OrderDetail WHERE OrderID = @OrderID
```

We transformed this into a subquery by transforming the result of this query into a field of the main query:

```
SELECT OrderID,
     (SELECT SUM(UnitCost*Quantity)
      FROM OrderDetail WHERE OrderID = @OrderID) as TotalAmount,
        DateCreated, DateShipped, Verified, Completed, Canceled, Comments,
CustomerName, ShippingAddress, CustomerEmail
FROM Orders
WHERE OrderID = @OrderID
```

GetOrderDetails

GetOrderDetails returns the list of products that belong to a specific order. This will be used to populate the data grid containing the order details, situated at the bottom of the control.

```
CREATE PROCEDURE GetOrderDetails
(@OrderID int)
AS

SELECT Orders.OrderID, ProductID, ProductName,
        Quantity, UnitCost, Quantity*UnitCost as Subtotal
FROM OrderDetail JOIN Orders
ON Orders.OrderID = OrderDetail.OrderID
WHERE Orders.OrderID = @OrderID
```

UpdateOrder

This procedure updates the order when the Update button is clicked (this is possible only when the order is in edit mode, after the Edit button was clicked).

```
CREATE PROCEDURE UpdateOrder
(@OrderID int,
 @DateCreated smalldatetime,
 @DateShipped smalldatetime = NULL,
 @Verified bit,
 @Completed bit,
 @Canceled bit,
 @Comments varchar(200),
 @CustomerName varchar(50),
 @ShippingAddress varchar(200),
 @CustomerEmail varchar(50))
AS

UPDATE Orders
SET DateCreated=@DateCreated,
        DateShipped=@DateShipped,
```

```
            Verified=@Verified,
            Completed=@Completed,
            Canceled=@Canceled,
            Comments=@Comments,
            CustomerName=@CustomerName,
            ShippingAddress=@ShippingAddress,
            CustomerEmail=@CustomerEmail
WHERE OrderID = @OrderID
```

MarkOrderAsVerified

This is called when the Mark this order as Verified button is clicked.

```
CREATE PROCEDURE MarkOrderAsVerified
(@OrderID int)
AS

UPDATE Orders
SET Verified = 1
WHERE OrderID = @OrderID
```

MarkOrderAsCompleted

This is called when the administrator clicks the Mark this order as Completed button. It not only sets the Completed bit to 1, but also updates the DateShipped field because an order is completed just after the shipment has been done.

```
CREATE PROCEDURE MarkOrderAsCompleted
(@OrderID int)
AS

UPDATE Orders
SET Completed = 1,
    DateShipped = getdate()
WHERE OrderID = @OrderID
```

MarkOrderAsCanceled

This is called when the Mark this order as Canceled button is clicked.

```
CREATE PROCEDURE MarkOrderAsCanceled
(@OrderID int)
AS

UPDATE Orders
SET Canceled = 1
WHERE OrderID = @OrderID
```

The Business Layer

Here, apart from the usual methods that pass data back and forth between the user interface and the database stored procedures, we create an additional class named OrderInfo. Objects of this class will store order information and will be used to fill the form with order information.

In this case, it is simpler to pass a data storage class to the user control than a `SqlDataReader` because the constituent controls are not data-bound and we need to manually fill them with data.

The OrderInfo Class

Add this to the `OrderManager.vb` file, but not inside the `OrderManager` class.

In fact, file location isn't important as long as it is located directly under the `WroxJokeShop` project, not inside any other class. If you prefer having each class in its separate file, feel free to add a new class file to your `BusinessObjects` folder.

```
Imports System.Data.SqlClient
```

```
Public Class OrderInfo
  Public OrderID As String
  Public TotalAmount As String
  Public DateCreated As String
  Public DateShipped As String
  Public Verified As String
  Public Completed As String
  Public Canceled As String
  Public Comments As String
  Public CustomerName As String
  Public ShippingAddress As String
  Public CustomerEmail As String
End Class
```

```
Public Class OrderManager
  ' ...
```

After this class is in place, please add the following methods to the `OrderManager` class:

GetOrderInfo

Here we use a `SqlDataReader` to read a row from the database containing information about a particular order. Note that we use `ToString` for each read field because some fields may have a `NULL` value, which cannot be stored into a string variable. `NULL` fields are transformed to empty strings when `ToString` is called on them.

```
Public Function GetOrderInfo(ByVal orderId As String) As OrderInfo
  ' Create the Connection object
  Dim connection As New SqlConnection(connectionString)

  ' Create and initialize the Command object
  Dim command As New SqlCommand("GetOrderInfo", connection)
  command.CommandType = CommandType.StoredProcedure

  ' Add an input parameter and set a value for it
  command.Parameters.Add("@OrderID", SqlDbType.Int)
  command.Parameters("@OrderID").Value = orderId
```

329

```
    ' Get the command results as a SqlDataReader
    connection.Open()
    Dim reader As SqlDataReader
    reader = command.ExecuteReader(CommandBehavior.CloseConnection)

    ' We move to the first (and only) record in the reader object
    ' and store the information in an OrderInfo object.
    Dim orderInfo As New OrderInfo()
    If reader.Read() Then ' returns true if there are records
      orderInfo.OrderID = reader("OrderID").ToString()
      orderInfo.TotalAmount = reader("TotalAmount").ToString()
      orderInfo.DateCreated = reader("DateCreated").ToString()
      orderInfo.DateShipped = reader("DateShipped").ToString()
      orderInfo.Verified = reader("Verified").ToString()
      orderInfo.Completed = reader("Completed").ToString()
      orderInfo.Canceled = reader("Canceled").ToString()
      orderInfo.Comments = reader("Comments").ToString()
      orderInfo.CustomerName = reader("CustomerName").ToString()
      orderInfo.ShippingAddress = reader("ShippingAddress").ToString()
      orderInfo.CustomerEmail = reader("CustomerEmail").ToString()
      ' Close the reader and its connection
      reader.Close()
      connection.Close()
    End If
    ' Return the information in the form of an OrderInfo object
    Return orderInfo
End Function
```

GetOrderDetails

`GetOrderDetails` returns the order details of the specified order.

```
Public Function GetOrderDetails(ByVal orderId As String) As SqlDataReader
    ' Create the Connection object
    Dim connection As New SqlConnection(connectionString)

    ' Create and initialize the Command object
    Dim command As New SqlCommand("GetOrderDetails", connection)
    command.CommandType = CommandType.StoredProcedure

    ' Add an input parameter and set a value for it
    command.Parameters.Add("@OrderID", SqlDbType.Int)
    command.Parameters("@OrderID").Value = orderId

    ' Get the command results as a SqlDataReader
    connection.Open()
    Return command.ExecuteReader(CommandBehavior.CloseConnection)
End Function
```

UpdateOrder

This stored procedure updates an order, and it is called when the **Update** button in `OrderDetailsAdmin` is clicked.

330

```vbnet
Public Sub UpdateOrder(ByVal orderInfo As OrderInfo)
  ' Create the Connection object
  Dim connection As New SqlConnection(connectionString)

  ' Create and initialize the Command object
  Dim command As New SqlCommand("UpdateOrder", connection)
  command.CommandType = CommandType.StoredProcedure

  ' We need to make sure orderInfo.Verified is a bit value
  If orderInfo.Verified.ToUpper = "TRUE" Or orderInfo.Verified = "1" Then
    command.Parameters.Add("@Verified", SqlDbType.Bit)
    command.Parameters("@Verified").Value = 1
  Else
    command.Parameters.Add("@Verified", SqlDbType.Bit)
    command.Parameters("@Verified").Value = 0
  End If

  ' We need to make sure orderInfo.Completed is a bit value
  If orderInfo.Completed.ToUpper = "TRUE" Or orderInfo.Completed = "1"
      Then
    command.Parameters.Add("@Completed", SqlDbType.Bit)
    command.Parameters("@Completed").Value = 1
  Else
    command.Parameters.Add("@Completed", SqlDbType.Bit)
    command.Parameters("@Completed").Value = 0
  End If

  ' We need to make sure orderInfo.Canceled is a bit value
  If orderInfo.Canceled.ToUpper = "TRUE" Or orderInfo.Canceled = "1" Then
    command.Parameters.Add("@Canceled", SqlDbType.Bit)
    command.Parameters("@Canceled").Value = 1
  Else
    command.Parameters.Add("@Canceled", SqlDbType.Bit)
    command.Parameters("@Canceled").Value = 0
  End If

  command.Parameters.Add("@OrderID", SqlDbType.Int)
  command.Parameters("@OrderID").Value = orderInfo.OrderID

  command.Parameters.Add("@DateCreated", SqlDbType.SmallDateTime)
  command.Parameters("@DateCreated").Value = orderInfo.DateCreated

  ' @DateShipped will be sent only if the user typed a date in that
  ' checkbox; otherwise we don't send this parameter, as its default
  ' value in the stored procedure is NULL
  If orderInfo.DateShipped.Trim <> "" Then
    command.Parameters.Add("@DateShipped", SqlDbType.SmallDateTime)
    command.Parameters("@DateShipped").Value = orderInfo.DateShipped
  End If

  command.Parameters.Add("@Comments", SqlDbType.VarChar, 200)
  command.Parameters("@Comments").Value = orderInfo.Comments
```

```
        command.Parameters.Add("@CustomerName", SqlDbType.VarChar, 50)
        command.Parameters("@CustomerName").Value = orderInfo.CustomerName

        command.Parameters.Add("@ShippingAddress", SqlDbType.VarChar, 200)
        command.Parameters("@ShippingAddress").Value = orderInfo.ShippingAddress

        command.Parameters.Add("@CustomerEmail", SqlDbType.VarChar, 50)
        command.Parameters("@CustomerEmail").Value = orderInfo.CustomerEmail

        ' Execute the command
        connection.Open()
        command.ExecuteNonQuery()
        connection.Close()
    End Sub
```

MarkOrderAsVerified

This method is called when the Mark this Order as Verified button is clicked, and sets the Verified bit of the specified order to 1.

```
    Public Sub MarkOrderAsVerified(ByVal orderId As String)
        ' Create the Connection object
        Dim connection As New SqlConnection(connectionString)

        ' Create and initialize the Command object
        Dim command As New SqlCommand("MarkOrderAsVerified", connection)
        command.CommandType = CommandType.StoredProcedure

        ' Add an input parameter and set a value for it
        command.Parameters.Add("@OrderID", SqlDbType.Int)
        command.Parameters("@OrderID").Value = orderId

        ' Execute the Command
        connection.Open()
        command.ExecuteNonQuery()
        connection.Close()
    End Sub
```

MarkOrderAsCompleted

This method is called when the Mark this Order as Completed button is clicked, and sets the Completed bit of the specified order to 1.

```
    Public Sub MarkOrderAsCompleted(ByVal orderId As String)
        ' Create the Connection object
        Dim connection As New SqlConnection(connectionString)

        ' Create and initialize the Command object
        Dim command As New SqlCommand("MarkOrderAsCompleted", connection)
        command.CommandType = CommandType.StoredProcedure
```

```
         ' Add an input parameter and set a value for it
         command.Parameters.Add("@OrderID", SqlDbType.Int)
         command.Parameters("@OrderID").Value = orderId

         ' Execute the Command
         connection.Open()
         command.ExecuteNonQuery()
         connection.Close()
      End Sub
```

MarkOrderAsCanceled

This method is called when the Mark this Order as Canceled button is clicked, and sets the `Canceled` bit of the specified order to 1.

```
      Public Sub MarkOrderAsCanceled(ByVal orderId As String)
         ' Create the Connection object
         Dim connection As New SqlConnection(connectionString)

         ' Create and initialize the Command object
         Dim command As New SqlCommand("MarkOrderAsCanceled", connection)
         command.CommandType = CommandType.StoredProcedure

         ' Add an input parameter and set a value for it
         command.Parameters.Add("@OrderID", SqlDbType.Int)
         command.Parameters("@OrderID").Value = orderId

         ' Execute the Command
         connection.Open()
         command.ExecuteNonQuery()
         connection.Close()
      End Sub
```

The Presentation Tier: OrderDetailsAdmin.ascx

Once again, we have reached the place where we wrap up all the data tier and business tier functionality and package it into a nice looking user interface.

Let's create this user control in the following *Try It Out* exercise.

Try It Out – Creating the OrderDetailsAdmin Web User Control

1. Right-click on the UserControls folder in Solution Explorer and select Add | New Web User Control. Choose `OrderDetailsAdmin.ascx` as for the name of the new user control.

2. Open the control in Design View and add labels, buttons and a data grid, as shown in the following screenshot:

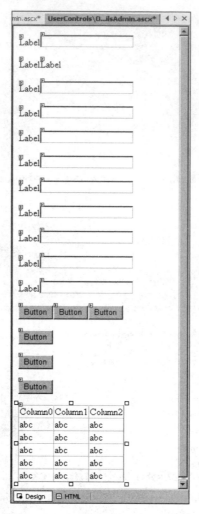

3. Set the properties for each constituent control as shown in the following table. Note that Visual Studio allows you to set properties on more than one control at a time – so you can select, for example, all the label controls in the left and set their CssClass and Width properties:

Control Type	ID	Text	CssClass	Width
Label	(doesn't matter)	Order ID:	AdminPageText	150px
TextBox	orderIdTextBox			400px
Label	(doesn't matter)	Total Amount:	AdminPageText	150px
Label	totalAmountLabel	(empty)	ProductPrice	

Control Type	ID	Text	CssClass	Width
Label	(doesn't matter)	Date Created:	AdminPageText	150px
TextBox	dateCreatedTextBox			400px
Label	(doesn't matter)	Date Shipped:	AdminPageText	150px
TextBox	dateShippedTextBox			400px
Label	(doesn't matter)	Verified:	AdminPageText	150px
TextBox	verifiedTextBox			400px
Label	(doesn't matter)	Completed:	AdminPageText	150px
TextBox	completedTextBox			400px
Label	(doesn't matter)	Canceled:	AdminPageText	150px
TextBox	canceledTextBox			400px
Label	(doesn't matter)	Comments:	AdminPageText	150px
TextBox	commentsTextBox			400px
Label	(doesn't matter)	Customer Name:	AdminPageText	150px
TextBox	customerNameTextBox			400px
Label	(doesn't matter)	Shipping Address:	AdminPageText	150px
TextBox	shippingAddressTextBox			400px
Label	(doesn't matter)	Customer Email:	AdminPageText	150px
TextBox	customerEmailTextBox			400px
Button	editButton	Edit	AdminButtonText	100px
Button	updateButton	Update	AdminButtonText	100px
Button	cancelButton	Cancel	AdminButtonText	100px
Button	markAsVerifiedButton	Mark this order as Verified	AdminButtonText	302px
Button	markAsCompletedButton	Mark this order as Completed	AdminButtonText	302px
Button	markAsCanceledButton	Mark this order as Canceled	AdminButtonText	302px
DataGrid	grid			100%

4. After setting the properties, the user control should look like this when seen in Design view:

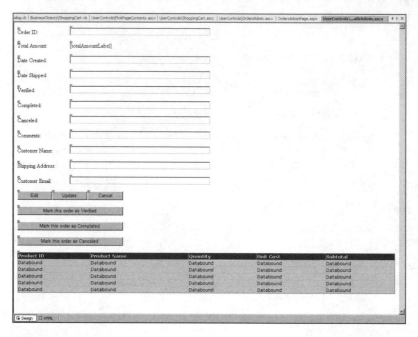

5. Open the Property Builder for the data grid, click the Columns link and unselect Create columns automatically at runtime checkbox. Now add the following fields to the data grid:

Column Type	Header Text	Data Field
Bound Column	Product ID	ProductID
Bound Column	Product Name	ProductName
Bound Column	Quantity	Quantity
Bound Column	Unit Cost	UnitCost
Bound Column	Subtotal	Subtotal

6. Now let's set the colors. Click on the Format link on the left and select the Header tab. Set its properties as shown:

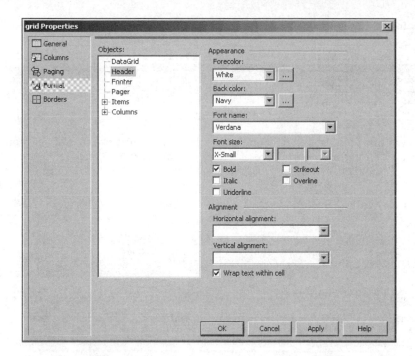

7. Then open the Normal Items template and set its properties as shown below:

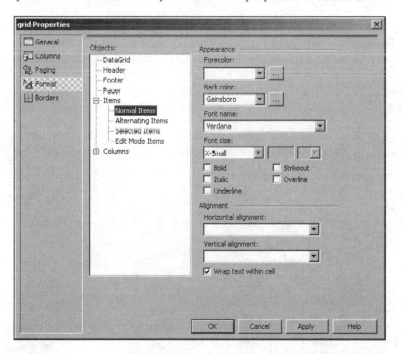

After setting all of the properties, the grid should look like this when viewed in **Design** view:

Also, at this point we can do a quick test and execute the project. After clicking on the *View Details* button for one of the orders, check to make sure that the *OrderDetailsAdmin* user control is loaded.

8. Let's start writing the code-behind logic now. First we modify the `Page_Load`:

```
Private Sub Page_Load(ByVal sender As System.Object, _
    ByVal e As System.EventArgs) Handles MyBase.Load
    If Not Page.IsPostBack Then
        ' Update information in all controls
        PopulateControls()

        ' Initially Edit mode should be disabled
        ' (administrator can't change order information)
        SetEditMode(False)
    End If
End Sub
```

In the `Page_Load` function we make use of two additional methods: `PopulateControls`, which populates with data all the controls on the form, and `SetEditMode`, which disables the textboxes for editing. These should allow editing only after the **Edit** button is clicked, as we'll see. Let's first implement the `PopulateControls` method:

9. Add `PopulateControls` just below `Page_Load`:

```
Private Sub PopulateControls()
    ' Create the OrderManager object which has the GetOrderDetails method
    Dim om As New OrderManager()

    ' The OrderInfo object will be populated by calling
    ' om.GetOrderDetails
    Dim orderInfo As OrderInfo

    ' We receive the order ID in the query string
    Dim orderId As String = Request.Params("OrderID")

    ' Populate the text boxes with order information
    orderInfo = om.GetOrderInfo(orderId)
    orderIdTextBox.Text = orderInfo.OrderID
    totalAmountLabel.Text = String.Format("{0:c}", orderInfo.TotalAmount)
    dateCreatedTextBox.Text = orderInfo.DateCreated
    dateShippedTextBox.Text = orderInfo.DateShipped
```

```
        verifiedTextBox.Text = orderInfo.Verified
        completedTextBox.Text = orderInfo.Completed
        canceledTextBox.Text = orderInfo.Canceled
        commentsTextBox.Text = orderInfo.Comments
        customerNameTextBox.Text = orderInfo.CustomerName
        shippingAddressTextBox.Text = orderInfo.ShippingAddress
        customerEmailTextBox.Text = orderInfo.CustomerEmail

        ' By default the Edit button is enabled
        ' and the Update and Cancel buttons are disabled
        editButton.Enabled = True
        updateButton.Enabled = False
        cancelButton.Enabled = False

        ' The Order ID can't be changed so we disable its textbox
        ' (alternatively we could have used Label instead of TextBox)
        orderIdTextBox.Enabled = False
        ' Decide which one of the other three buttons
        ' should be enabled and which should be disabled
        If canceledTextBox.Text = "True" Or completedTextBox.Text = "True" Then
            ' if the order was canceled or completed ...
          markAsVerifiedButton.Enabled = False
          markAsCompletedButton.Enabled = False
          markAsCanceledButton.Enabled = False
        ElseIf verifiedTextBox.Text = "True" Then
            ' if the order was not canceled but is verified ...
          markAsVerifiedButton.Enabled = False
          markAsCompletedButton.Enabled = True
          markAsCanceledButton.Enabled = True
        Else
            ' if the order was not canceled and is not verified ...
          markAsVerifiedButton.Enabled = True
          markAsCompletedButton.Enabled = False
          markAsCanceledButton.Enabled = True
        End If

        ' Fill the data grid with orderdetails
        grid.DataSource = om.GetOrderDetails(orderId)
        grid.DataKeyField = "OrderID"
        grid.DataBind()
End Sub
```

There isn't anything extraordinary about this method. It simply gets the order information in an `OrderInfo` object which was especially created for this task, by calling the `GetOrderInfo` method of the `OrderManager` class. Using the information from that object, the method fills the textboxes and the total amount label with data.

At the end, `OrderManager.GetOrderDetails()` is called to populate the data grid with the order details for the selected order.

10. Let's write the `SetEditMode` method now, which enables or disables edit mode for the information textboxes.

```
Private Sub SetEditMode(ByVal value As Boolean)
  dateCreatedTextBox.Enabled = value
  dateShippedTextBox.Enabled = value
  verifiedTextBox.Enabled = value
  completedTextBox.Enabled = value
  canceledTextBox.Enabled = value
  commentsTextBox.Enabled = value
  customerNameTextBox.Enabled = value
  shippingAddressTextBox.Enabled = value
  customerEmailTextBox.Enabled = value

  editButton.Enabled = Not value
  updateButton.Enabled = value
  cancelButton.Enabled = value
End Sub
```

As you can see this method receives a `Boolean` parameter that specifies if we enter or exit edit mode. When entering edit mode, all textboxes and the update and cancel buttons become enabled, while the edit button is disabled. The reverse happens when exiting edit mode, which happens when either the cancel or update button is clicked.

At this moment the project is compilable again, so we can see how our form looks when it's populated with some order information:

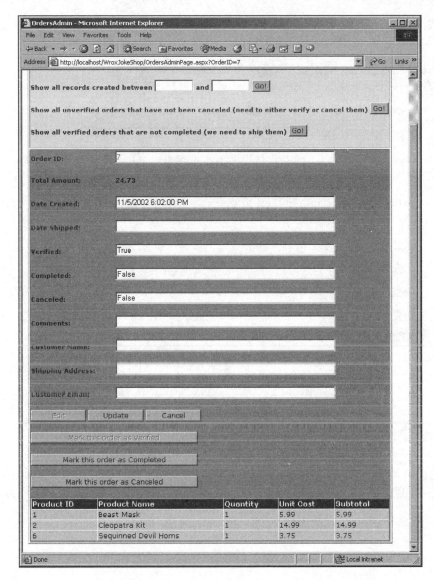

11. Let's start implementing the code that allows the administrator to edit order information. To make your life easier, first double-click on each of the buttons in design view to let Visual Studio generate the signatures of the event handlers. We start with the Click event of the Edit button, which simply enters the user control into edit mode:

```
Private Sub editButton_Click(ByVal sender As System.Object, _
    ByVal e As System.EventArgs) Handles editButton.Click
    SetEditMode(True)
End Sub
```

12. Here's the `Click` event handler for the Cancel button. Here we first exit edit mode and then call `PopulateControls` which restores the correct data in the form.

```
Private Sub cancelButton_Click(ByVal sender As System.Object, _
    ByVal e As System.EventArgs) Handles cancelButton.Click
  SetEditMode(False)
  PopulateControls()
End Sub
```

13. Finally let's deal with the `updateButton_Click` event handler. This one first creates and populates an `OrderInfo` object with the data gathered from the textboxes and then sends it as a parameter to the `OrderManager.UpdateOrder` business-tier method. This takes care of updating the order info. In the end we exit edit mode and call `PopulateControls` once again; this way, in case the update failed, the original information appears again in the form.

```
Private Sub updateButton_Click(ByVal sender As System.Object, _
    ByVal e As System.EventArgs) Handles updateButton.Click
  ' Store the new order details in an OrderInfo object
  Dim orderInfo As New OrderInfo()
  orderInfo.OrderID = orderIdTextBox.Text
  orderInfo.DateCreated = dateCreatedTextBox.Text
  orderInfo.DateShipped = dateShippedTextBox.Text
  orderInfo.Verified = verifiedTextBox.Text
  orderInfo.Completed = completedTextBox.Text
  orderInfo.Canceled = canceledTextBox.Text
  orderInfo.Comments = commentsTextBox.Text
  orderInfo.CustomerName = customerNameTextBox.Text
  orderInfo.ShippingAddress = shippingAddressTextBox.Text
  orderInfo.CustomerEmail = customerEmailTextBox.Text

  Try
    ' Update the order
    Dim om As New OrderManager()
    om.UpdateOrder(orderInfo)
  Catch
    ' Do nothing in case the update fails
  End Try

  ' Exit edit mode and update controls' information
  SetEditMode(False)
  PopulateControls()
End Sub
```

Note that here we didn't implement a mechanism to let the administrator know why the update failed – if something happens, we just ignore the error. We learned various error handling techniques in this chapter and in the previous ones, and you can choose to implement whichever technique you think is best for your application. In this case we preferred to focus on the task at hand, so we didn't implement a serious, user-friendly error-handling technique.

14. Finally, let's take care of the Click event handlers for the final three buttons. Here are the three of them, since they are all very alike:

```
Private Sub markAsVerifiedButton_Click(ByVal sender As System.Object, _
    ByVal e As System.EventArgs) Handles markAsVerifiedButton.Click
  Dim om As New OrderManager()
  Dim orderId As String = orderIdTextBox.Text
  om.MarkOrderAsVerified(orderId)
  PopulateControls()
End Sub

Private Sub markAsCompletedButton_Click(ByVal sender As System.Object, _
    ByVal e As System.EventArgs) Handles markAsCompletedButton.Click
  Dim om As New OrderManager()
  Dim orderId As String = orderIdTextBox.Text
  om.MarkOrderAsCompleted(orderId)
  PopulateControls()
End Sub

Private Sub markAsCanceledButton_Click(ByVal sender As System.Object, _
    ByVal e As System.EventArgs) Handles markAsCanceledButton.Click
  Dim om As New OrderManager()
  Dim orderId As String = orderIdTextBox.Text
  om.MarkOrderAsCanceled(orderId)
  PopulateControls()
End Sub
```

How it Works

Whew, we have written a lot of code for this control. The code itself isn't complicated but we had to deal with a lot of user interface elements.

Since we talked about each method while writing the code, it should be pretty clear how the page works. Please run it now and play with the buttons to make sure everything works as it should.

Summary

We covered a lot of ground in this chapter. We implemented a system by which we can both take orders and manually administer them.

We accomplished this in two separate stages. We added a **Place Order** button onto the shopping cart control, to allow the visitor to order the products in the shopping cart. We implemented a simple orders administration page, where the site administrator could view and handle pending orders.

In addition we looked at the use of validation controls and also, importantly, set the scene for entirely automating our entire order system. We will look at how we go about this in the next section of the book.

Customer Details

So far in this book we've built a basic (but functional) site, and have hooked it into PayPal for taking payments and confirming orders. In this section of the book we'll take things a little further. By cutting out PayPal from our ordering process we can obtain much better control over things – as well as reducing overheads. Doing this isn't as complicated as you might think, but we do have to be careful to do things right.

In this chapter we'll be laying out the groundwork for this, by implementing a customer account system

In order to make e-commerce sites more user friendly it is usual to store details such as credit card numbers in a database, so that users don't have to re-type this information each time they place an order. The customer account system we'll implement will do this, and will include all of the web pages required for the entry of such details.

As well as implementing these web pages, we'll need to take several other factors into account. First, simply placing credit card numbers, expiry dates, etc. into a database in plain text isn't ideal. If we do so then we may unwittingly be exposing this data to unscrupulous people with access to the database. This could occur remotely or be perpetrated by individuals within our organization. Rather than enforcing a prohibitively restrictive access policy to such data, it can be a lot easier simply to encrypt sensitive information, and retrieve it programmatically when required. We'll create a security library to ease this functionality.

Secondly, secure communications are important since we will be capturing sensitive information such as credit card details via the Web. We can't simply put a form up for people to access via HTTP and allow them to post it to us, as it is possible for such data to be intercepted. We'll look at the solution to this: using SSL over HTTPS connections.

We'll be taking the WroxJokeShop application to the point where we can move on and implement our own back-end order pipeline in the next chapter.

Customer Accounts

There are many ways to handle customer account functionality in web sites. In general, though, they share the following features:

❑ Customers log in via a login page or dialog in order to get access to secured areas of the web site

❑ Once logged in, the web application remembers the customer until they log out (either manually via a Log Out button, or automatically if their session times out or a server error occurs)

❑ All secure pages in a web application need to check whether a customer is logged in before allowing access

First, let's look at the general implementation details for the WroxJokeShop e-commerce site.

WroxJokeShop Customer Account Scheme

One simple way of enabling a check for a logged in customer is to store the customer ID in the session state. We can then check to see if a value is present here at the start of our secured pages, and redirect to a login form if not. The login form itself can then authenticate a user and store a value in the session state if successful, ready for later retrieval. To log a user out we simply remove the ID from session state.

To log in a customer needs to supply a username (we'll use their e-mail address here, since it is guaranteed to be unique) and a password. Sending this information over the Internet is a sensitive issue, since it may be possible for third parties to eavesdrop and capture it. Later in this chapter we'll look at secure communications over the Internet, and implement them for this information. For now, though, we'll concentrate on the authentication side of things, which is unaffected by the type of connection used to transmit the e-mail address and password of the customer.

Another issue related to security is the storage of user passwords. It isn't a good idea to store user passwords in our database in plain text, since this information is a potential target for attack. Instead we should store what is known as the **hash** of the password. A hash is a unique string that represents the password, but cannot be converted back into the password itself. To validate the password entered by the user, then, we simply need to generate a hash for the password entered and compare it with the hash stored in our database. If the hashes match then the passwords entered match as well, so we can be sure that the customer is who they say they are.

This leads us to another important task – we need to supply a method by which new users can register. The result of registration is to add a new customer to our database, including username and password hash information.

The specifics of the implementation of this scheme in our application will be as follows:

❑ A new database table to hold customer details called `Customer`, with associated stored procedures to add, modify, and retrieve information from customer records

❑ Modifications to `ShoppingCart.ascx`, which will now redirect the user to a checkout page called `Checkout.aspx`

❑ A customer login page called `CustomerLogin.aspx`

❑ A customer registration page called `CustomerNew.aspx`

Along the way we'll also implement the following:

❑   A page for customers to edit their basic details, `CustomerEdit.aspx`

❑   A page for customers to enter their credit card details, `CustomerCreditCard.aspx`

❑   A page for customers to enter their shipping address, `CustomerAddress.aspx`

The Customer Table

So, let's build our first table. Once again, there is a SQL script in the code download for this chapter that will build this table for you, or you can build it yourself in MSDE or SQL Enterprise Manager manually. The `Customer` table in the `WroxJokeShop` database is as follows:

Column Name	Column Type	Description
CustomerID	int(4)	Primary key, also set as table identity – this column should not allow nulls
Name	varchar(50)	Customer name – should not allow nulls
Email	varchar(50)	Customer e-mail address – should not allow nulls
Password	varchar(50)	Customer password, stored as a hash – should not allow nulls
CreditCard	varchar(512)	Customer credit card details
Address1	varchar(100)	First line of customer address
Address2	varchar(100)	Second line of customer address
City	varchar(100)	Customer address town/city information
Region	varchar(100)	Customer address region/state information
PostalCode	varchar(100)	Customer address postal code/ZIP information
Country	varchar(100)	Customer address country information
Phone	varchar(100)	Customer phone number

The credit card information for the customer is stored in an encrypted format. This is necessary since it is undesirable that we should store plain credit card details in our database, for the same reason that we don't want plain text passwords in there. Unlike passwords, however, we need to be able to retrieve this credit card information when required by the order pipeline, so we can't simply use a hash. The facilities for achieving this are contained in a new class library called `SecurityLib`, which we should look at now.

The SecurityLib Class Library

There are two areas we've seen so far where security functionality is required:

- ❑ Password hashing
- ❑ Credit card encryption

Both these tasks are carried out by classes in the `SecurityLib` class library. The reason for separating out this functionality is that we are likely to want access to it from outside of the WroxJokeShop application. In addition, it makes good logical sense not to bundle all this together in one place.

The `SecurityLib` class library project will consist of the following files:

- ❑ `PasswordHasher.vb` – contains the `PasswordHasher` class, containing the shared method `Hash()` that returns a hash for the password supplied.

- ❑ `SecureCard.vb` – contains the `SecureCard` class, which represents a credit card. This class can be initialized with credit card information, which is then accessible in encrypted format. Alternatively, it can be initialized with encrypted credit card data, and supply access to the decrypted information contained therein.

- ❑ `SecureCardException.vb` – should there be any problems during encryption or decryption then the exception contained in this file, `SecureCardException`, is thrown by `SecureCard`.

- ❑ `StringEncryptor.vb` – the class contained in this file, `StringEncryptor`, is used by `SecureCard` to encrypt and decrypt data. This means that if we want to change the encryption method then we only need to modify the code here, leaving the `SecureCard` class untouched.

- ❑ `StringEncryptorException.vb` – contains the `StringEncryptorException` exception, thrown by `StringEncryptor` if an error occurs.

We'll look at the code for hashing first, followed by encryption.

Hashing

Hashing, as has already been noted, is a means by which a unique value can be obtained that represents an object. In practice this means doing the following:

- ❑ First, we need to serialize the object being hashed into a byte array
- ❑ Second, we hash the byte array, obtaining a new, hashed byte array
- ❑ Third, we convert the hashed byte array into the format required for storage

For passwords this is quite simple, since converting a string (which is an array of characters) into a byte array is no problem. Converting the resultant hashed byte array into a string for database storage and quick comparison is also simple.

The actual method used to convert the source byte array into a hashed byte array can vary. The `System.Security.Cryptography` namespace in .NET contains several different algorithms for hashing, and allows us to provide our own if necessary, although I won't go into details of this here. The two main hashing algorithms found in the .NET Framework are SHA1 (which stands for Secure Hash Algorithm) and MD5 (which stands for Message Digest, another name for the hash code generated). SHA1 generates a 160 bit hash (regardless of the size of the input data), while MD5 generates a 128 bit hash, so SHA1 is generally agreed to be more secure (although slower) than MD5. The Framework also contains other versions of the SHA1 hash algorithm that generate longer hashes, up to 512 bits, as well as hash algorithms that work using a key (shared secret) as well as the data to be hashed.

In our implementation we'll use SHA1, although it is easy to change this if you require stronger security. We'll see the code that achieves this, in the `PasswordHasher` class, shortly.

Try It Out – Implementing the PasswordHasher Class

1. Create a new Class Library project called `SecurityLib` in the directory `C:\BegECom\Chapter10`.

2. Delete `Class1.vb` and add a new class file called `PasswordHasher.vb` with code as follows:

```
Imports System.Security.Cryptography

Public Class PasswordHasher
  Private Shared hasher As SHA1Managed = New SHA1Managed()

  Private Sub New()
    ' do nothing, make class uncreatable
  End Sub

  Public Shared Function Hash(ByVal password As String) As String
    ' convert password to byte array
    Dim passwordBytes() As Byte = _
        System.Text.ASCIIEncoding.ASCII.GetBytes(password)

    ' generate hash from byte array of password
    Dim passwordHash() As Byte = hasher.ComputeHash(passwordBytes)

    ' convert hash to string
    Return Convert.ToBase64String(passwordHash, 0, passwordHash.Length)
  End Function
End Class
```

3. Add a new Console Application project to the solution, called `SecurityLibTester`, and make this project the startup project (right-click on it and select **Set as StartUp Project**).

4. Add a project reference to `SecurityLibTester`, referencing the `SecurityLib` project. To do this, right-click on the references folder of the `SecurityLibTester` project, select **Add Reference...**, select the **Projects** tab of the dialog that appears, and select the only item that appears in the list – `SecurityLib`.

5. Modify `Module1.vb` as follows:

```
Imports SecurityLib

Module Module1

   Sub Main()
      Console.WriteLine("Enter your password:")
      Dim password1 As String = Console.ReadLine()
      Dim hash1 As String = PasswordHasher.Hash(password1)
      Console.WriteLine("The hash of this password is: {0}", hash1)
      Console.WriteLine("Enter your password again:")
      Dim password2 As String = Console.ReadLine()
      Dim hash2 As String = PasswordHasher.Hash(password2)
      Console.WriteLine("The hash of this password is: {0}", hash2)
      If hash1 = hash2 Then
         Console.WriteLine("The passwords match! Welcome!")
      Else
         Console.WriteLine("Password invalid. Armed guards are on their way.")
      End If
   End Sub

End Module
```

6. Execute the application (note that to avoid the window being closed as some as the code executes you can start without debugging by pressing *Ctrl-F5*, build the project and run `SecurityTestLib.exe` from the command line, or add a `Console.ReadLine()` statement at the end of the code):

```
C:\BegECom\Chapter10\SecurityLibTester\bin\SecurityLibTester.exe
Enter your password:
Chips&Beans
The hash of this password is: K3Q4yv0l4tMCXny0luKF9reue7k=
Enter your password again:
Beans&Chips
The hash of this password is: zq8fQrRRRH7lTtieNQnfbFUOL8k=
Password invalid. Armed guards are on their way.
Press any key to continue
```

How It Works

The code in the `PasswordHasher` class follows the steps that were discussed earlier. First we use the utility function `System.Text.ASCIIEncoding.ASCII.GetBytes()` to convert the password string into a byte array:

```
' convert password to byte array
Dim passwordBytes() As Byte = _
    System.Text.ASCIIEncoding.ASCII.GetBytes(password)
```

Next we use the private shared member hasher, an instance of `SHA1Managed`, to generate a hash byte array:

```
' generate hash from byte array of password
Dim passwordHash() As Byte = hasher.ComputeHash(passwordBytes)
```

Finally we convert the hash back into a string, using the utility function `Convert.ToBase64String()` and return the result:

```
' convert hash to string
Return Convert.ToBase64String (passwordHash, 0, passwordHash.Length)
```

All the hash algorithm classes in the .NET Framework use this `ComputeHash()` method to get a hash from an input array of bytes. If we wanted to increase the size of the hash we could simply replace the hasher with another one of these, for example:

```
Public Class PasswordHasher
    Private Shared hasher As SHA512Managed = New SHA512Managed()

    ...

End Class
```

The above change would result in a 512 bit hash, which is probably a bit excessive in this application!

The client application, `SecurityLibTest`, simply hashes two passwords and compares the result. The code is basic enough for us to ignore for now. What is worth mentioning, though, is that the generated hashes vary a great deal for even simple changes to the input data – one of the defining features of good hash generation.

Encryption

Encryption comes in many shapes and sizes, and continues to be a hot topic. As such there is no definitive solution to encrypting data, although there is plenty of advice that can be given. In general terms there are two forms of encryption:

- ❑ Symmetric encryption – a single key is used both to encrypt and decrypt data.
- ❑ Asymmetric encryption – separate keys are used to encrypt and decrypt data. The encryption key is commonly known as the public key, and anyone can use it to encrypt information. The decryption key is known as the private key, since only it can be used to decrypt data that has been encrypted using the public key.

Symmetric encryption is faster, but can be less secure since it involves both the encryptor and decryptor having knowledge of a single key. With Internet communications there is often no way of ensuring that this key remains a secret from third parties when it is sent to the encryptor.

Asymmetric encryption gets round this by its key pair method of operation, since there is never a need for the private key to be divulged, so a third party will find it much more difficult to break the encryption. Since it requires a lot more processing power, though, the normal method of operation is to use asymmetric encryption to exchange a symmetric key over the internet, which is then used for symmetric encryption safe in the knowledge that this key has not been exposed to third parties.

In the `WroxJokeShop` application things are much simpler than with Internet communications. We just need to encrypt data for storage in the database and decrypt it again when required, so we can use a symmetric algorithm.

Behind the scenes there is asymmetric encryption going on, though, since that is the method we use to encrypt the credit card details that are sent over the Internet. We, however, don't need to do very much to enable this, as we will see in the Secure Connections *section later in this chapter.*

As with hashing, there are several algorithms that can be used for both symmetric and asymmetric encryption. The .NET Framework contains implementations of several of these in the `System.Security.Cryptography` namespace.

The two available asymmetric algorithms are DSA (Digital Signature Algorithm) and RSA (Rivest-Shamir-Adleman, from the names of its inventors, Ronald Rivest, Adi Shamir, and Leonard Adleman). Of these, DSA can only be used to "sign" data such that its authenticity can be verified, while RSA is more versatile (although slower than DSA when used to generate digital signatures). DSA is the current standard for digital authentication used by the US government.

The symmetric algorithms found in the .NET Framework are DES (Data Encryption Standard), Triple DES (3DES), RC2 ("Ron's Code", or "Rivest's Cipher" depending on who you ask, also from Ronald Rivest), and Rijndael (from the names of its inventors, John Daemen and Vincent Rijman). DES has been the standard for some time now, although this is gradually changing. It uses a 64 bit key, although in practice only 56 of these bits are used as 8 are "parity" bits, and as such is often seen to be not strong enough to avoid being broken using today's computers (there are reports that a setup costing £250K managed to break DES encryption in three days). Both Triple DES and RC2 are variations of DES. Triple DES effectively encrypts data using three separate DES encryptions, using three keys totalling 168 bits when parity bits are subtracted. RC2 is a variant where key lengths up to 128 bits are possible (longer keys are also possible using RC3, RC4, etc.), so can be made weaker or stronger than DES depending on the key size. Rijndael is a completely separate encryption method, and has now been accepted as the new AES (Advanced Encryption Standard) standard. This standard is intended to replace DES, and several competing algorithms were considered before Rijndael was chosen. This is the standard that is gradually replacing DES as the most used symmetric encryption algorithm.

The tasks that must be carried out when encrypting and decrypting data are a little more involved than with hashing. The classes in the .NET Framework are optimized to work with data streams so we have a bit more work to do with data conversion. We also have to define both a key and an initialization vector (IV) to perform encryption and decryption. The initialization vector is required due to the nature of encryption: calculating the encrypted values for one sequence of bits involves using the encrypted values of the immediately preceding sequence of bits. Since there are no such values at the start of encryption an initialization vector is used instead. In practice both the initialization vector and the key can be represented as a byte array, which in the case of DES encryption are 64 bits (8 bytes) long.

The steps required for encrypting a string into an encrypted string are as follows:

- ❑ Convert the source string into a byte array.
- ❑ Initialize an encryption algorithm class.
- ❑ Use the encryption algorithm class to generate an encryptor object, supporting the `ICryptoTransform` interface. This requires key and IV values.
- ❑ Use the encryptor object to initialize a cryptographic stream (`CryptoStream` object). This stream also needs to know that we are encrypting data, and needs a target stream to write encrypted data to.
- ❑ Use the cryptographic stream to write encrypted data to a target memory stream, using the source byte array created above.
- ❑ Extract the byte data stored in the stream.
- ❑ Convert the byte data into a string.

Decryption follows a similar scheme:

- ❑ Convert source string into byte array.

- ❑ Fill a memory stream with the contents of the byte array.

- ❑ Initialize an encryption algorithm class.

- ❑ Use the encryption algorithm class to generate a decryptor object, supporting the `ICryptoTransform` interface. This requires key and IV values.

- ❑ Use the decryptor object to initialize a cryptographic stream (`CryptoStream` object). This stream also needs to know that we are decrypting data, and needs a source stream to read encrypted data from.

- ❑ Use the cryptographic stream to read decrypted data (can use the `StreamReader.ReadToEnd()` method to get the result as a string).

In our code we'll use DES, but the code in the `StringEncryptor` class could be replaced with code to use any of the algorithms specified above.

Try It Out – Implementing the StringEncryptor Class

1. Add a new class to the `SecurityLib` class library called `StringEncryptorException` with code as follows:

```
Public Class StringEncryptorException
    Inherits Exception

    Public Sub New(ByVal message As String)
        MyBase.New(message)
    End Sub
End Class
```

2. Add another new class to the `SecurityLib` class library called `StringEncryptor` with code as follows:

```
Imports System.Security.Cryptography
Imports System.IO

Public Class StringEncryptor
    Private Sub New()
        ' do nothing, make class uncreatable
    End Sub

    Public Shared Function Encrypt(ByVal sourceData As String) As String
        ' set key and initialization vector values
        Dim key() As Byte = New Byte() {1, 2, 3, 4, 5, 6, 7, 8}
        Dim iv() As Byte = New Byte() {1, 2, 3, 4, 5, 6, 7, 8}
        Try
            ' convert data to byte array
            Dim sourceDataBytes() As Byte = _
```

```vb
            System.Text.ASCIIEncoding.ASCII.GetBytes(sourceData)

        ' get target memory stream
        Dim tempStream As MemoryStream = New MemoryStream()

        ' get encryptor and encryption stream
        Dim encryptor As DESCryptoServiceProvider = _
            New DESCryptoServiceProvider()
        Dim encryptionStream As CryptoStream = _
            New CryptoStream(tempStream, encryptor.CreateEncryptor(key, iv), _
                             CryptoStreamMode.Write)

        ' encrypt data
        encryptionStream.Write(sourceDataBytes, 0, sourceDataBytes.Length)
        encryptionStream.FlushFinalBlock()

        ' put data into byte array
        Dim encryptedDataBytes() As Byte = tempStream.GetBuffer()

        ' convert encrypted data into string
        Return Convert.ToBase64String(encryptedDataBytes, 0, tempStream.Length)
    Catch
        Throw New StringEncryptorException("Unable to encrypt data.")
    End Try
End Function

Public Shared Function Decrypt(ByVal sourceData As String) As String
    ' set key and initialization vector values
    Dim key() As Byte = New Byte() {1, 2, 3, 4, 5, 6, 7, 8}
    Dim iv() As Byte = New Byte() {1, 2, 3, 4, 5, 6, 7, 8}
    Try
        ' convert data to byte array
        Dim encryptedDataBytes() As Byte = Convert.FromBase64String(sourceData)

        ' get source memory stream and fill it
        Dim tempStream As MemoryStream = _
            New MemoryStream(encryptedDataBytes, 0, encryptedDataBytes.Length)

        ' get decryptor and decryption stream
        Dim decryptor As DESCryptoServiceProvider = _
            New DESCryptoServiceProvider()
        Dim decryptionStream As CryptoStream = _
            New CryptoStream(tempStream, decryptor.CreateDecryptor(key, iv), _
                             CryptoStreamMode.Read)

        ' decrypt data
        Dim allDataReader As StreamReader = New StreamReader(decryptionStream)
        Return allDataReader.ReadToEnd()
    Catch
        Throw New StringEncryptorException("Unable to decrypt data.")
    End Try
End Function
End Class
```

3. Modify the code in `Module1.vb` in `SecurityLibTester` as follows:

```
Sub Main()
    Console.WriteLine("Enter data to encrypt:")
    Dim stringToEncrypt As String = Console.ReadLine()
    Dim encryptedString = StringEncryptor.Encrypt(stringToEncrypt)
    Console.WriteLine("Encrypted data: {0}", encryptedString)
    Console.WriteLine( _
        "Enter data to decrypt (hit enter to decrypt above data):")
    Dim stringToDecrypt As String = Console.ReadLine()
    If stringToDecrypt = "" Then
        stringToDecrypt = encryptedString
    End If
    Dim decryptedString As String = StringEncryptor.Decrypt(stringToDecrypt)
    Console.WriteLine("Decrypted data: {0}", decryptedString)
End Sub
```

4. Execute the code:

How It Works

The `StringEncryptor` class has two shared methods, `Encrypt()` and `Decrypt()`, which encrypt and decrypt data respectively. We'll look at each of these in turn.

`Encrypt()` starts by defining two hard-coded byte arrays for the key and initialization vector used in encryption:

```
Public Shared Function Encrypt(ByVal sourceData As String) As String
    ' set key and initialization vector values
    Dim key() As Byte = New Byte() {1, 2, 3, 4, 5, 6, 7, 8}
    Dim iv() As Byte = New Byte() {1, 2, 3, 4, 5, 6, 7, 8}
```

Both these arrays are set to temporary values here. They could just as easily take any other values, depending on the key you want to use. Alternatively, they could be loaded from disk, although I find that having the values compiled into your code in this way could stop people from discovering the values used quite effectively. Note that we initialize these values each time the method is called rather than using constant values. One reason for this is that the `iv` array is modified as part of the encryption process, so the values would be different if we didn't re-initialize it. In effect this would mean that the first few bytes of the decrypted data would be garbled. The important point to note here is that you should use your own values, not the temporary ones used above. There are classes and methods in the `System.Security.Cryptography` namespace that you can use to generate such values automatically, or you can just insert random numbers.

355

You could restrict access to this assembly to code that has been compiled using a particular key. This is possible if you strongly name your assemblies and configure code access security yourself, and would prevent people from using the `SecurityLib` *assembly to decrypt credit card details from outside the WroxJokeShop application, unless they had access to the signature key. However, this is an advanced topic and won't be covered here. For more information on code-access security see* Visual Basic .NET Code Security Handbook *published by Wrox Press (ISBN – 1-86100-747-7).*

Next we come to the encryption code itself, all of which is contained in a `Try...Catch` block in case an error occurs. The code follows the steps laid out earlier, starting with the conversion of the source string into a byte array:

```
Try
  ' convert data to byte array
  Dim sourceDataBytes() As Byte = _
      System.Text.ASCIIEncoding.ASCII.GetBytes(sourceData)
```

Next we initialize a `MemoryStream` object, which will be used to store to encrypted data:

```
  ' get target memory stream
  Dim tempStream As MemoryStream = New MemoryStream ()
```

Next we get the encryptor object, in this case an instance of the `DESCryptoServiceProvider` class, and use it with the key and IV created earlier to generate a `CryptoStream` object (specifying an encryption operation via the `CreateEncryptor()` method and `CryptoStreamMode.Write` mode):

```
  ' get encryptor and encryption stream
  Dim encryptor As DESCryptoServiceProvider = New DESCryptoServiceProvider()
  Dim encryptionStream As CryptoStream = _
      New CryptoStream(tempStream, encryptor.CreateEncryptor(key, iv), _
      CryptoStreamMode.Write)
```

This is the place where we'd change code if we wanted to substitute a different encryption algorithm (although we may also have to change the amount of data contained in the key and IV arrays if we did so).

Note that the suffix of this class is `CryptoServiceProvider`. *This indicates an unmanaged implementation of the DES encryption algorithm. There is no managed implementation of this algorithm in the .NET Framework, although there is a managed implementation of the Rijndael algorithm. In practice, though, this makes little (if any) difference to application performance.*

The next section of code performs the actual encryption, writing the resultant byte array to the `MemoryStream` created earlier:

```
  ' encrypt data
  encryptionStream.Write(sourceDataBytes, 0, sourceDataBytes.Length)
  encryptionStream.FlushFinalBlock()
```

The `FlushFinalBlock()` call here is essential. Without this call there might be unwritten data left in the buffer of the `CryptoStream`. This call forces the stream writing to complete such that all the data we require is contained in the `MemoryStream` object.

Next we grab the data from the `MemoryStream` and place it into a byte array:

```
' put data into byte array
Dim encryptedDataBytes() As Byte = tempStream.GetBuffer()
```

Finally, we convert the resultant byte array into a string and return it:

```
' convert encrypted data into string
Return Convert.ToBase64String(encryptedDataBytes, 0, tempStream.Length)
```

Should anything go wrong during this process we throw a `StringEncryptorException` exception:

```
Catch
  Throw New StringEncryptorException("Unable to encrypt data.")
End Try
End Function
```

Note that this exception class doesn't do very much, and you might think that just throwing a standard `Exception` would be good enough. However, by creating our own type it is possible for SEII code that uses this class to test for the specific type of this new exception, filtering out `StringEncryptorException` exceptions from other exceptions that might occur.

The `Decrypt()` method is very similar to `Encrypt()`. We start in the same way by initializing the key and IV before moving into a `Try...Catch` block and converting the source string into a byte array:

```
Public Shared Function Decrypt(ByVal sourceData As String) As String
  ' set key and initialization vector values
  Dim key() As Byte = New Byte() {1, 2, 3, 4, 5, 6, 7, 8}
  Dim iv() As Byte = New Byte() {1, 2, 3, 4, 5, 6, 7, 8}
  Try
    ' convert data to byte array
    Dim encryptedDataBytes() As Byte = Convert.FromBase64String(sourceData)
```

This time, though, we need a stream that is filled with this source byte array, since the `CryptoStream` will be reading from a stream rather than writing to one:

```
' get source memory stream and fill it
Dim tempStream As MemoryStream = _
New MemoryStream(encryptedDataBytes, 0, encryptedDataBytes.Length)
```

The next code is similar, although we use the `CreateDecryptor()` method and `CryptoStreamMode.Read` mode to specify decryption:

```
' get decryptor and decryption stream
Dim decryptor As DESCryptoServiceProvider = New DESCryptoServiceProvider()
Dim decryptionStream As CryptoStream = _
  New CryptoStream(tempStream, decryptor.CreateDecryptor(key, iv), _
  CryptoStreamMode.Read)
```

Finally we get the decrypted data out of the `CryptoStream` using a `StreamReader` object, which handily allows us to grab the data straight into a string for returning. As with `Encrypt()`, the last step is to add the code that throws a `StringEncryptorException` exception if anything goes wrong:

```
    ' decrypt data
    Dim allDataReader As StreamReader = New StreamReader(decryptionStream)
    Return allDataReader.ReadToEnd()
  Catch
    Throw New StringEncryptorException("Unable to decrypt data.")
  End Try
End Function
End Class
```

The client code for this class simply encrypts and decrypts data, demonstrating that things are working properly. The code for this is very simple, and we won't detail it here.

Now we have the `StringEncryptor` class code, the last step in creating the `SecureLib` library is to add the `SecureCard` class.

Try It Out – Implementing the SecureCard Class

1. Add a new class to the `SecurityLib` class library called `SecureCardException.vb` with code as follows:

```
Public Class SecureCardException
    Inherits Exception

    Public Sub New(ByVal message As String)
        MyBase.New(message)
    End Sub
End Class
```

2. Add another new file to the `SecurityLib` class library called `SecureCard.vb` with code as follows:

```
Imports System.Xml

Public Class SecureCard
  Private isDecrypted As Boolean = False
  Private isEncrypted As Boolean = False
  Private _cardHolder As String
  Private _cardNumber As String
  Private _issueDate As String
  Private _expiryDate As String
  Private _issueNumber As String
  Private _cardType As String
  Private _encryptedData As String
  Private _xmlCardData As XmlDocument
```

```
Private Sub New()
  ' private default constructor
End Sub

Public Sub New(ByVal newEncryptedData As String)
  ' constructor for use with encrypted data
  _encryptedData = newEncryptedData
  DecryptData()
End Sub

Public Sub New(ByVal newCardHolder As String, ByVal newCardNumber As String, _
    ByVal newIssueDate As String, ByVal newExpiryDate As String, _
    ByVal newIssueNumber As String, ByVal newCardType As String)
  ' constructor for use with decrypted data
  _cardHolder = newCardHolder
  _cardNumber = newCardNumber
  _issueDate = newIssueDate
  _expiryDate = newExpiryDate
  _issueNumber = newIssueNumber
  _cardType = newCardType
  EncryptData()
End Sub

Private Sub CreateXml()
  ' encode card details as XML document
  _xmlCardData = New XmlDocument()
  Dim documentRoot As XmlElement = _xmlCardData.CreateElement("CardDetails")
  Dim child As XmlElement

  child = _xmlCardData.CreateElement("CardHolder")
  child.InnerXml = _cardHolder
  documentRoot.AppendChild(child)

  child = _xmlCardData.CreateElement("CardNumber")
  child.InnerXml = _cardNumber
  documentRoot.AppendChild(child)

  child = _xmlCardData.CreateElement("IssueDate")
  child.InnerXml = _issueDate
  documentRoot.AppendChild(child)

  child = _xmlCardData.CreateElement("ExpiryDate")
  child.InnerXml = _expiryDate
  documentRoot.AppendChild(child)

  child = _xmlCardData.CreateElement("IssueNumber")
  child.InnerXml = _issueNumber
  documentRoot.AppendChild(child)

  child = _xmlCardData.CreateElement("CardType")
  child.InnerXml = _cardType
  documentRoot.AppendChild(child)
```

```
      _xmlCardData.AppendChild(documentRoot)
End Sub

Private Sub ExtractXml()
   ' get card details out of XML document
   _cardHolder = _xmlCardData.GetElementsByTagName("CardHolder").Item(0).InnerXml
   _cardNumber = _
       _xmlCardData.GetElementsByTagName("CardNumber").Item(0).InnerXml
   _issueDate = _
       _xmlCardData.GetElementsByTagName("IssueDate").Item(0).InnerXml
   _expiryDate = _
       _xmlCardData.GetElementsByTagName("ExpiryDate").Item(0).InnerXml
   _issueNumber = _
       _xmlCardData.GetElementsByTagName("IssueNumber").Item(0).InnerXml
   _cardType = _xmlCardData.GetElementsByTagName("CardType").Item(0).InnerXml
End Sub

Private Sub EncryptData()
   Try
      ' stuff data into XML doc
      CreateXml()

      ' encrypt data
      _encryptedData = StringEncryptor.Encrypt(_xmlCardData.OuterXml)

      ' set encrypted flag
      isEncrypted = True
   Catch
      Throw New SecureCardException("Unable to encrypt data.")
   End Try
End Sub

Private Sub DecryptData()
   Try
      ' decrypt data
      _xmlCardData = New XmlDocument()
      _xmlCardData.InnerXml = StringEncryptor.Decrypt(_encryptedData)

      ' extract data from XML
      ExtractXml()

      ' set decrypted flag
      isDecrypted = True
      Catch
         Throw New SecureCardException("Unable to decrypt data.")
   End Try
End Sub

Public ReadOnly Property CardHolder() As String
   Get
      If isDecrypted Then
         Return _cardHolder
      Else
```

```
        Throw New SecureCardException("Data not decrypted.")
      End If
    End Get
End Property


Public ReadOnly Property CardNumber() As String
  Get
    If isDecrypted Then
      Return _cardNumber
    Else
      Throw New SecureCardException("Data not decrypted.")
    End If
  End Get
End Property


Public ReadOnly Property CardNumberX() As String
  Get
    If isDecrypted Then
     Return "XXXX-XXXX-XXXX-" & _cardNumber.Substring(_cardNumber.Length - 4, 4)
    Else
      Throw New SecureCardException("Data not decrypted.")
    End If
  End Get
End Property


Public ReadOnly Property IssueDate() As String
  Get
    If isDecrypted Then
      Return _issueDate
    Else
      Throw New SecureCardException("Data not decrypted.")
    End If
  End Get
End Property


Public ReadOnly Property ExpiryDate() As String
  Get
    If isDecrypted Then
      Return _expiryDate
    Else
      Throw New SecureCardException("Data not decrypted.")
    End If
  End Get
End Property


Public ReadOnly Property IssueNumber() As String
  Get
    If isDecrypted Then
      Return _issueNumber
    Else
      Throw New SecureCardException("Data not decrypted.")
    End If
  End Get
```

```
      End Property

   Public ReadOnly Property CardType() As String
     Get
       If isDecrypted Then
         Return _cardType
       Else
         Throw New SecureCardException("Data not decrypted.")
       End If
     End Get
   End Property

   Public ReadOnly Property EncryptedData() As String
     Get
       If isEncrypted Then
         Return _encryptedData
       Else
         Throw New SecureCardException("Data not encrypted.")
       End If
     End Get
   End Property
End Class
```

3. Modify the code in `Module1.vb` as follows:

```
Sub Main()
   Console.WriteLine("Enter data to encrypt:")
   Console.WriteLine("Card Holder:")
   Dim cardHolder As String = Console.ReadLine()
   Console.WriteLine("Card Number:")
   Dim expiryDate As String = Console.ReadLine()
   Console.WriteLine("Issue Date:")
   Dim cardNumber As String = Console.ReadLine()
   Console.WriteLine("Expiry Date:")
   Dim issueDate As String = Console.ReadLine()
   Console.WriteLine("Issue Number:")
   Dim issueNumber As String = Console.ReadLine()
   Console.WriteLine("Card Type:")
   Dim cardType As String = Console.ReadLine()

   Dim encryptedCard As SecureCard = _
       New SecureCard(cardHolder, cardNumber, issueDate, expiryDate, _
       issueNumber, cardType)
   Console.WriteLine("Encrypted data: {0}", encryptedCard.EncryptedData)

   Console.WriteLine( _
       "Enter data to decrypt (hit enter to decrypt above data):")
   Dim stringToDecrypt As String = Console.ReadLine()
   If stringToDecrypt = "" Then
       stringToDecrypt = encryptedCard.EncryptedData
   End If
```

```
        Dim decryptedCard As SecureCard = New SecureCard(stringToDecrypt)
        Console.WriteLine("Decrypted data: {0}, {1}, {2}, {3}, {4}, {5}", _
            decryptedCard.CardHolder, decryptedCard.CardNumber, _
            decryptedCard.IssueDate, decryptedCard.ExpiryDate, _
            decryptedCard.IssueNumber, decryptedCard.CardType)
    End Sub
```

4. Execute:

How It Works

There is a bit more code here than in previous examples, but it is all quite simple. First we have the private member variables to hold the card details as individual strings, as an encrypted string, and in an intermediate XML document. We also have Boolean flags indicating whether the data has been successfully encrypted or decrypted:

```
Imports System.Xml

Public Class SecureCard
    Private isDecrypted As Boolean = False
    Private isEncrypted As Boolean = False
    Private _cardHolder As String
    Private _cardNumber As String
    Private _issueDate As String
    Private _expiryDate As String
    Private _issueNumber As String
    Private _cardType As String
    Private _encryptedData As String
    Private _xmlCardData As XmlDocument
```

Next we have three constructors, a private default one (since we don't want the class to be instantiated with no data), and two for encrypting or decrypting credit card data:

```
    Private Sub New()
        ' private default constructor
    End Sub
```

```
Public Sub New(ByVal newEncryptedData As String)
  ' constructor for use with encrypted data
  _encryptedData = newEncryptedData
  DecryptData()
End Sub

Public Sub New(ByVal newCardHolder As String, ByVal newCardNumber As String, _
    ByVal newIssueDate As String, ByVal newExpiryDate As String, _
    ByVal newIssueNumber As String, ByVal newCardType As String)
  ' constructor for use with decrypted data
  _cardHolder = newCardHolder
  _cardNumber = newCardNumber
  _issueDate = newIssueDate
  _expiryDate = newExpiryDate
  _issueNumber = newIssueNumber
  _cardType = newCardType
  EncryptData()
End Sub
```

The main work is carried out in the private `EncryptData()` and `DecryptData()` methods, which we'll come to shortly. First we have two utility methods for packaging and unpackaging data in XML format (which makes it easier for us to get at the bits we want when exchanging data with the encrypted format):

```
Private Sub CreateXml()
  ' encode card details as XML document
  _xmlCardData = New XmlDocument()
  Dim documentRoot As XmlElement = _xmlCardData.CreateElement("CardDetails")
  Dim child As XmlElement

  child = _xmlCardData.CreateElement("CardHolder")
  child.InnerXml = _cardHolder
  documentRoot.AppendChild(child)

  child = _xmlCardData.CreateElement("CardNumber")
  child.InnerXml = _cardNumber
  documentRoot.AppendChild(child)

  child = _xmlCardData.CreateElement("IssueDate")
  child.InnerXml = _issueDate
  documentRoot.AppendChild(child)

  child = _xmlCardData.CreateElement("ExpiryDate")
  child.InnerXml = _expiryDate
  documentRoot.AppendChild(child)

  child = _xmlCardData.CreateElement("IssueNumber")
  child.InnerXml = _issueNumber
  documentRoot.AppendChild(child)

  child = _xmlCardData.CreateElement("CardType")
  child.InnerXml = _cardType
  documentRoot.AppendChild(child)
```

```
    _xmlCardData.AppendChild(documentRoot)
End Sub

Private Sub ExtractXml()
  ' get card details out of XML document
  _cardHolder = _xmlCardData.GetElementsByTagName("CardHolder").Item(0).InnerXml
  _cardNumber = _
      _xmlCardData.GetElementsByTagName("CardNumber").Item(0).InnerXml
  _issueDate = _
      _xmlCardData.GetElementsByTagName("IssueDate").Item(0).InnerXml
  _expiryDate = _
      _xmlCardData.GetElementsByTagName("ExpiryDate").Item(0).InnerXml
  _issueNumber = _
      _xmlCardData.GetElementsByTagName("IssueNumber").Item(0).InnerXml
  _cardType = _xmlCardData.GetElementsByTagName("CardType").Item(0).InnerXml
End Sub
```

These methods use simple XML syntax to address data elements.

The `EncryptData()` method starts by using the above `CreateXml()` method to package the details supplied in the `SecureCard` constructor into XML format:

```
Private Sub EncryptData()
  Try
    ' stuff data into XML doc
    CreateXml()
```

Next, the XML string contained in the resultant XML document is encrypted into a single string and stored in the `_encryptedData` member:

```
    ' encrypt data
    _encryptedData = StringEncryptor.Encrypt(_xmlCardData.OuterXml)
```

Finally, we set the `isEncrypted` flag to `True` to indicate success – or throw a `SecureCardException` exception if anything goes wrong:

```
    ' set encrypted flag
    isEncrypted = True
  Catch
    Throw New SecureCardException("Unable to encrypt data.")
  End Try
End Sub
```

The `DecryptData()` method gets the XML from its encrypted form and uses it to populate a new XML document:

```
Private Sub DecryptData()
  Try
    ' decrypt data
    _xmlCardData = New XmlDocument()
    _xmlCardData.InnerXml = StringEncryptor.Decrypt(_encryptedData)
```

Then it gets the data in the XML document into the private member variables for card details using `ExtractXml()`, and either sets the `isDecrypted` flag to `True` or throws an exception depending on whether the code succeeds:

```
    ' extract data from XML
    ExtractXml()

    ' set decrypted flag
    isDecrypted = True
    Catch
      Throw New SecureCardException("Unable to decrypt data.")
    End Try
  End Sub
```

Next we come to the publicly accessible properties of the class. There are quite a few of these so I won't show them all. Several are for reading card detail data, such as `CardHolder`:

```
Public ReadOnly Property CardHolder() As String
  Get
    If isDecrypted Then
      Return _cardHolder
    Else
      Throw New SecureCardException("Data not decrypted.")
    End If
  End Get
End Property
```

Note that the data is only accessible when `isDecrypted` is `True`, so if an exception has been thrown during decryption then no data is available here (an exception is thrown instead). Also, note that the data isn't accessible after encryption – the data used to initialize a `SecureCard` object is only accessible in encrypted form. This is more a use-case decision than anything else, since this class is only really intended for encryption and decryption, not for persistently representing credit card details. Once a `SecureCard` instance has been used to encrypt card details we shouldn't subsequently need access to the unencrypted data, only the encrypted string.

One interesting property here is `CardNumberX`, which displays only a portion of the number on a credit card. This is handy when showing a user existing details, and is becoming standard practice since it lets the customer know what card they have stored without exposing the details to prying eyes:

```
Public ReadOnly Property CardNumberX() As String
  Get
    If isDecrypted Then
     Return "XXXX-XXXX-XXXX-" & _cardNumber.Substring(_cardNumber.Length - 4, 4)
    Else
      Throw New SecureCardException("Data not decrypted.")
    End If
  End Get
End Property
```

The last property worth looking at is `EncryptedData`, used when extracting the encrypted credit card details for database storage:

```
    Public ReadOnly Property EncryptedData() As String
      Get
        If isEncrypted Then
          Return _encryptedData
        Else
          Throw New SecureCardException("Data not encrypted.")
        End If
      End Get
    End Property
End Class
```

The structure here is much like the other properties, although this time the isEncrypted flag restricts access rather than the isDecrypted flag.

Before moving on to the client code it is worth explaining and justifying one important design consideration that you have probably already noticed. At no point are any of the card details validated. In fact, this class will work perfectly well with empty strings for any properties. This is so the class can remain as versatile as possible. It is more likely that credit card details will be validated as part of the UI used to enter them, or even not at all. This isn't at all dangerous – if invalid details are used then the credit card transaction will simply fail, and we handle that using very similar logic to that required to deal with lack of funds (that is, we notify the customer of failure and ask them to try another card). Of course, there are also simple data formatting issues (dates are usually MM/YY for example), but as noted, these can be dealt with externally to the SecureCard class.

The client code for this class simply allows you to see how an encrypted card looks. As you can see, quite a lot of data is generated, hence the rather large column size in the Customer database. We can also see that both encryption and decryption are working perfectly, and can now move on to the customer account section of this chapter.

The Customer Login Page

Currently, ShoppingCart.ascx has the following code when we hit the **Place Order** button:

```
Private Sub placeOrderButton_Click(ByVal sender As System.Object, _
    ByVal e As System.EventArgs) Handles placeOrderButton.Click
  ' The Shopping Cart object
  Dim cart As New ShoppingCart()

  ' We need to store the total amount because the shopping cart
  ' is emptied when creating the order
  Dim amount As Decimal = cart.GetTotalAmount()

  ' Create the order and store the order ID
  Dim orderId As String = cart.CreateOrder()

  ' After saving the order into our database, we need to
  ' redirect to a page where the customer can pay for the
  ' order. Please take a look at the "Single Item Purchases"
  ' section of the PayPal appendix to see how you can
  ' integrate PayPal here
```

```
    ' Right now we redirect to default.aspx
    Response.Redirect("default.aspx")
End Sub
```

This creates an entry in the Orders table using the contents of the current shopping cart then uses this in a call to PayPal (details not shown here). After this processing, we have a new order and an empty shopping cart.

In our new system we'll be removing this code from this class (although much of it will reappear later). Instead, we redirect the user to our new page, Checkout.aspx. This page will check for a logged on user by examining the session state for a variable called WroxJokeShop_CustomerID, and will redirect the user to another new web page, CustomerLogin.aspx, if this variable isn't found (meaning that the user isn't logged in). The checkout page itself will allow users to edit their details, including credit card details, and place the order. Alternatively, they can cancel the order in progress at any time, return to the shop front, add more items to the shopping cart (which will be preserved until the order is placed), and place the order later.

In this section we'll make the required modification to ShoppingCart.ascx, add the basic login check portion of Checkout.aspx, and implement CustomerLogin.aspx.

Try it Out – Adding the Customer Login Page

1. Add a reference to the WroxJokeShop project to the SecurityLib assembly created earlier.

2. Modify ShoppingCart.ascx as follows:

```
Private Sub placeOrderButton_Click(ByVal sender As System.Object, _
    ByVal e As System.EventArgs) Handles placeOrderButton.Click
    ' Redirect to checkout page
    Response.Redirect("Checkout.aspx")
End Sub
```

3. Modify the text on the **Place Order** button so it says **Checkout**.

4. Add a new Web Form to the WroxJokeShop application called Checkout.aspx.

5. Modify the code in Checkout.aspx.vb as follows:

```
Public Class Checkout
    Inherits System.Web.UI.Page
    Private customerID As Integer

    ...Web Form Designer Generated Code...

    Private Sub Page_Load(ByVal sender As System.Object, _
        ByVal e As System.EventArgs) Handles MyBase.Load
        If Not Page.IsPostBack Then
            If Context.Session("WroxJokeShop_CustomerID") Is Nothing Then
```

```
            Response.Redirect("CustomerLogin.aspx?ReturnPage=Checkout.aspx")
        Else
            customerID = _
                Convert.ToInt32(Context.Session("WroxJokeShop_CustomerID"))
        End If
    Else
        customerID = Convert.ToInt32(Context.Session("WroxJokeShop_CustomerID"))
    End If
End Sub
```

6. Add a new Web Form to the `WroxJokeShop` application called `CustomerLogin.aspx`.

7. Modify the ASP.NET code as follows:

```
<!DOCTYPE HTML PUBLIC "-//W3C//DTD HTML 4.0 Transitional//EN">
<HTML>
  <HEAD>
    <title>Customer Login</title>
    <meta content="Microsoft Visual Studio.NET 7.0" name="GENERATOR">
    <meta content="Visual Basic 7.0" name="CODE_LANGUAGE">
    <meta content="JavaScript" name="vs_defaultClientScript">
    <meta content="http://schemas.microsoft.com/intellisense/ie5"
        name="vs_targetSchema">
  </HEAD>
  <body>
    <form id="Form1" method="post" runat="server">
        <p>If you are a returning customer please enter your login details
            here:</p>
        <P>
          <table>
            <tr>
              <td><asp:label id="Label1" runat="server"
                  text="E-Mail Address:"/></td>
              <td><asp:textbox id="txtEmail" runat="server"/></td>
            </tr>
            <tr>
              <td><asp:label id="Label2" runat="server" text="Password:"/></td>
              <td><asp:textbox id="txtPassword" runat="server"
                  TextMode="Password"/></td>
            </tr>
          </table>
        </P>
        <P><asp:button id="btnLogin" runat="server" Text="Login"></asp:button></P>
        <P><asp:label id="lblLoginMsg" runat="server"></asp:label></P>
        <P>If you are a new customer please press the following button to
            register:</P>
        <P><asp:button id="btnRegister" runat="server"
            Text="Register"></asp:button></P>
    </form>
  </body>
</HTML>
```

8. Add the following `Imports` statements to `CustomerLogin.aspx.vb`:

```
Imports System.Data.SqlClient
Imports SecurityLib
```

9. Add event handlers for the two buttons on the form as follows:

```
Private Sub btnLogin_Click(ByVal sender As System.Object, _
    ByVal e As System.EventArgs) Handles btnLogin.Click
  ' create instance of Connection and Command objects
  Dim connection As SqlConnection = _
      New SqlConnection(ConfigurationSettings.AppSettings("ConnectionString"))
  Dim command As SqlCommand = _
      New SqlCommand("GetCustomerIDPassword", connection)
  command.CommandType = CommandType.StoredProcedure
  command.Parameters.Add("@Email", txtEmail.Text)

  ' execute command, checking for a user with the e-mail entered
  connection.Open()
  Dim customerReader As SqlDataReader = command.ExecuteReader()
  If customerReader.Read = False Then
    ' display error, close connection, and exit method
    lblLoginMsg.Text = "Unrecognized Email."
    connection.Close()
    Return
  End If

  ' extract user information and close connection
  Dim customerID As Integer = customerReader("CustomerID")
  Dim hashedPassword As String = customerReader("Password")
  connection.Close()

  ' check password
  If PasswordHasher.Hash(txtPassword.Text) <> hashedPassword Then
    ' display error
    lblLoginMsg.Text = "Unrecognized password."
  Else
    ' set session variable, storing customer ID for later retrieval
    Context.Session("WroxJokeShop_CustomerID") = customerID

    ' redirect user
    If Not Context.Request.QueryString("ReturnPage") Is Nothing Then
      Response.Redirect(Context.Request.QueryString("ReturnPage"))
    Else
      Response.Redirect("default.aspx")
    End If
  End If
End Sub

Private Sub btnRegister_Click(ByVal sender As System.Object, _
    ByVal e As System.EventArgs) Handles btnRegister.Click
```

```
    ' redirect user
    If Not Context.Request.QueryString("ReturnPage") Is Nothing Then
      Response.Redirect("CustomerNew.aspx?ReturnPage=" _
          & Context.Request.QueryString("ReturnPage"))
    Else
      Response.Redirect("CustomerNew.aspx")
    End If
  End Sub
```

10. Add the following stored procedure to the database:

```
CREATE PROCEDURE GetCustomerIDPassword
(@Email varchar(50))
AS

SELECT CustomerID, [Password]
FROM Customer
WHERE Email = @Email
GO
```

11. Compile and point your browser at the Checkout.aspx page, or go via the store front, add some items to a cart, then click on the **Checkout** button to take you to Checkout.aspx automatically.

12. You will be redirected to the new login page, although as yet you will be unable to log in as you haven't registered any customers:

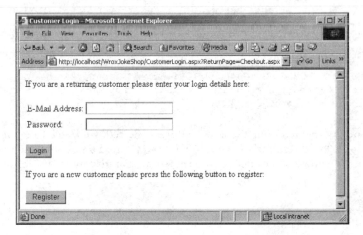

How It Works

As noted above, the code entered isn't a great deal of help at this stage as there are no customers to log in and we won't be adding the customer registration page until the next section. However, we can still look through the code for the page to see how it works.

First, let's have a quick look at what happens in our basic `Checkout.aspx` page. When this page is loaded a check is made for a logged on user. This is achieved by examining the `Session` variable `WroxJokeShop_CustomerID`. If this value is present then a user is logged in, otherwise we redirect the browser to the login page:

```
Private Sub Page_Load(ByVal sender As System.Object, _
    ByVal e As System.EventArgs) Handles MyBase.Load
  If Not Page.IsPostBack Then
    If Context.Session("WroxJokeShop_CustomerID") Is Nothing Then
      Response.Redirect("CustomerLogin.aspx?ReturnPage=Checkout.aspx")
    Else
      customerID = _
          Convert.ToInt32(Context.Session("WroxJokeShop_CustomerID"))
    End If
  Else
    customerID = Convert.ToInt32(Context.Session("WroxJokeShop_CustomerID"))
  End If
End Sub
```

If a customer is logged in then this code also stores the ID retrieved from the `Session` variable in the private member `CustomerID`. Now, let's move on to look at `CustomerLogin.aspx`.

After the user has entered their e-mail address and password the code starts by checking to see if there is a user with the e-mail address entered. It does this using the `GetCustomerIDPassword` stored procedure, which returns the ID and (hashed) password for a given customer e-mail address:

```
Private Sub btnLogin_Click(ByVal sender As System.Object, _
                        ByVal e As System.EventArgs) Handles btnLogin.Click
  ' create instance of Connection and Command objects
  Dim connection As SqlConnection = _
    New SqlConnection(ConfigurationSettings.AppSettings("ConnectionString"))
  Dim command As SqlCommand = _
    New SqlCommand("GetCustomerIDPassword", connection)
  command.CommandType = CommandType.StoredProcedure
  command.Parameters.Add("@Email", txtEmail.Text)
```

After the command is executed using the e-mail address entered, we check to see if a customer has been found by testing for a `True` result when we call the `Read()` method on the data reader obtained. If we don't get this then we know that no such user exists, so we can display an appropriate message and exit the event handler:

```
  ' execute command, checking for a user with the e-mail entered
  connection.Open()
  Dim customerReader As SqlDataReader = command.ExecuteReader()
  If customerReader.Read = False Then
    ' display error, close connection, and exit method
    lblLoginMsg.Text = "Unrecognized Email."
    connection.Close()
    Return
  End If
```

If a user does exist then we get the ID and password information out of the data reader for further processing:

```
' extract user information and close connection
Dim customerID As Integer = customerReader("CustomerID")
Dim hashedPassword As String = customerReader("Password")
connection.Close()
```

The next step is to check the password entered against the password stored. This requires us to hash the entered password, since the stored password is also hashed. Again, if no match is found then we display a message and exit:

```
' check password
If PasswordHasher.Hash(txtPassword.Text) <> hashedPassword Then
  ' display error
  lblLoginMsg.Text = "Unrecognized password."
```

Alternatively, if the passwords do match then we can set the session variable `WroxJokeShop_CustomerID` to the value extracted from the database and redirect the user to the page that originally sent us to the login page (or the `default.aspx` page if the `ReturnPage` querystring parameter was omitted):

```
Else
  ' set session variable, storing customer ID for later retrieval
  Context.Session("WroxJokeShop_CustomerID") = customerID

  ' redirect user
  If Not Context.Request.QueryString("ReturnPage") Is Nothing Then
    Response.Redirect(Context.Request.QueryString("ReturnPage"))
  Else
    Response.Redirect("default.aspx")
  End If
End If
End Sub
```

The other event handler, for the Register button, simply redirects to the customer registration page, `CustomerNew.aspx`, forwarding the `ReturnPage` querystring parameter. The URL `CustomerLogin.aspx?returnPage=Checkout.aspx` is used so that the login page knows where to redirect to.

The Customer Registration Page

The customer registration page is already hooked up to the customer login page, we just need to add the code itself.

Try It Out – Adding the Customer Registration Page

1. Add a new Web Form to the `WroxJokeShop` application called `CustomerNew.aspx`.

2. Modify the ASP.NET code as follows:

```html
<HTML>
  <HEAD>
    <title>New Customer</title>
      <meta content="Microsoft Visual Studio.NET 7.0" name="GENERATOR">
      <meta content="Visual Basic 7.0" name="CODE_LANGUAGE">
      <meta content="JavaScript" name="vs_defaultClientScript">
      <meta content="http://schemas.microsoft.com/intellisense/ie5"
        name="vs_targetSchema">
  </HEAD>
  <body>
    <form id="Form1" method="post" runat="server">
      <p>Please enter your details:</p>
      <P>
        <table>
          <tr>
            <td><asp:label id="Label3"
                runat="server">Username:</asp:label></td>
            <td><asp:textbox id="txtUserName"
                runat="server"></asp:textbox></td>
            <td><asp:requiredfieldvalidator id="validateUserName"
                ErrorMessage="You must enter a user name."
                ControlToValidate="txtUserName"
                Runat="server"></asp:requiredfieldvalidator></td>
          </tr>
          <tr>
            <td><asp:label id="Label1"
                runat="server">E-Mail Address:</asp:label></td>
            <td><asp:textbox id="txtEmail"
                runat="server"></asp:textbox></td>
            <td><asp:requiredfieldvalidator id="validateEmail"
                ErrorMessage="You must enter an e-mail address."
                ControlToValidate="txtEmail"
                Runat="server"></asp:requiredfieldvalidator></td>
          </tr>
          <tr>
            <td><asp:label id="Label2"
                runat="server">Password:</asp:label></td>
            <td><asp:textbox id="txtPassword" runat="server"
                TextMode="Password"></asp:textbox></td>
            <td><asp:requiredfieldvalidator id="validatePassword"
                ErrorMessage="You must enter a password."
                ControlToValidate="txtPassword"
                Runat="server"></asp:requiredfieldvalidator></td>
          </tr>
          <tr>
            <td><asp:label id="Label4"
                runat="server">Re-enter Password:</asp:label></td>
            <td><asp:textbox id="txtPasswordConfirm"
                runat="server" TextMode="Password"></asp:textbox></td>
            <td><asp:requiredfieldvalidator id="validatePasswordReEntry"
                ErrorMessage="You must re-enter your password."
                ControlToValidate="txtPasswordConfirm"
                Runat="server"></asp:requiredfieldvalidator>
```

```
                    <asp:comparevalidator id="validatePasswordMatch"
                        ErrorMessage="You must re-enter the same password."
                        ControlToValidate="txtPassword" Runat="server"
                        Operator="Equal"
                        ControlToCompare="txtPasswordConfirm"/></td>
                </tr>
                <tr>
                    <td><asp:label id="Label5"
                        runat="server">Phone Number:</asp:label></td>
                    <td><asp:textbox id="txtPhone"
                        runat="server"></asp:textbox></td>
                    <td><asp:requiredfieldvalidator id="validatePhone"
                        ErrorMessage="You must enter a phone number."
                        ControlToValidate="txtPhone"
                        Runat="server"></asp:requiredfieldvalidator></td>
                </tr>
            </table>
        </P>
        <P><asp:button id="btnConfirm" runat="server"
            Text="Confirm"></asp:button></P>
        <P><asp:label id="lblMsg" runat="server"></asp:label></P>
    </form>
  </body>
</HTML>
```

3. Add the following Imports statements to CustomerNew.aspx.vb:

```
Imports System.Data.SqlClient
Imports SecurityLib
```

4. Add the following event handler for the Confirm button:

```
Private Sub btnConfirm_Click(ByVal sender As System.Object, _
    ByVal e As System.EventArgs) Handles btnConfirm.Click
    ' Create instance of Connection and Command Object, check for existing user
    Dim connection As SqlConnection = _
        New SqlConnection(ConfigurationSettings.AppSettings("ConnectionString"))
    Dim command As SqlCommand = _
        New SqlCommand("GetCustomerIDPassword", connection)
    command.CommandType = CommandType.StoredProcedure
    command.Parameters.Add("@Email", txtEmail.Text)

    connection.Open()
    Dim customerReader As SqlDataReader = command.ExecuteReader()
    If customerReader.Read = True Then
        lblMsg.Text = "A user with that Email address already exists."
        connection.Close()
        Return
    End If
    connection.Close()
```

```
    ' Add user
    command = New SqlCommand("AddCustomer", connection)
    command.CommandType = CommandType.StoredProcedure
    command.Parameters.Add("@Name", txtUserName.Text)
    command.Parameters.Add("@Email", txtEmail.Text)
    command.Parameters.Add("@Password", PasswordHasher.Hash(txtPassword.Text))
    command.Parameters.Add("@Phone", txtPhone.Text)
    Dim customerID As Integer
    connection.Open()
    customerID = command.ExecuteScalar()
    connection.Close()
    Context.Session("WroxJokeShop_CustomerID") = customerID
    If Not Context.Request.QueryString("ReturnPage") Is Nothing Then
      Response.Redirect(Context.Request.QueryString("ReturnPage"))
    Else
      Response.Redirect("default.aspx")
    End If
  End Sub
```

5. Add the following stored procedure to the database:

```
CREATE PROCEDURE AddCustomer
(@Name varchar(50),
 @Email varchar(50),
 @Password varchar(50),
 @Phone varchar(100))
AS

DECLARE @CustomerID AS int

INSERT INTO Customer ([Name], Email, [Password], Phone)
VALUES (@Name, @Email, @Password, @Phone)
SET @CustomerID = @@IDENTITY

SELECT @CustomerID
GO
```

6. Add a customer using the new page, via Checkout.aspx and the **Register** button of CustomerLogin.aspx:

How it Works

At this point the basis of our customer account system is in place. We can now add customers and log in as a specific customer. As yet we haven't provided a means to add more customer details (address and credit card information) but that's not a big problem.

Before moving on let's look at the code for adding a customer. This code starts in a very similar way to the code for logging in a customer, since the first step is to ensure that no existing customer has the e-mail address entered. This code uses the GetCustomerIDPassword stored procedure from the last section, and we needn't look at this in any more depth.

Assuming that a new e-mail address has been entered, the next step is to add the details:

```
' Add user
command = New SqlCommand("AddCustomer", connection)
command.CommandType = CommandType.StoredProcedure
command.Parameters.Add("@Name", txtUserName.Text)
command.Parameters.Add("@Email", txtEmail.Text)
command.Parameters.Add("@Password", PasswordHasher.Hash(txtPassword.Text))
command.Parameters.Add("@Phone", txtPhone.Text)
Dim customerID As Integer
connection.Open()
customerID = command.ExecuteScalar()
connection.Close()
```

This uses the stored procedure AddCustomer, which returns the ID of the new customer as a result. We can then use this ID to set as the session variable for customer ID, thus removing the need for customers to log in after entering their details:

```
Context.Session("WroxJokeShop_CustomerID") = customerID
```

Finally, we redirect the user using the ReturnPage querystring parameter as before:

```
            If Not Context.Request.QueryString("ReturnPage") Is Nothing Then
                Response.Redirect(Context.Request.QueryString("ReturnPage"))
            Else
                Response.Redirect("default.aspx")
            End If
        End Sub
```

Customer Detail Modification Pages

There are three pages for modifying customer details:

❑ `CustomerEdit.aspx` – modifies basic customer information, including e-mail address, password, and phone number

❑ `CustomerAddress.aspx` – modifies customer address

❑ `CustomerCreditCard.aspx` – modifies customer credit card information

These function in a very similar way. Each of these pages displays a simple form using ASP.NET code much like that we've seen above, allowing the customer to edit various pieces of information. Each of them uses the following stored procedure, `GetCustomer`, to get the details it needs to populate text boxes with existing details:

```
CREATE PROCEDURE GetCustomer
(@CustomerID varchar(50))
AS

SELECT CustomerID, [Name], [Password], Email, CreditCard, Address1, Address2,
City,
 Region, PostalCode, Country, Phone
FROM Customer
WHERE CustomerID = @CustomerID
GO
```

The following three stored procedures, `UpdateCustomerDetails`, `UpdateAddress`, and `UpdateCreditCard`, are used to make changes to the information in the database. `UpdateCustomerDetails` changes the entries for the `Name`, `Email`, `Password`, and `Phone` columns:

```
CREATE PROCEDURE UpdateCustomerDetails
(@CustomerID int,
 @Name varchar(50),
 @Email varchar(50),
 @Password varchar(50),
 @Phone varchar(100))

AS
UPDATE Customer
SET [Name] = @Name, Email = @Email, [Password] = @Password, Phone = [Phone]
WHERE CustomerID = @CustomerID
GO
```

UpdateAddress changes the entries for the Address1, Address2, City, Region, PostalCode, and Country columns:

```
CREATE PROCEDURE UpdateAddress
(@CustomerID int,
 @Address1 varchar(100),
 @Address2 varchar(100),
 @City varchar(100),
 @Region varchar(100),
 @PostalCode varchar(100),
 @Country varchar(100)
)

AS
UPDATE Customer
SET Address1 = @Address1, Address2 = @Address2, City = @City, Region = @Region,
 PostalCode = @PostalCode, Country = @Country
WHERE CustomerID = @CustomerID
GO
```

UpdateCreditCard changes the entry for the CreditCard column:

```
CREATE PROCEDURE UpdateCreditCard
(@CustomerID int,
 @CreditCard varchar(512))

AS
UPDATE Customer
SET CreditCard = @CreditCard
WHERE CustomerID = @CustomerID
GO
```

Other than that, there is very little to say about this section of the code. Since there is nothing new to learn here, please refer to the downloadable code for a look at these pages, which contain comments to guide you through.

The Checkout Page

We are now in a position to add to the checkout page (so far all it does is redirect users to CustomerLogin.aspx if they aren't logged in). This page will look similar to the ShoppingCart.ascx control, as we are displaying the items ordered, but will also display additional information. Since we have access to a logged in user we can display user information, and can also include buttons for modifying address and credit card information. For new customers, neither address nor credit card information will have been added, so we can also disable the order button until such time as this information has been added.

We will take some of the ASP.NET code from default.aspx, such that we include the same color scheme, header, and so on, although we won't include the list of links on the left-hand side.

Try It Out – Updating the Checkout Page

1. Modify the ASP.NET code for `Checkout.aspx` as follows:

```
<%@ Register TagPrefix="uc1" TagName="Header" Src="UserControls/Header.ascx" %>
<%@ Page Language="vb" AutoEventWireup="false" Codebehind="Checkout.aspx.vb"
    Inherits="WroxJokeShop.Checkout"%>
<!DOCTYPE HTML PUBLIC "-//W3C//DTD HTML 4.0 Transitional//EN">
<HTML>
  <HEAD>
    <title>Checkout</title>
    <meta name="GENERATOR" content="Microsoft Visual Studio.NET 7.0">
    <meta name="CODE_LANGUAGE" content="Visual Basic 7.0">
    <meta name="vs_defaultClientScript" content="JavaScript">
    <meta name="vs_targetSchema"
        content="http://schemas.microsoft.com/intellisense/ie5">
      <link href="WroxJokeShop.css" type="text/css" rel="stylesheet">
  </HEAD>
  <body>
    <form id="Form1" runat="server">
      <table height="100%" cellSpacing="0" cellPadding="0" width="770"
          border="0">
        <tr>
          <td width="200" height="100%">
          <table background="Images/backgr.gif" height="100%" width="100%"
              cellspacing="0" cellpadding="0">
          <tr>
            <td vAlign="top" height="100%">
            </td>
          </tr>
          <tr>
            <td>
              <IMG src="Images/wrox.jpg" height="369" width="197"border="0">
            </td>
          </tr>
        </table>
        </td>
        <td vAlign="top" width="550"><br>
        <table>
          <tr>
            <td>
              <uc1:Header id="Header1" runat="server"></uc1:Header>
            </td>
          <tr>
            <td>
              <p align="right">
              <b>User logged in:</b>
              <asp:label id="txtUserName" runat="server"></asp:label><br>
              <asp:button id="logOutButton" runat="server"
                  Text="Log Out"></asp:button><br>
              <img src="Images/1n.gif" border="0" width="350" height="1">
              </p>
            </td>
```

```
      </tr>
      <tr>
        <td id="pageContentsCell" runat="server">
          <P><asp:label id="Label1" runat="server" CssClass="ListDescription">
              Your order consists of the following items:
            </asp:label></P>
          <P><asp:datagrid id="grid" runat="server"
                AutoGenerateColumns="False" Width="100%">
              <ItemStyle Font-Size="X-Small" Font-Names="Verdana"
                BackColor="Gainsboro"></ItemStyle>
              <HeaderStyle Font-Size="X-Small"
                  Font-Names="Verdana" Font-Bold="True"
                  ForeColor="White" BackColor="Navy"></HeaderStyle>
                <Columns>
                  <asp:BoundColumn DataField="Name"
                      ReadOnly="True" HeaderText="Product Name">
                  </asp:BoundColumn>
                  <asp:BoundColumn DataField="Price" ReadOnly="True"
                      HeaderText="Price"></asp:BoundColumn>
                  <asp:BoundColumn DataField="Quantity" ReadOnly="True"
                      HeaderText="Quantity"></asp:BoundColumn>
                  <asp:BoundColumn DataField="Subtotal" ReadOnly="True"
                      HeaderText="Subtotal"></asp:BoundColumn>
                </Columns>
              </asp:datagrid></P>
            <P>
            Total amount:
            <asp:label id="totalAmountLabel" runat="server"
                CssClass="ProductPrice"></asp:label>
            <br><br>
            <asp:label id="lblCreditCardNote"
                Runat="server"></asp:label>
            <br><br>
            <asp:label id="lblAddress" Runat="server"></asp:label>
            <br><br>
            <asp:button id="changeDetailsButton" runat="server"
                Text="Change Customer Details"></asp:button>
            <asp:button id="addCreditCardButton" runat="server"
                Text="Add Credit Card"></asp:button>
            <asp:button id="addAddressButton" runat="server"
                Text="Add Address"></asp:button>
            <br><br>
            <asp:button id="placeOrderButton" runat="server"
                Text="Place Order"></asp:button>
            <asp:button id="cancelOrderButton" runat="server"
                Text="Continue Shopping"></asp:button>
            </P>
          </td>
        </tr>
      </table>
    </td>
  </tr>
</table>
```

381

```
        </form>
      </body>
    </HTML>
```

2. Add the following `Imports` statements to `Checkout.aspx.vb`:

```
Imports System.Data.SqlClient
Imports SecurityLib
Imports System.Text
```

3. Add the following private methods for displaying user and shopping cart details (`BindShoppingCart()` is very similar to the method of the same name in `ShoppingCart.ascx`):

```
Private Sub BindShoppingCart()
  ' Populate the data grid and set its DataKey field
  Dim cart As New ShoppingCart()
  grid.DataSource = cart.GetProducts
  grid.DataKeyField = "ProductID"
  grid.DataBind()

  ' Set the total amount label using the Currency format
  totalAmountLabel.Text = String.Format("{0:c}", cart.GetTotalAmount())
End Sub

Private Sub BindUserDetails()
  ' Create Instance of Connection and Command Object
  Dim connection As SqlConnection = _
      New SqlConnection(ConfigurationSettings.AppSettings("ConnectionString"))
  Dim command As SqlCommand = New SqlCommand("GetCustomer", connection)
  command.CommandType = CommandType.StoredProcedure
  command.Parameters.Add("@CustomerID", customerID)

  ' get customer details
  connection.Open()
  Dim customerReader As SqlDataReader = command.ExecuteReader()
  If customerReader.Read = False Then
      Response.Redirect("CustomerLogin.aspx?returnPage=Checkout.aspx")
  End If

  ' set customer data display
  txtUserName.Text = customerReader("Name")
  If customerReader("CreditCard").GetType() Is GetType(DBNull) Then
      lblCreditCardNote.Text = "No credit card details stored."
      orderButton.Visible = False
  Else
    Dim cardDetails As SecureCard = _
        New SecureCard(customerReader("CreditCard"))
    lblCreditCardNote.Text = "Credit card to use: " & cardDetails.CardType _
        & ", Card number: " & cardDetails.CardNumberX()
```

```
          addCreditCardButton.Text = "Change Credit Card"
        End If
        If customerReader("Address1").GetType() Is GetType(DBNull) Then
          lblAddress.Text = "Shipping address required to place order."
          orderButton.Visible = False
        Else
          Dim addressBuilder As StringBuilder = New StringBuilder()
          addressBuilder.Append("Shipping address:<br><br>")
          addressBuilder.Append(customerReader("Address1"))
          addressBuilder.Append("<br>")
          If Not customerReader("Address2").GetType() Is GetType(DBNull) Then
            If customerReader("Address2") <> "" Then
              addressBuilder.Append(customerReader("Address2"))
              addressBuilder.Append("<br>")
            End If
          End If
          addressBuilder.Append(customerReader("City"))
          addressBuilder.Append("<br>")
          addressBuilder.Append(customerReader("Region"))
          addressBuilder.Append("<br>")
          addressBuilder.Append(customerReader("PostalCode"))
          addressBuilder.Append("<br>")
          addressBuilder.Append(customerReader("Country"))
          lblAddress.Text = addressBuilder.ToString()
          addAddressButton.Text = "Change Address"
        End If
        connection.Close()
      End Sub
```

4. Modify the code in `Page_Load()` to call the above methods:

```
Private Sub Page_Load(ByVal sender As System.Object, _
    ByVal e As System.EventArgs) Handles MyBase.Load
  If Not Page.IsPostBack Then
    If Context.Session("WroxJokeShop_CustomerID") Is Nothing Then
      Response.Redirect("CustomerLogin.aspx?returnPage=Checkout.aspx")
    Else
      customerID = _
      Convert.ToInt32(Context.Session("WroxJokeShop_CustomerID"))
    End If
    BindShoppingCart()
    BindUserDetails()
  Else
    customerID = Convert.ToInt32(Context.Session("WroxJokeShop_CustomerID"))
  End If
End Sub
```

5. Add the following button event handlers for customer detail modification:

```
Private Sub addCreditCardButton_Click(ByVal sender As System.Object, _
    ByVal e As System.EventArgs) Handles addCreditCardButton.Click
  Response.Redirect("CustomerCreditCard.aspx?ReturnPage=Checkout.aspx")
End Sub

Private Sub addAddressButton_Click(ByVal sender As System.Object, _
    ByVal e As System.EventArgs) Handles addAddressButton.Click
  Response.Redirect("CustomerAddress.aspx?ReturnPage=Checkout.aspx")
End Sub

Private Sub changeDetailsButton_Click(ByVal sender As System.Object, _
    ByVal e As System.EventArgs) Handles changeDetailsButton.Click
  Response.Redirect("CustomerEdit.aspx?ReturnPage=Checkout.aspx")
End Sub

Private Sub logOutButton_Click(ByVal sender As System.Object, _
    ByVal e As System.EventArgs) Handles logOutButton.Click
  Context.Session("WroxJokeShop_CustomerID") = Nothing
  Response.Redirect("default.aspx")
End Sub

Private Sub cancelOrderButton_Click(ByVal sender As System.Object, _
    ByVal e As System.EventArgs) Handles cancelOrderButton.Click
  Response.Redirect("default.aspx")
End Sub
```

6. Add the following event handler for the **Place Order** button:

```
Private Sub placeOrderButton_Click(ByVal sender As System.Object, _
    ByVal e As System.EventArgs) Handles placeOrderButton.Click
  ' The Shopping Cart object
  Dim cart As New ShoppingCart()

  ' We need to store the total amount because the shopping cart
  ' is emptied when creating the order
  Dim amount As Decimal = cart.GetTotalAmount()

  ' Create the order and store the order ID
  Dim orderId As String = cart.CreateOrder()

  ' After saving the order into our database, we need to
  ' redirect to a page where the customer can pay for the
  ' order. Please take a look at the "Single Item Purcases"
  ' section of the PayPal appendix to see how you can
  ' integrate PayPal here

  ' Right now we redirect to default.aspx
  Response.Redirect("default.aspx")
End Sub
```

7. This is the logic for the main checkout page. The other three ASP pages necessary to run this application are:

- ❏ `CustomerAddress.aspx`
- ❏ `CustomerCreditCard.aspx`
- ❏ `CustomerEdit.aspx`

These should be added to the project from the code download file for the chapter. None of them contain anything that we haven't seen before, so merely add them to your project by right-clicking on the project name and selecting **Add | Add Existing Item** and copying them into your working project.

8. Compile, login as the customer registered in the last section, add all customer details, and check out the results:

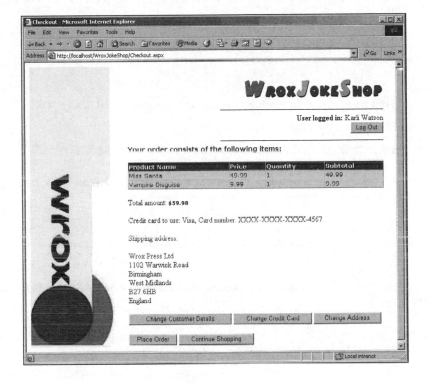

How it Works

Again, we haven't introduced any earth-shattering new code here. All we've done is to use the `GetCustomer` stored procedure to get customer details and format the checkout display accordingly. If either the address or credit card information is not present then we hide the **Order Now** button, since placing an order requires this information. Since `BindShoppingCart()` is practically identical to the version in `ShoppingCart.ascx` (the only difference being that we don't bother to check for items since users will only get to this stage via `ShoppingCart.ascx`) we only need to look through `BindUserDetails()`. This method starts by getting information about the current customer from the `Customer` table:

```
Private Sub BindUserDetails()
  ' Create Instance of Connection and Command Object
  Dim connection As SqlConnection = _
      New SqlConnection(ConfigurationSettings.AppSettings("ConnectionString"))
  Dim command As SqlCommand = New SqlCommand("GetCustomer", connection)
  command.CommandType = CommandType.StoredProcedure
  command.Parameters.Add("@CustomerID", customerID)

  ' get customer details
  connection.Open()
  Dim customerReader As SqlDataReader = command.ExecuteReader()
```

If no customer is found then there is a problem with the login, so we redirect the user to the
CustomerLogin.aspx page:

```
If customerReader.Read = False Then
  Response.Redirect("CustomerLogin.aspx?returnPage=Checkout.aspx")
End If
```

Otherwise, we begin extracting information, starting with the name of the user:

```
' set customer data display
txtUserName.Text = customerReader("Name")
```

Next we try to get the credit card details, which may or may not be present. If no data is present then
we hide the order button and display an appropriate message:

```
If customerReader("CreditCard").GetType() Is GetType(DBNull) Then
  lblCreditCardNote.Text = "No credit card details stored."
  orderButton.Visible = False
```

Alternatively, we display the required details and modify the text on the **Add Credit Card** button to
Change Credit Card:

```
Else
  Dim cardDetails As SecureCard = _
      New SecureCard(customerReader("CreditCard"))
  lblCreditCardNote.Text = "Credit card to use: " & cardDetails.CardType _
      & ", Card number: " & cardDetails.CardNumberX()
  addCreditCardButton.Text = "Change Credit Card"
End If
```

Next we check for an address by looking at the Address1 column and seeing if it contains any data. If it
doesn't then we display a message and disable the **Place Order** button, as we did for credit card details:

```
If customerReader("Address1").GetType() Is GetType(DBNull) Then
  lblAddress.Text = "Shipping address required to place order."
  orderButton.Visible = False
```

If an address is present then we use a `StringBuilder` instance to assemble the address data into an HTML string for displaying on the web page:

```
Else
   Dim addressBuilder As StringBuilder = New StringBuilder()
   addressBuilder.Append("Shipping address:<br><br>")
   addressBuilder.Append(customerReader("Address1"))
   addressBuilder.Append("<br>")
   If Not customerReader("Address2").GetType() Is GetType(DBNull) Then
      If customerReader("Address2") <> "" Then
         addressBuilder.Append(customerReader("Address2"))
         addressBuilder.Append("<br>")
      End If
   End If
   addressBuilder.Append(customerReader("City"))
   addressBuilder.Append("<br>")
   addressBuilder.Append(customerReader("Region"))
   addressBuilder.Append("<br>")
   addressBuilder.Append(customerReader("PostalCode"))
   addressBuilder.Append("<br>")
   addressBuilder.Append(customerReader("Country"))
   lblAddress.Text = addressBuilder.ToString()
   addAddressButton.Text = "Change Address"
End If
```

When we have all the information we need, we close the connection:

```
   connection.Close()
End Sub
```

Currently, the code that is called when the **Place Order** button is clicked is identical to the old code in `ShoppingCart.ascx`. We'll get onto this and change things in the next chapter when we implement our order pipeline.

Secure Connections

It is now possible for customers to register on our site, log in, and change details. However, the current system involves sending potentially sensitive information over HTTP. This protocol isn't secure, and it is possible that it could be intercepted and stolen. To avoid this we need to set up our application to work with secure SSL connections, using the HTTPS protocol.

In order to do this we have a bit of groundwork to get through first. Unless you have already been using SSL connection on your web server you are unlikely to have the correct configuration to do so. This configuration involves obtaining a security certificate for your server and installing it via IIS management.

Security certificates are basically public-private key pairs of similar form to those discussed earlier in the chapter relating to asynchronous encryption. It is possible to generate these yourself if your domain controller is configured as a certification authority, but this has its problems. Digital signing of SSL certificates is such that browsers using such a certificate will not be able to verify the identity of your certification authority, and may therefore doubt your security. This isn't disastrous, but may affect consumer confidence, as they will be presented with a warning message when they attempt to establish a secure connection.

The alternative is to obtain SSL certificates from a known and respected organization that specializes in web security, such as VeriSign. Web browsers such as Internet Explorer have built in root certificates from organizations such as this, and are able to authenticate the digital signature of SSL certificates supplied by them. This means that no warning message will appear, and SSL secured connection will be available with the minimum of fuss.

In this section I'll assume that you take this latter option, although if you want to create your own certificates that won't affect the end result.

Obtaining a SSL Certificate from VeriSign

Obtaining a certificate from VeriSign is a relatively painless experience, and full instructions are available on the VeriSign web site, http://www.verisign.com/. It is also possible to get test certificates from VeriSign, which are free to use for a trial period. The basic steps are as follows:

- ❑ Sign up for a trial certificate on the VeriSign web site.

- ❑ Generate a Certificate Signing Request (CSR) via IIS management on your web server. This involves filling out various personal information, including the name of your web site etc.

- ❑ Copy the contents of the generated CSR into the VeriSign request system.

- ❑ Shortly afterwards, you will receive a certificate from VeriSign that you copy into IIS Management to install the certificate.

There is a little more to it than that, but as noted above, detailed instructions are available on the VeriSign web site, and you shouldn't run into any difficulties.

Enforcing SSL Connections

Once installed, you will find that you can access any web pages on your web server using an SSL connection, simply by replacing the http:// part of the URL used to access the page with https:// (assuming that your firewall is set up to allow SSL connection, which by default uses port 443, if you use a firewall – this doesn't apply to local connections). Obviously, we don't need SSL connections for all areas of the site, and shouldn't enforce it in all places as it can reduce performance. However, we *do* want to make sure that the checkout, customer login, customer registration, and customer detail modification pages are accessible only via SSL.

To achieve this we need to configure the individual pages via IIS management. Looking at the properties for one of these pages in IIS management, Checkout.aspx for example, shows us a File Security tab:

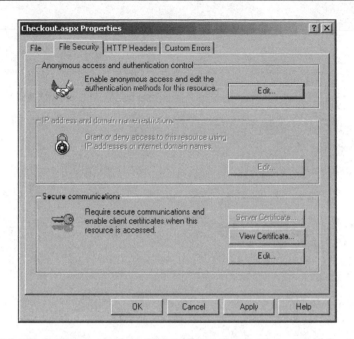

To get this dialog, open IIS manager from the Administrative Tools section of Control Panel, navigate through the tree view through IIS | Local Computer | Web Sites | Default Web Site | WroxJokeShop, and get the properties for `Checkout.aspx`.

From here we can click on the Edit button in the Secure communications section and tick the Require Secure Channel (SSL) box in the dialog that appears (we don't need to worry about the other options):

After clicking on **OK**, attempts to access the `Checkout.aspx` page using HTTP will be rejected.

You should go ahead and make the same modification to all the pages where security is essential:

- ❑ `Checkout.aspx`
- ❑ `CustomerAddress.aspx`
- ❑ `CustomerCreditCard.aspx`
- ❑ `CustomerEdit.aspx`
- ❑ `CustomerLogin.aspx`
- ❑ `CustomerNew.aspx`

Modifying Redirections to Use SSL Connections

Currently we redirect pages using the following syntax (taking the code in `ShoppingCart.ascx.vb` as an example):

```
Private Sub placeOrderButton_Click(ByVal sender As System.Object, _
    ByVal e As System.EventArgs) Handles placeOrderButton.Click
  ' Redirect to checkout page
  Response.Redirect("Checkout.aspx")
End Sub
```

Unfortunately, there is no easy way to change the connection to an SSL one and keep this simple virtual path syntax. Instead we need to provide a full URL to the page, including the `https://` string at the start of the URL. Now, this is all very well for published web sites where we have a mapped domain name, but slightly trickier for testing. The following might seem OK:

```
Private Sub placeOrderButton _Click(ByVal sender As System.Object, _
    ByVal e As System.EventArgs) Handles placeOrderButton.Click
  ' Redirect to checkout page
  Response.Redirect("https://localhost/WroxJokeShop/Checkout.aspx")

End Sub
```

However, this restricts the users that can use the site to those that are accessing it locally on the web server. This is fine for testing, but won't work when we deploy the application.

The solution to this is to extract the host used in the current request (which might be localhost, www.wroxjokeshop.com, or whatever) to build the URL, using code as follows:

```
Private Sub placeOrderButton _Click(ByVal sender As System.Object, _
    ByVal e As System.EventArgs) Handles placeOrderButton.Click
  ' Redirect to checkout page
  Response.Redirect("https://" & Request.Url.Host _
      & "/WroxJokeShop/Checkout.aspx")
End Sub
```

We also have something else to consider – in Chapter 8 we changed things a bit by storing session information without using cookies, instead including the session ID in the URL. Unfortunately, the code shown above won't cope with this. Instead, we need to check if this scheme is being used and include the session ID if necessary, using the following code:

```
Private Sub placeOrderButton_Click(ByVal sender As System.Object, _
    ByVal e As System.EventArgs) Handles placeOrderButton.Click
  ' Redirect to checkout page
  If Session.IsCookieless Then
    Response.Redirect("https://" & Request.Url.Host _
        & "/WroxJokeShop/(" & Session.SessionID & ")/Checkout.aspx")
  Else
    Response.Redirect("https://" & Request.Url.Host _
        & "/WroxJokeShop/Checkout.aspx")
  End If
End Sub
```

The `Session.IsCookieless` property is a Boolean one that reflects the configured behavior in `Web.config`. This change keeps the same URL format that we've seen in earlier examples, and makes sure we don't lose the shopping cart between pages.

Further redirects will keep using the HTTPS protocol even if they are just redirects to virtual paths, so this is the only place we need to make this change. However, we don't want to continue using HTTPS when we return to `default.aspx`, since there is an appreciable overhead when using a secure connection. Instead we modify the code in `default.aspx.vb` to detect and redirect secure connections, using similar code to that shown above:

```
Private Sub Page_Load(ByVal sender As System.Object, _
    ByVal e As System.EventArgs) Handles MyBase.Load
  ' Check for HTTPS (SSL) connection
  If Context.Request.IsSecureConnection Then
    ' Redirect to standard HTTP
    If Session.IsCookieless Then
      Response.Redirect("http://" & Request.Url.Host _
          & "/WroxJokeShop/(" & Session.SessionID & ")/default.aspx")
    Else
      Response.Redirect("http://" & Request.Url.Host _
          & "/WroxJokeShop/default.aspx")
    End If
  End If
End If
```

This ensures the persistence of shopping cart data and ends secure connections.

Summary

In this chapter we have implemented a customer account system that customers can use to store their details ready for use during order processing. We've looked at many aspects of this, including the encryption of sensitive data, and secure web connections for obtaining it.

We started by looking at a new table in our database, `Customer`, with fields for storing customer information.

Next we created a `SecurityLib` class library, containing classes for hashing and encrypting strings, and a secure credit card representation that makes it easy for us to exchange credit card details between encrypted and decrypted format.

After this we used this library to assist us in creating login, registration, and customer detail editing web pages. This required a few more stored procedures to be added, but the actual code turned out to be quite simple.

Finally, we looked at how we can secure data passing over the Internet using secure SSL connections. This involved obtaining a certificate from a known certification authority (VeriSign was used as an example), installing it, restricting access to SSL where appropriate, and modifying our redirection code slightly to use SSL connections.

In the next chapter we'll be looking at how we can create the framework for the order-processing pipeline, enabling us to automate even more of our supply process.

Order Pipeline

Our e-commerce application is shaping up nicely. Now we have added customer account functionality, and we are keeping track of customer addresses and credit card information, which is stored in a secure way. However, we are not currently using this information – currently we are delegating responsibility for this to PayPal.

In this chapter we will build our own order processing pipeline that deals with credit card authorization, stock checking, shipping, e-mail notification, and so on. In actual fact, we'll leave the credit card processing specifics until the next chapter, but we will show where this process fits in here.

Order pipeline functionality is an extremely useful capability for an e-commerce site. The reason for this is that it allows us to keep track of orders at every stage in the process, and leaves us with auditing information that we can refer to at a later date, or if something goes wrong during the order processing. We do all this without having to rely on a third party's accounting system, which can also reduce costs. The first section of this chapter will discuss what we actually mean by an order pipeline, and the specifics that apply to our WroxJokeShop application.

There are many ways of implementing such a system, and many people recommend that you use a transactional system such as MTS, or COM+ in more recent operating systems. However, this adds its own complications, and frankly doesn't give us that much that we can't achieve using standard .NET assemblies. While it is possible to create COM+ components using .NET, the code implementation is more complicated, and debugging code can be very tricky. For this reason we will stick with the .NET platform here – which has the added advantage that it makes code easier to understand and debug. The bulk of this chapter will deal with the construction of such a system, which will also involve a small amount of modification to the way things currently work, and some additions to the database we've been using. However, the code in this chapter isn't much more complicated than the code we've already been using. The real challenges are in the design of our system.

By the end of this chapter, customers will be able to place orders into our pipeline, and we'll be able to follow the progress of these orders as they pass through various stages. Although no real credit card processing will take place, we'll end up with a fairly complete system, including a new administration web page that can be used by suppliers to confirm that they have items in stock and to confirm that orders have been shipped. To start with, though, we need a bit more background about what we are actually trying to achieve.

What is an Order Pipeline?

Any commercial transaction, whether in a high street shop, over the Internet, or anywhere else, has several related tasks that must be carried out before it can be considered complete. For example, you can't simply remove an item of clothing from a fashion boutique without paying for it and say that you have bought it – remuneration is (unfortunately!) an integral part of any purchase. In addition, a transaction may only complete successfully if each of the tasks carried out completes successfully. If a customer's credit card is rejected, for example, then no funds can be taken from it, so a purchase can't be made.

The sequence of tasks carried out as part of a transaction is often thought of in terms of a pipeline. In this analogy, orders start at one end of the pipe and come out of the other end when they are completed. Along the way they must pass through several pipeline sections, each of which is responsible for a particular task, or a related group of tasks. If any pipeline section fails to complete, then the order 'gets stuck', and may require outside interaction before it can move further along the pipeline, or it may be canceled completely.

For example, the following simple pipeline applies to high street transactions:

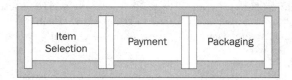

Here the last section might be optional, and might involve additional tasks such as gift-wrapping. The payment stage might also take one of several methods of operation, since the customer could pay using cash, credit card, gift vouchers, and so on.

When we look at e-commerce purchasing, the pipeline becomes longer, but isn't really any more complicated.

The WroxJokeShop Order Pipeline

In our e-commerce application the pipeline will look like this:

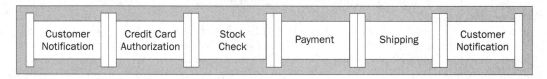

The tasks carried out in these pipeline sections are as follows:

❏ **Customer Notification** – an e-mail is sent to the customer notifying them that order processing has started, and confirming the items to be sent, and the address that goods will be sent to.

❏ **Credit Card Authorization** – the credit card used for purchasing is checked, and the total order amount is set aside (although no payment is taken at this stage).

- ❏ **Stock Check** – an e-mail is sent to the supplier with a list of the items that have been ordered. Processing continues when the supplier confirms that the goods are available.

- ❏ **Payment** – the credit card transaction is completed using the funds set aside earlier.

- ❏ **Shipping** – an e-mail is sent to the supplier confirming that payment for the items ordered has been taken. Processing continues when the supplier confirms that the goods have been shipped.

- ❏ **Customer Notification** – an e-mail is sent to the customer notifying them that the order has been shipped, and thanking them for using the WroxJokeShop web site.

In terms of implementation, as we will see shortly, we will actually have more stages than this, since the stock check and shipping stages actually consist of two pipeline sections – one for sending the e-mail, and one that waits for confirmation.

As orders flow through this pipeline, entries will be added to a new database table called `Audit`. These entries can be examined to see what has happened to an order, and are an excellent way of identifying problems if they occur. Each entry in the `Orders` database will also be flagged with a status, identifying which point in the pipeline it has reached.

Building the Pipeline

To process the pipeline, we will create classes representing each stage. These classes will carry out the required processing and then modify the status of the order in the `Orders` database to advance the order. We'll also need a coordinating class (or processor), which can be called for any order and will execute the appropriate pipeline stage class. This processor will be called once when the order is placed, and in normal operation will be called twice more – once for stock confirmation and once for shipping confirmation.

To make life easier, we'll also define a common interface supported by each pipeline stage class. This will enable the order processor class to access each stage in a standard way. We'll also define several utility functions and expose several common properties in the order processor class, which will be used as and when necessary by the pipeline stages. For example, the ID of the order should be accessible to all pipeline stages, and to save code duplication, we'll put that information in the order processor class.

Now, on to the specifics. We'll build an assembly called `CommerceLib` containing all our classes, which we'll reference from `WroxJokeShop`. `CommerceLib` will contain the following:

- ❏ `OrderProcessor` – the main class for processing orders

- ❏ `OrderProcessorConfiguration` – structure containing various configuration details for the `OrderProcessor` class, including administrator e-mail address, SQL connection string, and so on

- ❏ `OrderProcessorException` – custom exception class for use in the order processor and pipeline sections

- ❏ `IPipelineSection` – interface definition for pipeline sections.

- ❏ `Customer`, `OrderDetails`, `OrderDetail` – classes used to store data extracted from the database, for ease of access

- ❏ `PSInitialNotification`, `PSCheckFunds`, `PSCheckStock`, `PSStockOK`, `PSTakePayment`, `PSShipGoods`, `PSShipOK`, `PSFinalNotification` – pipeline section classes

The progress of an order through the pipeline as mediated by the order processor relates to the pipeline shown earlier as follows:

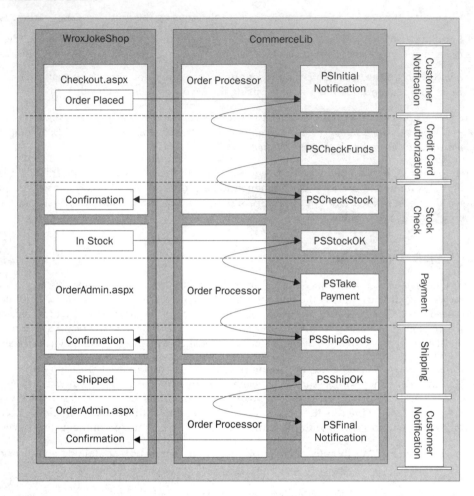

The process shown in this diagram is divided into three sections as follows:

- ❑ Customer places order
- ❑ Supplier confirms stock
- ❑ Supplier confirms shipping

The first stage is as follows:

- ❑ When the customer confirms an order, Checkout.aspx creates the order in the database and calls OrderProcessor to begin order processing.
- ❑ OrderProcessor detects that the order is new and calls PSInitialNotification.

- ❑ `PSInitialNotification` sends an e-mail to the customer confirming the order, and advances the order stage. It also instructs `OrderProcessor` to continue processing.

- ❑ `OrderProcessor` detects the new order status and calls `PSCheckFunds`.

- ❑ `PSCheckFunds` checks that funds are available on the customer's credit card, and stores the details required to complete the transaction if funds are available. If this is successful, then the order stage is advanced and `OrderProcessor` is told to continue.

- ❑ `OrderProcessor` detects the new order status and calls `PSCheckStock`.

- ❑ `PSCheckStock` sends an e-mail to the supplier with a list of the items ordered, instructs the supplier to confirm via `OrderAdmin.aspx`, and advances the order status.

- ❑ `OrderProcessor` terminates.

The second stage:

- ❑ When the supplier confirms that stock is available `OrderAdmin.aspx` calls `OrderProcessor` to continue order processing.

- ❑ `OrderProcessor` detects the new order status and calls `PSStockOK`.

- ❑ `PSStockOK` advances the order status and tells `OrderProcessor` to continue.

- ❑ `OrderProcessor` detects the new order status and calls `PSTakePayment`.

- ❑ `PSTakePayment` uses the transaction details stored earlier by `PSCheckFunds` to complete the transaction, then advances the order status and tells `OrderProcessor` to continue.

- ❑ `OrderProcessor` detects the new order status and calls `PSShipGoods`.

- ❑ `PSShipGoods` sends an e-mail to the supplier with a confirmation of the items ordered, instructs the supplier to ship these goods to the customer, and advances the order status.

- ❑ `OrderProcessor` terminates.

The third stage:

- ❑ When the supplier confirms that the goods have been shipped, `OrderAdmin.aspx` calls `OrderProcessor` to continue order processing.

- ❑ `OrderProcessor` detects the new order status and calls `PSShipOK`.

- ❑ `PSShipOK` enters the shipment date in the database, advances the order status, and tells `OrderProcessor` to continue.

- ❑ `OrderProcessor` detects the new order status and calls `PSFinalNotification`.

- ❑ `PSFinalNotification` sends an e-mail to the customer confirming that the order has been shipped and advances the order stage.

- ❑ `OrderProcessor` terminates.

If anything goes wrong at any point in the pipeline processing, such as a credit card being declined, an e-mail is sent to an administrator. This administrator then has all the information necessary to check what has happened, get in contact with the customer involved, and cancel or replace the order if necessary.

At no point in this process do we do anything particularly complicated, it's just that there's quite a lot of code required to put this into action!

Groundwork

Before we start building the components described above, there are a few modifications that we need to make to the WroxJokeShop database and web application.

The Audit Table

During order processing, one of the most important functions of the pipeline is to maintain an up-to-date audit trail. The implementation of this will involve adding records to a new database table called Audit. We need to create this table with fields as follows:

Column Name	Column Type	Description
AuditID	int(4)	Primary key, also set as table identity
OrderID	int(4)	The ID of the order that the audit entry applies to
DateStamp	datetime(8)	The date and time that the audit entry was created
Message	varchar(512)	The text of the audit entry
MessageNumber	int(4)	An identifying number for the audit entry type

Entries will be added by OrderProcessor and by individual pipeline stages to indicate successes and failures. These can then be examined to see what has happened to an order, an important function when it comes to error checking.

The MessageNumber column is an interesting one. This allows us to associate specific messages with an identifying number. It would be possible to have another database table allowing us to match these message numbers with descriptions, although this isn't really necessary, since the scheme used for numbering (as we will see later in the chapter) is in itself quite descriptive. In addition, we have the Message column, which already provides human-readable information.

The Orders Table

Currently the Orders table doesn't allow for as much information as we will need to implement our order-processing pipeline. We will need to add the following new columns to the Orders table:

Column Name	Column Type	Description
Status	int(4)	The current status of the order, which is equivalent to what pipeline section the order has reached
CustomerID	int(4)	The ID of the customer that placed the order
AuthCode	varchar(50)	The authentication code used to complete the customer credit card transaction
Reference	varchar(50)	The unique reference code of the customer credit card transaction

The first two of these columns are self-explanatory, but the next two are related to credit card transactions, which we'll look at in the next chapter.

Note that we won't be using some of the columns that already exist in the Orders table, such as Verified and Completed. This is because this information is now encapsulated in the Status column. We are also using a CustomerID column to link to the Customer table, rather than including customer name information in CustomerName.

The CreateCustomerOrder Stored Procedure

Currently we use the CreateOrder stored procedure to add orders to the database:

```
CREATE PROCEDURE CreateOrder
(@CartID varchar(50))
AS

DECLARE @OrderID int
INSERT INTO Orders (DateCreated, Verified, Completed, Canceled)
VALUES (GETDATE(), 0, 0, 0)
SET @OrderID = @@IDENTITY

INSERT INTO OrderDetail
    (OrderID, ProductID, ProductName, Quantity, UnitCost)
SELECT
    @OrderID, Product.ProductID, Product.[Name],
    ShoppingCart.Quantity, Product.Price
FROM Product JOIN ShoppingCart
ON Product.ProductID = ShoppingCart.ProductID
WHERE ShoppingCart.CartID = @CartID

EXEC EmptyShoppingCart @CartID

SELECT @OrderID
GO
```

Now we have more data to add to the database when we create an order, so we need to use a different (although very similar) stored procedure, CreateCustomerOrder (the differences are highlighted):

```
CREATE PROCEDURE CreateCustomerOrder
(@CartID varchar(50),
 @CustomerID int)
AS

DECLARE @OrderID int
INSERT INTO Orders (DateCreated, Verified, Completed, Canceled, CustomerID,
Status)
VALUES (GETDATE(), 0, 0, 0, @CustomerID, 0)
SET @OrderID = @@IDENTITY

INSERT INTO OrderDetail
    (OrderID, ProductID, ProductName, Quantity, UnitCost)
```

```
SELECT
    @OrderID, Product.ProductID, Product.[Name],
    ShoppingCart.Quantity, Product.Price
FROM Product JOIN ShoppingCart
ON Product.ProductID = ShoppingCart.ProductID
WHERE ShoppingCart.CartID = @CartID

EXEC EmptyShoppingCart @CartID

SELECT @OrderID
GO
```

The two new bits here are as follows:

❑   Including a `CustomerID` value with the order.

❑   Setting the `Status` column to 0, signifying that the order needs processing from the start of the order pipeline.

WroxJokeShop Modification

To make use of the new stored procedure we need to overload a method on the `ShoppingCart` class in the `WroxJokeShop` application. Insert the following method into this class:

```vb
Public Function CreateOrder(ByVal customerID As Integer) As Integer
    ' Create the connection object
    Dim connection As New SqlConnection(connectionString)

    ' Create and initialize the command object
    Dim command As New SqlCommand("CreateCustomerOrder", connection)
    command.CommandType = CommandType.StoredProcedure

    ' Add input parameters and supply values for them
    command.Parameters.Add("@CartID", SqlDbType.VarChar, 50)
    command.Parameters("@CartID").Value = shoppingCartId
    command.Parameters.Add("@CustomerID", SqlDbType.Int, 4)
    command.Parameters("@CustomerID").Value = customerID

    ' Save the value that needs to be returned to a variable
    Dim orderId As Integer
    connection.Open()
    orderId = Convert.ToInt32(command.ExecuteScalar())

    ' Close the connection
    connection.Close()

    ' Return the saved value
    Return orderId
End Function
```

This is simply a new overload for the `CreateOrder()` method used earlier in the book. We'll use this version later, when we modify the `Checkout.aspx` page to utilize the order-processing pipeline.

Utility Classes

The first classes we'll look at are the `OrderProcessorException` exception class and the utility classes for database objects, `Customer`, `OrderDetail`, and `OrderDetails`. We're looking at these first as the other classes use them, so having the types defined will make entering the code for later classes easier.

Try It Out – CommerceLib Utility Classes

1. Create a new Class Library project called `CommerceLib` in the directory `C:\BegECommerce\Chapter11`, and remove the `Class1.vb` class.

2. Add a reference to the `SecurityLib` assembly created in the last chapter.

3. Add a new class called `OrderProcessorException` with code as follows:

```
Public Class OrderProcessorException
    Inherits Exception

    Public Sub New(ByVal message As String, ByVal sourceStage As Integer)
        MyBase.New(message)
        _sourceStage = sourceStage
    End Sub

    Private _sourceStage As Integer

    Public ReadOnly Property SourceStage() As Integer
        Get
            Return _sourceStage
        End Get
    End Property
End Class
```

4. Add a new class called `Customer` with code as follows:

```
Imports SecurityLib
Imports System.Text
Imports System.Data.SqlClient

Public Class Customer
    Public CustomerID As Integer
    Public Name As String
    Public Email As String
    Public CreditCard As SecureCard
    Public Address1 As String
    Public Address2 As String
    Public City As String
    Public Region As String
    Public PostalCode As String
    Public Country As String
```

```
    Public Phone As String
    Public AddressAsString As String

    Public Sub New(ByVal reader As SqlDataReader)
        ' check for customer
        If reader.Read = False Then
            Throw New OrderProcessorException( _
                "Unable to obtain customer information.", 100)
        End If

        ' initialize data
        CustomerID = reader("CustomerID")
        Name = reader("Name")
        Email = reader("Email")
        Address1 = reader("Address1")
        Address2 = reader("Address2")
        City = reader("City")
        Region = reader("Region")
        PostalCode = reader("PostalCode")
        Country = reader("Country")
        Phone = reader("Phone")

        ' get credit card details
        Try
            CreditCard = New SecureCard(reader("CreditCard"))
        Catch
            Throw New OrderProcessorException( _
                "Unable to retrieve credit card details.", 100)
        End Try

        ' construct address string
        Dim builder As StringBuilder = New StringBuilder()
        builder.Append(Name)
        builder.Append(Chr(10))
        builder.Append(Address1)
        builder.Append(Chr(10))
        If Address2 <> "" Then
            builder.Append(Address2)
            builder.Append(Chr(10))
        End If
        builder.Append(City)
        builder.Append(Chr(10))
        builder.Append(Region)
        builder.Append(Chr(10))
        builder.Append(PostalCode)
        builder.Append(Chr(10))
        builder.Append(Country)
        AddressAsString = builder.ToString()
    End Sub
End Class
```

5. Add a new class called `OrderDetail` with code as follows:

```
Imports System.Text

Public Class OrderDetail
    Public ProductID As String
    Public ProductName As String
    Public Quantity As Double
    Public UnitCost As Double
    Public ItemAsString As String
    Public Cost As Double

    Public Sub New(ByVal newProductID As String, ByVal newProductName As String, _
                   ByVal newQuantity As Double, ByVal newUnitCost As Double)
        ' Initialize data
        ProductID = newProductID
        ProductName = newProductName
        Quantity = newQuantity
        UnitCost = newUnitCost
        Cost = UnitCost * Quantity

        ' construct item string for use in e-mails etc.
        Dim builder As StringBuilder = New StringBuilder()
        builder.Append(Quantity.ToString())
        builder.Append(" ")
        builder.Append(ProductName)
        builder.Append(", $")
        builder.Append(UnitCost.ToString())
        builder.Append(" each, total cost $")
        builder.Append(Cost.ToString())
        ItemAsString = builder.ToString()
    End Sub
End Class
```

6. Add a new class called `OrderDetails` with code as follows:

```
Imports System.Collections
Imports System.Text
Imports System.Data.SqlClient

Public Class OrderDetails
    Inherits CollectionBase

    Public TotalCost As Double = 0
    Public ListAsString As String

    Public Sub New(ByVal reader As SqlDataReader)
        ' check for details
        If reader.Read = False Then
            Throw New OrderProcessorException("Unable to obtain order details.", 100)
        End If
```

```
          ' construct string for item list and calculate total cost
        Dim builder As StringBuilder = New StringBuilder()
        Dim newOrderDetail As OrderDetail
        Dim productsRemaining As Boolean = True
        While productsRemaining
            newOrderDetail = _
                New OrderDetail(reader("ProductID"), reader("ProductName"), _
                                Convert.ToDouble(reader("Quantity")), _
                                Convert.ToDouble(reader("UnitCost")))
            List.Add(newOrderDetail)
            builder.Append(newOrderDetail.ItemAsString)
            TotalCost += newOrderDetail.Cost
            builder.Append(Chr(10))
            productsRemaining = reader.Read()
        End While
        builder.Append(Chr(10))
        builder.Append("Total order cost: $")
        builder.Append(TotalCost.ToString())
        ListAsString = builder.ToString()
    End Sub

    Default Public Property Item(ByVal index As Integer) As OrderDetail
        Get
            Return CType(List(index), OrderDetail)
        End Get
        Set(ByVal Value As OrderDetail)
            List(index) = Value
        End Set
    End Property
End Class
```

7. Compile the above, and add a new Console Application project to the solution to test the code, called `CommerceLibTest`.

8. Add references to `CommerceLib` and `SecurityLib` to `CommerceLibTest`, and make it the startup project.

9. Add the following code to `Module1.vb`, replacing the values for `customerID` and `orderID` with IDs of existing items in the `WroxJokeShop` database, and changing the connection string to the one you've been using in previous chapters (if you've forgotten what it is, check out `web.config` for the `WroxJokeShop` application):

```
Imports System.Data.SqlClient
Imports CommerceLib

Module Module1

    Sub Main()
        Dim customerID As Integer = 5
        Dim orderID As Integer = 25
```

```
        Dim Connection As SqlConnection = _
          New SqlConnection( _
             "server=(local);Integrated Security=SSPI;database=WroxJokeShop")

        Dim customerCommand As SqlCommand = _
          New SqlCommand("GetCustomer", Connection)
        customerCommand.CommandType = CommandType.StoredProcedure
        customerCommand.Parameters.Add("@CustomerID", customerID)
        Connection.Open()
        Dim customerObj As Customer = New Customer(customerCommand.ExecuteReader)
        Connection.Close()
        Console.WriteLine("Customer found. Address:")
        Console.WriteLine(customerObj.AddressAsString)
        Console.WriteLine("Customer credit card number: {0}", _
                          customerObj.CreditCard.CardNumberX)
        Console.WriteLine()

        Dim orderCommand As SqlCommand = _
          New SqlCommand("GetOrderDetails", Connection)
        orderCommand.CommandType = CommandType.StoredProcedure
        orderCommand.Parameters.Add("@OrderID", orderID)
        Connection.Open()
        Dim orderObj As OrderDetails = New OrderDetails(orderCommand.ExecuteReader)
        Connection.Close()
        Console.WriteLine("Order found. Details:")
        Console.WriteLine(orderObj.ListAsString)
        Console.WriteLine()
        Console.WriteLine("List of item names:")
        Dim item As OrderDetail
        For Each item In orderObj
           Console.WriteLine(item.ProductName)
        Next
      End Sub

End Module
```

10. Execute the application:

How It Works

We've added quite a lot of code here, but much of it is similar to code we've already seen. First we have the `OrderProcessorException` class, which is simply a class derived from `System.Exception` that adds the `Integer` property `SourceStage`. This will be used by pipeline stages to identify the source of the exception. A value of `100` (used in the `Customer` and `OrderDetails` classes) is arbitrarily chosen as meaning "no stage", since the numbering of pipeline sections starts with 0. There is no code in the definition of this exception that requires further analysis.

The `Customer` class is simply a wrapper around a row of data from the `Customer` table. To initialize a `Customer` object we pass a `SqlDataReader` to the class constructor, where this `SqlReader` contains all the fields in the `Customer` table. The test console application code uses the `GetCustomer` stored procedure from the last chapter to achieve this.

The constructor starts by checking for customer data in the `SqlReader`, and throwing an exception if no data row is encountered:

```
If reader.Read = False Then
    Throw New OrderProcessorException( _
        "Unable to obtain customer information.", 100)
End If
```

Next it reads most of the data from the `Customer` table row into public fields, for example:

```
CustomerID = reader("CustomerID")
```

When it comes to credit-card data, though, we need to decrypt the data – hence the reference to the `SecurityLib` assembly. If an error occurs during decryption, we throw an exception:

```
Try
    CreditCard = New SecureCard(reader("CreditCard"))
Catch
    Throw New OrderProcessorException( _
        "Unable to retrieve credit card details.", 100)
End Try
```

The `Customer` class has one extra public field: `AddressAsString`. This provides direct access to a formatted string representing the address of the customer – which will be very useful later on when we need to notify our supplier of the address to send an order to! This string is built up from the data already stored using a `StringBuilder` object to maximize performance, which is why we have the reference to the `System.Text` namespace. The console application used to test this class displays the value of this field to show typical output.

The `OrderDetails` class is slightly more complicated, since it is actually a strongly typed collection of individual `OrderDetail` objects. For this reason we'll look at `OrderDetail` first.

The `OrderDetail` class is a fairly standard looking one that simply groups the data for an order item in one place. The constructor for this class is simpler than that of `Customer`, since it simply takes the values to use for this data. As with `Customer`, however, this class also exposes data that is built from order item properties rather than being part of them. There are two such public fields this time, `Cost` (the product of the `Quantity` and `UnitCost` for the item), and `ItemAsString` (which is a formatted string suitable for displaying item properties in a readable way). The code for all this won't teach us anything new, so we won't examine it in any more depth here.

`OrderDetails` inherits from the `CollectionBase` class in the `System.Collections` namespace, which is a great starting point for strongly typed collection classes. If you haven't come across this class before, it should be noted that it has a protected member called `List` that stores a list of objects. This member has methods including `Add()`, to add an object to a list, that we'll make use of here. It also has an indexer, handy for iterating through items where appropriate.

The constructor for the `OrderDetails` class starts in a similar way to that of `Customer`, as it checks for existing data before progressing:

```
If reader.Read = False Then
    Throw New OrderProcessorException("Unable to obtain order details.", 100)
End If
```

The remainder of the constructor reads each item from the `SqlReader`, which contains a list of records from the `OrderDetails` table. The constructor adds the items found in the `SqlReader` to the `List` member as `OrderDetail` objects, and builds another of our handy public fields: `ListAsString`. This time, the public field is a combination of the `ItemAsString` fields of each `OrderDetail` stored and a "Total cost" string. This will come in handy when confirming orders with customers, and passing lists of items to suppliers. The code to achieve this is as follows:

```
Dim builder As StringBuilder = New StringBuilder()
Dim newOrderDetail As OrderDetail
Dim productsRemaining As Boolean = True
While productsRemaining
    newOrderDetail =
        New OrderDetail(reader("ProductID"), reader("ProductName"), _
                        Convert.ToDouble(reader("Quantity")), _
                        Convert.ToDouble(reader("UnitCost")))
    List.Add(newOrderDetail)
    builder.Append(newOrderDetail.ItemAsString)
    TotalCost += newOrderDetail.Cost
    builder.Append(Chr(10))
    productsRemaining = reader.Read()
End While
builder.Append(Chr(10))
builder.Append("Total order cost: $")
builder.Append(TotalCost.ToString())
ListAsString = builder.ToString()
```

This code uses a `StringBuilder` like the other string creating code in the classes we've seen, which is why this class also has a reference to the `System.Text` namespace. The code consists mainly of a single `While` loop, which executes until no more items are found in the `SqlReader`, that is, until the `reader.Read()` method returns `False`.

The `OrderDetails` class also includes an indexer. This is implemented as the default public property `Item`, in standard VB.NET fashion, which will allow us to use the handy `For Each` syntax to access the `OrderDetail` objects contained in the collection (we do this in `CommerceLibTest`):

```
Default Public Property Item(ByVal index As Integer) As OrderDetail
    Get
        Return CType(List(index), OrderDetail)
    End Get
    Set(ByVal Value As OrderDetail)
        List(index) = Value
    End Set
End Property
```

Note that we must change the type of the objects returned to `OrderDetail` – `List` contains `Object` items.

The console application uses the `GetOrderDetails` stored procedure used in earlier chapters to initialize an instance of `OrderDetails`. This stored procedure simply gets all the rows in the `OrderDetails` table that have a specific `OrderID` value, supplied as a parameter. This gets all the information required for the `OrderDetails` constructor to carry out its data extraction.

The code in the console application tests all of the data classes added by reading data in and displaying a few properties. It also uses the indexer of `OrderDetails` to iterate through the `OrderDetail` objects it contains. If you want to make sure the `OrderProcessorException` class is working, simply choose a value for `customerID` or `orderID` that doesn't have associated data in the database – an `OrderProcessorException` exception will be thrown!

The OrderProcessor Class

As is probably apparent now, the `OrderProcessor` class (which is the class responsible for moving an order through the pipeline) will contain quite a bit of code. However, we can start simply, and build up additional functionality as we need it. To start with, we'll create a version of the `OrderProcessor` class with the following functionality:

❑   Includes full configuration, whereby information such as the connection string to use, the mail server to send mail via, the required e-mail addresses, and so on is loaded into the order processor when it is instantiated

❑   Dynamically selects a pipeline section supporting `IPipelineSection`

❑   Adds basic auditing data

❑   Gives access to the current order details

❑   Gives access to the customer for the current order

❑   Gives access to administrator mailing

❑   Mails the administrator in case of error

The configuration is carried out via a structure called `OrderProcessorConfiguration`. A structure is used rather than a class since the data required consists of simple values. This is a somewhat subtle distinction, but is the correct choice here.

We'll also create a single pipeline section, `PSDummy`, which makes use of some of this functionality.

In order to implement the above functionality, we'll also need to add three new stored procedures:

❑   GetOrderStatus – returns the status of an order with the given order ID

❑   AddAudit – adds an entry to the Audit table

❑   GetCustomerByOrderID – returns customer data associated with an order with a given order ID

We'll see the code for these stored procedures below.

Try It Out – The Basic OrderProcessor Class

1. Add a new structure to the CommerceLib project called OrderProcessorConfiguration with code as follows (to create a structure, merely select **Add New Item | Add Class**, renaming the class and deleting the contents before replacing them with the following):

```
' Configuration details for order processor
Public Structure OrderProcessorConfiguration
    Public ConnectionString As String
    Public MailServer As String
    Public AdminEmail As String
    Public CustomerServiceEmail As String
    Public OrderProcessorEmail As String
    Public SupplierEmail As String

    Public Sub New(ByVal newConnectionString As String, _
                   ByVal newMailServer As String, _
                   ByVal newAdminEmail As String, _
                   ByVal newCustomerServiceEmail As String, _
                   ByVal newOrderProcessorEmail As String, _
                   ByVal newSupplierEmail As String)
        ConnectionString = newConnectionString
        MailServer = newMailServer
        AdminEmail = newAdminEmail
        CustomerServiceEmail = newCustomerServiceEmail
        OrderProcessorEmail = newOrderProcessorEmail
        SupplierEmail = newSupplierEmail
    End Sub
End Structure
```

2. Add new stored procedures to the WroxJokeShop database as follows:

```
CREATE PROCEDURE GetOrderStatus
(@OrderID int)
AS

SELECT Status
FROM Orders
WHERE OrderID = @OrderID
GO
```

411

```
CREATE PROCEDURE AddAudit
(@OrderID int,
 @Message nvarchar(512),
 @MessageNumber int)
AS

INSERT INTO Audit (OrderID, DateStamp, Message, MessageNumber)
VALUES (@OrderID, GetDate(), @Message, @MessageNumber)
GO
```

```
CREATE PROCEDURE GetCustomerByOrderID
(@OrderID int)
AS

SELECT Customer.CustomerID, Customer.[Name], Customer.Email, Customer.[Password],
  Customer.CreditCard, Customer.Address1, Customer.Address2, Customer.City,
  Customer.Region, Customer.PostalCode, Customer.Country, Customer.Phone
FROM Customer INNER JOIN Orders
ON Customer.CustomerID = Orders.CustomerID
WHERE Orders.OrderID = @OrderID
GO
```

3. Add a new class to the `CommerceLib` project called `OrderProcessor` with code as follows:

As an aside, many people have had trouble using the `System.Web.Mail` namespace, specifically because the error "Could not create CDO.Message object" occurs, particularly on W2K systems.

The VS7 installation tries to replace the `cdosys.dll` file that the namespace depends upon with a file called `cdoex.dll`, which always fails. In the process, however, `cdosys.dll` is unregistered, and the infamous error message will then haunt you forever after. If this happens, simply typing in `regsvr32 cdosys.dll` at a command prompt will solve the problem.

*Also, unless the SMTP service on the developer's machine is set to accept relays from itself (in the **Access** tab of the SMTP server's IIS properties window, click the **Relay** button and grant access to `127.0.0.1`, or `localhost`), the same error will occur (and it is not set to accept relays from itself by default).*

In addition to the above, you may have to add `System.Web.Mail` as a reference to the project, depending upon your installation.

```
Imports System.Data.SqlClient
Imports System.Web.Mail

' Main class, used to obtain order information, run pipeline sections, audit
' orders, etc.
Public Class OrderProcessor
   Friend OrderID As Integer
   Friend OrderStatus As Integer
   Friend Connection As SqlConnection
   Friend Configuration As OrderProcessorConfiguration
```

```vb
Friend CurrentPipelineSection As IPipelineSection
Friend ContinueNow As Boolean
Private _currentCustomer As Customer
Private _currentOrderDetails As OrderDetails

Public Sub Process(ByVal newOrderID As Integer, _
                   ByVal newConfiguration As OrderProcessorConfiguration)
    ' set order ID
    OrderID = newOrderID

    ' configure processor
    Configuration = newConfiguration
    ContinueNow = True

    ' open connection, to be shared by all data access code
    Connection = New SqlConnection(Configuration.ConnectionString)
    Connection.Open()

    ' log start of execution
    AddAudit("Order Processor started.", 10000)

    ' obtain status of order
    Dim command As SqlCommand = New SqlCommand("GetOrderStatus", Connection)
    command.CommandType = CommandType.StoredProcedure
    command.Parameters.Add("@OrderID", OrderID)
    OrderStatus = CType(command.ExecuteScalar(), Integer)

    ' process pipeline section
    Try
        While ContinueNow
            ContinueNow = False
            GetCurrentPipelineSection()
            CurrentPipelineSection.Process(Me)
        End While
    Catch e As OrderProcessorException
        MailAdmin("Order Processing error occured.", e.Message, e.SourceStage)
        AddAudit("Order Processing error occured.", 10002)
        Throw New OrderProcessorException( _
        "Error occured, order aborted. Details mailed to administrator.", 100)
    Catch e As Exception
        MailAdmin("Order Processing error occured.", e.Message, 100)
        AddAudit("Order Processing error occured.", 10002)
        Throw New OrderProcessorException( _
        "Unknown error, order aborted. Details mailed to administrator.", 100)
    Finally
        AddAudit("Order Processor finished.", 10001)
        Connection.Close()
    End Try
End Sub

Private Function GetCurrentPipelineSection() As IPipelineSection
    ' select pipeline section to execute based on order status
    ' for now just provide a dummy
```

```
            CurrentPipelineSection = New PSDummy()
    End Function

    Friend Sub MailAdmin(ByVal subject As String, ByVal message As String, _
                         ByVal sourceStage As Integer)
        ' Send mail to administrator
        SmtpMail.SmtpServer = Configuration.MailServer
        Dim notificationMail As MailMessage = New MailMessage()
        notificationMail.To = Configuration.AdminEmail
        notificationMail.From = Configuration.OrderProcessorEmail
        notificationMail.Subject = subject
        notificationMail.Body = "Message: " & message & Chr(10) & "Source: " _
                                & sourceStage.ToString() & Chr(10) & "Order ID: " _
                                & OrderID.ToString()
        SmtpMail.Send(notificationMail)
    End Sub

    Friend Sub AddAudit(ByVal message As String, ByVal messageNumber As Integer)
        ' add audit to database
        Dim command As SqlCommand = New SqlCommand("AddAudit", Connection)
        command.CommandType = CommandType.StoredProcedure
        command.Parameters.Add("@OrderID", OrderID)
        command.Parameters.Add("@Message", message)
        command.Parameters.Add("@MessageNumber", messageNumber)
        command.ExecuteNonQuery()
    End Sub

    Friend ReadOnly Property CurrentCustomer() As Customer
        Get
            If _currentCustomer Is Nothing Then
                ' Use ID of order to obtain customer information
                Dim command As SqlCommand = _
                    New SqlCommand("GetCustomerByOrderID", Connection)
                command.CommandType = CommandType.StoredProcedure
                command.Parameters.Add("@OrderID", OrderID)
                Dim reader As SqlDataReader = command.ExecuteReader()
                Try
                    _currentCustomer = New Customer(reader)
                Catch
                    Throw
                Finally
                    reader.Close()
                End Try
            End If
            Return _currentCustomer
        End Get
    End Property

    Friend ReadOnly Property CurrentOrderDetails() As OrderDetails
        Get
            If _currentOrderDetails Is Nothing Then
                ' Get list of items in order
                Dim command As SqlCommand = _
```

```
                New SqlCommand("GetOrderDetails", Connection)
            command.CommandType = CommandType.StoredProcedure
            command.Parameters.Add("@OrderID", OrderID)
            Dim reader As SqlDataReader = command.ExecuteReader()
            Try
                _currentOrderDetails = New OrderDetails(reader)
            Catch
                Throw
            Finally
                reader.Close()
            End Try
        End If
        Return _currentOrderDetails
    End Get
  End Property
End Class
```

4. Add a new interface to the CommerceLib project called IPipelineSection with code as follows:

```
Public Interface IPipelineSection
    Sub Process(ByVal processor As OrderProcessor)
End Interface
```

5. Add a new class to the CommerceLib project called PSDummy with code as follows:

```
Public Class PSDummy
    Implements IPipelineSection

    Public Sub Process(ByVal processor As OrderProcessor) _
        Implements IPipelineSection.Process

        processor.AddAudit("PSDoNothing started.", 99999)
        processor.AddAudit("Customer: " & processor.CurrentCustomer.Name, 99999)
        processor.AddAudit("First item in order: " _
                        & processor.CurrentOrderDetails(0).ItemAsString, 99999)
        processor.MailAdmin("Test.", "Test mail from PSDummy.", 99999)
        processor.AddAudit("PSDoNothing finished.", 99999)
    End Sub
End Class
```

6. Modify the code in Module1 in the CommerceLibTest project as follows, customizing the data with your own SMTP server for MailServer, your own e-mail addresses for AdminEMail and SupplierEMail, and an OrderID that exists in the database:

```
Sub Main()
    Dim configuration As OrderProcessorConfiguration = _
        New OrderProcessorConfiguration( _
            "server=(local);Integrated Security=SSPI;database=WroxJokeShop", _
            "MailServer", _
```

```
            "AdminEMail", _
            "customerservice@wroxjokeshop.com", _
            "orderprocessor@wroxjokeshop.com", _
            "SupplierEMail")
    Dim processor As New OrderProcessor()
' processor.Process(ByVal orderID As Integer, ByVal configuration As
' OrderProcessorConfiguration)
        processor.Process(1, configuration)
    End Sub
```

7. If necessary, modify the `Status` field in the `WroxJokeShop` database for `Orders` for the order selected above, giving it a value of 0 to move it back to the start of the pipeline.

8. Modify the `CustomerID` filed in the `WroxJokeShop` database for the order selected above, giving it a value for a customer in the `Customers` table (necessary as we haven't yet modified `Checkout.aspx` to place orders that include this information).

9. Execute the application.

10. Check your inbox for new mail:

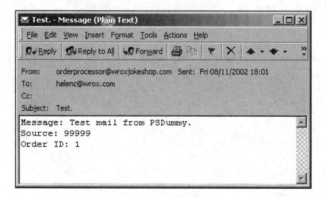

11. Examine the `Audit` table in the database to see the new entries:

How It Works

The first code added above was for the OrderProcessorConfiguration structure. This is a simple structure for grouping together the various pieces of information required to allow the OrderProcessor class to function. There are alternatives to this, such as storing this data in the registry, but this method works fine and makes our code simple. It also allows the same component library to be used in multiple e-commerce applications, as it takes its configuration dynamically. Later we'll see how we can store this data in the web.config file of our WroxJokeShop application before retrieving it when we place an order.

The information stored in the OrderProcessorConfiguration structure, and its use, is as follows:

❑ Connection string – used in all database communications.

❑ Mail server – the name of the SMTP server used to send e-mail messages. This is required by the classes in the System.Web.Mail namespace, which we use as a simple method of sending e-mail. This parameter can be left empty, in which case the local server is used, which is enough in many situations.

❑ Administrator e-mail – the e-mail address to send mail to if something goes wrong during order processing. This will include messages in the case of lack of funds available, allowing the administrator to take corrective action, and maybe contact the customer directly.

❑ Customer server e-mail – the return address for e-mail sent to customers and suppliers.

❑ Order processor e-mail – the return address for e-mail sent to the administrator.

❑ Supplier e-mail – the address for e-mail sent to the supplier.

For demonstration purposes, we set the administrator and supplier e-mail addresses to our own e-mail address, which should also be the address of the customer used to generate test orders. That way we can check that everything is working properly before sending mail to the outside world.

Next we come to the stored procedures mentioned before the code. These all involve simple code and we don't need to go into any more detail.

It is, however, worth stepping through all of the code for the OrderProcessor class. To start with, we have the Imports statements for the namespaces required for database access and e-mail functionality:

```
Imports System.Data.SqlClient
Imports System.Web.Mail
```

Following on from this, we have the class definition itself, starting with field definitions:

```
' Main class, used to obtain order information, run pipeline sections, audit
' orders, etc.
Public Class OrderProcessor
    Friend OrderID As Integer
    Friend OrderStatus As Integer
    Friend Connection As SqlConnection
    Friend Configuration As OrderProcessorConfiguration
    Friend CurrentPipelineSection As IPipelineSection
    Friend ContinueNow As Boolean = True
    Private _currentCustomer As Customer
    Private _currentOrderDetails As OrderDetails
```

Note that many of these have the `Friend` access modifier. This is a quick way of enabling access only to the other classes in the project, which includes all the pipeline section classes. These are all simple variables, so there is no real need to define full property access, but we do want to prevent code from outside from accessing this data. We can rely on the pipeline sections not to do anything they shouldn't do with this data, as we're writing them ourselves!

The two `Private` members are instances of the `Customer` and `OrderDetails` utility classes examined earlier. These are exposed as properties, and we'll see why this is necessary a little later.

The main body of the `OrderProcessor` class is the `Process()` method, which will be called by the `Checkout.aspx` and `OrderAdmin.aspx` pages to process an order. The order to be processed is indicated by its ID, and the configuration to use is set via an `OrderProcessorConfiguration` parameter:

```
Public Sub Process(ByVal newOrderID As Integer, _
                   ByVal newConfiguration As OrderProcessorConfiguration)
    ' set order ID
    OrderID = newOrderID

    ' configure processor
    Configuration = newConfiguration
    ContinueNow = True
```

We'll see how `ContinueNow` fits in shortly.

In order to simplify our code a little, we provide a single connection to the database, used by the `OrderProcessor` component and all pipeline sections. Since the order processor doesn't take long to function and isn't likely to be called as often as, say, a web page listing items in a department, this makes good sense. Remember that the .NET Framework carries out connection pooling automatically. Doing things this way means that we don't have to take a connection from the pool every time we access the database – we just do it once, then use it until we're finished. This will prevent other processes emptying the connection pool when we're half way through processing, which might cause the `OrderProcessor` to pause for longer than we'd like. In practice, perhaps this isn't as crucial as all that, but it also has the advantage of shortening our code somewhat, as we won't be creating new connections and calling `Open()` and `Close()` all the time!

```
    ' open connection, to be shared by all data access code
    Connection = New SqlConnection(Configuration.ConnectionString)
    Connection.Open()
```

Here we simply open the connection using the connection string supplied in the configuration for the order processor.

Next we use the `AddAudit()` method (which we'll come to shortly) to add an audit entry indicating that the `OrderProcessor` has started:

```
    ' log start of execution
    AddAudit("Order Processor started.", 10000)
```

10000 is the message number to store for the audit entry – we'll look at these codes in more detail shortly.

As detailed earlier, the processing of an order depends on its status, so the first thing to do is to get the status of the order, using the new GetOrderStatus stored procedure:

```
' obtain status of order
Dim command As SqlCommand = New SqlCommand("GetOrderStatus", Connection)
command.CommandType = CommandType.StoredProcedure
command.Parameters.Add("@OrderID", OrderID)
OrderStatus = CType(command.ExecuteScalar(), Integer)
```

The status is stored in the OrderStatus field we saw earlier.

Next we come to the order processing itself. The model we use here is to check the Boolean ContinueNow field before processing a pipeline section. This allows sections to specify either that processing should continue when they're finished with the current task (by setting ContinueNow to True) or that processing should pause (by setting ContinueNow to False). This is necessary because we need to wait for external input at certain points along the pipeline, such as checking whether stock is available.

The pipeline section to process is selected by the private GetCurrentPipelineSection() method, which will eventually select a section based on the status of the order, but currently just has the job of setting the CurrentPipelineSection field to an instance of PSDummy:

```
Private Function GetCurrentPipelineSection() As IPipelineSection
    ' select pipeline section to execute based on order status
    ' for now just provide a dummy
    CurrentPipelineSection = New PSDummy()
End Function
```

Back to Process(), we see this method being called in a Try block:

```
' process pipeline section
Try
    While ContinueNow
        ContinueNow = False
        GetCurrentPipelineSection()
```

Note that ContinueNow is set to False in the While loop – the default behavior is to stop after each pipeline section.

Once we have a pipeline section we need to process it. All sections support the simple IPipelineSection interface, defined as follows:

```
Public Interface IPipelineSection
    Sub Process(ByVal processor As OrderProcessor)
End Interface
```

Here we can see that all pipeline sections will use a `Process()` method to perform their work, and that this method required an `OrderProcessor` reference. This is because the pipeline sections will need access to the `Friend` fields, methods, and properties exposed by the order processor.

The last part of the `While` loop in `OrderProcessor` calls this method:

```
        CurrentPipelineSection.Process(Me)
    End While
```

We'll come back to the `Process()` method in `PSDummy` shortly.

The last part of the `Process()` method in `OrderProcessor` involves catching exceptions, which might be `OrderProcessorException` instances or other exception types. In either case, we send an e-mail to the administrator using the `MailAdmin()` method we'll cover in a little while, add an audit entry, and throw a new `OrderProcessorException` that can be caught by users of the `OrderProcessor` class:

```
        Catch e As OrderProcessorException
          MailAdmin("Order Processing error occured.", e.Message, e.SourceStage)
          AddAudit("Order Processing error occured.", 10002)
          Throw New OrderProcessorException( _
         "Error occured, order aborted. Details mailed to administrator.", 100)
        Catch e As Exception
          MailAdmin("Order Processing error occured.", e.Message, 100)
          AddAudit("Order Processing error occured.", 10002)
          Throw New OrderProcessorException( _
         "Unknown error, order aborted. Details mailed to administrator.", 100)
```

Regardless of whether processing is successful, we add a final audit entry saying that the processing has completed, and close the shared connection:

```
      Finally
        AddAudit("Order Processor finished.", 10001)
        Connection.Close()
      End Try
    End Sub
```

Next we have the `MailAdmin()` method. This simply takes a subject and message for the basic e-mail properties, and appends an identifier for the pipeline stage that sent the mail and the ID of the order being processed. Note that the calls to this method from the `Process()` method above used a pipeline stage ID of `100`, arbitrarily chosen as meaning "no pipeline stage" as mentioned earlier in the chapter. Even if we add new pipeline sections to the order pipeline, we are unlikely to have a hundred of them, so this is a safe choice!

```
    Friend Sub MailAdmin(ByVal subject As String, ByVal message As String, _
                        ByVal sourceStage As Integer)
      ' Send mail to administrator
      SmtpMail.SmtpServer = Configuration.MailServer
      Dim notificationMail As MailMessage = New MailMessage()
```

```
        notificationMail.To = Configuration.AdminEmail
        notificationMail.From = Configuration.OrderProcessorEmail
        notificationMail.Subject = subject
        notificationMail.Body = "Message: " & message & Chr(10) & "Source: " _
                        & sourceStage.ToString() & Chr(10) & "Order ID: " _
                            & OrderID.ToString()
    SmtpMail.Send(notificationMail)
End Sub
```

This e-mailing code is the standard .NET way of sending e-mail, and I won't go into more details here, other than to point out that the mail server used is identified via the appropriate entry in the configuration of the order processor.

The AddAudit() method is also a simple one, and simply calls the AddAudit stored procedure shown earlier:

```
Friend Sub AddAudit(ByVal message As String, ByVal messageNumber As Integer)
    ' add audit to database
    Dim command As SqlCommand = New SqlCommand("AddAudit", Connection)
    command.CommandType = CommandType.StoredProcedure
    command.Parameters.Add("@OrderID", OrderID)
    command.Parameters.Add("@Message", message)
    command.Parameters.Add("@MessageNumber", messageNumber)
    command.ExecuteNonQuery()
End Sub
```

At this point it is worth examining the message number scheme I've chosen for order processing audits. In all cases, the audit message number will be a 5-digit number. The first digit of this number will either be 1 in the case of an audit being added by OrderProcessor, or 2 if the audit is added by a pipeline section. The next two digits are used for the pipeline stage that added the audit (which maps directly to the status of the order when the audit was added). The final two digits uniquely identify the message within this scope. For example, so far we've seen the following message numbers:

❑   10000 – order processor started

❑   10001 – order processor finished

❑   10002 – order processor error occurred

Later we'll see a lot of these that start with 2, as we get on to pipeline sections, and include the necessary information for identifying the pipeline section as noted above. Hopefully you'll agree that this scheme allows for plenty of flexibility, although you can, of course, use whatever numbers you see fit. As a final note, numbers ending in 00 and 01 are used for starting and finishing messages for both the order processor and pipeline stages, while 02 and above are for other messages. There is no real reason for this apart from consistency between the components.

The last part of the OrderProcessor class is the code for the CurrentCustomer and CurrentOrderDetails properties. Earlier I promised to explain why the fields for this information were Private and required property accessors, rather than simply being Friend like the other fields. The reason is to cut back on database access. Not every pipeline stage will require this information, and it makes little sense to access it if it isn't required. Instead, both these properties obtain their data only when needed. Once they have been called, their data is stored in the private fields, and there is no need to repeat database access.

As an aside, this method of only getting information when needed is often known as 'lazy initialization', which is one of those bits of computer programming terminology that always makes me grin.

The code for both properties is simple, using the new `GetCustomerByOrderID` for `CurrentCustomer`, and the `GetOrderDetails` stored procedure from earlier in the chapter in `CurrentOrderDetails`:

```
    Friend ReadOnly Property CurrentCustomer() As Customer
        Get
            If _currentCustomer Is Nothing Then
                ' Use ID of order to obtain customer information
                Dim command As SqlCommand = _
                    New SqlCommand("GetCustomerByOrderID", Connection)
                command.CommandType = CommandType.StoredProcedure
                command.Parameters.Add("@OrderID", OrderID)
                Dim reader As SqlDataReader = command.ExecuteReader()
                Try
                    _currentCustomer = New Customer(reader)
                Catch
                    Throw
                Finally
                    reader.Close()
                End Try
            End If
            Return _currentCustomer
        End Get
    End Property

    Friend ReadOnly Property CurrentOrderDetails() As OrderDetails
        Get
            If _currentOrderDetails Is Nothing Then
                ' Get list of items in order
                Dim command As SqlCommand = _
                    New SqlCommand("GetOrderDetails", Connection)
                command.CommandType = CommandType.StoredProcedure
                command.Parameters.Add("@OrderID", OrderID)
                Dim reader As SqlDataReader = command.ExecuteReader()
                Try
                    _currentOrderDetails = New OrderDetails(reader)
                Catch
                    Throw
                Finally
                    reader.Close()
                End Try
            End If
            Return _currentOrderDetails
        End Get
    End Property
End Class
```

One point to note here is the unusual way that these properties use exception handling. The reason for this is that having an open `SqlReader` object completely blocks our database connection. Until we close the `SqlReader` for either of these properties, we won't be able to do anything using this connection – including adding audit entries! To get round this, we use an exception handling `Finally` block to ensure that the `SqlReaders` are closed before the property finishes processing, regardless of whether the data reading is successful. If an exception is thrown we simply re-throw it – the code using the property is given the responsibility of dealing with it.

The PSDummy class that is used in this skeleton processor performs some basic functions to check that things are working correctly:

```
Public Class PSDummy
    Implements IPipelineSection

    Public Sub Process(ByVal processor As OrderProcessor) _
        Implements IPipelineSection.Process

        processor.AddAudit("PSDoNothing started.", 99999)
        processor.AddAudit("Customer: " & processor.CurrentCustomer.Name, 99999)
        processor.AddAudit("First item in order: " _
                        & processor.CurrentOrderDetails(0).ItemAsString, 99999)
        processor.MailAdmin("Test.", "Test mail from PSDummy.", 99999)
        processor.AddAudit("PSDoNothing finished.", 99999)
    End Sub
End Class
```

The code here uses the AddAudit() and .MailAdmin() methods of OrderProcessor to generate something to show that the code has executed correctly. Note that the numbering schemes outlined above aren't used there, as this isn't a real pipeline section!

That was quite a lot of code to get through, but it did have the effect of making the client code very simple indeed:

```
Dim configuration As OrderProcessorConfiguration =
    New OrderProcessorConfiguration( _
        "server=(local);Integrated Security=SSPI;database=WroxJokeShop", _
        "MailServer", _
        "AdminEMail", _
        "customerservice@wroxjokeshop.com", _
        "orderprocessor@wroxjokeshop.com", _
        "SupplierEMail")
Dim processor As New OrderProcessor()
processor.Process(1, configuration)
```

Short of setting all the configuration details, there is very little to do, since OrderProcessor does a *lot* of work for us. It is worth noting at this point that the code we have ended up with is for the most part a consequence of the design choices made earlier. This is an excellent example of how a strong design can lead us straight to powerful and robust code.

Adding More Functionality to OrderProcessor

There are a few more bits and pieces that we need to add to the OrderProcessor class, but it hardly seems worth going through another *Try It Out* section to do so. Instead I'll simply go through the code briefly here.

We need to look at:

❑ Updating the status of an order

❑ Setting and getting credit card authentication details

❑ Setting the order shipment date

Updating the Status of an Order

Each pipeline section needs the ability to change the status of an order, advancing it to the next pipeline section. Rather than simply incrementing the status, this functionality is kept flexible, just in case you end up with a more complicated branched pipeline. This requires a new stored procedure, `UpdateOrderStatus`:

```
CREATE PROCEDURE UpdateOrderStatus
(@OrderID int,
 @Status int)
AS

UPDATE Orders
SET Status = @Status
WHERE OrderID = @OrderID
GO
```

The method that calls this stored procedure is another one with `Friend` access, such that it can be used from pipeline sections, and acts in much the same way as some of the other methods we've seen already:

```
Friend Sub UpdateOrderStatus(ByVal newStatus As Integer)
    ' change status of order, called by pipeline sections
Dim command As SqlCommand = New SqlCommand("UpdateOrderStatus", Connection)
    command.CommandType = CommandType.StoredProcedure
    command.Parameters.Add("@OrderID", OrderID)
    command.Parameters.Add("@Status", newStatus)
    command.ExecuteNonQuery()
    OrderStatus = newStatus
End Sub
```

Setting and Getting Credit Card Authentication Details

In the next chapter, when we deal with credit card usage, we'll need to set and retrieve data in the `AuthCode` and `Reference` fields in the `Orders` table.

Setting requires a new stored procedure, `SetOrderAuthCode`:

```
CREATE PROCEDURE SetOrderAuthCode
(@OrderID int,
 @AuthCode nvarchar(50),
 @Reference nvarchar(50))
AS

UPDATE Orders
SET AuthCode = @AuthCode, Reference = @Reference
WHERE OrderID = @OrderID
GO
```

The authorization and reference codes will be stored in private fields, as we will use a similar method of access to that for the `Customer` and `OrderDetails` information covered earlier:

```
        Private _authCode As String
        Private _reference As String
```

The code to set these values in the database is as follows:

```
    Friend Sub SetOrderAuthCodeAndReference(ByVal newAuthCode As String, _
                                     ByVal newReference As String)
       ' update order authorization code and reference
      Dim command As SqlCommand = New SqlCommand("SetOrderAuthCode", Connection)
        command.CommandType = CommandType.StoredProcedure
        command.Parameters.Add("@OrderID", OrderID)
        command.Parameters.Add("@AuthCode", newAuthCode)
        command.Parameters.Add("@Reference", newReference)
        command.ExecuteNonQuery()
        _authCode = newAuthCode
        _reference = newReference
    End Sub
```

This code also sets the private fields, just in case they are required before the `OrderProcessor` terminates. In this situation, it wouldn't make much sense to get these values from the database when we already know what the result will be.

Getting the data out also requires a new stored procedure, `GetOrderAuthCode`:

```
    CREATE PROCEDURE GetOrderAuthCode
    (@OrderID int)
    AS

    SELECT AuthCode,   Reference
    FROM Orders
    WHERE OrderID = @OrderID
    GO
```

Both `AuthCode` and `Reference` will be available as properties, but will only perform a database read if no data is currently available. Since the values of these items are linked, we supply the data-access code in one place:

```
    Private Sub GetOrderAuthCodeAndReference()
       ' get order authorization code and reference
      Dim command As SqlCommand = New SqlCommand("GetOrderAuthCode", Connection)
        command.CommandType = CommandType.StoredProcedure
        command.Parameters.Add("@OrderID", OrderID)
        Dim reader As SqlDataReader = command.ExecuteReader()
        Try
           reader.Read()
           _authCode = reader("AuthCode")
           _reference = reader("Reference")
        Catch
           Throw
        Finally
           reader.Close()
        End Try
    End Sub
```

This code handles the `SqlReader` returned in an exception handling block for the same reason as mentioned earlier – we don't want to block our connection by leaving a `SqlReader` open.

The properties themselves are as follows:

```
Friend ReadOnly Property AuthCode()
   Get
       If _authCode Is Nothing Then
           GetOrderAuthCodeAndReference()
       End If
       Return _authCode
   End Get
End Property

Friend ReadOnly Property Reference()
   Get
       If _reference Is Nothing Then
           GetOrderAuthCodeAndReference()
       End If
       Return _reference
   End Get
End Property
```

It would also be possible to configure read-write properties for this data, but having one method to set the values cuts down on database accesses.

Setting the Order Shipment Date

When an order is shipped, we should update the shipment date in the database, which can simply be the current date. The new stored procedure to do this, `SetDateShipped`, is as follows:

```
CREATE PROCEDURE SetDateShipped
(@OrderID int)
AS

UPDATE Orders
SET DateShipped = GetDate()
WHERE OrderID = @OrderID
GO
```

The code to call this stored procedure is very simple:

```
Friend Sub SetDateShipped()
    ' set the shipment date of the order
    Dim command As SqlCommand = New SqlCommand("SetDateShipped", Connection)
    command.CommandType = CommandType.StoredProcedure
    command.Parameters.Add("@OrderID", OrderID)
    command.ExecuteNonQuery()
End Sub
```

Summary

We've begun to build the backbone of our application, and prepared it for the lion's share of the order pipeline processing functionality, which we will implement in our next chapter.

Specifically, we've covered:

❑   Modifications to the WroxJokeShop application to enable our own pipeline processing

❑   The basic framework for our order pipeline

❑   The database additions for auditing data and storing additional required data in the Orders table

In the next chapter, we'll go on to implement our order pipeline.

Implementing the Pipeline

In the last chapter we completed the basic functionality of our `OrderProcessor` component, which is responsible for moving orders through pipeline stages. We've seen a quick demonstration of this using a dummy pipeline section, but we haven't yet implemented the pipeline discussed at the start of the last chapter.

In this chapter we'll add the required pipeline sections. Once we have done this we'll be able to process orders from start to finish, although we won't be adding full credit card transaction functionality until the next chapter.

We'll also look at web administration of orders by modifying the order admin pages added earlier in the book. We need to make changes that take account of our new order processing system.

The Pipeline Sections

Now we have completed the code in `OrderProcessor` apart from one important section – the pipeline stage selection. Rather than forcing the processor to use `PSDummy`, we actually want to select one of the pipeline stages outlined earlier, depending on the status of the order. Before we do this, let's run through the code for each of the pipeline sections in turn, which will take us to the point where our order pipeline will be complete apart from actual credit card authorization.

As you go through the following sections, create a new class in the `CommerceLib`, using the name of the section as the class name. It follows that the code beneath the heading should be entered into the class (remember that this code is available in the download). By the time you get to the next *Try It Out*, you should have eight new classes with the following names:

- ❑ PSInitialNotification
- ❑ PSCheckFunds
- ❑ PSCheckStock
- ❑ PSStockOK
- ❑ PSTakePayment
- ❑ PSShipGoods

❑   PSShipOK

❑   PSFinalNotification

We'll discuss the classes we are creating as we go.

PSInitialNotification

This is the first pipeline stage, and is responsible for sending an e-mail to the customer confirming that the order has been placed. The code for this class starts off in what will soon become a very familiar fashion:

```
Imports System.Text
Imports System.Web.Mail

' 1st pipeline stage - used to send a notification email to
' the customer, confirming that the order has been received
Public Class PSInitialNotification
    Implements IPipelineSection

    Private _processor As OrderProcessor
    Private _currentCustomer As Customer
    Private _currentOrderDetails As OrderDetails

    Public Sub Process(ByVal processor As OrderProcessor) _
        Implements IPipelineSection.Process

        _processor = processor
        _processor.AddAudit("PSInitialNotification started.", 20000)
```

First we have the required `Imports` statements, then the class itself, which implements the `IPipelineSection` interface, then some private fields for storing important references, then the `IPipelineSection.Process()` method implementation. This method starts by storing the reference to `OrderProcessor` – which all of our pipeline sections will do since using the methods it exposes (either in the `Process()` method or in other methods) is essential. We also add an audit entry, using the numbering scheme introduced earlier (the initial 2 as it is coming from a pipeline section, the next 00 as it is the first pipeline section, and the final 00 as it is the start message for the pipeline section).

Next we get the customer and order details required by the pipeline section, using the appropriate properties of `OrderProcessor`:

```
        ' get customer details
        _currentCustomer = _processor.CurrentCustomer

        ' get order details
        _currentOrderDetails = _processor.CurrentOrderDetails
```

The remainder of the `Process()` method sends the e-mail. This requires information from the customer and configuration data, which we have easy access to. We also use a private method to build a message body, which we'll look at shortly:

```
Try
    ' Send mail to customer
    SmtpMail.SmtpServer = _processor.Configuration.MailServer
    Dim notificationMail As MailMessage = New MailMessage()
    notificationMail.To = _currentCustomer.Email
    notificationMail.From = _processor.Configuration.CustomerServiceEmail
    notificationMail.Subject = "Order received."
    notificationMail.Body = GetMailBody()
    SmtpMail.Send(notificationMail)
```

Once the mail is sent we add an audit message change the status of the order, and tell the order processor that it's OK to move straight on to the next pipeline section:

```
_processor.AddAudit("Notification e-mail sent to customer.", 20002)

_processor.UpdateOrderStatus(1)
_processor.ContinueNow = True
```

If an error occurs then we throw an `OrderProcessor` exception:

```
Catch
    ' mail sending failure
    Throw _
        New OrderProcessorException("Unable to send e-mail to customer.", 0)
End Try
```

If all goes according to plan, the `Process()` method finishes by adding a final audit entry:

```
_processor.AddAudit("PSInitialNotification finished.", 20001)
End Sub
```

The `GetMailBody()` method is used to build up an e-mail body to send to the customer, using a `StringBuilder` object for efficiency. The text uses customer and order data, but follows a generally accepted e-commerce e-mail format:

```
Private Function GetMailBody() As String
    ' construct message body
    Dim bodyBuilder As StringBuilder = New StringBuilder()
    bodyBuilder.Append("Thank you for your order! The products you have " _
                        & "ordered are as follows:")
    bodyBuilder.Append(Chr(10))
    bodyBuilder.Append(Chr(10))
    bodyBuilder.Append(_currentOrderDetails.ListAsString)
    bodyBuilder.Append(Chr(10))
    bodyBuilder.Append(Chr(10))
    bodyBuilder.Append("Your order will be shipped to: ")
    bodyBuilder.Append(Chr(10))
    bodyBuilder.Append(Chr(10))
    bodyBuilder.Append(_currentCustomer.AddressAsString)
    bodyBuilder.Append(Chr(10))
```

```
            bodyBuilder.Append(Chr(10))
            bodyBuilder.Append("Order reference number: ")
            bodyBuilder.Append(_processor.OrderID.ToString())
            bodyBuilder.Append(Chr(10))
            bodyBuilder.Append(Chr(10))
            bodyBuilder.Append("You will receive a confirmation e-mail when this " _
                            & "order has been dispatched. Thank you for shopping " _
                            & "at WroxJokeShop.com!")
        Return bodyBuilder.ToString()
    End Function
End Class
```

When this pipeline stage finishes, processing will move straight on to `PSCheckFunds`.

PSCheckFunds

This pipeline stage is responsible for making sure that the customer has the required funds available on a credit card. For now we'll provide a dummy implementation of this, and just assume that these funds are available.

The code starts in the same way as `PSInitialNotification`:

```
Imports SecurityLib

' 2nd pipeline stage - used to check that the customer
' has the required funds available for purchase
Public Class PSCheckFunds
    Implements IPipelineSection

    Private _processor As OrderProcessor

    Public Sub Process(ByVal processor As OrderProcessor) _
        Implements IPipelineSection.Process

        _processor = processor
        _processor.AddAudit("PSCheckFunds started.", 20100)
```

Even though we aren't actually performing a check, we'll set the authorization and reference codes for the transaction to make sure that code in `OrderProcessor` works properly:

```
        Try
            ' check customer funds
            ' assume they exist for now

            ' set order authorization code and reference
            _processor.SetOrderAuthCodeAndReference("AuthCode", "Reference")
```

We finish up with some auditing, the code required for continuation, and error checking:

```
            ' audit and continue
            _processor.AddAudit("Funds available for purchase.", 20102)
            _processor.UpdateOrderStatus(2)
            _processor.ContinueNow = True
        Catch
            ' fund checking failure
            Throw _
                New OrderProcessorException("Error occured while checking funds.", 1)
        End Try
        _processor.AddAudit("PSCheckFunds finished.", 20101)
    End Sub
End Class
```

When this pipeline stage finishes, processing will move straight on to PSCheckStock.

PSCheckStock

This pipeline stage sends a mail to the supplier instructing them to check stock availability.

```
Imports System.Text
Imports System.Web.Mail

' 3rd pipeline stage - used to send a notification email to
' the supplier, asking whether goods are available
Public Class PSCheckStock
    Implements IPipelineSection

    Private _processor As OrderProcessor
    Private _currentOrderDetails As OrderDetails

    Public Sub Process(ByVal processor As OrderProcessor) _
        Implements IPipelineSection.Process

        _processor = processor
        _processor.AddAudit("PSCheckStock started.", 20200)
```

This time we need access to order details, although there is no real need to get the customer details, as the supplier isn't interested in who has placed the order at this stage:

```
        ' get order details
        _currentOrderDetails = _processor.CurrentOrderDetails
```

Mail is sent in a similar way to PSInitialNotification, using a private method to build up the body:

```
        Try
            ' Send mail to supplier
            SmtpMail.SmtpServer = _processor.Configuration.MailServer
            Dim notificationMail As MailMessage = New MailMessage()
            notificationMail.To = _processor.Configuration.SupplierEmail
            notificationMail.From = _processor.Configuration.AdminEmail
            notificationMail.Subject = "Stock check."
            notificationMail.Body = GetMailBody()
            SmtpMail.Send(notificationMail)
```

433

As before, we finish by auditing and updating the status, although this time we don't tell the order processor to continue straight away:

```
        _processor.AddAudit("Notification e-mail sent to supplier.", 20202)

        _processor.UpdateOrderStatus(3)
    Catch
        ' mail sending failure
        Throw _
            New OrderProcessorException("Unable to send e-mail to supplier.", 2)
    End Try
    _processor.AddAudit("PSCheckStock finished.", 20201)
End Sub
```

The code for building the message body is simple; it just lists the items in the order and tells the supplier to confirm via the `WroxJokeShop` web site (using the order administration page `OrdersAdminPage.aspx`, which we'll modify later):

```
    Private Function GetMailBody() As String

        ' construct message body
        Dim bodyBuilder As StringBuilder = New StringBuilder()
        bodyBuilder.Append("The following goods have been ordered:")
        bodyBuilder.Append(Chr(10))
        bodyBuilder.Append(Chr(10))
        bodyBuilder.Append(_currentOrderDetails.ListAsString)
        bodyBuilder.Append(Chr(10))
        bodyBuilder.Append(Chr(10))
        bodyBuilder.Append("Please check availability and confirm via " _
                        & "http://www.wroxjokeshop.com/OrdersAdminPage.aspx")
        bodyBuilder.Append(Chr(10))
        bodyBuilder.Append(Chr(10))
        bodyBuilder.Append("Order reference number: ")
        bodyBuilder.Append(_processor.OrderID.ToString())
        Return bodyBuilder.ToString()
    End Function
End Class
```

When this pipeline stage finishes, processing pauses. Later, when the supplier confirms that stock is available, processing moves on to `PSStockOK`.

PSStockOK

This pipeline section doesn't do very much at all. It just confirms that the supplier has the product in stock and moves on. Its real purpose is to look for orders that have a status corresponding to this pipeline section and know that they are currently awaiting stock confirmation.

```
' 4th pipeline stage - after confirmation that supplier has goods available
Public Class PSStockOK
    Implements IPipelineSection
```

```
        Private _processor As OrderProcessor

        Public Sub Process(ByVal processor As OrderProcessor) _
            Implements IPipelineSection.Process

            _processor = processor
            _processor.AddAudit("PSStockOK started.", 20300)

            ' the method is called when the supplier confirms that stock is available,
            ' so we don't have to do anything else here.
            _processor.AddAudit("Stock confirmed by supplier.", 20302)
            _processor.UpdateOrderStatus(4)
            _processor.ContinueNow = True
            _processor.AddAudit("PSStockOK finished.", 20301)
        End Sub
    End Class
```

When this pipeline stage finishes, processing will move straight on to `PSTakePayment`.

PSTakePayment

This pipeline section completes the transaction started by `PSCheckFunds`. As with that section, we only provide a dummy implementation here, although we do retrieve the authorization and reference codes to check that part of `OrderProcessor`.

```
' 5th pipeline stage - takes funds from customer
Public Class PSTakePayment
    Implements IPipelineSection

    Private _processor As OrderProcessor
    Private _authCode As String
    Private _reference As String

    Public Sub Process(ByVal processor As OrderProcessor) _
        Implements IPipelineSection.Process

        _processor = processor
        _processor.AddAudit("PSTakePayment started.", 20400)

        ' get authorization code and reference
        _authCode = _processor.AuthCode
        _reference = _processor.Reference

        Try
            ' take customer funds
            ' assume success for now

            ' audit and continue
            _processor.AddAudit("Funds deducted from customer credit card " _
                            & "account.", 20402)
            _processor.UpdateOrderStatus(5)
            _processor.ContinueNow = True
```

```
        Catch
            ' fund checking failure
            Throw _
                New OrderProcessorException("Error occured while taking payment.", 4)
        End Try
        _processor.AddAudit("PSTakePayment finished.", 20401)
    End Sub
End Class
```

When this pipeline stage finishes, processing will move straight on to PSShipGoods.

PSShipGoods

This pipeline section is remarkably similar to PSCheckStock, as it sends a mail to the supplier and stops the pipeline until the supplier has confirmed that stock has shipped. This time we do need customer information, though, as the supplier needs to know where to ship the order! This section should not be combined with PSCheckStock because once we have checked the goods are in stock, we need to take payment before we ship the goods.

```
Imports System.Text
Imports System.Web.Mail

' 6th pipeline stage - used to send a notification email to
' the supplier, stating that goods can be shipped
Public Class PSShipGoods
    Implements IPipelineSection

    Private _processor As OrderProcessor
    Private _currentCustomer As Customer
    Private _currentOrderDetails As OrderDetails

    Public Sub Process(ByVal processor As OrderProcessor) _
        Implements IPipelineSection.Process

        _processor = processor
        _processor.AddAudit("PSShipGoods started.", 20500)

        ' get customer details
        _currentCustomer = _processor.CurrentCustomer

        ' get order details
        _currentOrderDetails = _processor.CurrentOrderDetails
        Try
            ' Send mail to supplier
            SmtpMail.SmtpServer = _processor.Configuration.MailServer
            Dim notificationMail As MailMessage = New MailMessage()
            notificationMail.To = _processor.Configuration.SupplierEmail
            notificationMail.From = _processor.Configuration.AdminEmail
            notificationMail.Subject = "Ship Goods."
            notificationMail.Body = GetMailBody()
            SmtpMail.Send(notificationMail)
            _processor.AddAudit("Ship goods e-mail sent to supplier.", 20502)
```

```
            _processor.UpdateOrderStatus(6)
        Catch
            ' mail sending failure
            Throw _
                New OrderProcessorException("Unable to send e-mail to supplier.", 5)
        End Try
        _processor.AddAudit("PSShipGoods finished.", 20501)
    End Sub
```

As before, a private method called GetMailBody() is used to build the message body for the e-mail sent to the supplier:

```
    Private Function GetMailBody() As String
        ' construct message body
        Dim bodyBuilder As StringBuilder = New StringBuilder()
        bodyBuilder.Append("Payment has been received for the following goods:")
        bodyBuilder.Append(Chr(10))
        bodyBuilder.Append(Chr(10))
        bodyBuilder.Append(_currentOrderDetails.ListAsString)
        bodyBuilder.Append(Chr(10))
        bodyBuilder.Append(Chr(10))
        bodyBuilder.Append("Please ship to:")
        bodyBuilder.Append(Chr(10))
        bodyBuilder.Append(Chr(10))
        bodyBuilder.Append(_currentCustomer.AddressAsString)
        bodyBuilder.Append(Chr(10))
        bodyBuilder.Append(Chr(10))
        bodyBuilder.Append("When goods have been shipped, please confirm via " _
                        & "http://www.wroxjokeshop.com/OrdersAdminPage.aspx")
        bodyBuilder.Append(Chr(10))
        bodyBuilder.Append(Chr(10))
        bodyBuilder.Append("Order reference number: ")
        bodyBuilder.Append(_processor.OrderID.ToString())
        Return bodyBuilder.ToString()
    End Function
End Class
```

When this pipeline stage finishes, processing pauses. Later, when the supplier confirms that the order has been shipped, processing moves on to PSShipOK.

PSShipOK

This pipeline section is very similar to PSStockOK, although it has slightly more to do. Since we know that items have shipped, we can add a shipment date value to the Orders table. Technically, this isn't really necessary, since all audit entries are dated. However, this method means that we have all the information easily accessible in one database table.

```
    ' 7th pipeline stage - after confirmation that supplier has shipped goods
    Public Class PSShipOK
        Implements IPipelineSection
```

```
    Private _processor As OrderProcessor

    Public Sub Process(ByVal processor As OrderProcessor) _
        Implements IPipelineSection.Process

        _processor = processor
        _processor.AddAudit("PSShipOK started.", 20600)
        ' set order shipment date
        _processor.SetDateShipped()
        _processor.AddAudit("Order dispatched by supplier.", 20602)
        _processor.UpdateOrderStatus(7)
        _processor.ContinueNow = True
        _processor.AddAudit("PSShipOK finished.", 20601)
    End Sub
End Class
```

When this pipeline stage finishes, processing will move straight on to `PSFinalNotification`.

PSFinalNotification

This last pipeline section is very similar to the first, as it sends e-mail to the customer. This time we are confirming that the order has shipped:

```
Imports System.Text
Imports System.Web.Mail

' 8th pipeline stage - used to send a notification email to
' the customer, confirming that the order has been shipped
Public Class PSFinalNotification
    Implements IPipelineSection

    Private _processor As OrderProcessor
    Private _currentCustomer As Customer
    Private _currentOrderDetails As OrderDetails

    Public Sub Process(ByVal processor As OrderProcessor) _
        Implements IPipelineSection.Process

        _processor = processor
        _processor.AddAudit("PSFinalNotification started.", 20700)

        ' get customer details
        _currentCustomer = _processor.CurrentCustomer

        ' get order details
        _currentOrderDetails = _processor.CurrentOrderDetails

        Try
            ' Send mail to customer
            SmtpMail.SmtpServer = _processor.Configuration.MailServer
            Dim notificationMail As MailMessage = New MailMessage()
            notificationMail.To = _currentCustomer.Email
```

```
              notificationMail.From = _processor.Configuration.CustomerServiceEmail
              notificationMail.Subject = "Order dispatched."
              notificationMail.Body = GetMailBody()
              SmtpMail.Send(notificationMail)
              _processor.AddAudit("Dispatch e-mail sent to customer.", 20702)

              _processor.UpdateOrderStatus(8)
          Catch
              ' mail sending failure
              Throw _
                New OrderProcessorException("Unable to send e-mail to customer.", 7)
          End Try
          _processor.AddAudit("PSFinalNotification finished.", 20701)
      End Sub
```

It uses a familiar-looking `GetMailBody()` method to build the body of the e-mail:

```
      Private Function GetMailBody() As String
          ' construct message body
          Dim bodyBuilder As StringBuilder = New StringBuilder()
          bodyBuilder.Append("Your order has now been dispatched! The following " _
                            & "products have been shipped:")
          bodyBuilder.Append(Chr(10))
          bodyBuilder.Append(Chr(10))
          bodyBuilder.Append(_currentOrderDetails.ListAsString)
          bodyBuilder.Append(Chr(10))
          bodyBuilder.Append(Chr(10))
          bodyBuilder.Append("Your order has beenshipped to: ")
          bodyBuilder.Append(Chr(10))
          bodyBuilder.Append(Chr(10))
          bodyBuilder.Append(_currentCustomer.AddressAsString)
          bodyBuilder.Append(Chr(10))
          bodyBuilder.Append(Chr(10))
          bodyBuilder.Append("Order reference number: ")
          bodyBuilder.Append(_processor.OrderID.ToString())
          bodyBuilder.Append(Chr(10))
          bodyBuilder.Append(Chr(10))
          bodyBuilder.Append("Thank you for shopping at WroxJokeShop.com!")
          Return bodyBuilder.ToString()
      End Function
  End Class
```

When this pipeline section finishes, the order status is changed to 8, which represents a completed order. Further attempts to process the order using `OrderProcessor` will result in an exception being thrown.

Try It Out – The PipeLine in Action

1. If you haven't already done so, ensure that the utility methods and pipeline stage classes detailed above have been added to the `CommerceLib` project.

2. Modify the code of the `GetCurrentPipelineSection()` method in `OrderProcessor` as follows:

```
Private Function GetCurrentPipelineSection() As IPipelineSection
    ' select pipeline section to execute based on order status
    Select Case OrderStatus
        Case 0
            CurrentPipelineSection = New PSInitialNotification()
        Case 1
            CurrentPipelineSection = New PSCheckFunds()
        Case 2
            CurrentPipelineSection = New PSCheckStock()
        Case 3
            CurrentPipelineSection = New PSStockOK()
        Case 4
            CurrentPipelineSection = New PSTakePayment()
        Case 5
            CurrentPipelineSection = New PSShipGoods()
        Case 6
            CurrentPipelineSection = New PSShipOK()
        Case 7
            CurrentPipelineSection = New PSFinalNotification()
        Case 8
            Throw New OrderProcessorException( _
                "Order has already been completed.", 100)
        Case Else
            Throw New OrderProcessorException( _
                "Unknown pipeline section requested.", 100)
    End Select
End Function
```

3. Modify the code in `Module1.vb` as follows, using the same values you used in the last example for the configuration:

```
Sub Main()
    Dim configuration As OrderProcessorConfiguration = _
        New OrderProcessorConfiguration( _
            "server=(local);Integrated Security=SSPI;database=WroxJokeShop", _
            "MAILSERVER", _
            "AdminEMail", _
            "customerservice@wroxjokeshop.com", _
            "orderprocessor@wroxjokeshop.com", _
            "SupplierEMail")
    Dim processor As New OrderProcessor()
    ' 1st call to OrderProcessor, normally from Checkout.aspx
    processor.Process(1, configuration)
    Console.ReadLine()
    ' 2nd call to OrderProcessor, normally from OrdersAdminPage.aspx
    processor.Process(1, configuration)
    Console.ReadLine()
    ' 3rd call to OrderProcessor, normally from OrdersAdminPage.aspx
    processor.Process(1, configuration)
End Sub
```

4. Execute the code, calling `OrderProcessor.Process()` for the first time.

5. Check your mail for the customer notification e-mail:

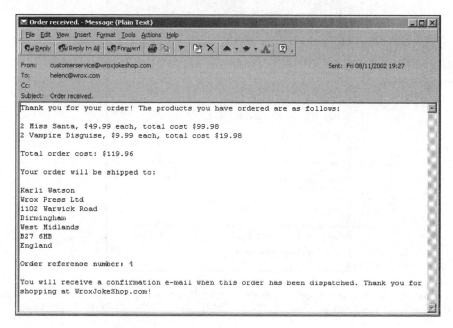

```
Order received. - Message (Plain Text)
File  Edit  View  Insert  Format  Tools  Actions  Help

Reply   Reply to All   Forward         X

From:    customerservice@wroxjokeshop.com                    Sent: Fri 08/11/2002 19:27
To:      helenc@wrox.com
Cc:
Subject: Order received.

Thank you for your order! The products you have ordered are as follows:

2 Miss Santa, $49.99 each, total cost $99.98
2 Vampire Disguise, $9.99 each, total cost $19.98

Total order cost: $119.96

Your order will be shipped to:

Karli Watson
Wrox Press Ltd
1102 Warwick Road
Birmingham
West Midlands
B27 6HB
England

Order reference number: 1

You will receive a confirmation e-mail when this order has been dispatched. Thank you for
shopping at WroxJokeShop.com!
```

6. Check your mail for the stock check e-mail:

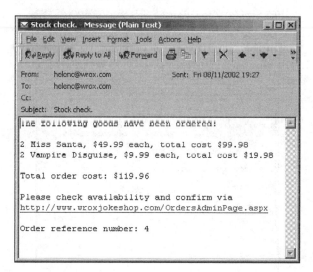

```
Stock check. - Message (Plain Text)
File  Edit  View  Insert  Format  Tools  Actions  Help

Reply   Reply to All   Forward       X

From:    helenc@wrox.com              Sent: Fri 08/11/2002 19:27
To:      helenc@wrox.com
Cc:
Subject: Stock check.

The following goods have been ordered:

2 Miss Santa, $49.99 each, total cost $99.98
2 Vampire Disguise, $9.99 each, total cost $19.98

Total order cost: $119.96

Please check availability and confirm via
http://www.wroxjokeshop.com/OrdersAdminPage.aspx

Order reference number: 4
```

7. Continue processing in the `CommerceLibTest` application by hitting enter, calling
`OrderProcessor.Process()` for the second time.

8. Check your mail for the ship goods e-mail:

9. Continue processing in the `CommerceLibTest` application by hitting enter, calling `OrderProcessor.Process()` for the third time and finishing the application.

10. Check your mail for the shipping confirmation e-mail:

11. Examine the new audit entries for the order:

How It Works

We've covered how the order pipeline works; so all that needs looking at here is what is going on with the new code added to OrderProcessor. We changed the code in the GetCurrentPipelineSection() method, which is responsible for selecting the pipeline section that needs to be executed.

The change is simply a Select Case block that assigns a pipeline section to CurrentPipelineSection:

```
Private Function GetCurrentPipelineSection() As IPipelineSection
    ' select pipeline section to execute based on order status
    Select Case OrderStatus
        Case 0
            CurrentPipelineSection = New PSInitialNotification()
        Case 1
            CurrentPipelineSection = New PSCheckFunds()
        Case 2
            CurrentPipelineSection = New PSCheckStock()
        Case 3
            CurrentPipelineSection = New PSStockOK()
        Case 4
            CurrentPipelineSection = New PSTakePayment()
        Case 5
            CurrentPipelineSection = New PSShipGoods()
        Case 6
            CurrentPipelineSection = New PSShipOK()
        Case 7
            CurrentPipelineSection = New PSFinalNotification()
        Case 8
```

```
            Throw New OrderProcessorException( _
                "Order has already been completed.", 100)
        Case Else
            Throw New OrderProcessorException( _
                "Unknown pipeline section requested.", 100)
        End Select
    End Function
```

If the order has been completed or an unknown section is requested then we generate an exception.

The test code gives us the additional opportunity of testing this exception generation, since if we run it again we will be processing an already completed order. Execute the application again and you should get an exception as follows:

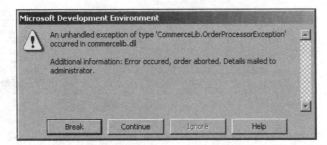

If you check your mail you'll see the details:

The error message mailed to the administrator should be enough to get started in detective work, finding out what has happened.

WroxJokeShop Modifications

In the last example we were forced to call the `OrderProcessor.Process()` method three times in a row from our test code. In practice this won't happen – it will be called once by `Checkout.aspx` when a customer places an order, and twice more by the supplier in `OrdersAdminPage.aspx`. We'll need to modify these web pages to enable the web interface.

Both these pages will need to configure the order processor as well, so a good starting point is to add the configuration details to web.config as follows:

```
<appSettings>
    <add key="ConnectionString"
     value="server=(local);Integrated Security=SSPI;database=WroxJokeShop" />
    <add key="MailServer" value="MailServer" />
    <add key="AdminEmail" value="AdminEMail" />
    <add key="CustomerServiceEmail"
     value="customerservice@wroxjokeshop.com" />
    <add key="OrderProcessorEmail" value="orderprocessor@wroxjokeshop.com" />
    <add key="SupplierEmail" value="SupplierEmail" />
</appSettings>
```

Again, you'll need to modify these settings to match your configuration.

We also need to add a reference to our new CommerceLib assembly.

The Checkout.aspx Web Page

The modifications to this page are as follows:

```
Private Sub placeOrderButton_Click(ByVal sender As System.Object, _
    ByVal e As System.EventArgs) Handles placeOrderButton.Click
  ' The Shopping Cart object
  Dim cart As New ShoppingCart()

  ' Create the order and store the order ID
  Dim orderId As Integer = cart.CreateOrder(customerID)

  ' Get configuration for order processor
  Dim processorConfiguration As OrderProcessorConfiguration = _
    New OrderProcessorConfiguration( _
      ConfigurationSettings.AppSettings("ConnectionString"), _
      ConfigurationSettings.AppSettings("MailServer"), _
      ConfigurationSettings.AppSettings("AdminEmail"), _
      ConfigurationSettings.AppSettings("CustomerServiceEmail"), _
      ConfigurationSettings.AppSettings("OrderProcessorEmail"), _
      ConfigurationSettings.AppSettings("SupplierEmail"))

  ' Process order
  Try
    Dim processor As OrderProcessor = New OrderProcessor()
    processor.Process(orderId, processorConfiguration)
  Catch ex As OrderProcessorException
    ' If an error occurs head to an error page
    Response.Redirect("OrderError.aspx?message=" & ex.Message)
  End Try

  ' On success head to an order successful page
  Response.Redirect("OrderDone.aspx")
End Sub
```

We simply use the values from `web.config` to initialize an `OrderProcessor` instance, and process the order in the same way we've seen earlier in this chapter. To round things off we redirect the customer to `OrderDone.aspx`, the following simple page that you can create adding the following code to its body:

```
<form id="Form1" method="post" runat="server">
    <p>Thank you for your order!</p>
    <p>A confirmation e-mail should arrive shortly.</p>
    <p><a href="default.aspx">Back to shop</a></p>
</form>
```

Alternatively, if an error occurs we redirect to another page we create now, `OrderError.aspx`:

```
<form id="Form1" method="post" runat="server">
    <p>An error has occured during the processing of your order.</p>
    <p>Details:
        <asp:Label Runat="server" ID="errorLabel"></asp:Label></p>
    <p>If you have an enquiry regarding this message please e-mail
        <a href="mailto:customerservice@wroxjokeshop.com">
        customerservice@wroxjokeshop.com</a></p>
    <p><a href="default.aspx">Back to shop</a></p>
</form>
```

This page also has code in its `Page_Load()` event handler:

```
Private Sub Page_Load(ByVal sender As System.Object, _
    ByVal e As System.EventArgs) Handles MyBase.Load
    errorLabel.Text = Request.Params("message")
End Sub
```

We can now use the `WroxJokeShop` web application to place orders, but they will pause when it gets to stock confirmation. To continue, we need to implement the interface for suppliers and administrators to use to force orders to continue processing.

Modifications to OrdersAdminPage.aspx

There are all manner of ways that this page could be implemented. In fact, in some setups it might be better to implement this as a Windows Forms application, for example, if your suppliers are in-house and on the same network. Or it might be better to combine this approach with web services.

Whichever method you choose, the basic functionality is the same: suppliers and administrators should be able to view a list of orders that need attention, and advance them in the pipeline manually. This is simply a case of calling the `OrderProcess.Process()` method as described earlier.

To simplify things in this section, we'll supply a single page for both administrators and suppliers. This may not be ideal in all situations, since you might not want to expose all order details and audit information to external suppliers. However, for demonstration purposes this is fine, and reduces the amount of code we have to get through. We'll also tie in the security for this page with the administrator forms-based security used earlier in the book, assuming that people with permission to edit the site data will also have permission to administer orders. In a more advanced setup we could modify this slightly, providing roles for different types of users, and restricting the functionality available to users in different roles.

As a starting point we'll take the existing `OrdersAdminPage.aspx` and associated user controls and classes, and rewrite them to give us the functionality we require. In actual fact we can simplify the code slightly to achieve this, as we won't need the ability to update order data in such a complete way as we did before. However, there are quite a lot of code modifications to get through, so we won't look at this example in the context of a *Try It Out* section.

The first thing to do is to add a new database table.

The Status Table

This table contains human-readable strings describing the status of orders. This is necessary, as when filtering orders it is a lot better to filter by an order stage description than via a status number, since it is easier to remember a description such as "Order Completed" than the number 8, for example. Placing this data in our database allows for future extensibility.

The new table, `Status`, has columns as follows:

Column Name	Column Type	Description
StatusID	int(4)	Primary key – also set as table identity. Corresponds to a status number.
Description	varchar(50)	The human-readable description of the status.

Add data to this table as shown in the following screenshot:

Stored Procedures

We'll need to add several new stored procedures, which will be used by the `OrderManager` data object to get the data required for displaying order information.

Note that many of these stored procedures will be used in place of some of the stored procedures previously used by the older version of this page (or, more specifically, by the `OrderManager` class). This is because we are now interested in different columns since our order data storage system has changed a little.

❑ `GetStatuses` – gets the list of statuses from the `Status` table

```
CREATE PROCEDURE GetStatuses
AS

SELECT StatusID, [Description]
FROM Status
GO
```

❏   GetOrders – gets all orders

```
CREATE PROCEDURE GetOrders
AS

SELECT Orders.OrderID, Orders.DateCreated, Orders.DateShipped, Orders.Status,
Orders.CustomerID, Orders.AuthCode, Orders.Reference, Status.[Description],
Customer.[Name]
FROM Orders INNER JOIN Customer
ON Customer.CustomerID = Orders.CustomerID
INNER JOIN Status
ON Status.StatusID = Orders.Status
GO
```

❏   GetOrder – gets a specific order

```
Create PROCEDURE GetOrder
(@OrderID as int)
AS

SELECT Orders.OrderID, Orders.DateCreated, Orders.DateShipped, Orders.Status,
Orders.CustomerID, Status.[Description], Customer.[Name]
FROM Orders INNER JOIN Customer
ON Customer.CustomerID = Orders.CustomerID
INNER JOIN Status
ON Status.StatusID = Orders.Status
WHERE Orders.OrderID = @OrderID
GO
```

❏   GetOrdersByRecent – gets specified number of most recent orders

```
CREATE PROCEDURE GetOrdersByRecent
(@Count int)
AS

SET ROWCOUNT @Count

SELECT Orders.OrderID, Orders.DateCreated, Orders.DateShipped, Orders.Status,
Orders.CustomerID, Status.[Description], Customer.[Name]
FROM Orders INNER JOIN Customer
ON Customer.CustomerID = Orders.CustomerID
INNER JOIN Status
ON Status.StatusID = Orders.Status
ORDER BY DateCreated DESC
```

```
SET ROWCOUNT 0

GO
```

❑   GetOrdersByCustomer – gets all orders placed by a specified customer

```
CREATE PROCEDURE GetOrdersByCustomer
(@CustomerID int)
AS

SELECT Orders.OrderID, Orders.DateCreated, Orders.DateShipped, Orders.Status,
Orders.CustomerID, Status.[Description], Customer.[Name]
FROM Orders INNER JOIN Customer
ON Customer.CustomerID = Orders.CustomerID
INNER JOIN Status
ON Status.StatusID = Orders.Status
WHERE Orders.CustomerID = @CustomerID
GO
```

❑   GetOrdersByDate – gets orders between two specified dates

```
CREATE PROCEDURE GetOrdersByDate
(@StartDate datetime,
 @EndDate datetime)
AS

SELECT Orders.OrderID, Orders.DateCreated, Orders.DateShipped, Orders.Status,
Orders.CustomerID, Status.[Description], Customer.[Name]
FROM Orders INNER JOIN Customer
ON Customer.CustomerID = Orders.CustomerID
INNER JOIN Status
ON Status.StatusID = Orders.Status
WHERE Orders.DateCreated > @StartDate AND Orders.DateCreated < @EndDate
GO
```

❑   GetOrdersByStatus – gets all orders with a specific status

```
CREATE PROCEDURE GetOrdersByStatus
(@Status int)
AS

SELECT Orders.OrderID, Orders.DateCreated, Orders.DateShipped, Orders.Status,
Orders.CustomerID, Status.[Description], Customer.[Name]
FROM Orders INNER JOIN Customer
ON Customer.CustomerID = Orders.CustomerID
INNER JOIN Status
ON Status.StatusID = Orders.Status
WHERE Orders.Status = @Status
GO
```

❑   `GetAuditTrail` – gets the `Audit` table entries associated with a specific order

```
CREATE PROCEDURE GetAuditTrail
(@OrderID int)
AS

SELECT DateStamp, MessageNumber, Message
FROM Audit
WHERE OrderID = @OrderID
GO
```

OrderManager Modifications

We will also have to add several new methods to the `OrderManager` class to cater for the stored procedures listed above (and, optionally, remove the ones we no longer require).

The first stored procedure, `GetStatuses`, is accessed using a new method also called `GetStatuses()`:

```
Public Function GetStatuses() As SqlDataReader
    ' Create the connection object
    Dim connection As New SqlConnection(connectionString)

    ' Create and initialize the command object
    Dim command As New SqlCommand("GetStatuses", connection)
    command.CommandType = CommandType.StoredProcedure

    ' Return the results
    connection.Open()
    Return command.ExecuteReader(CommandBehavior.CloseConnection)
End Function
```

The code here looks almost identical to the code for some of the methods already included in `OrderManager`, and is made even simpler by virtue of the fact that this stored procedure requires no parameters.

Next we have the `GetOrder` stored procedure, also accessed by a method with the same name:

```
Public Function GetOrder(ByVal orderID As Integer) As SqlDataReader
    ' Create the connection object
    Dim connection As New SqlConnection(connectionString)

    ' Create and initialize the command object
    Dim command As New SqlCommand("GetOrder", connection)
    command.CommandType = CommandType.StoredProcedure

    ' Add an input parameter and supply a value for it
    command.Parameters.Add("@OrderID", SqlDbType.Int, 4)
    command.Parameters("@OrderID").Value = orderID

    ' Return the results
    connection.Open()
    Return command.ExecuteReader(CommandBehavior.CloseConnection)
End Function
```

Again, there isn't anything new here, we simply pass the ID of the order we want to retrieve to the stored procedure and return the result in `SqlDataReader` form.

The code for the methods that use the rest of the stored procedures listed above follows the same format. We have `GetOrders()`:

```
Public Function GetOrders() As SqlDataReader
    ' Create the connection object
    Dim connection As New SqlConnection(connectionString)

    ' Create and initialize the command object
    Dim command As New SqlCommand("GetOrders", connection)
    command.CommandType = CommandType.StoredProcedure

    ' Return the results
    connection.Open()
    Return command.ExecuteReader(CommandBehavior.CloseConnection)
End Function
```

`GetOrdersByRecent()`:

```
Public Function GetOrdersByRecent(ByVal count As Integer) As SqlDataReader
    ' Create the connection object
    Dim connection As New SqlConnection(connectionString)

    ' Create and initialize the command object
    Dim command As New SqlCommand("GetOrdersByRecent", connection)
    command.CommandType = CommandType.StoredProcedure

    ' Add an input parameter and supply a value for it
    command.Parameters.Add("@Count", SqlDbType.Int, 4)
    command.Parameters("@Count").Value = count

    ' Return the results
    connection.Open()
    Return command.ExecuteReader(CommandBehavior.CloseConnection)
End Function
```

`GetOrdersByCustomer()`:

```
Public Function GetOrdersByCustomer(ByVal customerID As Integer) _
        As SqlDataReader
    ' Create the connection object
    Dim connection As New SqlConnection(connectionString)

    ' Create and initialize the command object
    Dim command As New SqlCommand("GetOrdersByCustomer", connection)
    command.CommandType = CommandType.StoredProcedure

    ' Add an input parameter and supply a value for it
    command.Parameters.Add("@CustomerID", SqlDbType.Int, 4)
```

```
    command.Parameters("@CustomerID").Value = customerID

    ' Return the results
    connection.Open()
    Return command.ExecuteReader(CommandBehavior.CloseConnection)
End Function
```

GetOrdersByDate():

```
Public Function GetOrdersByDate(ByVal startDate As String, _
    ByVal endDate As String) As SqlDataReader
    ' Create the connection object
    Dim connection As New SqlConnection(connectionString)

    ' Create and initialize the command object
    Dim command As New SqlCommand("GetOrdersByDate", connection)
    command.CommandType = CommandType.StoredProcedure

    ' Add an input parameter and supply a value for it
    command.Parameters.Add("@StartDate", SqlDbType.SmallDateTime)
    command.Parameters("@StartDate").Value = startDate

    ' Add an input parameter and supply a value for it
    command.Parameters.Add("@EndDate", SqlDbType.SmallDateTime)
    command.Parameters("@EndDate").Value = endDate

    ' Return the results
    connection.Open()
    Return command.ExecuteReader(CommandBehavior.CloseConnection)
End Function
```

GetOrdersByStatus():

```
Public Function GetOrdersByStatus(ByVal status As Integer) As SqlDataReader
    ' Create the connection object
    Dim connection As New SqlConnection(connectionString)

    ' Create and initialize the command object
    Dim command As New SqlCommand("GetOrdersByStatus", connection)
    command.CommandType = CommandType.StoredProcedure

    ' Add an input parameter and supply a value for it
    command.Parameters.Add("@Status", SqlDbType.Int, 4)
    command.Parameters("@Status").Value = status

    ' Return the results
    connection.Open()
    Return command.ExecuteReader(CommandBehavior.CloseConnection)
End Function
```

GetAuditTrail():

```
Public Function GetAuditTrail(ByVal orderID As Integer) As SqlDataReader
    ' Create the connection object
    Dim connection As New SqlConnection(connectionString)

    ' Create and initialize the command object
    Dim command As New SqlCommand("GetAuditTrail", connection)
    command.CommandType = CommandType.StoredProcedure

    ' Add an input parameter and supply a value for it
    command.Parameters.Add("@OrderID", SqlDbType.Int, 4)
    command.Parameters("@OrderID").Value = orderID

    ' Return the results
    connection.Open()
    Return command.ExecuteReader(CommandBehavior.CloseConnection)
End Function
```

We also have one more new method that uses a stored procedure introduced in the last chapter, GetCustomerByOrderID():

```
Public Function GetCustomerByOrderID(ByVal orderId As String) As SqlDataReader
    ' Create the Connection object
    Dim connection As New SqlConnection(connectionString)

    ' Create and initialize the Command object
    Dim command As New SqlCommand("GetCustomerByOrderID", connection)
    command.CommandType = CommandType.StoredProcedure

    ' Add an input parameter and set a value for it
    command.Parameters.Add("@OrderID", SqlDbType.Int)
    command.Parameters("@OrderID").Value = orderId

    ' Get the command results as a SqlDataReader
    connection.Open()
    Return command.ExecuteReader(CommandBehavior.CloseConnection)
End Function
End Class
```

The only method in OrderManager that we need to leave in is GetOrderDetails():

```
Public Function GetOrderDetails(ByVal orderId As String) As SqlDataReader
    ' Create the Connection object
    Dim connection As New SqlConnection(connectionString)

    ' Create and initialize the Command object
    Dim command As New SqlCommand("GetOrderDetails", connection)
    command.CommandType = CommandType.StoredProcedure

    ' Add an input parameter and set a value for it
    command.Parameters.Add("@OrderID", SqlDbType.Int)
    command.Parameters("@OrderID").Value = orderId
```

```
      ' Get the command results as a SqlDataReader
      connection.Open()
      Return command.ExecuteReader(CommandBehavior.CloseConnection)
   End Function
```

All the rest can be removed – including the `OrderInfo` class definition at the start of the file.

OrdersAdmin.ascx Modifications

Next we have `OrdersAdmin.ascx`, the user control that displays a list of orders meeting certain criteria, such as orders placed between certain dates. Now we have changed the way orders are processed there are some filters here that we no longer require, such as searching for unverified, uncanceled orders. Instead we add filters that take into account the new structure of our data, such as filtering orders by status or by customer ID. We also need to change what data is displayed in the data grid. This requires several modifications to the ASP.NET code for the page.

Note that some of the changes shown here are changes to the IDs of items. This is to keep things in line with the names of our new stored procedures, so it is easier to see which component relates to what.

First we have changes to the list of filters at the top of the control:

```
<%@ Control Language="vb" AutoEventWireup="false" Codebehind="OrdersAdmin.ascx.vb"
   Inherits="WroxJokeShop.OrdersAdmin1"
   TargetSchema="http://schemas.microsoft.com/intellisense/ie5" %>
<P><asp:label id="Label1" CssClass="AdminPageText" runat="server">
   Show the most recent</asp:label>
   <asp:textbox id="recordCountTextBox" runat="server"Width="35px">
   20</asp:textbox>
   <asp:label id="Label2" CssClass="AdminPageText"runat="server">
   orders</asp:label>
   <asp:button id="ordersByRecentButton" CssClass="AdminButtonText" runat="server"
   Text="Go!"></asp:button></P>
<P><asp:label id="Label3" CssClass="AdminPageText" runat="server">
   Show all orders created between</asp:label>
   <asp:textbox id="startDateTextBox" runat="server" Width="70px"></asp:textbox>
   <asp:label id="Label4" CssClass="AdminPageText" runat="server">
   and</asp:label>
   <asp:textbox id="endDateTextBox" runat="server" Width="70px"></asp:textbox>
   <asp:button id="ordersByDateButton" CssClass="AdminButtonText" runat="server"
   Text="Go!"></asp:button></P>
<P><asp:label id="Label5" CssClass="AdminPageText" runat="server">
   Show orders by status</asp:label>
   <asp:dropdownlist id="statusList" Runat="server"></asp:dropdownlist>
   <asp:button id="ordersByStatusButton" CssClass="AdminButtonText" runat="server"
   Text="Go!"></asp:button></P>
<P><asp:label id="Label6" CssClass="AdminPageText" runat="server">
   Show orders for customer with CustomerID</asp:label>
   <asp:textbox id="customerIDTextBox" runat="server" Width="35px">
   1</asp:textbox>
   <asp:button id="ordersByCustomerButton" CssClass="AdminButtonText"
   runat="server" Text="Go!"></asp:button></P>
```

```
<P><asp:label id="Label7" CssClass="AdminPageText" runat="server">
    Show order with OrderID</asp:label>
  <asp:textbox id="orderIDTextBox" runat="server" Width="35px">
    1</asp:textbox>
  <asp:button id="orderByIDButton" CssClass="AdminButtonText" runat="server"
    Text="Go!"></asp:button></P>
```

We also need to add the required validators for these new filters:

```
<P><asp:label id="errorLabel" CssClass="AdminErrorText" runat="server">
  </asp:label>
  <asp:requiredfieldvalidator id="recordCountValidator" runat="server"
    Display="None" ControlToValidate="recordCountTextBox"
    ErrorMessage="Invalid record count.">
  </asp:requiredfieldvalidator>
  <asp:rangevalidator id="startDateValidator" runat="server" Display="None"
    ControlToValidate="startDateTextBox" ErrorMessage="Invalid start date."
    Type="Date" MinimumValue="1/1/1999" MaximumValue="1/1/2005">
  </asp:rangevalidator>
  <asp:rangevalidator id="endDateValidator" runat="server" Display="None"
    ControlToValidate="endDateTextBox" ErrorMessage="Invalid end date."
    Type="Date" MinimumValue="1/1/1999" MaximumValue="1/1/2005">
  </asp:rangevalidator>
  <asp:requiredfieldvalidator id="customerIDValidator" Display="None"
    ControlToValidate="customerIDTextBox"
    ErrorMessage="You must enter a customer ID." Runat="server">
  </asp:requiredfieldvalidator>
  <asp:requiredfieldvalidator id="orderIDValidator" Display="None"
    ControlToValidate="orderIDTextBox"
    ErrorMessage="You must enter an order ID." Runat="server">
  </asp:requiredfieldvalidator>
  <asp:comparevalidator id="compareDatesValidator" runat="server" Display="None"
    ControlToValidate="startDateTextBox"
    ErrorMessage="End date should be more recent than start date." Type="Date"
    Operator="LessThan" ControlToCompare="endDateTextBox">
  </asp:comparevalidator>
  <asp:validationsummary id="ValidationSummary" CssClass="AdminErrorText"
    runat="server" HeaderText="Validation errors:">
  </asp:validationsummary>
```

Next we have the datagrid, which now needs to show a status description, customer ID, and customer name from a different column (from the data extracted from the `Customer` table by the stored procedures, rather than from the now redundant `CustomerName` field in the `Orders` table):

```
<asp:datagrid id="grid" runat="server" Width="100%"
  AutoGenerateColumns="False">
  <ItemStyle Font-Size="X-Small" Font-Names="Verdana"
    BackColor="Gainsboro"></ItemStyle>
  <HeaderStyle Font-Size="X-Small" Font-Names="Verdana" Font-Bold="True"
    ForeColor="White" BackColor="Navy"></HeaderStyle>
  <Columns>
```

```
            <asp:BoundColumn DataField="OrderID"
                HeaderText="Order ID"></asp:BoundColumn>
            <asp:BoundColumn DataField="DateCreated"
                HeaderText="Date Created"></asp:BoundColumn>
            <asp:BoundColumn DataField="DateShipped"
                HeaderText="Date Shipped"></asp:BoundColumn>
            <asp:BoundColumn DataField="Description"
                HeaderText="Status"></asp:BoundColumn>
            <asp:BoundColumn DataField="CustomerID"
                HeaderText="Customer ID"></asp:BoundColumn>
            <asp:BoundColumn DataField="Name"
                HeaderText="Customer Name"></asp:BoundColumn>
            <asp:ButtonColumn Text="View Details" ButtonType="PushButton"
                CommandName="Select"></asp:ButtonColumn>
    </Columns>
</asp:datagrid></P>
```

Next we have the code behind this form, OrdersAdmin.ascx.vb. This requires a little extra work in the Page_Load() handler to list an individual order if the OrderID querystring parameter is used, and to get a list of status descriptions for drop-down list selection:

```
    Private Sub Page_Load(ByVal sender As System.Object, _
        ByVal e As System.EventArgs) Handles MyBase.Load
        errorLabel.Text = ""

        If Not IsPostBack Then
            Dim om As New OrderManager()
            If Not Request.Params("OrderID") Is Nothing Then
                ' Set OrderID text box to selected order
                orderIDTextBox.Text = Request.Params("OrderID")

                ' Get selected Order
                grid.DataSource = _
                    om.GetOrder(Convert.ToInt32(Request.Params("OrderID")))
                grid.DataKeyField = "OrderID"
                grid.DataBind()
            End If

            statusList.DataSource = om.GetStatuses()
            statusList.DataTextField = "Description"
            statusList.DataValueField = "StatusID"
            statusList.DataBind()
        End If
    End Sub
```

The SelectedIndexChanged() method is the only other one of the existing methods we require:

```
    Private Sub grid_SelectedIndexChanged(ByVal sender As System.Object, _
        ByVal e As System.EventArgs) Handles grid.SelectedIndexChanged
        Dim orderId As String
        orderId = grid.DataKeys(grid.SelectedIndex)
        Response.Redirect("OrdersAdminPage.aspx?OrderID=" & orderId)
    End Sub
```

Next we have the various button click handlers for the Go! buttons on the form. These are all very similar, like the methods we looked at for `OrderManager`. First we have `ordersByStatusButton_Click()`:

```
Private Sub ordersByStatusButton_Click(ByVal sender As System.Object, _
        ByVal e As System.EventArgs) Handles ordersByStatusButton.Click
    Dim om As New OrderManager()
    Dim status As Integer

    Try
        status = statusList.SelectedItem.Value

        grid.DataSource = om.GetOrdersByStatus(status)
        grid.DataKeyField = "OrderID"
        grid.DataBind()
    Catch
        errorLabel.Text = "Could not get the requested data!"
    End Try
End Sub
```

Here we get the status value from the drop-down list `statusList` and use that in the `OrderManager.GetOrdersByStatus()` method to get a `SqlDataReader` containing a list of orders with the specified status. This is then bound to the data grid to display them.

Next we have `ordersByCustomerButton_Click()`, which works in the same way:

```
Private Sub ordersByCustomerButton_Click(ByVal sender As System.Object, _
        ByVal e As System.EventArgs) Handles ordersByCustomerButton.Click
    Dim om As New OrderManager()
    Dim customerID As Integer

    Try
        customerID = Int32.Parse(customerIDTextBox.Text)

        grid.DataSource = om.GetOrdersByCustomer(customerID)
        grid.DataKeyField = "OrderID"
        grid.DataBind()
    Catch
        errorLabel.Text = "Could not get the requested data!"
    End Try
End Sub
```

`orderByIDButton_Click()`:

```
Private Sub orderByIDButton_Click(ByVal sender As System.Object, _
        ByVal e As System.EventArgs) Handles orderByIDButton.Click
    Dim om As New OrderManager()
    Dim orderID As Integer

    Try
        orderID = Int32.Parse(orderIDTextBox.Text)
```

```
            grid.DataSource = om.GetOrder(orderID)
            grid.DataKeyField = "OrderID"
            grid.DataBind()
        Catch
            errorLabel.Text = "Could not get the requested data!"
        End Try
    End Sub
```

`ordersByRecentButton_Click()`:

```
    Private Sub ordersByRecentButton_Click(ByVal sender As System.Object, _
        ByVal e As System.EventArgs) Handles ordersByRecentButton.Click
        Dim om As New OrderManager()
        Dim recordCount As Integer

        Try
            recordCount = Int32.Parse(recordCountTextBox.Text)

            grid.DataSource = om.GetOrdersByRecent(recordCount)
            grid.DataKeyField = "OrderID"
            grid.DataBind()
        Catch
            errorLabel.Text = "Could not get the requested data!"
        End Try
    End Sub
```

Finally, `ordersByDateButton_Click()`:

```
    Private Sub ordersByDateButton_Click(ByVal sender As System.Object, _
        ByVal e As System.EventArgs) Handles ordersByDateButton.Click
        Dim om As New OrderManager()
        Dim startDate As String
        Dim endDate As String

        Try
            startDate = startDateTextBox.Text
            endDate = endDateTextBox.Text

            grid.DataSource = om.GetOrdersByDate(startDate, endDate)
            grid.DataKeyField = "OrderID"
            grid.DataBind()
        Catch
            errorLabel.Text = "Could not get the requested data!"
        End Try
    End Sub
```

OrderDetailsAdmin.ascx Modifications

The last control to modify is `OrderDetailsAdmin.ascx`, which shows the details of an order. Earlier in the book this control also included the ability to modify order data, but we're removing this here. Instead, we provide the ability for orders to be pushed along the pipeline when they are stuck at the Awaiting confirmation of stock and Awaiting confirmation of shipment stages.

There are also a few other modifications. Now we have more detailed customer information we display all available data (apart from credit card and password information) for the customer who placed the order in a new data grid. We also display all the audit information for the order in another new data grid. Since we have these new sources of information we also cut back a little on the other information displayed for the order, which is displayed in read-only textboxes above the data grids:

```
<%@ Control Language="vb" AutoEventWireup="false"
    Codebehind="OrderDetailsAdmin.ascx.vb"
    Inherits="WroxJokeShop.OrderDetailsAdmin"
    TargetSchema="http://schemas.microsoft.com/intellisense/ie5" %>
<P><asp:label id="Label1" CssClass="AdminPageText" Width="150px" runat="server">
    Order ID:</asp:label>
    <asp:textbox id="orderIdTextBox" Width="400px" runat="server"
    ReadOnly="True"></asp:textbox></P>
<P><asp:label id="Label4" CssClass="AdminPageText" Width="150px" runat="server">
    Date Created:</asp:label>
    <asp:textbox id="dateCreatedTextBox" Width="400px" runat="server"
    ReadOnly="True"></asp:textbox></P>
<P><asp:label id="Label5" CssClass="AdminPageText" Width="150px" runat="server">
    Date Shipped:</asp:label>
    <asp:textbox id="dateShippedTextBox" Width="400px" runat="server"
    ReadOnly="True"></asp:textbox></P>
```

However, we do add files to display the order status, `AuthCode`, and `Reference`:

```
<P><asp:label id="Label6" CssClass="AdminPageText" Width="150px" runat="server">
    Status:</asp:label>
    <asp:textbox id="statusTextBox" Width="400px" runat="server"
    ReadOnly="True"></asp:textbox></P>
<P><asp:label id="Label7" CssClass="AdminPageText" Width="150px" runat="server">
    AuthCode:</asp:label>
    <asp:textbox id="authCodeTextBox" Width="400px" runat="server"
    ReadOnly="True"></asp:textbox></P>
<P><asp:label id="Label8" CssClass="AdminPageText" Width="150px" runat="server">
    Reference:</asp:label>
    <asp:textbox id="referenceTextBox" Width="400px" runat="server"
    ReadOnly="True"></asp:textbox></P>
```

Next we have the button for processing orders in the pipeline, which is only displayed for orders with the statuses noted above:

```
<P><asp:button id="processButton" CssClass="AdminButtonText" Width="302px"
    runat="server" Text="Process Button"></asp:button></P>
```

After this we have the list of items in the order, which is one section of code we don't need to modify. However, we can add a descriptive label since we will now have three datagrids and we don't want to get them mixed up:

```
<P><asp:label id="Label2" CssClass="AdminPageText" Width="150px" runat="server">
    Order Details:</asp:label>
```

```
<asp:datagrid id="orderDetailsGrid" Width="100%" runat="server"
    AutoGenerateColumns="False">
    <ItemStyle Font-Size="X-Small" Font-Names="Verdana"
        BackColor="Gainsboro"></ItemStyle>
    <HeaderStyle Font-Size="X-Small" Font-Names="Verdana" Font-Bold="True"
        ForeColor="White" BackColor="Navy"></HeaderStyle>
    <Columns>
        <asp:BoundColumn DataField="ProductID"
            HeaderText="Product ID"></asp:BoundColumn>
        <asp:BoundColumn DataField="ProductName"
            HeaderText="Product Name"></asp:BoundColumn>
        <asp:BoundColumn DataField="Quantity"
            HeaderText="Quantity"></asp:BoundColumn>
        <asp:BoundColumn DataField="UnitCost"
            HeaderText="Unit Cost"></asp:BoundColumn>
        <asp:BoundColumn DataField="Subtotal"
            HeaderText="Subtotal"></asp:BoundColumn>
    </Columns>
</asp:datagrid></P>
```

Now we come to our two new datagrids, starting with the one for displaying customer information:

```
<P><asp:label id="Label11" CssClass="AdminPageText" Width="150px" runat="server">
    Customer Details:</asp:label>
    <asp:datagrid id="customerGrid" Width="100%" runat="server"
        AutoGenerateColumns="False">
        <ItemStyle Font-Size="X-Small" Font-Names="Verdana"
            BackColor="Gainsboro"></ItemStyle>
        <HeaderStyle Font-Size="X-Small" Font-Names="Verdana" Font-Bold="True"
            ForeColor="White" BackColor="Navy"></HeaderStyle>
        <Columns>
            <asp:BoundColumn DataField="CustomerID"
                HeaderText="ID"></asp:BoundColumn>
            <asp:BoundColumn DataField="Name"
                HeaderText="Name"></asp:BoundColumn>
            <asp:BoundColumn DataField="EMail"
                HeaderText="EMail"></asp:BoundColumn>
            <asp:BoundColumn DataField="Address1"
                HeaderText="Address1"></asp:BoundColumn>
            <asp:BoundColumn DataField="Address2"
                HeaderText="Address2"></asp:BoundColumn>
            <asp:BoundColumn DataField="City"
                HeaderText="Town/City"></asp:BoundColumn>
            <asp:BoundColumn DataField="Region"
                HeaderText="Region/State"></asp:BoundColumn>
            <asp:BoundColumn DataField="PostalCode"
                HeaderText="Postal Code/ZIP"></asp:BoundColumn>
            <asp:BoundColumn DataField="Country"
                HeaderText="Country"></asp:BoundColumn>
            <asp:BoundColumn DataField="Phone"
                HeaderText="Phone"></asp:BoundColumn>
        </Columns>
    </asp:datagrid></P>
```

Finally, the data grid for showing the audit trail for the order:

```
<P><asp:label id="Label3" CssClass="AdminPageText" Width="150px" runat="server">
    Audit Trail:</asp:label>
  <asp:datagrid id="auditGrid" Width="100%" runat="server"
    AutoGenerateColumns="False">
    <ItemStyle Font-Size="X-Small" Font-Names="Verdana"
      BackColor="Gainsboro"></ItemStyle>
    <HeaderStyle Font-Size="X-Small" Font-Names="Verdana" Font-Bold="True"
      ForeColor="White" BackColor="Navy"></HeaderStyle>
    <Columns>
      <asp:BoundColumn DataField="DateStamp"
        HeaderText="Date Recorded"></asp:BoundColumn>
      <asp:BoundColumn DataField="Message"
        HeaderText="Message"></asp:BoundColumn>
      <asp:BoundColumn DataField="MessageNumber"
        HeaderText="Message Number"></asp:BoundColumn>
    </Columns>
  </asp:datagrid></P>
```

Next we come to the code behind `OrderDetailsAdmins.ascx`. The first modification here is to add the following:

```
Imports System.Data
Imports CommerceLib
```

This is necessary since we will need to use `OrderProcessor` to push orders along the pipeline.

For the rest of the code we take out almost as much as we add. The `Page_Load()` event handler no longer needs to worry about whether the control is in edit mode or not, so we have shortened the code there:

```
Private Sub Page_Load(ByVal sender As System.Object, _
      ByVal e As System.EventArgs) Handles MyBase.Load
    'Put user code to initialize the page here
    If Not Page.IsPostBack Then
      ' Update information in all controls
      PopulateControls()
    End If
End Sub
```

The `PopulateControls()` method called here also changes. This time there are several reasons: we are no longer using the `OrderInfo` class, we have more data grids to populate, we don't worry about edit mode, and we have the **Process** button to consider.

Taking it from the top, we start by getting the data for the order selected, in the form of a `SqlDataReader`:

```
Private Sub PopulateControls()
    ' Create the OrderManager object which has the GetOrderDetails method
    Dim om As New OrderManager()
```

```
' Get orderID from request parameters
Dim orderID As Integer = Convert.ToInt32(Request.Params("OrderID"))
```

```
' The Order information is extracted using om.GetOrder
Dim orderReader As SqlDataReader = om.GetOrder(orderID)
```

First we check for data and abort if none is found:

```
If Not orderReader.Read() Then
    ' no data to display
    Return
End If
```

Next we extract order information for placing in the textboxes, first checking to see if certain fields are null (we only need to check this for the fields where null values are allowed):

```
' Populate the text boxes with order information
orderIdTextBox.Text = orderReader("OrderID")
dateCreatedTextBox.Text = orderReader("DateCreated")
If Not orderReader("DateShipped").GetType() Is GetType(DBNull) Then
    dateShippedTextBox.Text = orderReader("DateShipped")
End If
statusTextBox.Text = orderReader("Description")
If Not orderReader("AuthCode").GetType() Is GetType(DBNull) Then
    authCodeTextBox.Text = orderReader("AuthCode")
    referenceTextBox.Text = orderReader("Reference")
End If
```

Note that the AuthCode and Reference data fields are linked, so if one of them is null then the other one will be as well, hence the single check for a null value above rather than checking both fields.

The Process button will only be available for orders with a status of 3 or 6, and we format it accordingly:

```
' Name or hide Process button
If orderReader("Status") = 3 Then
    processButton.Text = "Confirm Stock"
ElseIf orderReader("Status") = 6 Then
    processButton.Text = "Confirm Shipment"
Else
    processButton.Visible = False
End If
```

Finally, we close the data reader.

```
' close reader
orderReader.Close()
```

The last part of this method populates the three datagrids using the following simple code:

```
            ' Fill the data grid with orderdetails
            orderDetailsGrid.DataSource = om.GetOrderDetails(orderID)
            orderDetailsGrid.DataKeyField = "OrderID"
            orderDetailsGrid.DataBind()

            ' Get full customer details
            customerGrid.DataSource = om.GetCustomerByOrderID(orderID)
            customerGrid.DataBind()

            ' Fill the audit trail with data
            auditGrid.DataSource = om.GetAuditTrail(orderID)
            auditGrid.DataKeyField = "DateStamp"
            auditGrid.DataBind()
        End Sub
```

The only user interaction that is now possible for an order is clicking on the **Process** button. When we do this we call code very similar to that in `Checkout.aspx.vb`, since we are using `OrderProcessor` to push an order along the pipeline:

```
    Private Sub processButton_Click(ByVal sender As System.Object, _
        ByVal e As System.EventArgs) Handles processButton.Click
        ' Get orderID from request parameters
        Dim orderID As Integer = Convert.ToInt32(Request.Params("OrderID"))

        ' Get configuration for order processor
        Dim processorConfiguration As OrderProcessorConfiguration = _
            New OrderProcessorConfiguration( _
                ConfigurationSettings.AppSettings("ConnectionString"), _
                ConfigurationSettings.AppSettings("MailServer"), _
                ConfigurationSettings.AppSettings("AdminEmail"), _
                ConfigurationSettings.AppSettings("CustomerServiceEmail"),
                ConfigurationSettings.AppSettings("OrderProcessorEmail"),
                ConfigurationSettings.AppSettings("SupplierEmail"))

        ' Process order, ignore errors as they will be apparent when
        ' nothing changes!
        Try
            Dim processor As OrderProcessor = New OrderProcessor()
            processor.Process(orderID, processorConfiguration)
        Catch ex As OrderProcessorException
            ' If an error occurs head to an error page
        End Try

        Response.Redirect("OrdersAdminPage.aspx?OrderID=" & orderID.ToString())
    End Sub
```

Testing the Order Administration Page

All that remains now is to check that everything is working properly. To do this, use the web interface to place an order, then check it out via the **orders admin** link on `default.aspx`. You should see that the order is awaiting confirmation of stock:

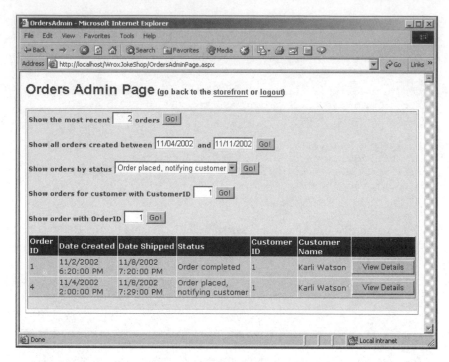

Click on View Details, and scroll down until the button for confirming stock appears:

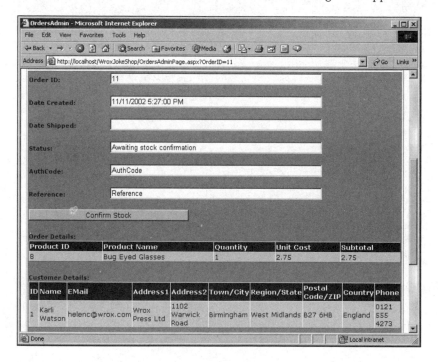

Click on the **Confirm Stock** button and the order is processed. Since this happens very quickly, we are soon presented with the next stage, a prompt to confirm shipment:

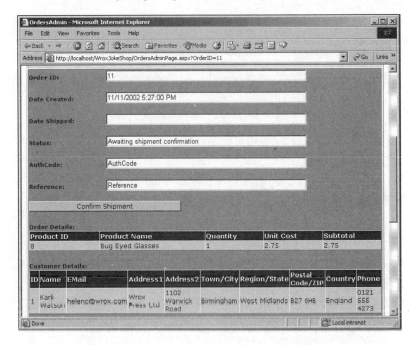

Clicking on **Confirm Shipment** shows us that the order has been completed:

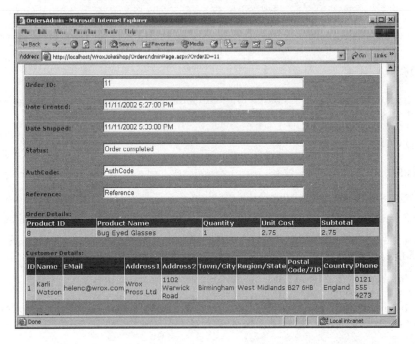

If we scroll down further we can see all audit trail messages that have been stored in the database concerning this order:

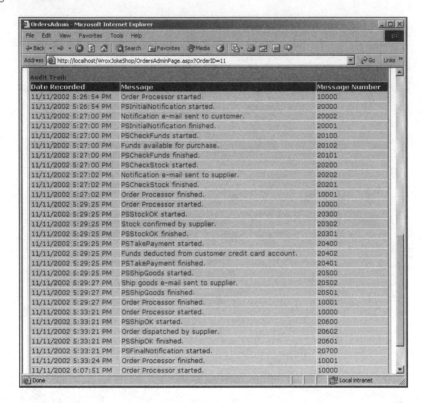

Summary

We've taken giant strides towards completing our e-commerce application in this chapter. Now we have a fully audited, secure backbone for our application.

Specifically, we've covered:

- ❑ Modifications to the WroxJokeShop application to enable our own pipeline processing

- ❑ The basic framework for our order pipeline

- ❑ The database additions for auditing data and storing additional required data in the Orders table

- ❑ The implementation of most of the order pipeline, apart from those sections that deal with credit cards

- ❑ A simple implementation of an order administration web page

The only thing missing that we need to add before we can deliver this application to the outside world is credit card processing functionality, which we'll look at in the next chapter.

Credit Card Transactions

There is one last thing we need to do before we can launch our e-commerce site: we need to enable credit card processing. In this chapter, we will look at how we can build this into the pipeline we created in the last chapter.

We'll start by looking at the theory behind credit card transactions, the sort of organizations that help us achieve this, and the sort of transactions that are possible. Moving on, we'll take an example organization and discuss the specifics of its transaction API (the means by which we access credit card transaction functionality). Once we have done this, we'll build a new class library that helps us to use the transaction API, and use it via some simple test code.

Finally, we'll integrate the API with the WroxJokeShop e-commerce application and order-processing pipeline.

Credit Card Transaction Fundamentals

Banks and other financial institutions use very secure networks for their transactions, based on the X.25 protocol rather than TCP/IP. X.25 isn't something you need to know anything about, apart from the fact that it is a different protocol for networking and isn't compatible with TCP/IP. As such, X.25 networks are completely separate from the Internet, and although it is possible to get direct access to them, this is unlikely to be a reasonable option. In order to do so, you may have to enter into some serious negotiation with the owner of the network you wish to use. They will want to be 100% sure that you are a reliable customer who is capable of enforcing the necessary safeguards to prevent an attack on their system. They won't be handing out these licenses to just anyone, since most people won't be able to afford the security measures required (which include locking your servers in a cage, sending daily backup tapes down a secure chute, having three individuals with separate keys to access these tapes, and so on).

The alternative is to go via a gateway provider. This enables you to perform your side of the credit card transaction protocol over the Internet (using a secure protocol), while relying on your chosen gateway to communicate with X.25 networks. Although there is likely to be a cost involved with this, the provider will have reached some deal with financial institutions that enables them to keep costs low, and this saving will be passed on to you (after the gateway takes its share), so it is likely to be much cheaper than having your own X.25 connection. This way of doing things is also likely to be cheaper than going via a third party such as PayPal, since you only need the minimum functionality when you are handling your own order pipeline. There is no need, for example, to use all the order auditing functionality offered by a company such as PayPal, since in the last chapter we built all this for ourselves.

Credit Card Payment Gateways

In order to work with a gateway organization you will first need to open a merchant bank account. This can be done at most banks, and will get you a merchant ID that you can use when signing up with the gateway. The next step is to find a suitable gateway. Unfortunately, this can be a lot of hard work!

It isn't hard to find a gateway; it is hard to find the right one. There are quite literally hundreds of companies that would like to be there to take a cut of your sales. A quick search on the Internet for a term such as 'credit card gateway' will get you a list as long as both your arms. The web sites of these companies are for the most part pure brochure-ware – you'll find yourself reading through pages of text about how they are the best and most secure at what they do, only to end up with a form to fill in so that a customer service representative can phone you back to 'discuss your needs'. This is a fact of life that we have to live with when dealing with the corporate world. In the long run, you can rest assured that at least you will probably only have to go through the procedure once.

When push comes to shove, you'll probably find that most of the organizations offering this service offer a very similar package, so there may be very little that influences your choice. However, key points to look for are which banks they will do business with (your merchant bank account will have to be at one of these), which currencies they deal in, and, of course, what the costs are.

In this book we will use one of the few organizations that is easy to deal with – DataCash.

Here is a table of some of the other Gateway services available:

United States		United Kingdom	
CyberCash	http://www.cybercash.com/	BT Ignite	http://www.btignite.com/uk/ products/cardpayments.html
First Data	http://www.firstdata.com/	Cable & Wireless	http://www.web-commerce.co.uk/
Cardservice International	http://www.cardservice.com/	WorldPay	http://www.worldpay.com/
IC *Verify*	http://www.icverify.com/	DataCash	http://www.datacash.com/

DataCash

DataCash is a UK-based credit card gateway organization. Unfortunately this means that you'll need a UK merchant bank account if you want to use it in your final application, but we don't have to worry about this for now. The reason for going with them in this chapter is that you don't have to do very much to get access to a rather useful test account – you don't even need a merchant bank account to get it. As we will see later in this chapter, we'll be able to perform test transactions using so-called 'magic' credit card numbers supplied by DataCash, which will accept or decline transactions without performing any actual financial transactions. This is fantastic for development purposes, since we don't really want to use our own credit cards for testing!

The important point to bear in mind is that the techniques covered in this chapter apply to every credit card gateway there is. The specifics may change slightly if you switch to a different organization, but you'll have done most of the hard work already.

Before you ask, no, we're not sales representatives for DataCash. It's just that we've spent many hours (days?) looking into credit card transactions, and so far we've yet to find a more developer-friendly way of getting started.

Credit Card Transactions

Whichever gateway you use; the basic principles of credit card transactions are the same. First off, the sort of transactions we will be dealing with in an e-commerce web site are known as Card Not Present (CNP) transactions. This is where you don't have the credit card in front of you, and you can't check the customer signature. This isn't a problem; after all you've probably been performing CNP transactions for some time now: online, over the phone, by mail, and so on. It's just something to be aware of should you see the CNP acronym.

Several advanced services are offered by various gateways, including cardholder address verification, security code checking, fraud screening, and so on. Each of these adds an additional layer of complexity to your credit card processing, and we're not going to go into details here. Rather, this chapter provides a starting point from which it is possible to add these services if required. With all of these optional extras, the choice will involve how much money is passing through your system, and a trade off between the costs of implementation and the potential costs if something goes wrong that could be prevented if you use them. If you are interested in these services, the "customer service representative" mentioned above will be happy to explain things...!

There are several types of transaction that we can perform, including:

- ❑ Authorisation – basic type, checks card for funds and deducts them.
- ❑ Pre-authorisation – checks cards for funds and allocates them if available, but doesn't deduct them straight away
- ❑ Fulfilment – completes a pre-authorisation transaction, deducting the funds already allocated
- ❑ Refund – refunds the funds from a completed transaction, or simply puts money on a credit card

Again, the specifics vary, but these are the basic types.

In this chapter we'll use the pre/fulfil model, where we don't take payment until just before we instruct our supplier to ship goods. This has been hinted at previously by the structure of the pipeline we created in the last chapter.

Implementing Credit Card Processing

Now we've covered the basics, we need to look at how we will go about getting things working in our WroxJokeShop application, using the DataCash system. The first thing to do, then, is to obtain a test account with DataCash. Do this as follows:

1. Point your browser at http://www.datacash.com/.

2. Head to the Support | Integration Info section of the web site.

3. Enter your details and submit.

4. From the e-mail you receive, make a note of your account username and password, as well as the additional information required for accessing the DataCash reporting system.

The next step would normally be to download one of DataCash's toolkits for easy integration. However, since it does not provide a .NET-compatible implementation we need to use the XML API for performing transactions. Basically, this involves sending XML requests to a certain URL using an SSL connection, and deciphering the XML result. This is a very easy thing to do in .NET.

The DataCash XML API

We'll be doing a lot of XML manipulation when communicating with DataCash, since we will need to create XML documents to send to them, and extract data from XML responses. In this section, we will take a quick look at the XML required for the operations we will be performing, and the responses we can expect.

Pre Request

When we send a pre-authentication request to DataCash we need to include the following information:

❑ DataCash username (known as the DataCash Client)

❑ DataCash password

❑ A unique transaction reference number (see below)

❑ The amount of money to be debited

❑ The currency used for the transaction (USD, GBP, and so on)

❑ The type of the transaction (for pre-authentication we use the code pre)

❑ The credit card number

❑ The credit card expiry date

❑ The credit card issue date (if applicable to the type of credit card being used)

❑ The credit card issue number (if applicable to the type of credit card being used)

The reference number must be a number between 6 and 12 digits long, and is chosen by us to uniquely identify the transaction with an order. Since we can't use a short number, we can't just use the order ID values we've been using up till now for orders. However, we can use this order ID as the starting point for creating a reference number, simply by adding a high number, such as 1000000. We can't duplicate the reference number in any future transactions, so we can be sure that once a transaction is completed it won't execute again, which might otherwise result in charging the customer twice. This does mean, though, that if a credit card is rejected, we may need to create a whole new order for the customer, but that shouldn't be a problem if required.

The XML request is formatted in the following way, with the values detailed above highlighted:

```xml
<?xml version="1.0" encoding="UTF-8"?>
<Request>
  <Authentication>
    <password>DataCash password</password>
    <client>DataCash client</client>
  </Authentication>
  <Transaction>
    <TxnDetails>
      <merchantreference>Unique reference number</merchantreference>
      <amount currency='Currency Type'>Cash amount</amount>
    </TxnDetails>
    <CardTxn>
      <method>pre</method>
      <Card>
        <pan>Credit card number</pan>
        <expirydate>Credit card expiry date</expirydate>
      </Card>
    </CardTxn>
  </Transaction>
</Request>
```

Pre Response

The response to a pre-authentication request includes the following information:

❑   Status code – a number indicating what happened; 1 if the transaction was successful, or one of several other codes if something else happens. For a complete list of return codes for a DataCash server see https://testserver.datacash.com/software/returncodes.html.

❑   A reason for the status, which is basically a string explaining the status in English. For a status of 1 this string is ACCEPTED.

❑   An authentication code, used to fulfill the transaction.

❑   A reference code for use by DataCash.

❑   The time that the transaction was processed.

❑   The mode of the transaction, which is TEST when using the test account.

❑   Confirmation of the type of credit card used.

❑   Confirmation of the country that the credit card was issued in.

❑   The authorization code used by the bank (for reference only).

The XML for this is formatted as follows:

```
<?xml version="1.0" encoding="utf-8"?>
<Response>
  <status>Status code</status>
  <reason>Reason</reason>
  <merchantreference>Authentication code</merchantreference>
  <datacash_reference>Reference number</datacash_reference>
  <time>Time</time>
  <mode>TEST</mode>
  <CardTxn>
    <card_scheme>Card Type</card_scheme>
    <country>Country</country>
    <authcode>Bank authorization code</authcode>
  </CardTxn>
</Response>
```

Fulfil Request

For a fulfillment request we need to send the following information:

- ❑ DataCash username (known as the DataCash Client)
- ❑ DataCash password
- ❑ The type of the transaction (for fulfillment we use the code `fulfil`)
- ❑ The authentication code received earlier
- ❑ The reference number received earlier

Optionally, we can include additional information, such as a confirmation of the amount to be debited from the credit card, although this isn't really necessary.

This is formatted as follows:

```
<?xml version="1.0" encoding="UTF-8"?>
<Request>
  <Authentication>
    <password>DataCash password</password>
    <client>DataCash client</client>
  </Authentication>
  <Transaction>
    <HistoricTxn>
      <reference>Reference Number</reference>
      <authcode>Authentication code</authcode>
      <method>fulfil</method>
    </HistoricTxn>
  </Transaction>
</Request>
```

Fulfil Response

The response to a fulfillment request includes the following information:

❏ Status code – a number indicating what happened; 1 if the transaction was successful, or one of several other codes if something else happens. Again for a complete list of the codes see https://testserver.datacash.com/software/returncodes.html.

❏ A reason for the status, which is basically a string explaining the status in English. For a status of 1 this string is FULFILLED OK.

❏ Two copies of the reference code for use by DataCash.

❏ The time that the transaction was processed.

❏ The mode of the transaction, which is TEST when using the test account.

The XML for this is formatted as follows:

```
<?xml version="1.0" encoding="utf-8"?>
<Response>
  <status>Status code</status>
  <reason>Reason</reason>
  <merchantreference>Reference Code</merchantreference>
  <datacash_reference>Reference Code</datacash_reference>
  <time>Time</time>
  <mode>TEST</mode>
</Response>
```

Exchanging XML Data

We could build up the XML documents shown above piece by piece, but the .NET Framework allows us to do things in a much better way. The solution presented here involves **XML serialization**. It is possible to configure any .NET class in such a way that it can be serialized as an XML document, and also that XML documents can be used to instantiate classes. This involves converting all public fields and properties into XML data, and is the basis for the web services functionality in .NET.

The default behavior for this is to create XML documents with elements named the same as the public fields and properties that we are serializing. For example, we might have the following class and member:

```
Public Class TestClass
  Public TestMember as String
End Class
```

This would be serialized as follows:

```
<?xml version="1.0" encoding="utf-8"?>
<TestClass>
  <TestMember>Value</TestMember>
</TestClass>
```

We can override this behavior using XML serialization attributes. We can force pieces of data to be formatted in elements with custom names, as attributes, as plain text, and so on.

For example, we could force the above class to serialize as an attribute as follows:

```
Public Class TestClass
   <XmlAttributeAttribute("TestAttribute")>
   Public TestMember as String
End Class
```

The `<XmlAttributeAttribute()>` part means that the member that follows should be serialized as an attribute, and the string parameter names the attribute. This class would now serialize as follows:

```
<?xml version="1.0" encoding="utf-8"?>
<TestClass TestAttribute="Value">
</TestClass>
```

There are several of these attributes that we can use, and we'll see some of them in the example that follows. This example demonstrates how we can create classes that represent DataCash requests and responses, which will be capable of serializing to and deserializing from an XML representation. This has two benefits:

- ❑ It makes it easy for us to send data to DataCash.
- ❑ We can use the full power of .NET classes to provide an intelligent way of accessing data.

In the example that follows we'll create the classes we need to exchange data with DataCash, and try out these classes using some simple client code. Note that we actually use several classes to build up our XML, since the structure involves several nested elements rather than a flat structure.

Try It Out – Communicating with DataCash

1. Create a new Class Library project in `C:\BegECom\Chapter13` called `DataCashLib`.

2. Remove the default `Class1` class.

3. Add the following classes starting with `AmountClass`:

```
Imports System.Xml.Serialization

Public Class AmountClass
   <XmlAttributeAttribute("currency")> _
   Public Currency As String

   <XmlText()> _
   Public Amount As String
End Class
```

4. Add the following class, `AuthenticationClass`:

```
Imports System.Xml.Serialization

Public Class AuthenticationClass
  <XmlElement("password")> _
  Public Password As String

  <XmlElement("client")> _
  Public Client As String
End Class
```

5. Add the following class, `CardClass`:

```
Imports System.Xml.Serialization

Public Class CardClass
  <XmlElement("pan")> _
  Public CardNumber As String

  <XmlElement("expirydate")> _
  Public ExpiryDate As String

  <XmlElement("startdate")> _
  Public StartDate As String

  <XmlElement("issuenumber")> _
  Public IssueNumber As String
End Class
```

6. Add the following class, `CardTxnRequestClass`:

```
Imports System.Xml.Serialization

Public Class CardTxnRequestClass
  <XmlElement("method")> _
  Public Method As String

  <XmlElement("Card")> _
  Public Card As CardClass = New CardClass()
End Class
```

7. Add the following class, `CardTxnResponseClass`:

```
Imports System.Xml.Serialization

Public Class CardTxnResponseClass
  <XmlElement("card_scheme")> _
  Public CardScheme As String
```

```
  <XmlElement("country")> _
  Public Country As String

  <XmlElement("issuer")> _
  Public Issuer As String

  <XmlElement("authcode")> _
  Public AuthCode As String
End Class
```

8. Add the following class, `HistoricTxnClass`:

```
Imports System.Xml.Serialization

Public Class HistoricTxnClass
  <XmlElement("reference")> _
  Public Reference As String

  <XmlElement("authcode")> _
  Public AuthCode As String

  <XmlElement("method")> _
  Public Method As String

  <XmlElement("tran_code")> _
  Public TranCode As String

  <XmlElement("duedate")> _
  Public DueDate As String
End Class
```

9. Add the following class, `TxnDetailsClass`:

```
Imports System.Xml.Serialization

Public Class TxnDetailsClass
  <XmlElement("merchantreference")> _
  Public MerchantReference As String

  <XmlElement("amount")> _
  Public Amount As AmountClass = New AmountClass()
End Class
```

10. Add the following class, `TransactionClass`:

```
Imports System.Xml.Serialization

Public Class TransactionClass
  <XmlElement("TxnDetails")> _
  Public TxnDetails As TxnDetailsClass = New TxnDetailsClass()
```

```
   Private _cardTxn As CardTxnRequestClass

   Private _historicTxn As HistoricTxnClass

   <XmlElement("CardTxn")> _
   Public Property CardTxn() As CardTxnRequestClass
     Get
       If _historicTxn Is Nothing Then
         If _cardTxn Is Nothing Then
           _cardTxn = New CardTxnRequestClass()
         End If
         Return _cardTxn
       Else
         Return Nothing
       End If
     End Get
     Set(ByVal Value As CardTxnRequestClass)
       _cardTxn = Value
     End Set
   End Property

   <XmlElement("HistoricTxn")> _
   Public Property HistoricTxn() As HistoricTxnClass
     Get
       If _cardTxn Is Nothing Then
         If _historicTxn Is Nothing Then
           _historicTxn = New HistoricTxnClass()
         End If
         Return _historicTxn
       Else
         Return Nothing
       End If
     End Get
     Set(ByVal Value As HistoricTxnClass)
       _historicTxn = Value
     End Set
   End Property
End Class
```

11. Add the following class, `DataCashRequest`:

```
Imports System.Net
Imports System.IO
Imports System.Text
Imports System.Xml.Serialization

<XmlRoot("Request")> _
Public Class DataCashRequest
  <XmlElement("Authentication")> _
  Public Authentication As AuthenticationClass = New AuthenticationClass()

  <XmlElement("Transaction")> _
  Public Transaction As TransactionClass = New TransactionClass()
```

```
Public Function GetResponse(ByVal url As String) As DataCashResponse
  ' Configure HTTP Request
  Dim httpRequest As HttpWebRequest
  httpRequest = WebRequest.Create(url)
  httpRequest.Method = "POST"

  ' Prepare correct encoding for XML serialization
  Dim encoding As UTF8Encoding = New UTF8Encoding()

  ' Use Xml property to obtain serialized XML data
  ' Convert into bytes using encoding specified above and get length
  Dim bodyBytes() As Byte = encoding.GetBytes(Xml)
  httpRequest.ContentLength = bodyBytes.Length

  ' Get HTTP Request stream for putting XML data into
  Dim httpRequestBodyStream As Stream = _
    httpRequest.GetRequestStream()

  ' Fill stream with serialized XML data
  httpRequestBodyStream.Write(bodyBytes, 0, bodyBytes.Length)
  httpRequestBodyStream.Close()

  ' Get HTTP Response
  Dim httpResponseStream As StreamReader
  Dim httpResponse As HttpWebResponse = httpRequest.GetResponse()
  httpResponseStream = _
    New StreamReader(httpResponse.GetResponseStream(), _
                     System.Text.Encoding.ASCII)

  Dim httpResponseBody As String

  ' Extract XML from response
  httpResponseBody = httpResponseStream.ReadToEnd()
  httpResponseStream.Close()

  ' Ignore everyhthing that isn't XML by removing headers
  httpResponseBody = _
    httpResponseBody.Substring(httpResponseBody.IndexOf("<?xml"))

  ' Deserialize XML into DataCashResponse
  Dim serializer As XmlSerializer = _
    New XmlSerializer(GetType(DataCashResponse))
  Dim responseReader As StringReader = New StringReader(httpResponseBody)

  ' Return DataCashResponse result
  Return CType(serializer.Deserialize(responseReader), DataCashResponse)
End Function

<XmlIgnore()> _
Public ReadOnly Property Xml()
  Get
    ' Prepare XML serializer
    Dim serializer As XmlSerializer = _
```

```
      New XmlSerializer(GetType(DataCashRequest))

    ' Serialize into StringBuilder
    Dim bodyBuilder As StringBuilder = New StringBuilder()
    Dim bodyWriter As StringWriter = New StringWriter(bodyBuilder)
    serializer.Serialize(bodyWriter, Me)

    ' Replace UTF-16 encoding with UTF-8 encoding
    Dim body As String = bodyBuilder.ToString()
    body = body.Replace("utf-16", "utf-8")
    Return body
  End Get
 End Property
End Class
```

12. Add the following class, `DataCashResponse`:

```
Imports System.IO
Imports System.Text
Imports System.Xml.Serialization

<XmlRoot("Response")> _
Public Class DataCashResponse
  <XmlElement("status")> _
  Public Status As String

  <XmlElement("reason")> _
  Public Reason As String

  <XmlElement("information")> _
  Public Information As String

  <XmlElement("merchantreference")> _
  Public MerchantReference As String

  <XmlElement("datacash_reference")> _
  Public DatacashReference As String

  <XmlElement("time")>
  Public Time As String

  <XmlElement("mode")> _
  Public Mode As String

  <XmlElement("CardTxn")> _
  Public CardTxn As CardTxnResponseClass

  <XmlIgnore()> _
  Public ReadOnly Property Xml()
    Get
      ' Prepare XML serializer
      Dim serializer As XmlSerializer = _
        New XmlSerializer(GetType(DataCashResponse))
```

```
         ' Serialize into StringBuilder
         Dim bodyBuilder As StringBuilder = New StringBuilder()
         Dim bodyWriter As StringWriter = New StringWriter(bodyBuilder)
         serializer.Serialize(bodyWriter, Me)

         ' Replace UTF-16 encoding with UTF-8 encoding
         Dim body As String = bodyBuilder.ToString()
         body = body.Replace("utf-16", "utf-8")
         Return body
      End Get
   End Property
End Class
```

13. Now we've finished adding the classes we can now add a new Console Application project to the solution called `DataCashLibTest`.

14. Add a reference to `DataCashLib` to the `DataCashLibTest` project, and set the project as the startup application.

15. Modify the code in `Module1.vb` as follows, replacing the values for `dataCashClient` and `dataCashPassword` with your own values (obtained when you signed up with DataCash). You will also have to change the Merchant Reference number to be a different value or else you will get a duplicate reference response returned to you:

```
Imports DataCashLib
Imports System.Xml.Serialization
Imports System.Text
Imports System.IO

Module Module1
   Sub Main()
      ' Initialize variables
      Dim request As DataCashRequest
      Dim requestSerializer As XmlSerializer = _
         New XmlSerializer(GetType(DataCashRequest))
      Dim response As DataCashResponse
      Dim responseSerializer As XmlSerializer = _
         New XmlSerializer(GetType(DataCashResponse))
      Dim xmlBuilder As StringBuilder
      Dim xmlWriter As StringWriter
      Dim dataCashUrl As String = "https://testserver.datacash.com/Transaction"
      Dim dataCashClient As String = "99110400"
      Dim dataCashPassword As String = "rUD27uD"

      ' Construct pre request
      request = New DataCashRequest()
      request.Authentication.Client = dataCashClient
      request.Authentication.Password = dataCashPassword
      request.Transaction.TxnDetails.MerchantReference = "9999999"
      request.Transaction.TxnDetails.Amount.Amount = "49.99"
      request.Transaction.TxnDetails.Amount.Currency = "GBP"
```

```
    request.Transaction.CardTxn.Method = "pre"
    request.Transaction.CardTxn.Card.CardNumber = "4444333322221111"
    request.Transaction.CardTxn.Card.ExpiryDate = "10/04"

    ' Display pre request
    Console.WriteLine("Pre Request:")
    xmlBuilder = New StringBuilder()
    xmlWriter = New StringWriter(xmlBuilder)
    requestSerializer.Serialize(xmlWriter, request)
    Console.WriteLine(xmlBuilder.ToString())
    Console.WriteLine()

    ' Get pre response
    response = request.GetResponse(dataCashUrl)

    ' Display pre response
    Console.WriteLine("Pre Response:")
    xmlBuilder = New StringBuilder()
    xmlWriter = New StringWriter(xmlBuilder)
    responseSerializer.Serialize(xmlWriter, response)
    Console.WriteLine(xmlBuilder.ToString())
    Console.WriteLine()

    ' Construct fulfil request
    request = New DataCashRequest()
    request.Authentication.Client = dataCashClient
    request.Authentication.Password = dataCashPassword
    request.Transaction.HistoricTxn.Method = "fulfill"
    request.Transaction.HistoricTxn.AuthCode = response.MerchantReference
    request.Transaction.HistoricTxn.Reference = response.DatacashReference

    ' Display fulfil request
    Console.WriteLine("Fulfil Request:")
    xmlBuilder = New StringBuilder()
    xmlWriter = New StringWriter(xmlBuilder)
    requestSerializer.Serialize(xmlWriter, request)
    Console.WriteLine(xmlBuilder.ToString())
    Console.WriteLine()

    ' Get fulfil response
    response = request.GetResponse(dataCashUrl)

    ' Display fulfil response
    Console.WriteLine("Fulfil Response:")
    xmlBuilder = New StringBuilder()
    xmlWriter = New StringWriter(xmlBuilder)
    responseSerializer.Serialize(xmlWriter, response)
    Console.WriteLine(xmlBuilder.ToString())
  End Sub
End Module
```

16. Now build the solution and run the program from the command line. Go to
C:\BegECom\Chapter11\DataCashLibTest\bin and enter DataCashLibTest:

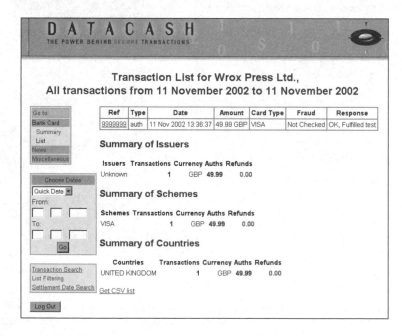

```
C:\BegECom\Chapter11\DataCashLibTest\bin\DataCashLibTest.exe                    _ □ ×
Pre Request:
<?xml version="1.0" encoding="utf-16"?>
<Request xmlns:xsd="http://www.w3.org/2001/XMLSchema" xmlns:xsi="http://www.w3.o
rg/2001/XMLSchema-instance">
  <Authentication>
    <password>rUD27uD</password>
    <client>99110400</client>
  </Authentication>
  <Transaction>
    <TxnDetails>
      <merchantreference>9999999</merchantreference>
      <amount currency="GBP">49.99</amount>
    </TxnDetails>
    <CardTxn>
      <method>pre</method>
      <Card>
        <pan>4444333322221111</pan>
        <expirydate>10/04</expirydate>
      </Card>
    </CardTxn>
  </Transaction>
</Request>

Pre Response:
<?xml version="1.0" encoding="utf-16"?>
<Response xmlns:xsd="http://www.w3.org/2001/XMLSchema" xmlns:xsi="http://www.w3.
org/2001/XMLSchema-instance">
  <status>1</status>
  <reason>ACCEPTED</reason>
  <merchantreference>9999999</merchantreference>
  <datacash_reference>9911040135657684</datacash_reference>
  <time>1033380002</time>
  <mode>TEST</mode>
  <CardTxn>
    <card_scheme>VISA</card_scheme>
    <country>United Kingdom</country>
    <authcode>903647</authcode>
  </CardTxn>
</Response>

Fulfil Request:
<?xml version="1.0" encoding="utf-16"?>
<Request xmlns:xsd="http://www.w3.org/2001/XMLSchema" xmlns:xsi="http://www.w3.o
rg/2001/XMLSchema-instance">
  <Authentication>
```

17. Log on to https://testserver.datacash.com/reporting to see the transaction log for your DataCash account:

DATACASH
THE POWER BEHIND SECURE TRANSACTIONS

Transaction List for Wrox Press Ltd.,
All transactions from 11 November 2002 to 11 November 2002

Go to:
Bank Card
Summary
List
News
Miscellaneous

Ref	Type	Date	Amount	Card Type	Fraud	Response
9999999	auth	11 Nov 2002 13:36:37	49.99 GBP	VISA	Not Checked	OK, Fulfilled test

Summary of Issuers

Issuers	Transactions	Currency	Auths	Refunds
Unknown	1	GBP	49.99	0.00

Summary of Schemes

Schemes	Transactions	Currency	Auths	Refunds
VISA	1	GBP	49.99	0.00

Summary of Countries

Countries	Transactions	Currency	Auths	Refunds
UNITED KINGDOM	1	GBP	49.99	0.00

Choose Dates
Quick Date
From:
To:
Go

Transaction Search
List Filtering
Settlement Date Search   Get CSV list

Log Out

Here is a more detailed view of the transaction:

How It Works

Here we've created code to represent the XML documents that we are exchanging. There are two root classes, `DataCashRequest` and `DataCashResponse` that encapsulate XML requests and responses respectively. These classes contain instances of the other classes defined, which contain instances of other classes, and so on, relating to the structure of the XML documents described earlier.

Each of the members of each of these classes has an associated XML serialization attribute, matching the data with the way it will be formatted when the request or response classes are serialized. For example, many of the `String` members appear as follows:

```
<XmlElement("status")> _
Public Status As String
```

Here the `Status` field will be formatted as follows:

```
<status>Status data</status>
```

Here the correct capitalization is included while at the same time allowing us to set the status data using standard Pascal Casing format.

Pascal Casing is where variable names start with a capital letter and each subsequent word in the name also has a capital letter, such as `ThisIsAVariable`. One alternative scheme is camel Casing, where the first word isn't capitalized, for example `thisIsAVariable`. The capitalization in the names of these casing schemes serves as a reminder of their usage.

One of the classes used, `TransactionClass`, is slightly more complicated than the others, since the `<Transaction>` element contains one of either `<CardTxn>` or `<HistoricTxn>`, depending on whether the request is a `pre` request or a `fulfil` request. Instead of using fields, this class uses properties that ensure that only one of these two elements is used.

The `DataCashRequest` class also has a method called `GetResponse()` which sends the request, and packages the returned response as a `DataCashResponse` class. In the code to do this we start by creating an `HttpWebRequest` instance for the URL supplied as a parameter:

```
Public Function GetResponse(ByVal url As String) As DataCashResponse
  Dim httpRequest As HttpWebRequest
  httpRequest = WebRequest.Create(url)
```

This request is then defined as a `POST` request with the appropriate encoding:

```
  httpRequest.Method = "POST"
  Dim encoding As UTF8Encoding = New UTF8Encoding()
```

HTTP requests can be sent in a number of formats, the most common being GET and POST. The difference here is that GET requests have just a URL and header information, POST requests have all this plus a message body. Think of an HTTP POST request as if it was an e-mail, with the HTTP response being the e-mail reply. In both cases, header information is like the address and subject of the e-mail, body information is like the message body of an e-mail.

Next we need to supply the body of the `POST` request, which is the XML document we wish to send. To do this we obtain the serialized version of the data contained in the object via the `Xml` property (which simply serializes the `DataCashRequest` instance into XML, making use of the XML serialization attributes):

```
  Dim bodyBytes() As Byte = encoding.GetBytes(Xml)
```

We also need to specify the length of the data contained in the HTTP header for the request:

```
  httpRequest.ContentLength = bodyBytes.Length
```

Next we take the XML data and place it into the request via standard stream manipulation code:

```
  Dim httpRequestBodyStream As Stream = httpRequest.GetRequestStream()
  httpRequestBodyStream.Write(bodyBytes, 0, bodyBytes.Length)
  httpRequestBodyStream.Close()
```

Once we have the request class we can obtain the response, also via stream manipulation:

```
  Dim httpResponseStream As StreamReader
  Dim httpResponse As HttpWebResponse = httpRequest.GetResponse()
  httpResponseStream = _
    New StreamReader(httpResponse.GetResponseStream(), _
                    System.Text.Encoding.ASCII)
```

```
Dim httpResponseBody As String
httpResponseBody = httpResponseStream.ReadToEnd()
httpResponseStream.Close()
```

We only need the XML data contained in this stream, so we clip off the headers at the beginning of the data returned before deserializing it. We do this using the `String.Substring()` method to obtain the section of the string that starts with "<?xml", the location of which is found using the `String.IndexOf()` method.

```
httpResponseBody = _
   httpResponseBody.Substring(httpResponseBody.IndexOf("<?xml"))
Dim serializer As XmlSerializer = _
   New XmlSerializer(GetType(DataCashResponse))
Dim responseReader As StringReader = New StringReader(httpResponseBody)
```

Finally, we cast the deserialized object into a `DataCashResponse` object for further manipulation:

```
   Return CType(serializer.Deserialize(responseReader), DataCashResponse)
End Function
```

Once the transaction has completed we can check that everything has worked properly via the DataCash reporting web interface.

Integration with WroxJokeShop

Now we have a new class library that we can use to perform credit card transactions. However, we need to modify a few things to integrate it with our existing e-commerce application and pipeline.

OrderProcessor Configuration Modification

We now have three new pieces of information that `CommerceLib` requires to operate:

❏ DataCash client

❏ DataCash password

❏ DataCash URL

We can place all this information into the `OrderProcessorConfiguration` class we are using to initialize `OrderProcessor` as follows:

```
' Configuration details for order processor
Public Structure OrderProcessorConfiguration
  Public ConnectionString As String
  Public MailServer As String
  Public AdminEmail As String
  Public CustomerServiceEmail As String
  Public OrderProcessorEmail As String
  Public SupplierEmail As String
```

```
    Public DataCashClient As String
    Public DataCashPassword As String
    Public DataCashUrl As String

    Public Sub New(ByVal newConnectionString As String, _
                   ByVal newMailServer As String, _
                   ByVal newAdminEmail As String, _
                   ByVal newCustomerServiceEmail As String, _
                   ByVal newOrderProcessorEmail As String, _
                   ByVal newSupplierEmail As String, _
                   ByVal newDataCashClient As String, _
                   ByVal newDataCashPassword As String, _
                   ByVal newDataCashUrl As String)
      ConnectionString = newConnectionString
      MailServer = newMailServer
      AdminEmail = newAdminEmail
      CustomerServiceEmail = newCustomerServiceEmail
      OrderProcessorEmail = newOrderProcessorEmail
      SupplierEmail = newSupplierEmail
      DataCashClient = newDataCashClient
      DataCashPassword = newDataCashPassword
      DataCashUrl = newDataCashUrl
    End Sub
  End Structure
```

Note that making this change will break any code that uses the CommerceLib *library. Don't worry about this for now though; by the time we use it we'll have corrected things. However, you might want to remove* CommerceLibTest *from the* CommerceLib *solution since we won't be needing it any more, and it will be annoying to see it fail to compile every time. Alternatively, you could modify* CommerceLibTest *to make it work with this new scheme and use it for testing, although this isn't really necessary at this stage. A version of* CommerceLib *that is compatible with this example is provided in the code download for this chapter.*

We can store this information in the web.config file of WroxJokeShop just as we did the other data:

```
<appSettings>
    <add key="ConnectionString"
     value="server=(local);Integrated Security=SSPI;database=WroxJokeShop" />
    <add key="MailServer" value="ALTAR1" />
    <add key="AdminEmail" value="karli@watsons.dnsalias.com" />
    <add key="CustomerServiceEmail"
     value="customerservice@wroxjokeshop.com" />
    <add key="OrderProcessorEmail" value="orderprocessor@wroxjokeshop.com" />
    <add key="SupplierEmail" value="karli@watsons.dnsalias.com" />
    <add key="DataCashClient" value="99110400" />
    <add key="DataCashPassword" value="rUD27uD" />
    <add key="DataCashUrl"
     value="https://testserver.datacash.com/Transaction" />
</appSettings>
```

We also need to change the placeOrderButton_Click() event handler in Checkout.aspx.vb to include this information:

```
Private Sub placeOrderButton_Click(ByVal sender As System.Object, _
    ByVal e As System.EventArgs) Handles orderButton.Click
  Dim cart As New ShoppingCart()
  Dim processorConfiguration As OrderProcessorConfiguration = _
    New OrderProcessorConfiguration( _
      ConfigurationSettings.AppSettings("ConnectionString"), _
      ConfigurationSettings.AppSettings("MailServer"), _
      ConfigurationSettings.AppSettings("AdminEmail"), _
      ConfigurationSettings.AppSettings("CustomerServiceEmail"), _
      ConfigurationSettings.AppSettings("OrderProcessorEmail"), _
      ConfigurationSettings.AppSettings("SupplierEmail"), _
      ConfigurationSettings.AppSettings("DataCashClient"), _
      ConfigurationSettings.AppSettings("DataCashPassword"), _
      ConfigurationSettings.AppSettings("DataCashUrl"))
  Dim processor As OrderProcessor = New OrderProcessor()
  processor.Process(cart.CreateOrder(customerID), processorConfiguration)
  Response.Redirect("OrderDone.aspx")
End Sub
```

Exactly the same change also needs to be made to the code in OrderDetailsAdmin.aspx.vb.

Pipeline Modification

The final modifications involve modifying the pipeline section classes that deal with credit card transactions. We've already included the infrastructure for storing and retrieving authentication code and reference information, via the OrderProcessor.SetOrderAuthCodeAndReference() method and the AuthCode and Reference properties.

After we add a reference to DataCashLib to CommerceLib, the modifications to PSCheckFunds are as follows:

```
' 2nd pipeline stage - used to check that the customer
' has the required funds available for purchase
Imports DataCashLib
Imports SecurityLib

Public Class PSCheckFunds
  Implements IPipelineSection

  Private _processor As OrderProcessor
  Private _currentCustomer As Customer
  Private _currentOrderDetails As OrderDetails

  Public Sub Process(ByVal processor As OrderProcessor) _
    Implements IPipelineSection.Process

    _processor = processor
    _processor.AddAudit("PSCheckFunds started.", 20100)
```

```vb
        ' get customer details
        _currentCustomer = _processor.CurrentCustomer

        ' get order details
        _currentOrderDetails = _processor.CurrentOrderDetails

    Try
        ' check customer funds via datacash gateway
        ' configure Datacash XML request
        Dim request As DataCashRequest = New DataCashRequest()
        request.Authentication.Client = _processor.Configuration.DataCashClient
        request.Authentication.Password = _
         _processor.Configuration.DataCashPassword
        request.Transaction.TxnDetails.MerchantReference = _
         _processor.OrderID.ToString().PadLeft(6, "0"c).PadLeft(7, "5"c)
        request.Transaction.TxnDetails.Amount.Amount = _
         _currentOrderDetails.TotalCost.ToString()
        request.Transaction.TxnDetails.Amount.Currency = "GBP"
        request.Transaction.CardTxn.Method = "pre"
        request.Transaction.CardTxn.Card.CardNumber = _
         _currentCustomer.CreditCard.CardNumber
        request.Transaction.CardTxn.Card.ExpiryDate = _
         _currentCustomer.CreditCard.ExpiryDate
        If _currentCustomer.CreditCard.IssueDate <> "" Then
          request.Transaction.CardTxn.Card.StartDate = _
           _currentCustomer.CreditCard.IssueDate
        End If
        If _currentCustomer.CreditCard.IssueNumber <> "" Then
          request.Transaction.CardTxn.Card.IssueNumber = _
           _currentCustomer.CreditCard.IssueNumber
        End If

        ' Get DataCash response
        Dim response As DataCashResponse = _
          request.GetResponse(_processor.Configuration.DataCashUrl)
        If response.Status = "1" Then
          ' update order authorization code and reference
          _processor.SetOrderAuthCodeAndReference(response.MerchantReference, _
                                          response.DatacashReference)

          ' audit and continue
          _processor.AddAudit("Funds available for purchase.", 20102)
          _processor.UpdateOrderStatus(2)
          _processor.ContinueNow = True
        Else
          _processor.AddAudit("Funds not available for purchase.", 20103)
          _processor.MailAdmin("Credit card declined.", "XML data exchanged:" _
            & Chr(10) & request.Xml & Chr(10) & Chr(10) & response.Xml, 1)
        End If
    Catch
        ' fund checking failure
        Throw _
          New OrderProcessorException("Error occured while checking funds.", 1)
    End Try
    _processor.AddAudit("PSCheckFunds finished.", 20101)
  End Sub
End Class
```

The modifications to PSTakePayment are as follows:

```vb
' 5th pipeline stage - takes funds from customer
Imports DataCashLib

Public Class PSTakePayment
  Implements IPipelineSection

  Private _processor As OrderProcessor
  Private _authCode As String
  Private _reference As String

  Public Sub Process(ByVal processor As OrderProcessor) _
    Implements IPipelineSection.Process

    _processor = processor
    _processor.AddAudit("PSTakePayment started.", 20400)

    ' get authorization code and reference
    _authCode = _processor.AuthCode
    _reference = _processor.Reference

    Try
      ' take customer funds via datacash gateway
      ' configure Datacash XML request
      Dim request As DataCashRequest = New DataCashRequest()
      request.Authentication.Client = _processor.Configuration.DataCashClient
      request.Authentication.Password = _
        _processor.Configuration.DataCashPassword
      request.Transaction.HistoricTxn.Method = "fulfill"
      request.Transaction.HistoricTxn.AuthCode = _authCode
      request.Transaction.HistoricTxn.Reference = _reference

      Dim response As DataCashResponse = _
        request.GetResponse(_processor.Configuration.DataCashUrl)
      If response.Status = "1" Then
        ' audit and continue
        _processor.AddAudit( _
          "Funds deducted from customer credit card account.", 20402)
        _processor.UpdateOrderStatus(5)
        _processor.ContinueNow = True
      Else
        _processor.AddAudit( _
          "Error taking funds from customer credit card account.", 20403)
        _processor.MailAdmin("Credit card fulfillment declined.", _
          "XML data exchanged:" & Chr(10) & request.Xml & Chr(10) & Chr(10) _
          & response.Xml, 1)
      End If
    Catch
      ' fund checking failure
      Throw _
        New OrderProcessorException("Error occured while taking payment.", 4)
    End Try
    _processor.AddAudit("PSTakePayment finished.", 20401)
  End Sub
End Class
```

Testing

Now we have all this in place it is worth testing with a few orders. This is easily achieved by making sure you create a customer with 'magic' credit card details. As mentioned earlier in the chapter, these are numbers that DataCash supplies for testing purposes, and can be used to obtain specific responses from DataCash. A sample of these is shown below; a full list is available on the DataCash web site:

Card Type	Card Number	Return Code	Description	Sample Message
Switch	4936000000000000001	1	Authorised with random auth code.	AUTH CODE ??????
	4936000000000000019	7	Decline the transaction.	DECLINED
	6333000000000005	1	Authorised with random auth code.	AUTH CODE ??????
	6333000000000013	7	Decline the transaction.	DECLINED
	6333000000123450	1	Authorised with random auth code.	AUTH CODE ??????
Visa	4242424242424242	7	Decline the transaction.	DECLINED
	4444333322221111	1	Authorised with random auth code.	AUTH CODE ??????
	4546389010000131	1	Authorised with random auth code.	AUTH CODE ??????

Going Live

Moving from the test account to the live one is now simply a matter of replacing the DataCash information in web.config. Once we have set up a merchant bank account we can use these details to set up a new DataCash account, obtaining new client and password data along the way. We also need to change the URL that we send data to, since it needs to be the live server. The URL for this is https://transaction.datacash.com/Transaction. Other than removing the test user accounts from the database, this is all we need to do before exposing our newly completed e-commerce application to customers.

Summary

In this chapter we have completed our e-commerce application by integrating it with credit card authorization. Short of putting your own products in, hooking it up with your suppliers, getting a merchant bank account, and putting it one web, you're ready to go. OK, so that's still quite a lot of work, but none of it is particularly difficult. We've done the hard work for you.

Specifically, in this chapter we have looked at the theory behind credit card transactions on the web and looked at one implementation – DataCash. We created a library that can be used to access DataCash and integrated it with our application.

The End

Over the last thirteen chapters we've designed and built a complete e-commerce web site. You should now be ready to develop your own site and unleash it on the world.

A true e-commerce site will continue to improve throughout its life, as customer expectations and business strategy changes. The site we've built in this book gives plenty of scope for modifications and expansions, and the way that we've worked in phases should give you all the guidance you need to add fourth, fifth, and sixth phases of your own.

Aside from building an e-commerce site, you've seen lots of techniques and examples that will prove useful in any medium-large sized application you build.

In this chapter, we'll take a look at some of the places you might like to look when considering the next step.

Join Our Community

We don't want you to develop alone. This book has its own aspnet_ecommerce forum at p2p.wrox.com, where you can discuss the site with other readers. This is a great way to get help with problems, share ideas, and find out if other people have already written the add-on that you need. Or you can just show off the sites you've developed! This service is free to all readers.

Through P2P, we hope to build a list of the best web sites built with the help of this book. Let us know if you build anything really impressive, and we'll be sure to add it to our hall of fame!

Stake Out IBuySpy

Microsoft has put together two of its own examples of ASP.NET in action – an e-commerce site and an intranet ('portal') for a seller of spy equipment. We formulated our own design with the help of these examples, and they are well worth checking out in order to find alternative ways of doing things and a few ideas that we didn't incorporate here. For example the IBuySpy portal enables administrators to choose which controls load where, effectively enabling them to redesign the layout of the site without doing any programming at all.

Both of these sites are available from www.ibuyspy.com. The documentation is a little dry, and can be hard to follow, but having read this book you should easily get an idea of what's going on.

Read More

This book has touched on a number of subjects: e-commerce methods, server controls, *n*-tier architecture, security, database design, and more. If you want to find out more about these subjects, there are several Wrox books that will help.

Server Controls

This book has presented several server controls, and used them extensively. However, there is lots more to server controls than we've covered here. Building good controls puts us in an excellent position to reuse functionality and save development effort. *Professional ASP.NET Server Controls* (ISBN– 1-86100-564-6) looks at how to build solid, reusable, and flexible controls for your ASP.NET projects.

Databases

Data access and manipulation has played a major part in developing our web site. Efficient use of databases is one of the best things we can do to ensure performance and scalability. *Professional ADO.NET* (ISBN – 1-86100-527-X) covers a wide range of data handling techniques, while *Professional SQL Server 2000* (ISBN –1-86100-448-6) gives information on setting up and using SQL Server in the most effective way.

ASP.NET

Even though we've built a powerful application, we've still only really touched on what ASP.NET can do. Wrox has lots of books on ASP.NET, ranging from the broad, essential Professional ASP.NET (ISBN –1-86100-703-5) (available online) to more specialized titles. *Professional ASP.NET Web Forms Techniques* (ISBN –1-86100-786-8), for example, shows you how to build attractive and flexible user interfaces for your application – incorporating dynamic graphics generation, and combining client-side scripts with ASP.NET code for maximum impact.

Security

Security is essential to e-commerce applications. If you're going to be extending the site significantly then you should really get a good grasp of the issues involved. *Professional ASP.NET Security* (ISBN –1-86100-620-9) delves deep into these topics, showing you how to build your own custom security frameworks. It also contains many tips on protecting your code from hackers and prying eyes.

Building Web Sites

This book has guided you through the process of developing an e-commerce web site – building everything yourself. Wrox's Problem, Design, Solution books take a different approach. We start off with a complete, professional-quality web application. We show how it was designed to fit requirements, and highlight the interesting and powerful code techniques that went into it. These titles save developers save hours of time by showing ready-made solutions to their programming and design problems, while introducing exciting new techniques and ideas.

The soon-to-be-released *ASP.NET E-Commerce Programming: Problem, Design, Solution* (ISBN – 1-86100-803-1) shows you how to build a highly advanced e-commerce site. You will see how to incorporate the advanced features that the most well-know e-commerce sites use to boost their revenue: recommendation engines, affiliate schemes, wish lists, discounting, and much more. This book will show you how to build a site that can give the big boys a real run for their money!

The first Problem, Design, Solution book – *ASP.NET Website Programming* (ISBN – 1-86100-693-4) – takes a similar approach to building a content-based web site. It includes features such as user accounts, forums, hosting advertising, and adding opinion polls and newsletters. These features will help you to develop a far richer browsing experience for your e-commerce customers, as well as showing you how to build an entirely different type of site.

We hope you have enjoyed this book, and that it proves useful as you go on to develop your own web sites. Good luck!

Installing IIS, MSDE, OSQL, and Creating Class Libraries

In this appendix, we will cover a few bits and pieces that you will need to know in order run the code in this book. You may or may not already be familiar with this material, so feel free to dip in and out for just what you need.

Let's begin by looking at how to install our IIS Web Server.

Installing the IIS 5.x Web Server

We'll look at the installation process for IIS on Windows 2000 Professional and Windows XP Professional together as they don't differ significantly. The main difference is that Windows 2000 installs IIS 5.0, while Windows XP installs IIS 5.1. The options for installing are exactly the same; the only thing that might differ is the look of the dialog boxes.

> *It's worth noting that you cannot install IIS on Windows XP Home Edition, and therefore you cannot run ASP.NET on it. It will only work on Windows XP Professional.*

Before you install it though, it's worth noting that you might not have to do much in this initial stage, as it's possible you're already running IIS 5.x. We'll describe a process for checking whether this is the case as part of the installation process. You should also note that to install anything (not just ASP.NET, but literally anything) on Windows 2000/XP you need to be logged in as a user with administrative rights. If you're uncertain of how to do this, we suggest you consult your Windows documentation.

Try It Out – Locating and/or Installing IIS 5.x on a Web Server Machine

1. Go to the control panel (Start | Settings | Control Panel) and select the Add/Remove Programs icon. The following dialog will appear, displaying a list of your currently installed programs:

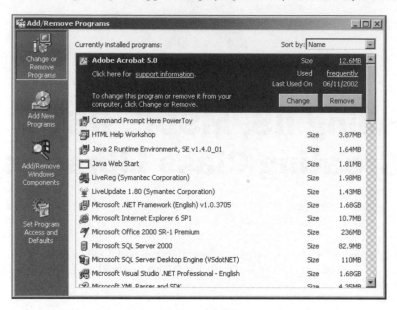

2. Select the Add/Remove Windows Components icon on the left side of the dialog to get to the screen that allows you to install new Windows components:

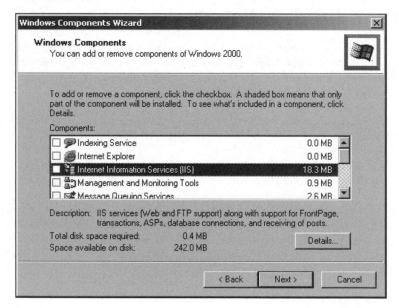

3. Locate the Internet Information Services (IIS) entry in the dialog, and note the checkbox that appears to its left. Unless you installed Windows 2000 via a custom install and specifically requested IIS, it's most likely that the checkbox will be unchecked (as shown).

4. If the checkbox is *cleared*, then check the checkbox and click on Next to load Internet Information Services 5.x. You might be prompted to place your Windows 2000/XP installation disk into your CD-ROM drive. It will take a few minutes to complete. Then go to Step 5.

OR

If the checkbox is *checked* then you won't need to install the IIS 5.*x* component – it's already present on your machine. Go to Step 6 instead.

5. Click on the Details button – this will take you to the dialog shown below. There are a few options here, for the installation of various optional bits of functionality. For example, if the World Wide Web Server option is checked then our IIS installation will be able to serve and manage web pages and applications. If you're planning to use FrontPage 2000 or Visual InterDev at any point, then you'll need to ensure that the FrontPage 2000 Server Extensions and Visual InterDev RAD Remote Deployment Support checkboxes are checked. The Internet Information Services Snap-In is also very desirable, as you'll see in the book, so ensure that this is checked too.

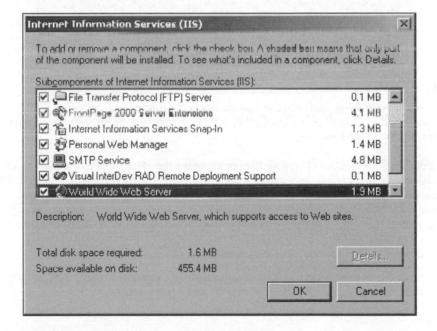

For the purpose of this installation, make sure all the checkboxes in this dialog are checked. Then click on OK to return to the previous dialog.

6. There's one other component that you might want to install – it's the Script Debugger. If you scroll to the foot of the Windows Components Wizard dialog that we showed above, you'll find a checkbox for Script Debugger. If it isn't already checked, check it now and click on Next to complete the installation. Otherwise, if both IIS 5.*x* and the script debugger are already present, you can click on Cancel to abort the process:

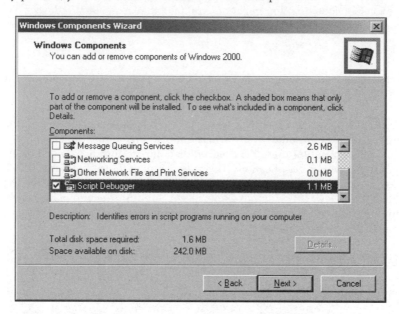

How It Works

IIS starts up automatically as soon as your installation is complete, and thereafter whenever you boot up Windows – so you don't need to run any further start-up programs, or click on any shortcuts as you would to start up Word or Excel.

IIS installs most of its bits and pieces on your hard drive, under the \WinNT\system32\inetsrv directory. However, more interesting to us at the moment is the \InetPub directory that is also created at this time. This directory contains subdirectories that will provide the home for the web page files that we create.

If you expand the InetPub directory, you'll find that it contains several subdirectories:

- ❏ \iissamples\homepage contains some example classic ASP pages.

- ❏ \iissamples\sdk contains a set of subdirectories that hold classic ASP pages that demonstrate the various classic ASP objects and components.

- ❏ \scripts is an empty directory, where ASP.NET programs can be stored.

- ❏ \webpub is also empty. This is a 'special' virtual directory, used for publishing files via the Publish wizard. Note that this directory only exists if you are using Windows 2000 Professional Edition.

- ❏ \wwwroot is the top of the tree for your web site (or web sites). This should be your default web directory. It also contains a number of subdirectories, which contain various bits and pieces of IIS. This directory is generally used to contain subdirectories that contain the pages that make up our web site – although, in fact, there's no reason why you can't store your pages elsewhere.

- ❏ \ftproot, \mailroot, and \nntproot should form the top of the tree for any sites that use FTP, mail, or news services, if installed.

- ❏ In some versions of Windows, you will find an \AdminScripts folder that contains various VBScript files for performing some common 'housekeeping' tasks on the web server, allowing you to stop and start services.

Working with IIS

Having installed IIS web server software onto our machine, we'll need some means of administering its contents and settings. In this section, we'll meet the user interface provided for IIS 5.*x*.

In fact, some versions of IIS 5.*x* provide two user interfaces, the MMC and the PWS interface. We're only going to look at one, as the other version is now obsolete. The version we will use is the **Microsoft Management Console (MMC)**, which is a generic way of managing all sorts of services. Let's take a quick look at it now.

The Microsoft Management Console (MMC)

The beauty of the MMC is that it provides a central interface for administrating all sorts of services that are installed on your machine. We can use it to administer IIS – but in fact, when we use it to administer other services the interface looks roughly the same. The MMC is provided as part of the Windows 2000 operating system, and also comes with older Windows server operating systems.

The MMC itself is just a shell – on its own, it doesn't do much at all. If we want to use it to administer a service, we have to add a **snap-in** for that service. The good news is that IIS 5.*x* has its own snap-in. Whenever you need to administer IIS, you can simply call up the Internet Services Manager MMC console by selecting Start | Settings | Control Panel | Administrative Tools | Internet Services Manager.

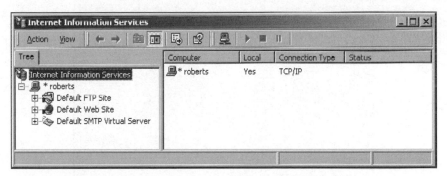

Having opened the IIS snap-in within the MMC, you can perform all of your web management tasks from this window. The properties of the web site are accessible via the Default Web Site node.

Testing your Installation

The next thing to do is test the web server to see if it is working correctly, and serving web pages. We've already noted that the IIS web service should start as soon as it has been installed, and will restart every time you start your machine. In this section, we'll try that out.

In order to test the web server, we'll start up a browser and try to view some web pages that we know are already placed on the web server. In order to do that, we'll need to type a URL into the browser's Address box, as we often do when browsing on the Internet. The URL is an http://... web page address that indicates which web server to connect to, and the page we want to view.

What URL do we use in order to browse to our web server? If your web server and web browser are connected by a local area network, or if you're using a single machine for both web server and browser, then it should be enough to specify the name of the web server machine in the URL.

Identifying your Web Server's Name

By default, IIS will take the name of your web server from the name of the computer. You can change this in the machine's network settings. If you haven't set one, then Windows will generate one automatically – note that this automatic name won't be terribly friendly; probably something along the lines of "P77RTQ7881". To find the name of your own web server machine, select Start | Settings | Network and Dial-up Connections and from the Advanced menu select Network Identification, or Start | Settings | Control Panel | System (depending on which operating system you are using – if it isn't in one, try the other). The Network Identification tab will display your machine name under the description Full computer name:

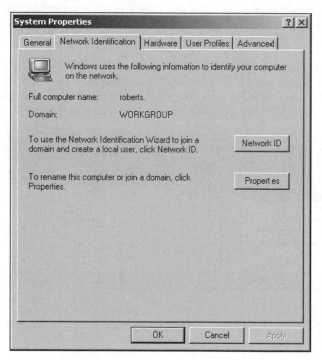

My machine has the name **roberts**, and (as you can see here and in the earlier screenshot of the MMC dialog) my web server has adopted the same name. On a computer within a domain you might see something different such as WROX_UK/roberts, if the computer was in the WROX_UK domain. However, this doesn't alter operations for ASP.NET. Browsing to pages on this machine across a local area network (or, indeed, from the same machine), I can use a URL that begins http://roberts/....

There are a couple of alternatives if you're using the same machine as both web server and browser. Try http://127.0.0.1/... – here, 127.0.0.1 is a default that causes requests to be sent to a web server on the local machine. Alternatively, try http://localhost/... – 'localhost' is an alias for the 127.0.0.1 address – you may need to check the LAN settings (in your browser's options) to ensure that local browsing is not through a proxy server (a separate machine that filters all incoming and outgoing web traffic employed at most workplaces, but not something that affects you if you are working from home).

> In the book, in any examples that require you to specify a web server name, the server name will be shown as **localhost**, implicitly assuming that your web server and browser are being run on the same machine. If they reside on different machines, then you simply need to substitute the computer name of the appropriate web server machine.

Let's now move on to look at installing MSDE.

MSDE: Introduction

The first thing to say about MSDE is that it's entirely compatible with SQL Server, which is truly an enterprise-class database server. This means that the things you learn while using MSDE will stand you in good stead when you come to use SQL Server itself – it behaves in exactly the same way. From our perspective here, though, the immediate benefits of MSDE are:

❑ It's freely distributable

❑ It's currently available on your Visual Studio .NET discs, you just need to install it

What this means is that as well as providing the perfect system for us to learn and experiment with, a complete web application can initially be produced and distributed without incurring any costs for the database server. If the system expands at a later date, it can be ported to the commercial distribution of SQL Server with next to no effort. The only features cut down from the full version of SQL Server are that the MSDE is optimized for (but not limited to) up to five connections at a time, that the maximum database size is limited to 2GB, and that some enterprise features are absent.

In this book, the code samples and text will assume that MSDE is being used as the data provider. To ensure that the code in the book will all function correctly, the next section details the installation of MSDE.

> All of the features that MSDE supports are also supported by SQL Server. The converse is not true, however; some of the richer functionality of SQL Server is not present in MSDE. However, none of this functionality is required for any of the code in this book to operate correctly.

Obtaining and Installing MSDE

When any of the various Visual Studio .NET products are installed, an item called Microsoft .NET Framework SDK is added to your Start | Programs menu. Beneath this is an item called Samples and QuickStart Tutorials; if you select it, this is what you'll see:

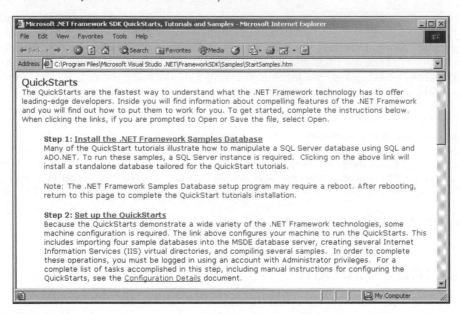

This page is self-explanatory: clicking on the first link will install the MSDE engine; clicking on the second will cause the sample databases – which we won't actually need for this book – to be created.

This page will only appear once, so if you (or someone else) have been here before, you won't see it. Don't worry: you'll find the instmsde.exe *and* configsamples.exe *files that these links invoke beneath the* FrameworkSDK\Samples *folder of your Visual Studio .NET installation.*

Ensure that you're logged on as a user with Administrator privileges on the current machine, and click on the first link (or run the executable). The following dialog will appear:

When this has finished, there's no need to restart your machine. You can go straight on to the next step, which will produce another dialog:

Once again, wait for this step to finish its work... and you're all done.

Using MSDE

Once it has been successfully installed on the local machine, you need to make sure that the MSDE service has started. This procedure differs slightly from platform to platform, but the instruction here, for Windows 2000, should tell you all you need to know. From the Start Menu, open the Control Panel, and go to Administrative Tools | Services:

The service called MSSQL$VSdotNET *is* MSDE. Make sure that the Status and Startup Type are set to Started and Automatic, as they are here, and you can rest assured that from now, when Windows is running, MSDE will also be running. Close this window, open Visual Studio .NET, and choose the View | Server Explorer menu item. Right-click on the Data Connections item at the top of the Server Explorer window, choose Add Connection from the context menu, and you'll see the following:

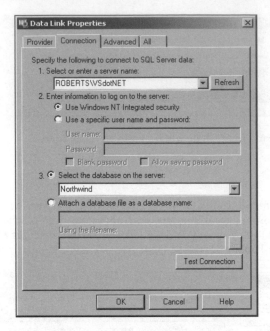

On choosing the appropriate settings in this dialog, the Server Explorer allows you to browse SQL Server databases, examining their content and performing some simple operations. When you return to the Server Explorer, you'll be rewarded with a view of the database (we show the Northwind database here, but the view for WroxJokeShop will be very similar):

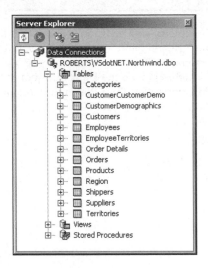

Having made it this far, you can be sure that the MSDE database is ready for action.

Finally, let's see how we can run our scripts using the `osql` command-line utility.

Running Scripts with osql

We can run the scripts to create and populate the database using the `osql` command-line utility. The syntax of the command is shown below. (Note – Ensure the case of the switches are exactly as shown):

```
osql -S localhost -d WroxJokeShop -E -i
C:\BegECom\Database\Chapter07\ShoppingCart.sql
```

Where:

Switch	Description
S	The name of the server on which your instance of SQL Server is running (Note – can also be *server name\instance name*)
U	User name (If not using integrated security for the database access)
P	Password (If not using integrated security for the database access)
d	The name of the database you want to use
E	This switch tells the program that you are using a trusted connection
i	Full path of the SQL script file you want to run

The result of the command above should be:

The SQL scripts for the book will be kept in the respective chapter sub-folders of the `BegECom\Database` directory.

Creating Class Libraries

Finally, we will go through the process required to build class libraries in Visual Basic .NET Standard Edition. We need to force Visual Basic .NET Standard Edition. to do some of the things that the full Visual Studio .NET does automatically.

Try It Out – Creating a Class Library in Visual Basic .NET Standard

1. In Visual Studio .NET, select File | New | Project.

2. Select Visual Basic Projects from the Project Types list, and then choose the Console Application icon from the Templates list. Enter the name MyClassLibrary:

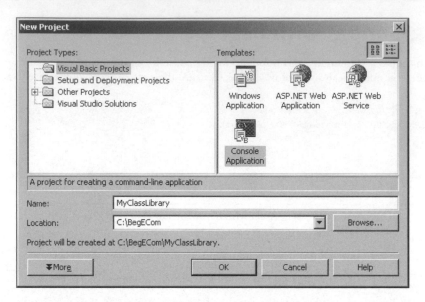

Select the whole content of the Location box and then press *Ctrl+C*. This will copy the location name to the Windows Clipboard, which we will use later. This example uses the location C:\BegECom, but of course you can locate it anywhere you like. Then click OK.

3. A new Console Application project will be created, with a default module called Module1.vb. Right-click on Module1.vb in the Solution Explorer and choose Delete. Then confirm the choice by clicking OK.

4. Now close the solution. Do this by selecting File | Close Solution. Select Yes to save changes.

5. Now, go to the Windows Start menu and select Programs | Accessories | Notepad. In the Notepad window select File | Open. Paste the Location from Step 2 into the File name box by selecting the textbox and pressing *Ctrl+V*. If this doesn't work, then just type the location in. Then click Open. This will take you to the folder that contains the project.

Go into the MyClassLibrary folder, and then from the Files of type dropdown select All Files. The Open dialog should now look like this:

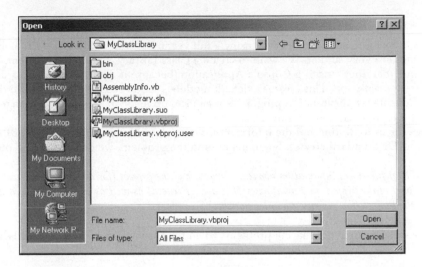

Select `MyClassLibrary.vbproj` and click **Open**. If your computer does not display file extensions, then you can identify the right file by its icon:

Then click **Open** to open the file in Notepad.

6. The VBPROJ file is an XML file that keeps track of all the files in the project, as well as settings that apply to the whole project. We are going to edit it. The line we are interested in is this one – about 19 lines down the file:

```
DelaySign = "false"
OutputType = "Exe"
OptionCompare = "Binary"
```

Change the highlighted line to:

```
OutputType = "Library"
```

Take care not to change anything else. Now save the file, close Notepad, and return to Visual Basic .NET.

7. Select **File | Recent Projects**. `MyClassLibrary.sln` should be first on the list. Select it. If it does not appear on the list then open it in the usual way.

How It Works – Creating a Class Library in Visual Basic .NET Standard Edition

This process is far more complicated than using a full version of Visual Studio .NET. Behind the scenes, however, things are very similar. We want to create a Class Library, but there is no template available. The closest one that does exist is a Console Application (because it does not bring up a designer, for example), so we create one. This creates a default module – Module1. We do not want this, so we delete it. A Console Application is a program – it can run on its own. We need to change it so that instead of it building to something runnable, it builds to a library. Visual Basic .NET Standard Edition offers no way for us to do this, but the information that makes the decision is in the VBPROJ file that Visual Basic .NET Standard creates. So, to get around the problem, we change the file ourselves.

> *The VBPROJ file stores information about the structure of the project (for example what source code files are part of the project, and what assemblies are referenced) as well as information needed to compile the project (for example compiler switches).*

We close the solution to avoid sharing problems when the file is open in Notepad, and then load up Notepad. Of course, any text editor would work here.

> *Text editors enable us to edit unformatted text files such as source code files, HTML files, and XML files. Having a good text editor is very useful, and an important part of a programmer's toolbox.*

The line that tells Visual Basic .NET to build this project into a program is the one that we edited:

```
OutputType = "Exe"
```

Here, Exe is short for executable. It is also the file extension for most programs that run under Windows. We changed it to Library. This tells Visual Basic .NET Standard that, when we build this project, it should be built into a class library instead of a program.

Now that you have the base template for a Class Library you can add the relevant code.

Indexes

Wrox Joke Shop Index

ASP Today

p2p.wrox.com
The programmer's resource centre

A unique free service from Wrox Press
With the aim of helping programmers to help each othe

Wrox Press aims to provide timely and practical information to today's programmer. P2P is a list server offering a host of targeted mailing lists where you can share knowledge with four fellow programmers and find solutions to your problems. Whatever the level of your programming knowledge, and whatever technology you use P2P can provide you with the information you need.

ASP
Support for beginners and professionals, including a resource page with hundreds of links, and a popular ASP.NET mailing list.

DATABASES
For database programmers, offering support on SQL Server, mySQL, and Oracle.

MOBILE
Software development for the mobile market is growing rapidly. We provide lists for the several current standards, including WAP, Windows CE, and Symbian.

JAVA
A complete set of Java lists, covering beginners, professionals, and server-side programmers (including JSP, servlets and EJBs)

.NET
Microsoft's new OS platform, covering topics such as ASP.NET, C#, and general .NET discussion.

VISUAL BASIC
Covers all aspects of VB programming, from programming Office macros to creating components for the .NET platform.

WEB DESIGN
As web page requirements become more complex, programmer's are taking a more important role in creating web sites. For these programmers, we offer lists covering technologies such as Flash, Coldfusion, and JavaScript.

XML
Covering all aspects of XML, including XSLT and schemas.

OPEN SOURCE
Many Open Source topics covered including PHP, Apache, Perl, Linux, Python and more.

FOREIGN LANGUAGE
Several lists dedicated to Spanish and German speaking programmers, categories include. NET, Java, XML, PHP and XML

How to subscribe:
Simply visit the P2P site, at http://p2p.wrox.com/

wrox

Programmer to Programmer™

Registration Code: 7507V0Y9Z0L13B01

Wrox writes books for you. Any suggestions, or ideas about how you want
information given in your ideal book will be studied by our team.
Your comments are always valued at Wrox.

Free phone in USA 800-USE-WROX
Fax (312) 893 8001

UK Tel.: (0121) 687 4100   Fax: (0121) 687 4101

Beginning ASP.NET E-Commerce – Registration Card

Name _____

Address _____

_____

_____

City _____ State/Region _____

Country _____ Postcode/Zip _____

E-Mail _____

Occupation _____

How did you hear about this book?

☐ Book review (name) _____

☐ Advertisement (name) _____

☐ Recommendation _____

☐ Catalog _____

☐ Other _____

Where did you buy this book?

☐ Bookstore (name) _____ City _____

☐ Computer store (name) _____

☐ Mail order _____

☐ Other _____

What influenced you in the purchase of this book?

☐ Cover Design   ☐ Contents   ☐ Other (please specify):

_____

How did you rate the overall content of this book?

☐ Excellent   ☐ Good   ☐ Average   ☐ Poor

What did you find most useful about this book? _____

_____

What did you find least useful about this book? _____

_____

Please add any additional comments. _____

_____

What other subjects will you buy a computer book on soon?

_____

What is the best computer book you have used this year?

_____

Programmer to Programmer™

Note: If you post the bounce back card below in the UK, please send it to:

Wrox Press Limited, Arden House, 1102 Warwick Road,
Acocks Green, Birmingham B27 6HB. UK.

Computer Book Publishers